'A book for our troubled times. Monaghan, Huq, and Flinders have convened an exceptional cast of contributors to illuminate the uses and abuses of impeachment in a comparative context. From Africa to the Americas and from Asia to Europe, this outstanding volume draws from doctrine, history, and theory to highlight understudied problems and questions through riveting case studies that expose the many functions of impeachment as a check on executive power, as a device for accountability, and as a weapon for retribution in constitutional politics. "Impeachment in a Global Context" is a home run study of impeachment around the world.'

Richard Albert, *Professor of World Constitutions, The University of Texas at Austin*

'Whether it is a judge, minister, or chief executive in removal proceedings, impeachment brings with it thorny legal questions and often intense political ramifications. Impeachment in a Global Context acknowledges and engages these difficulties by providing deeply contextualized accounts of impeachment within individual countries, set within a broader framing of comparative analysis and theoretical insight. From those systems in which impeachment is core to constitutional governance to countries where it is only newly emerging as a tool, the book's breadth is a boon for scholars and practitioners interested in constitutional design. And the book's empirical focus on how impeachment actually functions sheds important light on its normative desirability. In short, this deftly constructed volume will serve as an essential resource on impeachment long into the future.'

Erin F. Delaney, *Professor of Law, Northwestern University*

'Impeachment looms large in the current US political imaginary. It also shapes democratic politics across presidential systems worldwide: it has been deployed on almost every continent in the last decade, in ways that served both to bolster and undermine commitments to democracy and rule of law. In this important new volume, Monaghan, Huq, and Flinders bring together a star-studded list of contributors to survey these trends, their underpinnings, and significance for our understanding of democratic constitutional design and practice.'

Rosalind Dixon, *Professor of Law, University of New South Wales*

'Impeachment remains a central institution to constrain executive power, but it is often abused. This rich volume transcends the conventional study of impeachment proceedings in presidential regimes to show their role in semi-presidential and parliamentary systems across the world. The contributors address the impact of impeachment on democracy, human rights, and the rule of law.'

Aníbal Pérez-Liñán, *Professor of Political Science and Global Affairs, University of Notre Dame*

Impeachment in a Global Context

This volume considers the use of impeachment within a global context. The book brings together leading scholars and experts to give an insight into significant periods in the development of impeachment and its modern comparative use. Divided into five parts, the opening chapter introduces the topic and underlines its significance in terms of understanding the relationship and inter-dependence among politics, governance and the law. It also offers a novel conceptual framework that facilitates the global mapping of impeachment processes. Part I presents a thematic approach that explores the topic of impeachment through the lenses of democracy, human rights and the rule of law. With these themes in mind, Part II focuses on those parts of the world where impeachment is generally recognised as a core constitutional process including the United States, South Korea, Brazil and other countries in South America. Part III continues with the process of constitutional mapping by moving to a focus on those countries where impeachment is arguably an important but largely secondary or peripheral process. This includes chapters on Denmark, Iceland, Sri Lanka and the Philippines and flows through into Part IV's focus on areas of the world where impeachment matters and may even be increasing in terms of visibility but, for a number of reasons, arguably exists within a satellite status in terms of constitutional processes and safeguards. The fifth and final section steps back in an attempt to assess impeachment processes from a broad comparative perspective. The collection presents the definitive text on impeachment for students and scholars with an interest in comparative public law, politics and constitutional studies.

Chris Monaghan is Principal Lecturer in Law at the University of Worcester.

Matthew Flinders is Professor of Politics and Founding Director of the Sir Bernard Crick Centre at the University of Sheffield.

Aziz Z. Huq is the Frank and Bernice Greenberg Professor of Law, University of Chicago Law School.

Routledge Frontiers in Accountability Studies
Series Editors:
Matthew Flinders, *University of Sheffield, UK.*
Chris Monaghan, *University of Worcester, UK.*
Thomas Schillemans, *Utrecht University School of Governance, the Netherlands.*
Ellen Rock, *University of Technology, Sydney, Australia.*

Routledge Frontiers in Accountability Studies series promotes state-of-the-art analyses that reflect and interrogate the shifting accountability landscape from a range of perspectives.

The series welcomes proposals for monographs, edited collections and shorter works by established and early-career academics from a range of disciplines that span the arts, humanities and social sciences. Inter-disciplinary studies are particularly encouraged, as are approaches that seek to challenge dominant frameworks of 'self-evident' truths. The series is designed for a global audience, welcoming contributions that address national, comparative and international issues.

Other titles in this series:

Accountability, Impeachment and the Constitution
The Case for a Modernised Process in the United Kingdom
Chris Monaghan

British Origins and American Practice of Impeachment
Edited by Chris Monaghan and Matthew Flinders

Impeachment in a Global Context
Law, Politics, and Comparative Practice
Edited by Chris Monaghan, Matthew Flinders and Aziz Z. Huq

For more information about this series, please visit: www.routledge.com

Impeachment in a Global Context

Law, Politics, and Comparative Practice

Edited by Chris Monaghan, Matthew Flinders and Aziz Z. Huq

Routledge
Taylor & Francis Group
LONDON AND NEW YORK

First published 2024
by Routledge
4 Park Square, Milton Park, Abingdon, Oxon OX14 4RN

and by Routledge
605 Third Avenue, New York, NY 10158

Routledge is an imprint of the Taylor & Francis Group, an informa business

British Library Cataloguing-in-Publication Data
A catalogue record for this book is available from the British Library

Library of Congress Cataloging-in-Publication Data
Names: Monaghan, Christopher, editor. | Flinders, Matthew, editor. | Huq, Aziz Z., editor.
Title: Impeachment in a global context : law, politics, and comparative practice / edited by Chris Monaghan, Matthew Flinders, and Aziz Z. Huq.
Description: Abingdon, Oxon [UK] ; New York, NY : Routledge, 2024. | Series: Routledge frontiers in accountability studies | Includes bibliographical references and index.
Identifiers: LCCN 2023041488 | ISBN 9781032187402 (hardback) | ISBN 9781032187457 (paperback) | ISBN 9781003256007 (ebook)
Subjects: LCSH: Impeachments. | Impeachments—Political aspects.
Classification: LCC K3322 .I47 2024 | DDC 342/.068—dc23/eng/20231002
LC record available at https://lccn.loc.gov/2023041488

ISBN: 978-1-032-18740-2 (hbk)
ISBN: 978-1-032-18745-7 (pbk)
ISBN: 978-1-003-25600-7 (ebk)

DOI: 10.4324/9781003256007

Typeset in Galliard
by Apex CoVantage, LLC

Contents

Biographies of Contributors

Carina Barbosa Gouvêa is Professor permanent of the Graduate Program in Law, Master's and Doctorate at the Federal University of Pernambuco (PPGD/UFPE); she has a Post-Doctorate in Constitutional Law from the Federal University of Pernambuco (PPGD/UFPE) and holds a Doctorate and Master's in Law from UNESA. She is the Coordinator of the Study and Research Group "Theory of Separation of Powers and Crisis of the Brazilian Democratic System", which is linked to the PPGD/UFPE. She is the Deputy Leader of the International Law and Human Rights Research Group (UFPE).

Frank O. Bowman, III is Curators' Distinguished Professor Emeritus and Floyd R. Gibson Missouri Endowed Professor of Law Emeritus at the University of Missouri School of Law. Professor Bowman has written about impeachment since the Clinton affair. His work was widely cited during both impeachments of President Donald Trump, during which he consulted with members of both houses of Congress and appeared frequently as a commentator on both U.S. and international media outlets.

Imelda Deinla is Senior Lecturer at the School of Law, University of New England. She has published extensively on the rule of law and democracy in ASEAN and judicial politics, women judges and hybrid justice in the Philippines. She currently works on research projects on crime, punitiveness and electoral violence and on misinformation and democracy. She obtained her doctorate and master's degrees in law at the University of New South Wales, Australia.

Omololu Fagbadebo is Research Associate at the Durban University of Technology, South Africa. He holds a Ph.D. in Political Science from the University of KwaZulu-Natal, South Africa. He was a recipient of the Study of the United States Institutes (SUSI) on American Politics and Political Thought Fellowship at the University of Massachusetts, Amherst, USA, in 2010. His research focuses on comparative politics, legislative studies, public governance and institutions, public leadership, development studies and African government and politics.

Matthew Flinders is Professor of Politics and Founding Director of the Sir Bernard Crick Centre at the University of Sheffield. He is also Vice-President of the Political Studies Association and past Chair of the Universities Policy Engagement Network. A former special advisor in both the House of Lords and House of Commons, Prof. Flinders has published 14 books and over 200 peer-reviewed research articles and book chapters.

Tom Ginsburg is the Leo Spitz Distinguished Service Professor of International Law at the University of Chicago, where he also holds an appointment in the Political Science Department. He is also Research Professor at the American Bar Foundation. He holds B.A., J.D. and Ph.D. degrees from the University of California at Berkeley and currently co-directs the Comparative Constitutions Project, an NSF-funded data set cataloging the world's constitutions since 1789, that runs the award-winning Constitute website. His latest book is *Democracies and International Law* (2021), winner of the Best Book Prizes from the American Branch of the International Law Association and the American Society for International Law. He is also the author of *How to Save a Constitutional Democracy* (2018, with Aziz Z. Huq), winner of the Best Book Prize from the International Society for Constitutional Law; *Judicial Reputation: A Comparative Theory* (2015) (with Nuno Garoupa); *The Endurance of National Constitutions* (2009) (with Zachary Elkins and James Melton); and *Judicial Review in New Democracies* (2003), with the latter two winning best book awards from the American Political Science Association. He is a member of the American Academy of Arts and Sciences. Before entering law teaching, he served as a legal advisor at the Iran-U.S. Claims Tribunal, The Hague, Netherlands, and he has consulted with numerous international development agencies and governments on legal and constitutional reform. He currently serves as a senior advisor on Constitution Building to International IDEA.

Ragnhildur Helgadóttir (Cand jur. 1997, L.L.M. and S.J.D. 1999 and 2004) has been a Professor at Reykjavik University since 2006. She is the author of a number of books and articles on Constitutional Law and History and Administrative Law. Professor Helgadóttir has advised Parliament and been an ad hoc judge in the District Court, Supreme Court and European Court of Human Rights. She is Chair of the Science Committee of the Icelandic Science and Innovation Board 2016–2022 and has been Rector of Reykjavík University since 2021.

Dr. Young Hun Kim is Associate Professor of Political Science at North Carolina Wesleyan University and earned his Ph.D. in 2008 from The Pennsylvania State University. Dr. Kim's research and teaching focus is on comparative political institutions, democracy and democratization, East European politics, Russian Politics and East Asian Politics. His research has appeared in the *Journal of Politics*, *Cross-Cultural Research*,

Democratization, *Government and Opposition* and *Political Research Quarterly*.

Aziz Z. Huq is the Frank and Bernice Greenberg Professor of Law, University of Chicago Law School. His books include *The Collapse of Constitutional Remedies* (2021), *How to Save a Constitutional Democracy* (2018) (with Tom Ginsburg) and *The Rule of Law: A Very Short Introduction* (forthcoming 2024). His research focuses on U.S. and comparative constitutional law.

Philipp Köker is Lecturer in the Department of Political Science at Leibniz University Hannover, Germany. His research interests include presidential politics, political parties and comparative constitutional law. He is the author of *Presidential Activism and Veto Power in Central and Eastern Europe* (2017) and *Party People: Candidates and Party Evolution* (with Allan Sikk, 2023).

Yasser Kureshi is Department Lecturer in South Asian Studies at the Oxford School of Global and Area Studies at the University of Oxford. His book, *Seeking Supremacy: The Pursuit of Judicial Power in Pakistan* (2022), traces the evolution of the relationship between the judiciary and military in Pakistan. His work has also appeared in the *Journal of Comparative Politics*, the *Journal of Conflict Resolution* and *Democratization*.

David Landau is Mason Ladd Professor and Associate Dean for International Programs at Florida State University College of Law. His most recent book, *Abusive Constitutional Borrowing*, was coauthored with Rosalind Dixon. Since 2012, he has been a founding editor of ICONect, the blog of the *International Journal of Constitutional Law*. He holds an A.B., J.D. and Ph.D. (in political science) from Harvard University.

Youngjae Lee is Professor of Law and Associate Dean for Research at Fordham University School of Law and Director of the Fordham-Sungkyunkwan Summer Program in Seoul, Korea. Lee's research focuses on criminal law, criminal procedure, constitutional law and comparative constitutional law.

Chris Monaghan is Principal Lecturer in Law at the University of Worcester. He has recently published *Accountability, Impeachment and the Constitution: The Case for a Modernised Process in the United Kingdom* (Routledge 2022). He has previously written on the impeachment of Warren Hastings and publishes on constitutional law, accountability and the litigation surrounding the Chagos Islands.

Gerald L Neuman is the J. Sinclair Armstrong Professor of International, Foreign, and Comparative Law at Harvard Law School and Director of the school's Human Rights Program. From 2011 to 2014, he was a member of the UN Human Rights Committee, which monitors compliance with the International Covenant on Civil and Political Rights.

John Ohnesorge is the Bascom Professor in Business Law at the University of Wisconsin Law School, where he directs the East Asian Legal Studies Center and the Compliance Initiative. He teaches Administrative Law and Business Organizations and seminars in Compliance, Law & Development and Chinese Law. His is a graduate of St. Olaf College, the University of Minnesota Law School, and Harvard Law School. He is a 2023 Fulbright Scholar at Seoul's Yonsei University.

John Polga-Hecimovich is Associate Professor of Political Science at the United States Naval Academy, where he is also the director of the Forum for Latin American Studies. He previously taught at Wake Forest University, the College of William & Mary, and FLACSO-Ecuador. John has an M.A. in Latin American Studies from the Universidad Andina Simon Bolívar in Ecuador and received his Ph.D. in Political Science from the University of Pittsburgh. John's research studies the effects of political institutions on democratic stability, policymaking and governance, with a focus on Latin America. One of his primary areas of interest is how the executive branch of government exercises power and how presidents interact with legislatures and their own bureaucracies. John also studies presidential (in)stability, coalition dynamics under presidentialism and the design of electoral institutions. He has published peer-reviewed articles in places such as *The Journal of Politics*, *Political Research Quarterly*, *Democratization*, *Latin American Politics and Society* and the *Latin American Research Review*, including dozens more editor-reviewed articles, book chapters, policy papers and op-eds. Outside of the classroom, John has given briefings to the U.S. State Department, the Defense Intelligence Agency and U.S. Southern Command on issues related to Latin American politics.

Maria Lulu Reyes is Professor, School of Law, at Saint Lous University in Baguio City, the Philippines. She is Program Coordinator of the Master of Laws Program and currently completing her doctorate in juridical science at San Beda University where she also obtained her Master of Laws.

Geoffrey Robertson AO KC is founder and head of Doughty Street Chambers, Britain's leading human rights practice. He has argued many celebrated cases in constitutional criminal and media law and served as the first President of the U.N. war crimes court in Sierra Leone. He is the author of *Crimes Against Humanity* (1999) and of many other books and is a bencher of the Middle Temple and Visiting Professor at the College of Humanities. He conducted an inquiry into the impeachment of the Sri Lankan Chief Justice at the request of the human rights committee of the Bar of England and Wales.

Henrik Skovgaard-Petersen, Ph.D., L.L.M. (Cantab), was awarded a Ph.D. in European Union law from the University of Aarhus, Denmark, in 2016. In 2023, he was appointed Head of the Legal Department at the Prime

Minister's Office. He also holds a position as an external lecturer (constitutional law) at the University of Copenhagen. He has published several articles in international and Danish law reviews, including the *European Law Review* and *Legal Issues of European Integration*.

Pedro H. Villas Bôas Castelo Branco is Associate Professor at the Institute of Social and Political Studies at the State University of Rio de Janeiro (IESP-UERJ). He is Professor of the Graduate Program in Law, Master's and Doctorate at Veiga de Almeida University (PPGD-UVA). He holds a Doctorate in Political Science (IUPERJ) and a Master's in State Theory and Constitutional Law (Puc-Rio). He is Coordinator of the Laboratory of Political Studies of Defense and Public Security (LEPDESP-UERJ).

Foreword

Impeachment is an ancient institution, originating with the British Parliament in 1376 to combat perceived monarchical absolutism. It was subsequently borrowed by British colonists in North America and included in the United States Constitution of 1787 to remove officials who "commit, among other offenses, high crimes and misdemeanors." The institution of impeachment has since spread all over the world along with the written constitution. For countries with a directly elected president, it is nearly universal. Impeachment is also used in former British colonies and other countries to remove judges and other high officials.

One of the early scholars of impeachment, Theodore Plucknett, once described it as "the most powerful weapon in the political armory, short of civil war."[1] Perhaps because of its power, impeachment is somewhat Janus-faced in practice and application. On the one hand, it represents a crucial mechanism of accountability for chief executives and the primary mechanism for removal. It is deployed against judges with some regularity and is usually uncontroversial. On the other hand, impeachment can be prone to abuse. Although it is used only sparingly in some countries, in other countries, impeachment talk is a regular feature of political discourse, and its deployment is routine. As I write, Peru has just impeached President Pedro Castillo and removed him from office after two prior attempts. Two of Castillo's three predecessors were also threatened with impeachment and ended their terms early. The abuse of impeachment proceedings can create a permanent state of political crisis, and this seems especially likely to occur in countries with high levels of polarization. Too much impeachment is not a sign of democratic health.

When it occurs in someone else's country, the high political drama associated with removing a leader is interesting; but when it occurs in one's own country, as Americans have learned, it can be downright terrifying. In an era with serious and genuine governance challenges, the partisan warfare in the capital city can be frustrating and demoralizing. It can contribute to a sense

1 See TFT Plucknett, 'Presidential Address' (1953) 3 *Transactions of the Royal Historical Society* 145.

of alienation in politics among citizens. Still, confronted with a president who crosses red lines by, for example, trying to interfere with the succession process or elections, impeachment is surely necessary. Ideally, it is like a fire extinguisher: to be kept in reserve but hopefully never deployed.

To evaluate impeachment, a comparative and empirical approach is needed, and this is precisely what the editors of this volume have done. Presenting a mix of theoretical accounts, case studies, and broader comparative chapters, the authors collectively provide a richly textured account of impeachment. Methodologically, the editors' inductive approach to comparative law and politics is most welcome and the best way to make progress to a more complete understanding of what has become a central institution of democratic political life.

Tom Ginsburg
Leo Spitz Distinguished Service Professor of International Law
University of Chicago Law School

Preface

We would like to thank Alison Kirk, the Senior Commissioning Editor at Routledge, and Anna Gallagher, the Editorial Assistant for Law, for supporting us throughout the editorial process for *Impeachment in a Global Context: Law, Politics, and Comparative Practice*. The production and editorial team at Routledge, including our copyeditor Leslie Castro, have been supportive throughout the production process.

We are grateful to the series editors Ellen Rock and Thomas Schillemans for giving their full support for publishing this volume within the Routledge Frontiers in Accountability Studies series and to our colleagues at the University of Chicago, the University of Worcester, and the University of Sheffield for their help during the period when we were working on this volume. Thanks must go to our fantastic contributors who were a pleasure to work with and have each contributed excellent and thought-provoking chapters to the book. We would also like to acknowledge and thank the two reviewers who peer reviewed the initial proposal.

Finally, we would like to thank our friends and families for their support and understanding during the time that we spent on this volume.

Chris Monaghan
Worcester
Matthew Flinders
Sheffield
Aziz Z. Huq
Chicago

1 Understanding Impeachment

An Exercise in Comparative Cartography

Chris Monaghan, Aziz Z. Huq and Matthew Flinders

1.1 Introduction

The impetus for *Impeachment in a Global Context: Law, Politics, and Comparative Practice* arose as a result of the Questions of Accountability Conference that took place in late 2021. The conference featured a keynote lecture from Professor Tom Ginsburg, of the University of Chicago, on the comparative use of impeachment and a keynote panel discussion on impeachment featuring Professor Frank O. Bowman, III of the University of Missouri; Karen Popp, former Associate White House Counsel to the Clinton Administration; Joshua Matz, who had recently acted as the House Judiciary Committee's impeachment counsel for both Trump impeachment trials and would go on to represent E. Jean Carroll in her defamation case against Donald Trump; Professor Richard Albert, from the University of Texas; and Dr. Chris Monaghan, from the University of Worcester. Both the keynote lecture and panel served to underline the need for a wide-ranging book on impeachment that explored the use of impeachment from a global perspective. Over the following eighteen months, the editors of this volume (led by Chris Monaghan) assembled a team of experts from across the globe who could bring their knowledge of law and political science to bear on a series of chapters on their chosen country or region.

1.2 Mapping the Globe – Challenges and Opportunities

A book that purports to offer a global approach to impeachment sets itself an almost impossible task within the constraints of a standalone academic edited volume – namely, how to cover in sufficient detail the countries that have constitutions that contain an impeachment provision and that have used this provision. The aim of the editors is to offer a snapshot of diverse uses of impeachment from across the globe through a series of substantive chapters that not only consider specific countries or regions as case studies but also address the relationship between impeachment and human rights, the rule of law, and democracy. The challenge for the editors was to avoid a western-centred approach to impeachment but instead to ensure coverage of the use of

DOI: 10.4324/9781003256007-1

impeachment around the globe. To this end, we are excited that this volume looks at case studies including Sri Lanka, the Philippines, Pakistan, Nigeria, Latin America, and Brazil.

We begin here by offering a brief bibliographic survey of the global literature on impeachment. This body of scholarship is immense. It ranges over both present-day examples of impeachment and historical instances of impeachment. The phenomena of impeachment in the United States (both at a state and federal level) has seen a surge of books being published over the past decade, most notably on presidential impeachments. This has no doubt been caused by the feverous nature of the 2016 presidential election (where it looked likely that both major candidates – Hillary Rodham Clinton and Donald J. Trump – would be threatened by impeachment proceedings should they be elected). In many ways, the nadir of American political life under the shadow of Trump and his message of 'Make America Great Again' have done much to intensify political tensions, with the almost previously unimaginable storming of the United States (US) Capital Building in January 2021 by supporters of the outgoing President. Observers of US politics from around the world, who once consumed Aaron Sorkin's later-day Camelot of Jed Bartlett's fictional *West Wing*, may have struggled to ever imagine that such a thing could happen. Unsurprisingly, Trump was impeached twice.

Over the past decades, numerous books have been published in the US on impeachment. Examples include Jon Meacham, Timothy Naftali, Peter Baker, and Jeffery A. Engel's *Impeachment: An American History*,[1] which explores the earlier impeachments of Bill Clinton and Andrew Johnson, the resignation of Richard M. Nixon (in the face of impeachment), and the US Constitution under Trump, who had not yet been impeached when the book was published. Michael J. Gerhardt published *Impeachment: What Everyone Needs to Know*[2] and *The Law of Presidential Impeachment: A Guide for the Engaged Citizen*,[3] whilst Allan J. Lichtman laid out the case for proceeding against Trump in *The Case for Impeachment*.[4] In addition to these books, there are numerous books on impeaching previous presidents including George W. Bush and Barack Obama and a vast number of articles published in US law reviews and academic

1 (Random House 2018).
2 (OUP 2018).
3 (New York UP 2024).
4 (William Collins 2017). Other leading books on impeachment include David E. Kyvig's, *The Age of Impeachment: American Constitutional Culture Since 1960* (University Press of Kansas 2008) and H. Lowell Brown's wide-ranging *Prosecution of the President of the United States: The Constitution, Executive Power, and the Rule of Law* (Palgrave Macmillan 2022). The prospect of then-President Donald J. Trump being impeached accompanied the publication of Laurence Tribe and Joshua Matz's provocative and authoritative *To End a Presidency: The Power of Impeachment* (Basic Books 2018), Daniel P. Franklin and others, *The Politics of Presidential Impeachment* (SUNY Press 2020) and Frank O. Bowman III's extensive and authoritative, *High Crimes and Misdemeanors: A History of Impeachment for the Age of Trump* (2nd edn, CUP 2023).

journals. It is apparent that there is considerable academic interest in the use of impeachment in the United States.

In contrast, impeachment is regarded as something of a relic in its country of origin, the United Kingdom. For the most part, impeachment is explored by historians focused on particular periods of history or on the impeachment of specific individuals. There is a regular (but far from anything like the US) flow of academic articles on impeachment covering the Long Parliament, the impeachment trial of Warren Hastings, and the trial of Viscount Melville. A lone recent example of a book on impeachment is Rachel Carnell's *Backlash: Libel, Impeachment, and Populism in the Reign of Queen Anne*.[5] Brian Cowan and Scott Sowerby's *The State Trials and the Politics of Justice in Later Stuart England* is another noteworthy example.[6] Then, there is the question of how impeachment fits within the contemporary United Kingdom, a country that has witnessed a decade of constitutional strife and uncertainty, capped off with the rise and fall of Prime Minister Boris Johnson. These issues are addressed in Chris Monaghan's *Accountability, Impeachment and the Constitution: The Case For a Modernised Process in the United Kingdom*.[7] This book makes the case that impeachment, if modernised and reinvented for the 21st century, could be used to support existing accountability mechanisms and thus empower the House of Commons to hold the executive to account. This view is somewhat of an outlier. Although other academics have called for change and enhanced accountability of the executive, most scholars would initially regard impeachment as obsolete, especially given the weight of history and its legacy.

There has been considerable literature on impeachment from a Latin American perspective. A leading text is Anibal Pérez-Liñán's *Presidential Impeachment and the New Political Instability in Latin America*.[8] Another important text is Mariana Llanos and Leiv Marsteintredet's *Latin America in Times of Turbulence: Presidentialism under Stress*, in which the editors wrote a piece tellingly entitled 'The Limits of Presidential Impeachment: Lessons from Latin America'.[9] The impeachment of President Dilma Rousseff (now the former President of Brazil) also catalyzed the publication of several books exploring the consequences and causes of the impeachment and what it means for Brazilian politics. Examples include Mads Bjelke Damgaard *Media Leaks and Corruption in Brazil: The Infostorm of Impeachment and the Lava-Jato Scandal*,[10] Pedro A. G. dos Santos and Farida Jalalzai *Women's Empowerment and Disempowerment in Brazil: The Rise and Fall of President Dilma*

5 (U of Virginia P 2020).
6 (Boydell and Brewer 2021).
7 (Routledge 2022).
8 (CUP 2007).
9 (Routledge 2023).
10 (Routledge 2018).

Rousseff,[11] Fernando Limongi, *Operação impeachment: Dilma Rousseff e o Brasil da Lava Jato*,[12] and Peter Prenganan and Mauricio Savarese, *Dilma's Downfall: The Impeachment of Brazil's First Woman President and the Pathway to Power for Jair Bolsonaro's Far-Right*.[13] In addition to these books, academic articles on the topic include Mariana Llanos and Aníbal Pérez-Liñán's, 'Oversight or Representation? Public Opinion and Impeachment Resolutions in Argentina and Brazil',[14] Alexandra Rattinger's 'The Impeachment Process of Brazil: A Comparative Look at Impeachment in Brazil and the United States',[15] and Felipe Nunes and Carlos Ranulfo Melo 'Impeachment, Political Crisis and Democracy in Brazil'.[16]

Beyond Britain and the Americas, there is yet other rich literature on impeachment under quite different political and institutional conditions. A recent addition to the African literature on impeachment in Nigeria is Omololu Fagbadebo's *Impeachment in the Nigerian Presidential System: Challenges, Successes and the Way Forward*.[17] Academics have also published articles on the recent impeachment of President Geun-hye Park in South Korea, such as Hannes B. Mosler's 'The Institution of Presidential Impeachment in South Korea, 1992–2017'[18] and Sungmoon Kim's 'From Remonstrance to Impeachment: A Curious Case of "Confucian Constitutionalism" in South Korea'.[19] Within a European perspective, there is literature on the use of impeachment or the threatened use of impeachment. The Irish academics Conor Casey and Eoin Daly in 'Political Constitutionalism under a Culture of Legalism: Case Studies from Ireland'[20] explored the threatened use of impeachment against a Supreme Court Justice, Mr. Seamus Woulfe, in the wake of the 'golfgate' scandal. The push for impeachment here arose because Woulfe may have breached the law related to the Covid-19 pandemic. Casey and Daly observe that '[t]he controversy leading up to an unprecedented mooting of a Supreme Court judge being impeached by the Irish parliament arose in the very peculiar circumstances of legislative restrictions in effect during the Covid-19 pandemic.' Other examples of literature on impeachments in Europe include Jón Ólafsson's 'The Case Against Leaders: A Moral Reading of Geir Haarde's Conviction for Negligence of Ministerial Duties',[21] which explored the controversial impeachment of a prime minister of Iceland. Impeachment in the

11 (Temple UP 2021).
12 (Todavia 2023).
13 (Associated Press 2021).
14 (2021) 46(2) *Legislative Studies Quarterly* 357.
15 (2018) 49 *University of Miami Inter-American Law Review* 129.
16 (2017) 37(2) *Revista de Ciencia Politica* 281.
17 (Palgrave 2020).
18 (2017) 50(2) *Law and Politics in Africa, Asia and Latin America* 111.
19 (2019) 44(3) *Law and Social Inquiry* 586.
20 (2021) 17(2) *European Constitutional Law Review* 202.
21 [2021] *Frontiers in Political Science* <www.frontiersin.org/articles/10.3389/fpos.2021.619719/full>.

Philippines is considered in Yuko Kasuya's 'Patronage of the past and future: Legislators' decision to impeach President Estrada of the Philippines'.[22]

In terms of an attempt to provide a global overview of impeachment, Jody C. Baumgartner and Naoko Kada's *Checking Executive Power: Presidential Impeachment in Comparative Perspective*,[23] was published two decades ago. There have been influential attempts by academics to offer comparative analyses in academic journals, with Young Hun Kim's 'Impeachment and Presidential Politics in New Democracies'[24] in 2014 followed by Aziz Z. Huq, Tom Ginsburg and David Landau's, 'The Comparative Constitutional Law of Presidential Impeachment'[25] and John Ohnesorge's 'Comparing Impeachment Regimes',[26] both published in 2021. We hope that this book, *Impeachment in a Global Context: Law, Politics, and Comparative Practice*, will build upon this extant academic literature and deepen our understanding of impeachment as a global phenomenon by taking a comparative perspective not confined to country or region-specific silos. Although it presents a global overview, it is not exhaustive, as many other countries might have been included. But we hope that it enriches the dialogue among scholars around the globe.

1.3 Anglo-American Origins

Impeachment emerged from the Good Parliament that met in 1376 in medieval England. Although the Good Parliament can be said to have been crucial to the emergence of impeachment, the process of impeachment was refined and dramatically changed during the decades that followed. After a long period of desuetude, it was revived in the 1620s because of the efforts of parliamentarians including Sir Edward Coke, who had been dismissed in 1616 as Chief Justice of the King's Bench by James I. Impeachment continued to be used during the seventeenth century, most notably as a way for the Long Parliament to proceed against Charles I's unpopular advisers. After being revived yet again following the restoration of Charles II in 1660, impeachment continued being used as a means of removing officials well into the eighteenth century. Indeed, the early decades of that century saw impeachment transformed into a partisan weapon by the rival Whigs and Tories to deploy against their opponents once they were no longer in office. Impeachment was then sporadically used in the mid to latter part of the eighteenth century. Lord Lovat, for example, was impeached for supporting the Jacobite rebellion of 1745 (and therefore executed). Impeachment was also the vehicle used to proceed against Warren Hastings, the former and inaugural Governor-General of Bengal. Hastings' impeachment was accomplished in 1787, spearheaded by

22 (2005) 18(4) *The Pacific Review* 521.
23 (Praeger 2003).
24 (2014) 21 *Democratization* 519.
25 (2021) 88 *University of Chicago Law Review* 81.
26 (2021) 31 *Duke Journal of Comparative and International Law* 259.

Edmund Burke, Charles James Fox, and others. The final British impeachment took place in 1806, when Viscount Melville was tried by the House of Lords but was ultimately acquitted.

The framers of the US constitution were no strangers to impeachment as a part of both contemporaneous and then-historical British political practice. The inclusion of impeachment within the federal constitution of 1787 was a clear adoption and refinement of the British version of this practice. Although impeachment originated to serve a specific purpose in its parliamentary birth place – for accountability and to address grievances – the American framers believed that impeachment would prevent a president in particular from abusing that position in any one of several ways, thus destroying the young Republic. As Alexander Hamilton explained,

> The President of the United States would be liable to be impeached, tried, and, upon conviction of treason, bribery, or other high crimes or misdemeanors, removed from office; and would afterwards be liable to prosecution and punishment in the ordinary course of law.[27]

Drawing a direct comparison between the President and the British King, Hamilton further opined that

> The person of the king of Great Britain is sacred and inviolable; there is no constitutional tribunal to which he is amenable; no punishment to which he can be subjected without involving the crisis of a national revolution. In this delicate and important circumstance of personal responsibility, the President of Confederated America would stand upon no better ground than a governor of New York, and upon worse ground than the governors of Maryland and Delaware.[28]

On this view, impeachment offered a way to remove a president without having to resort to a popular insurrection. The power of the presidency would offer no defence to a conviction by the Senate.

In a similar vein, Benjamin Franklin said that he

> was for retaining the clause as favorable to the Executive. History furnishes one example only of a first Magistrate being formally brought to public Justice. Every body cried out agst. this as unconstitutional. What was the practice before this in cases where the chief Magistrate rendered himself obnoxious? Why recourse was had to assassination in wch. he was not only deprived of his life but of the opportunity of vindicating his character. It wd.. be the best way therefore to provide in

27 *The Federalist Papers: No 69*, Friday 14 March 1788.
28 ibid.

> the Constitution for the regular punishment of the Executive where his misconduct should deserve it, and for his honorable acquittal when he should be unjustly accused.[29]

Hence, impeachment would mean that a leaders' opponents would not need to resort to assassination and other violent methods in order to remove a controversial President. In the same debates, James Madison argued the importance of including impeachment within the proposed constitution because it was

> indispensable that some provision should be made for defending the Community agst. the incapacity, negligence or perfidy of the chief Magistrate. The limitation of the period of his service, was not a sufficient security. He might lose his capacity after his appointment. He might pervert his administration into a scheme of peculation or oppression.[30]

1.4 An Overview

This collection is divided into five parts. Part One explores the foundations of impeachment as a legal idea. It addresses the comparative use of impeachment through a consideration of impeachment and the rule of law, impeachment and democracy, and impeachment and human rights. In Chapter 2, Gerald L Neuman explores the theme of 'Impeachment as Cause or Cure of Human Rights Violations'. As Neuman states very clearly at the outset of his chapter, the process is always a two-edged sword:

> Impeachment is an extraordinary procedure for responding to abuse of government power by removing the abusive actor from office. It enables legislatures to play an important role in halting or preventing serious violations of human rights. Yet like all power, the authority to impeach can be abused.

Neuman explores precisely what is meant by impeachment, with reference to examples including the US federal constitution and Commonwealth constitutions, before addressing the question as to whether impeachment is a cure for human rights violations. In addressing this question, Neuman particularly reflects carefully on the examples of 'strongmen' including Peru's Alberto Fujimori and Paraguay's Raúl Cubas Grau and elected officials and judges in the countries such as the US and Japan. Neuman's chapter then explores the question as to whether impeachment can itself inflict a human rights violation. Neuman considers whether '[a]dditional human rights considerations apply in

29 *Madison Debates*, Friday 20 July 1787.
30 ibid.

the case of legislative removal of a judge.' He considers here the position of the Inter-American Court of Human Rights and the European Court of Human Rights by reflecting on his own experience in internal bodies.

Young Hun Kim in Chapter 3, 'Impeachment and Democracy: Does Impeachment Have an Effect on Democracy in Third Wave Presidentialism?', asks about the practice of impeachment in relatively new democracies. 'Since a growing number of presidential democracies have been relying on impeachment to remove the incumbent, it is important to ask what impacts impeachment may have on these new democracies.' He notes that the use of impeachment often results in clear political gains for those calling for a president to be impeached. An overtly partisan or instrumental use of impeachment could thus have the effect of undermining public confidence in democratic institutions and the 'legitimacy' of the decision to remove the president. To better understand this dilemma, Kim considers examples of the impeachment of President Fernando Lugo in Paraguay, President Dilma Rousseff in Brazil, and both President Park Geun-hye and President Roh Moo-hyun in South Korea.

In Chapter 4, 'Impeachment and the Rule of Law: It's Complicated', John Ohnesorge considers whether the rule of law can serve as an effectual constraint on impeachment. He outlines his view as to the role that the rule of law ought to play in impeachment proceedings, considers its relation to values such as due process, and offers a clear definition as to what will amount to an impeachable offence. He concludes in particular that '[a]n important Rule-of-Law value is that legal rules of conduct should be clear and knowable in advance.' Ohnesorge also asks whether impeachment could operate as a protector of the rule of law. He addresses the need to maintain judicial independence and the threat that impeachment could pose to this value. Related to this point, he explores how judges can be protected, especially in the US when the President disagrees with a judicial decision. Therefore, in this context, impeachment could be used against a president where the President is undermining judicial independence and/or the democratic order.

In Part Two of the book, the contributors explore countries and regions where impeachment has become a core feature of the political landscape. In Chapter 5, Youngjae Lee explores 'The Role of the Judiciary in the Presidential Impeachment Process in Korea'. His chapter reviews the role of the Constitution Court of Korea in presidential impeachments as set forth in a 1987 constitutional amendment. Lee provides an account of the inaugural use of impeachment in South Korea in 2004 when President Roh Moo-Hyun was impeached by the National Assembly of Korea. However, the motion for impeachment was subsequently dismissed by the Constitutional Court as legally insufficient. Lee explains that 'the Court held that none of the violations by Roh justified removing him from office'. He then considers the impeachment of Park Geun-hye and the circumstances that led to her impeachment in 2016–2017. The role of the press in sealing Park Geun-hye's fate is highlighted.

John Polga-Hecimovich looks at 'Latin America: Between Governability Crises and the Impeachment Trap' in Chapter 6. He asks whether 'impeachment [has] become more prevalent across Latin America in the 2010s and 2020s'. Polga-Hecimovich notes the influence of the US constitution (and the British historical tradition of impeachment) in the decision to include impeachment in a typical Latin American constitution. He contrasts the different types of models used, such as the American model (used in countries including Brazil and Chile) and the unicameral model (employed in countries such as Ecuador and Peru). Polga-Hecimovich observes that '[p]rior to the third wave of democratization, impeachments in Latin America were rare.' He also describes the increased use of impeachment in Latin America to remove a country's president and the key role played by the military pressuring politicians to bring these impeachments. In contrast, during the Cold War, the military used coups to remove democratically elected presidents, resulting in a predominance of military dictatorships over democracies in Latin America. Indeed, there is a sense in which the re-emergence of democracy in Latin America reignited the use of impeachment as a substitute for the military coup. Polga-Hecimovich observes that from 1991 to 2022, there were more than twenty impeachment trials. He notes the dangers of such frequent use of impeachment, which along with 'a high level of presidential instability is probably not healthy for Latin American democracy.'

Focusing on Brazil in Chapter 7, Carina Barbosa Gouvêa and Pedro H. Villas Bôas Castelo Branco discuss 'Contemporary Impeachment in Brazil: Political Time and Aporias'. They begin by addressing the history of impeachment in Brazil and the removal of President Café Filho and President Carlos Luz, which they regard as being irregular for their failure to comply with the legal and constitutional frameworks. In their view, it therefore 'cannot be treated as [an] instance[ ] of successful use of the impeachment process.' Barbosa Gouvêa and Villas Bôas Castelo Branco also explore the impeachment of President Fernando Collor de Melo in 1992 and President Dilma Rousseff in 2016. In the case of Collor de Melo, they underscore the key role played by the President's brother, Pedro Collor, who was also the first democratically elected president since the 1964 military coup. Barbosa Gouvêa and Villas Bôas Castelo Branco outline how an impeachment can occur. They explore the predicate for such action, which is known as a responsibility crime. In Rousseff's case, this was her use of the presidential decree power to supplement the Brazilian budget by 'more than R$95 billion'. This, it was argued, created an artificial fiscal surplus. Then, it was alleged that Rousseff provided misleading accounts to 'intentionally hide the real fiscal situation of the country.'

In Chapter 8, Frank O. Bowman, III explores 'Impeachment in the United States'. Looking past the recent visibility of impeachment in the American political culture, Bowman provides a clear account of the historical origins of impeachment in fourteenth-century England and its lessons for the American constitution-drafting process. He emphasises that 'the drafters of the American constitution were inheritors of Britain's constitutional tradition, familiar with its most notable incidents, and acutely conscious of what they took to be its strengths and weaknesses'. As a result, 'impeachment had come to seem so natural a feature of Anglo-American constitutional practice that ten of the thirteen new states which declared independence from Great Britain that year wrote impeachment into their state constitutions.' Bowman explores the founding-era debates as to whether impeachment should be included in the new federal constitution. Bowman notes that '[t]he most significant American deviation from British historical practice was to make impeachment applicable to the Chief Executive, not just his or her subordinates.' Bowman then provides an account of judicial impeachments, starting with that of Supreme Court Justice Samuel Chase, and the use of impeachment against presidents. Reviewing the case of President Nixon, who resigned before he could be impeached, Bowman observes that 'although Nixon was never formally impeached or tried, his forced resignation should be considered a success of the impeachment mechanism.' Bowman is critical of the Trump presidency. In his view, 'Trump was plainly unqualified to be president', and his presidency 'tested all the guardrails erected by the framers of America's constitution'. Commenting on Trump's two acquittals by the Senate, Bowman is clear that the fact that Trump could be elected is down to the 'flaws in the contemporary American political system' and that these flaws, in turn, have 'disabled impeachment as a dispositive remedy for presidential misconduct.'

Part Three moves beyond the traditional canon of cases to explore the use of impeachment in less familiar settings, particularly where it has been less of a historical presence in a nation's political culture. In Chapter 9, Ragnhildur Helgadóttir looks at 'Impeachment in Iceland' and the role that the Icelandic Constitution plays in providing the legal basis for impeachment. Helgadóttir notes that since 1904, Iceland has had a parliamentary system of government. As a result, a government that loses a parliamentary vote of no confidence must resign. This creates an alternative to impeachment: Helgadóttir hence observes that a confidence vote 'could indeed be a less cumbersome way of ousting a Cabinet minister who has committed (or is suspected of) an impeachable offense.' The grounds for which a minister may be impeached are outlined in the Ministerial Accountability Act no 4/1964. Helgadóttir notes growing support for revising the Ministerial Accountability Act no 4/1964 at the turn of the century. She then considers whether, in light of the parliamentary system of government in Iceland, impeachment is needed as an accountability mechanism. Specifically, Helgadóttir examines the impact of the financial collapse in 2008 and the subsequent decision to impeach the Icelandic Prime Minister Geir Haarde. Ultimately, Haarde was convicted by the Court of Impeachment. He subsequently challenged his conviction at the European Court of Human Rights. He argued that the conviction breached Articles 6 and 7 of the European Convention on Human Rights. Helgadóttir observes that although Geir Haarde was unsuccessful in the European Court of Human Rights, 'there were no celebrations, either in Parliament or elsewhere in the Icelandic government, when the ECtHR judgment was published.' Indeed, as Helgadóttir explains, there is now little appetite for using impeachment in the wake of the Haarde conviction.

Henrik Skovgaard-Petersen provides an account of 'Impeachment in Denmark: Law and Practice' in Chapter 10. Skovgaard-Petersen observes that '[u]ntil recently, impeachment was generally considered not just a peripheral but almost exotic phenomenon in Denmark.' This is despite the impeachment and conviction of a former Minister of Justice in the 1990s. Skovgaard-Petersen then provides an historical overview of impeachment in Denmark and the use of impeachment in the nineteenth and twentieth centuries. He notes that all three cases brought in the twentieth and twenty-first centuries 'have resulted in convictions'. According to him, all three emerged not from an 'institutional power struggle' but rather involved efforts to 'sanction alleged breaches of norms applicable to actions or omissions by ministers during their term of office.' The introduction of a parliamentary system of government to Denmark at the beginning of the twentieth century, in which ministers were expected to resign if they lost the confidence of the legislature, did not as in the case of the United Kingdom mean that 'impeachment became obsolete'. Skovgaard-Petersen explores the procedure for bringing an impeachment and the role played by the Court of Impeachment.

In Chapter 11, 'The Impeachment of the Chief Justice of Sri Lanka, Dr. Shirani Bandaranayake' is explored by Geoffrey Robertson KC. He outlines the background to the impeachment and the reasons why politicians decided to remove Sri Lanka's most senior judge. The impeachment was criticised internationally, with critics citing the threat it apparently posed to judicial independence. The author had been tasked at the time of the impeachment to conduct a review into whether the removal of Dr. Shirani Bandaranayake contravened Sri Lanka's obligations in international and Commonwealth law. Robertson sets out the impeachment charges against the Chief Justice connected to the Judicial Services Commission and the Divineguma Bill.

Imelda Deinla and Maria Lulu Reyes consider 'Impeachment in the Philippines: Politics, Institutions and Leadership' in Chapter 12. In the Philippines, impeachment was '[d]esigned as a mechanism of accountability', but the 'impeachment of judges in the highest court, the Supreme Court, has become a tool for consolidating strongmen rule.' Deinla and Lulu Reyes offer an account of how the Philippine Supreme Court has regained public confidence. They also discuss the judicial crises that resulted in the impeachments of Chief Justice Renato Corona in 2012 and Chief Justice Sereno in 2017. They consider the judiciary's role in removing fellow judges via the impeachment process and ask why judges are willing to remove their colleagues. After all, they note, 'the Justices' action in removing a colleague is not a unique phenomenon; this had happened in other jurisdictions where political and institutional support is weak for the courts and judges.' Deinla and Lulu Reyes are clear about not only the role a judiciary can play in limiting the excesses of 'strongman' style leaders but also the limits of this role.

Part Four explores the use of impeachment where it has been included within a country's constitution but has not been extensively used. In these contexts, impeachment is best understood as peripheral to the country's mainstream political life. Philipp Köker explores this in Chapter 13 'Impeachment in Central and Eastern Europe'. His chapter examines eleven countries that were formerly socialist and within the Soviet Union's sphere of influence. Crucially, all eleven countries joined the European Union after 2004. As Köker notes, these countries had to design a new constitutional framework. They 'faced similar challenges in creating democratic political systems in a short period of time.' However, Köker is clear that the systems they created varied greatly, so the expected role of impeachment in each country differs. Köker sets out the historical tradition of impeachment in Central and Eastern Europe following the end of the First World War. He points here to the Czechoslovak Constitutional Charter of 1920, which allowed the President to be impeached. He also establishes and distinguishes different ways in which impeachment operates in Central and Eastern Europe, particularly considering how it can be initiated and which institution has the final say as to whether a president can be removed. The case of Lithuanian president Rolandas Paksas, who was removed from office in 2004 after refusing to resign, is explored. Köker underscores that Paksas has been the only serving European head of state to have been removed from office via impeachment. Köker also considers the unsuccessful attempts to impeach presidents, such as Ion Iliescu, President of Romania in 1994, Traian Băsescu, President of Romania in both 2007 and 2012, and Václav Klaus, President of the Czech Republic in 2013.

In Chapter 14, Omololu Fagbadebo gives an account of 'Impeachment in Nigeria: Process, Practice and Failure'. His chapter sets out the political and constitutional history of Nigeria as context for its experiences with impeachment. As a cause and consequence of the political instability in Nigeria, Fagbadebo flags 'the attitudinal disposition of Nigeria's political leaders to power rather than the institutional system.' This, in his view, 'has remained the bane of political instability in the country.' He sets out how impeachment operates in Nigeria and the evolving nature of the Nigerian constitution and what it means for impeachment. His chapter offers an account of how impeachment has been used to remove regional premiers and governors such as Chief Akintolam who was the premier of the Western Region in Nigeria. It also discusses the unsuccessful attempt to remove Governor Peter Obi (the governor of Anambra State) between 2006 and 2007.

Yasser Kureshi considers 'The Politics of Impeachment in Pakistan's Hybrid Democracy' in Chapter 15. In his chapter, Kureshi explores the history of impeachment in Pakistan since 1973. He looks not only at attempts to impeach the President but also at votes of no confidence in the Prime Minister and the use of judicial disqualification to remove judges. The framework for impeachment is found in the 1973 constitution, which was introduced by a civilian-led government. Kureshi explains that a President can be removed under the 1973 constitution, and he details the steps needed to do this. He also explores how a vote of no confidence can be filed in the National Assembly to remove a Prime Minister. He then explores the 1985 constitutional reform allowing the judiciary to 'disqualify political officers including the Prime Minister'. As Kureshi observes, 'the recent history of impeachment proceedings in Pakistan . . . highlights the dynamic nature of Pakistan's hybrid politics and reveals the ways in which elected and tutelary institutions contest and negotiate over political authority, autonomy and legitimacy.' Finally, he considers attempts to remove then-Prime Minister Imran Khan in 2022; the judicial disqualification of Nawaz Sharif in 2017; and the effect of impeachment's threat on President Musharraf's decision to resign in 2008.

In Chapter 16, Chris Monaghan explores 'The United Kingdom and Impeachment: Justification, Renewal, and the House of Commons as a Guardian of the Constitution'. He sets out the history behind the development of impeachment in England and its later use through British history. In terms of historical practice, impeachment was first used in England in 1376 by the Good Parliament (with Lord Latimer being the first person to be impeached), and it ceased to be used after the acquittal of Henry Dundas, Viscount Melville in 1806. Although offering an account of the history, he is clear that '[t]his chapter does not seek to present a historical account of impeachment; rather, it seeks to ask whether impeachment could still serve a role in the 21st century United Kingdom.' Monaghan argues that impeachment could serve a purpose as a way of improving the accountability of the executive to the House of Commons. He bases his account on the rationale for modernising impeachment and for using it again in the United Kingdom. Monaghan argues that a modernised form of impeachment would enhance accountability, offer genuine democratic oversight, and provide a role for the House of Commons as the guardian of the constitution. In part, his argument is based on the fallout and constitutional 'crisis' that followed the Supreme Court's controversial decision in *R (on the application of Miller) v Prime Minister (No 2)*,[31] which was seen by some as a judicial intrusion into the workings of the political constitution. As Monaghan notes, 'there arguably needs to be a greater dialogue about who takes responsibility for the protection and development of the contemporary constitution.' His conclusion is that impeachment would serve a purpose here by empowering the House of Commons.

In the final chapter of the book, which explores the future of impeachment, Tom Ginsburg, Aziz Z. Huq, and David Landau consider 'Impeachment in Comparative Perspective: An Empirical View'. This chapter explores the use of impeachment around the globe and the reasons that it has been used, which is based on a consideration of why impeachment was included within a country's constitution and the particular national context. As Ginsburg, Huq, and Landau explain, '[p]residential impeachment in practice is about far more than removing criminals or other bad actors; it often serves as an exit from the deep

31 [2019] UKSC 41.

structural crises that presidential (and semi-presidential) systems of government sometimes undergo.' In terms of the global context, Ginsburg, Huq, and Landau acknowledge the trend of popular dissatisfaction with established systems of government and the subsequent fragility of the elected tenures of presidents and why their political opponents resort to impeachment as a method to circumvent term limits and preemptively remove a president.

Accordingly, the chapters of this book offer a comprehensive and varied view of the global landscape of impeachment. Plainly, this landscape reveals both promise and peril: impeachment can be both a wellspring of political crisis and a response. Much depends on context and the health of institutions such as the judiciary and parliament. The work collected in this volume, however, should enable a more sure-footed path through the risks and the democratic returns to be had from impeachment as a political practice.

Part I

Foundations

2 Impeachment as Cause or Cure of Human Rights Violations

Gerald L Neuman

2.1 Introduction

Impeachment is an extraordinary procedure for responding to abuse of government power by removing the abusive actor from office. It enables legislatures to play an important role in halting or preventing serious violations of human rights. Yet like all power, the authority to impeach can be abused.

Human rights analysis of impeachments has considered this unusual procedure from both perspectives. Groundless political trial or arbitrary and irregular proceedings may violate the rights of officials or the rights of the citizens who elected them and for whom they serve. Lawfully conducted impeachments with appropriate sanctions – especially against officials who are not otherwise subject to removal – may be essential for protecting human rights and democracy. This chapter discusses the virtues of the institution of impeachment and then examines the need for suitable limitations.

2.2 What Is Impeachment?

'Impeachment' historically denotes a form of legislative accusation and trial providing extraordinary redress for public wrongs. More generally, the term embraces a variety of mechanisms for the removal for cause of a public official singled out by the legislature. This chapter uses the term broadly to cover them all. Impeachment for cause differs from dismissal at will by a vote of no confidence in a parliamentary system, which may properly be based on simple policy disagreements or partisan alignments.

The United States (U.S.) federal constitution, which has had significant influence on numerous countries, limits the consequences of impeachment to removal from office and disqualification from future federal office. This procedure applies broadly to 'civil officers of the United States'[1] but not to state officials, whose removal is left to the respective state constitutions and laws. In other countries with systems of federalism, the impeachment of subnational

1 US Constitution, art II, s 4.

DOI: 10.4324/9781003256007-3

officials may be regulated and carried out at the subnational level or may involve the national legislature.[2]

In some countries and two U.S. states (Missouri and Nebraska), the legislature initiates the process, but a court holds the actual trial and makes the final decision on removal. Elsewhere, courts may play an advisory role or make intermediate decisions in a legislative impeachment process.

Some U.S. state constitutions and some Commonwealth constitutions have preserved a different version of legislative removal of judges, the resolution of 'address' by one or both houses. Address leads only to removal, not to disqualification. This procedure has fallen largely into disuse as modern independent judicial discipline developed. This chapter treats address as functionally another form of impeachment.

Ideally, impeachment provides a form of accountability for wrongdoing and prevents further wrongs. Moreover, the very possibility of impeachment may have a deterrent effect on officials who know that they are not guaranteed the completion of their designated terms of office. In evaluating the effects of an impeachment regime, completed removals should be considered alongside cases of resignation to avoid removal. Officials facing the prospect of impeachment may resign before trial or before formal accusation, and the proceeding may then be abandoned even in systems that allow it to continue after resignation. Threats of impeachment can thus achieve some of the benefits of actual impeachment.

Legislative removal serves other purposes of greater or lesser legitimacy. It enables the legislature to intervene in a particular major political scandal, demonstrating its responsiveness to public opinion and asserting its moral authority. Assigning the removal decision to the legislature may result in a sounder holistic judgment on whether the official's performance justifies termination. In some systems, legislative removal provides a method for compelling the retirement of officials who can no longer perform their duties.[3]

Impeachment can, however, be employed as a means of power struggle between rival parties or factions within a party. Removal for cause presupposes violation of a standard, not merely the preference of a majority (or supermajority) of the legislators that someone else should hold the position, as in a vote of no confidence. Nonetheless, impeachment may be misused by legislators who do not play by the rules. Some countries seek to prevent such misuse

2 See, e.g., Leonard Muye Mwakuni, 'Kenya's Gubernatorial Impeachments: Superior Courts as Guardians against Abuse of Power' (2020) 5 *Kabarak Journal of Law and Ethics* 221 (describing local accusation and trial by national Senate for county governors in Kenya).

3 This chapter does not discuss whether removing officials due to inability, or using less demanding removal procedures for doing so, may violate the human rights of persons with disabilities. For consideration of some of the issues, see David Bilchitz, 'Dignity, Fundamental Rights and Legal Capacity: Moving Beyond the Paradigm Set by the General Comment on Article 12 of the Convention on the Rights of Persons with Disabilities' [2016] *South African Journal on Human Rights* 410, 418–19.

by requiring a judicial determination that the accusation meets the governing standard as a necessary step in the impeachment process or by providing the weaker safeguard of an advisory report of a court or other body that does not bind the legislature. But assigning the impeachment decision to legislators entails political risks.

The compensating value of impeachment depends in part on the alternative methods available for removing the official from office. In the U.S., the president and vice president are elected to a four-year term. Impeachment is the only method provided to cut the term short for wrongdoing.[4] Federal judges are appointed with life tenure, although modern judicial discipline procedures now enable the judiciary to limit the authority of a lower court judge who does not resign after findings of misbehavior. In contrast, other federal officials are subject to removal by their superiors for misconduct, and the availability of impeachment reflects concern about negligence or complicity at higher levels of the executive. At the state level, more executive officials are separately elected and insulated from removal by higher officials, increasing the need for impeachment.

2.3 Impeachment as a 'Cure' for Human Rights Violations

As a historic remedy for abuse of power, impeachment has long provided an available means of responding to official depredations that would now be characterized as human rights violations. Removal from office serves both retrospective and prospective functions – it provides a form of accountability for violations that have already occurred, and it takes away the opportunity to commit similar or different violations in the future.

Of course, legislative removal does not fully cure violations. It does not remedy all the harm done to past victims. It does not address all the underlying causes of the violations. And it may only partially incapacitate the perpetrator who was removed. Impeachment may end the public career of the abusive official, or it may provide only a temporary interruption. There may also be negative downstream consequences in the particular context. Still, impeachment serves its purpose of terminating a specific current threat to human rights.

Moreover, impeaching one official who has violated human rights does not always reduce the number of violations. Legislative removals may amount to sporadic interventions in situations where more systematic enforcement is needed. The official's replacement may be worse than the official removed and yet not incur the same consequences. Nonetheless, complete insulation from removal, for life or for a term of years, is a dangerous temptation to abuse power.

4 In addition, the Twenty-Fifth Amendment to the Constitution creates a procedure for suspending a president's authority during inability to discharge the powers and duties of the office.

The legal grounds for legislative removal cover a wide range of infractions, in phrasing that differs from country to country. Often the constitutional provision refers to crimes and/or constitutional violations. These categories overlap considerably with international human rights conceptions.[5] The following examples, from the U.S. and elsewhere, illustrate successful or attempted impeachments that were prompted by abuse of human rights.

One stark example of a human rights impeachment involved Alberto Fujimori, who had subverted the Peruvian constitution and ruled as a strongman in reliance on his feared head of intelligence Vladimiro Montesinos. Shortly after Fujimori's dubious reelection in the spring of 2000, a videotape of Montesinos bribing a member of Congress to switch allegiances became available and created public outrage, greatly strengthening the opposition. In November 2000, Fujimori fled to Japan and submitted his resignation. The Congress rejected it and instead held a formal vote removing him on grounds of 'moral incapacity.' After his extradition, he was criminally convicted of responsibility for two episodes of mass murder and two incidents of kidnapping. The Supreme Court's judgment placed these violations in a context of systematic state violence and characterized the murders (and grievous bodily harm to additional victims) as crimes against humanity.[6]

Raúl Cubas Grau was elected president of Paraguay in 1998 amid factional disputes within the dominant Colorado party in the transition period following the dictatorship of Alfredo Stroessner. He defied Supreme Court decisions by freeing from prison a general who led his faction. Violence followed, including the murder of the vice president (from the opposing faction) and killings of demonstrators. Facing impeachment for his role in these events, Cubas Grau resigned and fled to Brazil.[7]

The resignation of Richard Nixon in 1974 provides the one successful example of a presidential impeachment process in the U.S. Although Nixon did resign, like Fujimori and Cubas Grau, it was the likelihood of removal by impeachment that prompted his departure. The central legal threat in Nixon's case was the technical accusation of obstruction of justice in relation to the investigation of his re-election campaign – the Watergate cover-up – clearly demonstrated by the audio tapes that the Supreme Court had ordered released. However, the House of Representatives was also considering a charge that he 'repeatedly engaged in conduct violating the constitutional rights of citizens,' including through tax authority retaliation against political opponents and unauthorized domestic surveillance.[8] Even if the Senate would

5 Tom Ginsburg, Aziz Z. Huq and David Landau, 'The Comparative Constitutional Law of Presidential Impeachment' (2021) 88 *The University of Chicago Law Review* 81, 127.

6 See Aimee Sullivan (tr), 'The Judgment Against Fujimori for Human Rights Violations' (2010) 25 *American University International Law* 657.

7 Aníbal S. Pérez-Liñán, *Presidential Impeachment and the New Political Instability in Latin America* (CUP 2007) 29–32.

8 House of Representatives, Report No 93–1305, 93d Cong, 2d Session (1974) (USA) 3.

only have reached the required two-thirds majority on the obstruction of justice charge, the end of the Nixon presidency terminated his abusive methods of governance and enabled legislative reforms.

The failed impeachment effort against U.S. President Andrew Johnson in 1868 would also have served a clear human rights purpose. The principal charges adopted by the House addressed Johnson's firing of his secretary of war, without congressional consent under the Tenure of Office Act, an undeniable fact of debated legal character. Congress's underlying motivation for impeachment, however, was not the control of personnel decisions for its own sake but Johnson's opposition to Reconstruction – his willingness to let the pre-civil war power structure of the southern states be reestablished and to abandon the fate of the newly freed slaves.[9]

As the Nixon and Johnson examples illustrate, removal does not always rest formally on an official's worst violations. The charges may instead address the violations most easily proven, to the satisfaction of the required number of legislators. The cover-up is not necessarily worse than the violation; rather, it may be documented and may be less subject to controversy.

The only impeached officials who have actually been convicted by the U.S. Senate have been life-tenured judges, primarily for corruption.[10] More impeachment proceedings have ended with resignation, either at the investigative stage before a House vote or before a Senate trial. It is worth pointing out that judicial corruption *is* a human rights violation, as it deprives litigants of fair trial rights, and removal of corrupt judges prevents them from committing further violations.

At the U.S. state level, there have been more convictions of more varied officials, for good or bad reasons. Several governors have been removed, and others have resigned under threat of impeachment. The resignees include the 2021 example of Andrew Cuomo of New York, who was accused of multiple instances of sexual harassment (which is also a human rights violation). Other kinds of officials removed by state legislatures include a lieutenant governor, an attorney general, secretaries of state, treasurers, a member of the governor's council, an auditor, a university regent, sheriffs, public surveyors, and higher and lower court judges. The most common theme has been financial dishonesty, including extortion, bribery, and embezzlement. Such abuses may amount to human rights violations depending on the circumstances. One South Carolina sheriff was impeached in 1811 for torturing a criminal suspect; he was convicted and disqualified for four years from holding office.[11] A county

9 See Annette Gordon-Reed, *Andrew Johnson* (Henry Holt 2011) 134–39.

10 See United States House of Representatives, List of Individuals Impeached by the House of Representatives <https://history.house.gov/Institution/Impeachment/Impeachment-List/> accessed 18 November 2022.

11 See James W Ely Jr, '"That No Office Whatever Be Held During Life or Good Behavior": Judicial Impeachments and the Struggle for Democracy in South Carolina' (1977) 30 *Vanderbilt Law Review* 167, 189–92.

judge in Virginia was removed by the legislature in 1903 for horsewhipping a preacher who had criticized him.[12] Massachusetts probate judge Edward Loring was removed by address from his state position in 1858 because he also served as a federal commissioner and in this capacity, ordered the return of Anthony Burns to slavery in Virginia; looking beyond the complexities of positive law in the 1850s, this was an impeachment for human rights purposes.[13] Texas governor James Ferguson's impeachment in 1917 resulted from his politically motivated assault on the University of Texas, which implicated freedom of expression and the right to education.[14] In Missouri, a secretary of state was impeached and removed for falsifying documents to favor her own son's political candidacy.[15]

In Japan, one judge was removed by impeachment in 2008 for the sexual harassment of a courthouse employee, and another was removed in 2001 for his involvement in child prostitution.[16] A federal judge in Australia resigned in 2021 after findings of sexual harassment led to a recommendation of proceedings for parliamentary removal.[17]

Corruption is a frequent basis for impeachment worldwide. Executive corruption can directly affect the human rights of individuals, and more generally, there is a growing trend to regard it as a human rights abuse per se, taking into account its indirect effects.[18] Corruption charges contributed to the impeachment of presidents such as Fernando Collor de Mello (Brazil, 1992), Carlos Andrés Pérez (Venezuela, 1993), Abdalá Bucaram (Ecuador, 1997), and Park Guen-Hye (South Korea, 2017).[19] In Peru in 2018, all the judges on the national council of magistrates were removed by the Congress for gross misconduct in the midst of a wide-ranging judicial corruption scandal that also resulted in the resignation of the president of the Supreme Court.[20] It should be recognized, however, that in a country where corruption is endemic, a

12 See Brent Tarter, 'Campbell, Clarence Jackson' in *Dictionary of Virginia Biography*, vol 2 (Library of Virginia 2001) 559.

13 See Mass Acts & Resolves 1858, 186 (Removal Message of Governor Banks Upon Address); Paul Finkelman, 'Legal Ethics and Fugitive Slaves: The Anthony Burns Case, Judge Loring, and Abolitionist Attorneys' (1995) 17 *Cardozo Law Review* 1793.

14 See John R Lundberg, 'The Great Texas "Bear Fight": Progressivism and the Impeachment of James E Ferguson' in Jessica Brannon-Wranosky and others (eds), *Impeached: The Removal of Texas Governor James E Ferguson* (Texas A&M UP 2017).

15 *State Ex Inf Nixon v Moriarty*, 893 SW2d 806 (Missouri Supreme Court, 1994).

16 See Noboru Yanase, 'Political Threats to Judicial Independence in Post-War Japan: Judging from Judge Impeachment Cases' (2021) 37 *Nihon University College of Law* 1, 7–8.

17 See Michael Pelly, 'Judge Resigns Over "Sexualised" Conduct' *Australian Financial Review* (Sydney, 8 July 2021) <www.afr.com/politics/federal/judge-resigns-over-sexualised-conduct-202107008-p587ve> accessed 18 November 2022.

18 See Anne Peters, 'Corruption as a Violation of International Human Rights' (2019) 29 *European Journal of International Law* 1251.

19 See Ginsburg, Huq and Landau (n 5); Pérez-Liñán (n 7).

20 See 'Judicial Crisis in Peru; the Congress Removed All the Magistrates of the CNM' *CE Noticias Financieras English* (21 July 2018); 'Peru Political Turmoil: Supreme Court President

well-founded corruption charge may provide a pretext for a shift in power that improves nothing.

Finally, it is worth saying explicitly that both impeachments of Donald Trump were about human rights violations. Both centrally involved his efforts to subvert the 2020 presidential election, first, by bribing Ukraine to fabricate evidence against the Democratic candidate who ultimately defeated him and second, by violent disruption of the congressional count of the electoral votes confirming that defeat.[21] The January 6 attack and the deaths and injuries it included only illustrate the range of human rights violations that could have been prevented if the first impeachment had succeeded.

2.4 Impeachment as a Cause of Human Rights Violations

Although impeachment can benefit human rights, human rights violations may arise as a direct result of the impeachment proceedings. Some of these violations have been addressed by international human rights courts or similar bodies.

In addition to direct violations, impeachment may also contribute to a worsening of the human rights situation in the particular empirical circumstances of the country. Indeed, even a meticulously lawful removal may have indirect negative consequences if it is poorly received by the public, if it shifts power to a less desirable successor, or if it destabilizes a fragile political system. This chapter, however, focuses on the violations inhering in the removal itself and leaves the discussion of when a justified impeachment is best avoided to other chapters.

This section first provides some examples of abusive impeachments before addressing some of the elements that could make an impeachment a human rights violation. It explains why impeachment proceedings should be constrained by human rights (1) and then considers violations of procedural rights (2), threats to judicial independence (3), and excessive restriction of political rights through disqualification (4). The jurisprudence mentioned comes primarily from the Inter-American Court of Human Rights (IACtHR), applying the American Convention on Human Rights; the European Court of Human Rights (ECtHR), applying the European Convention and its Protocols; and at the global level, the Human Rights Committee, applying the International Covenant on Civil and Political Rights (ICCPR).

It is unfortunately too easy to find examples of impeachments that violate human rights. In 1997, Fujimori had three judges of Peru's constitutional court impeached and removed for their decision finding him ineligible to run

---

Resigns Over Tapes Scandal' *BBC* (19 July 2018) <www.bbc.com/news/world-latin-america-44892884> accessed 3 December 2022.

21 H Res 755, 116th Cong, 1st Session (2019) (USA) (First Articles of Impeachment); H Res 24, 117th Cong, 1st Session (2021) (Second Articles of Impeachment).

for a third term as president.[22] Impeachment and threats of impeachment were among the methods by which Black politicians and judges in the southern U.S. were driven from office as the post-Civil War Reconstruction ended.[23] In 2012, after irritating his major coalition partner, Paraguay's president Fernando Lugo was impeached and removed in a 'hasty 24-hour process' that gave him only two hours to present his defense against charges largely based on policy disagreements.[24]

States in Nigeria have witnessed a grotesque series of impeachments of governors or deputy governors based on retaliation for political disloyalty. These were sometimes conducted irregularly by segments of the legislature meeting off-premises.[25] The charges were not necessarily groundless, but as Professor Omololu Fagbadebo has explained, given systemic corruption in Nigeria, impeachment can be selectively deployed as a political weapon.[26]

2.4.1 Is Impeachment Merely a No-confidence Vote?

Before discussing particular violations from impeachment, one should confront a basic issue about removal for cause. If it is legitimate for a parliamentary majority to remove a prime minister by a vote of no confidence as a simple matter of preference, then why should it be problematic from a human rights perspective for a legislative majority or supermajority to impeach and remove a president for whatever reason it likes?

There are several answers. First, parliamentary systems have rules that authorize subjective no-confidence votes, and if the majority follows the proper procedures, then it is staying within its power. When the legislature instead seeks to impeach, the legal system normally provides an objective standard of evaluation that should be met.

Second, in human rights terms, the officer being removed has political and personal rights at stake in serving out a term in accordance with the rules, and the voters have political rights at stake in the removal of an elected official. Impeachment that disregards these rules, merely by legislative will, would violate the officer's rights.[27] It would also vitiate the election, harming democracy itself.

22 *Case of the Constitutional Court v Peru*, Judgment No 71 (IACtHR, 31 January 2001).

23 See Eric Foner, *Reconstruction: America's Unfinished Revolution, 1863–1877* (Harper & Row 1988) 562.

24 Leiv Marsteintredet, Mariana Llanos and Detlef Nolte, 'Paraguay and the Politics of Impeachment' (2013) 24(4) *Journal of Democracy* 110.

25 See, e.g., Omololu Fagbadebo, *Impeachment in the Nigerian Presidential System: Challenges, Successes and the Way Forward* (Palgrave Macmillan 2020) 123, 342–53. The procedural transgressions ultimately drove the Supreme Court of Nigeria to revise its prior refusal to review the legality of impeachment. ibid 292–93.

26 ibid 42.

27 It may follow from this perspective that no-confidence votes are subject to some human rights constraints, for example, that legislators must not merely vote their preferences when these preferences amount to prohibited discrimination.

Third, some impeachment procedures impose consequences that go beyond removal, such as disqualification from future office or even criminal sanctions. These effects may require different protections compared with no-confidence votes that result only in removal.

2.4.2 Procedural Fairness in General

Different systems employ a wide variety of decisional structures for impeachment. In some systems, the process is wholly legislative, often with accusation voted by one chamber and adjudication by the other. In others, the judiciary plays a role, either binding or nonbinding. A court may act as a filter, deciding whether an adequate factual or legal basis exists before the process can go forward; it may provide a nonbinding report at an intermediate stage; the trial may be held in court rather than in a legislative body; or a more limited judicial review may follow the legislature's decision. Instead of a court, an independent outside committee may act as a filter or provide a nonbinding report.

The involvement of a court potentially ensures that a legal standard for impeachment is not misunderstood or ignored by the politicians and may thus protect the human rights of the accused official. However, filtering decisions by judges are less likely to protect against politicized selectivity regarding which well-founded cases to initiate or which cases would satisfy the standard that the legislature will actually convict.

When votes are taken in the legislative, judicial, or independent bodies, systems also vary in the size of the required majority.[28] In the U.S. Congress, a simple majority of the House of Representatives can accuse ('impeach'), but a two-thirds majority of the Senate is required to convict; Senate practice requires only a simple majority to specify sanctions other than removal after conviction. Some systems require larger majorities at one or both stages; other systems require smaller majorities than two-thirds to convict. Generally, higher majority requirements make impeachment more difficult and make partisan abuses of the process less likely, but they may lessen the opportunity for accountability.

Turning to comparative human rights jurisprudence, the regional and global tribunals have disagreed on how fair trial principles apply to impeachment proceedings. The Inter-American and African systems include generally phrased fair trial provisions, while the versions in the European system and the global ICCPR are directed to criminal prosecutions and an incomplete range of civil disputes.[29]

28 Ginsburg, Huq and Landau (n 5) 130.

29 American Convention on Human Rights (ACHR), art 8; African Charter on Human and Peoples' Rights (ACHPR), art 7; [European] Convention for the Protection of Human Rights and Fundamental Freedoms (ECHR), art 6; ICCPR, art 14.

The IACtHR has interpreted its fair trial provision broadly and has extended the minimum procedural guarantees for criminal proceedings to all forms of government adjudication. The court subjects impeachments to this provision because it imposes a sanction on individuals, even if it is conducted by the legislature.[30] Nonetheless, in 2018, the IACtHR backed away from an opportunity to issue an advisory opinion elaborating the human rights constraints on impeachment of democratically elected presidents. The court recognized the political delicacy of the question and showed unusual sensitivity to the range of practice among states in the hemisphere. Rather than 'reduce the inter-American standards to a minimum common denominator' in an advisory opinion, the court chose to leave evaluation to a 'detailed and contextualized analysis that can only be made in the context of a contentious case.'[31] Even allowing for variations depending on national historical context and the features of the particular office, the IACtHR's established doctrine regarding wide applicability of criminal trial-type procedures would suggest robust limitations on impeachment processes.

Within the African regional system, the subregional ECOWAS Community Court of Justice has held that the proceedings in the legislative impeachment of a Liberian Supreme Court judge violated the fair trial guarantee of the African Charter of Human and Peoples' Rights.[32] The Court found that the Senate did not comply with its own rules and that the judge had been denied the right to be heard at the impeachment stage before the House of Representatives. The analysis invoked criminal procedure notions of fair trial, but this may in part have been because the Liberian Senate rules did so expressly.

The ECtHR, in contrast, held in 2011 that the legislative impeachment and removal of Lithuanian president Rolandas Paksas fell outside the scope of the fair trial provision, as applied to either criminal or civil matters.[33] Moreover, the other rights relating only to criminal proceedings did not apply. However, when the ECtHR evaluated the disqualification that resulted from this impeachment (*discussed in section 4 later*), it did point to the significant procedural safeguards that had been provided, including an intermediate judicial ruling that the allegations met the constitutional standard for impeachment, and the use of criminal law procedures in the parliamentary trial. Moreover, the ECtHR has characterized impeachment proceedings in Iceland, which are initiated by the legislature before a hybrid court of impeachment empowered

30 *Constitutional Court* (n 22) [68–71].

31 *Order on Request for an Advisory Opinion Presented by the Inter-American Commission on Human Rights* (IACtHR, 29 May 2018) [14, 17] <corteidh.or.cr/solicitudoc/sor_01_18_ing.pdf> accessed 22 October 2009.

32 *Ja'neh v Liberia*, Judgment No ECW/CCJ/JUD/28/20 (ECOWAS Court, 10 November 2020). The Community Court of Justice of the Economic Community of West African States (ECOWAS) has jurisdiction to issue binding judgments on human rights issues involving ECOWAS member states.

33 *Paksas v Lithuania*, App No 34932/04 (ECHR, 6 January 2011) [GC].

to impose imprisonment, as a criminal process. The ECtHR upheld this process as fair. The hybrid court had a majority of lay judges appointed by parliament, but there were sufficient safeguards for its independence.[34]

At the global level, the Human Rights Committee has held that the ICCPR fair trial guarantee did not apply to the legislative impeachment procedure in Lithuania, which was a disciplinary-type procedure rather than a criminal trial or civil dispute.[35] However, Article 25(c) of the ICCPR sets forth a right of equal access to positions in public service; the European Convention lacks any such language. The Committee interprets this provision as prohibiting arbitrary dismissal of elected or appointed public officials. As the Committee explained in its General Comment on Article 25, '[t]he grounds for removal of elected officeholders should be established by laws based on objective and reasonable criteria and incorporating fair procedures,' while in appointive public service 'the criteria and processes for appointment . . . and dismissal must be objective and reasonable.'[36] In the Human Rights Committee's 2013 review of Paraguay, it criticized the rapid impeachment of president Lugo and recommended that the state should always ensure that impeachments accord with the basic principles of due process and the principles of Article 25.[37]

Stepping back to general human rights conceptions, regardless of whether a specific treaty provision on fair trial applies, impeachment proceedings should satisfy basic norms of fairness adapted to their character. Some departures from a judicial model may be necessary in order to empower a legislative body to provide an effective check on abuses by another branch. Nevertheless, procedures should provide structure that keeps impeachment within its assigned boundaries and that considers both the official and the public. Officials threatened with removal should have a right to be adequately heard on the truth of the allegations and on the appropriateness of the proposed consequences. If legislators are the ultimate decision-makers, then they should be obligated to decide objectively on the charges brought and on the public benefit of removal, not on their partisan advantage. More serious consequences beyond removal should require more robust procedures. But involving the legislature presupposes the value of having their political experience and judgment inform the decision, and professional standards of judicial conduct and recusal may be only partially relevant. When the consequences extend to criminal

34 *Haarde v Iceland*, App No 66847/12 (ECHR, 23 November 2017).

35 *Paksas v Lithuania*, UN Doc CCPR/C/110/D/2155/2012 (HRC, 25 March 2014) [7.7–7.8]. The author should disclose that, as a member of the Human Rights Committee in 2013 and 2014, he participated in this decision and in the adoption of the concluding observations on Paraguay and Sri Lanka cited in notes 36 and 45.

36 Human Rights Committee, General Comment No 25: Article 25 (1996) [16, 23], in Compilation of General Comments and General Recommendations Adopted by Human Rights Treaty Bodies, UN Doc HRI/GEN/1/Rev.9 (Vol. I) (2008); see, e.g., *Jagminas v Lithuania*, UN Doc CCPR/C/126/D/2670/2015 (HRC, 24 July 2019).

37 Human Rights Committee, Concluding Observations on the Third Periodic Report of Paraguay, UN Doc CCPR/C/PRY/CO/3 (2013) [24].

punishment, yet more stringent procedural protections are required, and one may doubt the propriety of allowing politicians to pass a sentence of imprisonment against their rivals.

2.4.3 Judicial Independence

Additional human rights considerations apply in the case of legislative removal of a judge. The independence of the judiciary is a key principle of human rights law. The Universal Declaration of Human Rights frames the right to fair trial in terms that include an 'independent and impartial tribunal,' as do several major human rights treaties.[38] Both international court jurisprudence and international declarations of principle have further addressed judicial independence in the context of removal.

In the U.S., the independence of the federal judiciary faced a crisis at the beginning of the nineteenth century, but the outcome produced a strong tradition that judges should not be impeached in retaliation for unpopular decisions or as a means of partisan control. There has been, however, greater tolerance for indirect interference through court reorganization, including variations in the size of the Supreme Court, and highly politicized appointment processes. State legislatures have not always been as respectful. For example, during much of the nineteenth century, political parties in New Hampshire used removal by address to replace state judges by their own partisans when control of state government shifted.[39]

The IACtHR has repeatedly imposed strict requirements on legislative removal of judges. Its first confrontation with impeachment involved the three constitutional court judges removed for deciding against Fujimori.[40] The IACtHR emphasized the need to protect judicial independence while also invoking its regional jurisprudence of adjudicatory due process. In a later case about legislative removal of judges in Ecuador, the IACtHR explained that judicial independence requires protection against external pressures on judges' decisions to ensure their ability to rule on specific disputes without fear of reprisals. Judges need not have absolute guarantees of tenure in their positions, but there must be clear procedures and objective criteria for dismissal.[41] Nonetheless, the American Convention does not totally prohibit involvement of legislators in a decision to remove a judge. The Court has upheld the removal of a judge by a mixed 'impeachment jury' (*jurado de enjuiciamiento*) composed of a presiding judge, four legislators, and four

38 ICCPR art 14(1), ACHR art 8(1), ECHR art 14(1). The ACHPR refers to an 'impartial tribunal' in the free trial provision, article 7, and imposes on states an obligation 'to guarantee the independence of the Courts' in article 26.

39 Richard F Upton, 'The Independence of the Judiciary in New Hampshire' (1959) 1(4) *New Hampshire Bar Journal* 28.

40 *Constitutional Court* (n 22).

41 *Quintano Coello v Ecuador*, Judgment No 266 (IACtHR, 23 August 2013) [143–55].

attorneys, in the absence of a concrete demonstration of improper pressures or unfair procedures.[42]

The ECtHR has also has emphasized the protection of judicial independence, in relation not only to judicial discipline procedures before various types of bodies but also to other actions by the legislature. The cases have not involved impeachment as such. One leading decision involved the demotion of the president of the Hungarian Supreme Court (without removing him from the court altogether) through legislation revising the courts as part of Viktor Orbán's consolidation of power.[43] Similarly, after the legislature of Poland set aside the appointments of constitutional court judges and chose its own adherents to replace them, the ECtHR held that the resulting recomposition of the court deprived litigants of their right to a 'tribunal established by law.'[44]

Both the European and Inter-American Courts have cited the interpretation of the fair trial provision at the global level by the Human Rights Committee. As the Committee explained in summarizing its jurisprudence, 'Judges may be dismissed only on serious grounds of misconduct or incompetence, in accordance with fair procedures ensuring objectivity and impartiality set out in the constitution or the law.'[45] In 2014, the Committee's review of Sri Lanka specifically expressed concern 'at the impeachment of the former Chief Justice [Bandaranayake], in January 2013, under circumstances that raised serious doubts about its consistency with basic principles of due process and judicial independence.'[46]

The IACtHR has also taken a strong position in favor of the institutional independence and tenure of prosecutors, viewed in a civil law manner as a branch of the judiciary.[47] The ECtHR has not gone as far, though it has noted the existence of a trend in this direction.[48] In contrast, the Human Rights Committee has noted the opposite risk of unchecked prosecutorial authority, expressing concern to Bulgaria about 'the weak accountability of the Prosecutor General, who is essentially immune from criminal prosecution and irremovable by means of impeachment for other misconduct.'[49]

2.4.4 Disqualification from Future Office

A substantial minority of constitutions list disqualification from future office as a required or authorized outcome of the impeachment process. Like removal

42 *Rico v Argentina*, Judgment No 383 (IACtHR, 2 September 2019).

43 *Baka v Hungary*, App No 20261/12 (ECHR, 23 June 2016) [GC].

44 *Xero Flor w Polsce v Poland*, App No 4907/18 (ECHR, 7 May 2021).

45 Human Rights Committee, General Comment No 32: Right to Equality Before Courts and Fair Trial (2007) [19–20] in *Compilation* (n 36).

46 Human Rights Committee, Concluding Observations on the Fifth Periodic Report of Sri Lanka, UN Doc CCPR/C/LKA/CO/5 (2014) [5].

47 *Martínez Esquivia v Colombia*, Judgment No 412 (IACtHR, 6 October 2020).

48 *Kövesi v Romania*, App No 3594/19 (ECHR, 5 May 2020).

49 Human Rights Committee, Concluding Observations on the Fourth Periodic Report of Bulgaria, UN Doc CCPR/C/BGR/CO/4 (2018) [43].

itself, disqualification serves to protect the public from further abuse of power. The provision may specify the duration and the scope of the positions covered or leave a range of discretion to the decisionmaker. The U.S. constitution permits the Senate to impose disqualification that is life-long and covers all federal offices. In some countries, disqualification applies only to the office previously held; in other countries, the duration of disqualification is short (e.g., five years).

Adding disqualification to removal raises both procedural and substantive human rights issues. One may ask whether the procedures used in the impeachment process are sufficient in light of the seriousness of the disqualification consequence. One may also ask whether barring the ex-official from future election or appointment exceeds the permissible limitations on that individual's right to political participation or the rights of the voters to choose their representative.[50]

Both the ECtHR and the Human Rights Committee examined issues about disqualification in proceedings arising from the 2004 impeachment of the president of Lithuania, Rolandas Paksas.[51] Paksas became the first European head of state to be impeached and removed due primarily to benefits he conferred on a Russian businessman who was a major donor to his campaign. After the removal vote, the constitutional court interpreted the Lithuanian constitution as implicitly requiring that an official impeached for gross violation of the constitution and breach of the constitutional oath be disqualified permanently from certain high offices, including being president or a member of the national legislature.

The ECtHR examined his disqualification only in relation to candidacy for the parliament due to the narrow framing of electoral rights in the European Convention. The Court approved of restricting the candidacy of a person who 'seriously abused a public position or whose conduct has threatened to undermine the rule of law or democratic foundations.'[52] But it found Paksas's permanent and irreversible disqualification from legislative office disproportionate. The ECtHR emphasized that the constitutional court's rule was categorical and that this rule had been adopted in the context of the particular impeachment as factors in its proportionality analysis. The ECtHR's 2011 judgment was referred to the Council of Europe to oversee implementation but did not

50 The electoral rights in article 25 ICCPR are expressly protected against 'unreasonable restrictions;' the corresponding provision in the European Convention is understood by the ECtHR as permitting proportionate limitations for legitimate purposes.

51 The subject of disqualification and the decisions involving Lithuania are discussed in greater depth in Gerald L Neuman, 'Impeachment, Disqualification and Human Rights' (2023) 54 *Columbia Human Rights Law Review* 627. For an account by a Lithuanian judge of the ECtHR, see Egidijus Kūris, 'On Lessons Learned and Yet to Be Learned: Reflections on the Lithuanian Cases in the Strasbourg Court's Grand Chamber' (2019) 2 *East European Yearbook on Human Rights* 3, 17–27.

52 *Paksas* (n 33) (ECHR) [101].

immediately produce a shortening of Paksas's disqualification or an amendment of the general rule.

Paksas next commenced a proceeding before the Human Rights Committee, invoking the broader right to stand as a candidate or enter public service that is protected by article 25 ICCPR. With regard to running for president or serving as a government minister, the Committee concluded in 2014 that lifelong disqualification was disproportionate under the specific circumstances, for reasons like those that the ECtHR had given.[53] The present author, a Committee member at the time, dissented in part, arguing that 'an impeachment is not merely a vote of no confidence that contemplates renewed elections to test the President's popular support.'[54] I defended the proportionality of a lifelong disqualification rule:

> If Presidents who have successfully completed one or more terms can be permanently ineligible for reelection for the sake of ensuring a healthy and competitive political system, then surely Presidents who have been removed for abusing their offices can also be permanently barred.[55]

Lithuania still failed to amend its constitution, and after a later impeachment, the issue returned to the ECtHR in a request for an advisory opinion providing guidance on the permissible length of disqualification. The 2022 opinion de-emphasized the case-specific features of the Paksas decision and expressed more generally the Court's objection to permanent, irreducible disqualification from legislative elections.[56] The ECtHR explained that proportionality required either a time limit on the disqualification set in advance or the opportunity for individualized review in later years by a judicial or similar independent body on whether disqualification was no longer needed. Lithuania then completed the process of amending its constitution to limit disqualification to ten years after impeachment, for legislative elections and for the other relevant offices, which went further than the ECtHR had required.

These human rights decisions accept disqualification as a possible consequence of impeachment proceedings but call for greater care in determining its extent. The human rights principle of proportionality involves tailoring the restriction to the need rather than unreflectively disqualifying from as many

53 *Paksas* (n 35) (HRC).

54 ibid 18.

55 ibid. On the permissibility or necessity of presidential term limits from a human rights perspective, see European Commission on Democracy Through Law, Report on Term Limits, Part I – Presidents, CDL-AD(2018)010 (20 March 2018); *Indefinite Presidential Re-Election in Presidential Systems in the Context of the Inter-American System of Human Rights*, Advisory Opinion OC-28/21 (Series A) (IACtHR, 7 June 2021).

56 *Advisory Opinion on the Assessment, Under Article 3 of Protocol No 1 to the Convention, of the Proportionality of a General Prohibition on Standing for Election After Removal from Office in Impeachment Proceedings*, Request No P16-2020-002 (ECHR, 8 April 2022) [GC].

offices as possible for as long as possible. Even in the U.S., where federal disqualification has been regarded as an all-or-nothing option, there is an older state practice, now largely forgotten, of partial disqualification. Nonetheless, the ex-official's rights do not require immediate eligibility to return to office. The same could be said for the voters' rights – they are not absolutely entitled to choose whomever they like, regardless of the effect on the rights of others or on the democratic system.

It is not clear whether the ECtHR's rejection of irreducible permanent disqualification from legislative elections extends to disqualification from executive office, which provides more opportunity for a single official to inflict harm. Either way, the court's absolute approach may be too strict, particularly in a period of assaults on democracy. Human rights may be better protected by preserving the possibility of lifelong disqualification, where it is needed, in Europe and other parts of the world alike.

2.5 Conclusion

Properly employed, impeachment provides an important defense for the protection of human rights and democracy. Human rights law also suggests needed guidelines for avoiding misuse of this power. Still, the availability of impeachment as a backstop is essential when officials, such as presidents, cannot otherwise be removed from office.

3 Impeachment and Democracy

Does Impeachment Have an Effect on Democracy in Third Wave Presidentialism?

Young Hun Kim

3.1 Introduction

Of the key characteristics of presidentialism, a fixed term of a president in office has been a focal point of scholarly criticism for the past several decades.[1] On the one hand, some argue that a fixed term may be a boon for new democracies by enhancing the government stability, accountability, and the quality of democracy.[2] Since new democracies are more likely to suffer from government instability, fluid horizontal and vertical accountability, and relatedly, a higher risk of democratic breakdown particularly in the early years after democratic transition, a fixed term may, as the argument goes, work as a safety valve for a fragile democracy. On the other hand, some contend that a fixed term in office makes removing an incompetent, incapable, and/or corrupt president almost impossible. Most presidential democracies have impeachment available, but the requirements and process are often too high and cumbersome to be met. Then, non-democratic actors such as the military may decide to intervene. As a result, a fixed term in office of presidentialism is a greater culprit of democratic breakdown than a promoter of democratic stability.[3]

However, recent comparative literature has shown that a fixed term in office and the resulting rigidity of presidentialism need to be revisited.[4] As a matter

1 Juan J. Linz, 'The Perils of Presidentialism' (1990) 1(1) *Journal of Democracy* 51–69; Juan J. Linz, 'Presidential or Parliamentary Democracy: Does It Make a Difference?' in Juan J. Linz and Valenzuela Arturo (eds), *The Failure of Presidential Democracy* (The Johns Hopkins UP 1994) 3–87.

2 See, for example, Young Hun Kim and Donna Bahry, 'Interrupted Presidencies in Third Wave Democracies' (2008) 70(3) *The Journal of Politics* 807–22.

3 See, for example, Linz, 'The Perils of Presidentialism' (n 1) 51–69; Alfred Stepan and Cindy Skach, 'Constitutional Frameworks and Democratic Consolidation: Parliamentarianism Versus Presidentialism' (1993) 46(1) *World Politics* 1–22.

4 Margaret E Edwards, 'Understanding Presidential Failure in South America' (2015) 57(2) *Latin American Politics and Society* 111–31; Kathryn Hochstetler, 'Rethinking Presidentialism: Challenges and Presidential Falls in South America' (2006) 38(4) *Comparative Politics* 401–18; Kathryn Hochstetler and Margaret E Edwards, 'Failed Presidencies: Identifying and Explaining a South American Anomaly' (2009) 1(2) *Journal of Politics in Latin America* 31–57; Kim and

DOI: 10.4324/9781003256007-4

of fact, not a small number of presidents have left office early before their term expired in new democracies,[5] and some have left by impeachment. Such constitutional removals of presidents have not been limited to certain regions. They have been observed in Asia, Africa, Europe, and Latin America. To list a few examples of successful impeachment, Lithuanian President Rolandas Paksas was removed from office in April 2004 for violating the constitution by granting Lithuanian citizenship to a businessman who had ties to the Russian mafia.[6] Fernando Lugo of Paraguay was another president whose term was cut short for 'poor performance of duties' in June 2012.[7] In addition, Brazilian President Dilma Rousseff was impeached for financial irregularities in August 2016.[8] In Asia, the Constitutional Court of South Korea made President Park Geun-hye the first impeached president of the country for charges of corruption and abuse of power in March 2017.[9] Finally, Malagasy President Albert Zafy became the first impeached president in Africa since the Third Wave democratization. The charges included abuses of power and violations of the constitution.[10] Furthermore, it has been found that impeachments have often been tried by legislators in many new democracies, although doing so did not always lead to successful removal.[11] In all, impeachment is not

Bahry (n 2) 807–22; Leiv Marsteintredet and Einar Berntzen, 'Reducing the Perils of Presidentialism in Latin America Through Presidential Interruptions' (2008) 41 *Comparative Politics* 83–101; Christopher A Martínez, 'Presidential Instability in Latin America: Why Institutionalized Parties Matter' (2021) 56(4) *Government and Opposition* 683–704; Aníbal S. Pérez-Liñán, 'Democratization and Constitutional Crises in Presidential Regimes: Toward Congressional Supremacy?' (2005) 38(1) *Comparative Political Studies* 51–74; Aníbal S. Pérez-Liñán, *Presidential Impeachment and the New Political Instability in Latin America* (CUP 2007).

5 See, for example, Kim and Bahry (n 2) 807–22; Leiv Marsteintredet, Mariana Llanos and Detlef Nolte, 'Paraguay and the Politics of Impeachment' (2013) 24(4) *Journal of Democracy* 110–23; Arturo Valenzuela, 'Latin American Presidencies Interrupted' (2004) 15(4) *Journal of Democracy* 5–19.

6 Kim Murphy, 'Lithuanian Lawmakers Vote to Impeach President; Rolandas Paksas Was Linked to a Businessman with Alleged Ties to the Russian Mafia' *Los Angeles Times* (2004) A.3.

7 Daniel Jatobá and Bruno Theodoro Luciano, 'The Deposition of Paraguayan President Fernando Lugo and Its Repercussions in South American Regional Organizations*' (2018) 12(1) *Brazilian Political Science Review* 1–26; Marsteintredet, Llanos and Nolte (n 5) 110–23.

8 Marina Lopes and Dom Phillips, 'Brazilian President Dilma Rousseff Faces Final Impeachment Vote: Her Former Vice-President, Michel Temer, Is Widely Expected to Assume Full Power' *The Washington Post (Online)* (2016) <www.proquest.com/central/docview/1815593672/citation/6DD359C432E84C87PQ/1> accessed 6 March 2023.

9 Jonathan Cheng, 'South Korean President Park Geun-Hye Ousted from Office; Snap Election Will Pick Scandal-Plagued Leader's Successor' *Wall Street Journal (Online)* (2017) n/a.

10 Philip M Allen, 'Madagascar: Impeachment as Parliamentary Coup d'Etat' in Jody C Baumgartner and Naoko Kada (eds), *Checking Executive Power: Presidential Impeachment in Comparative Perspective* (Praeger 2003) 81–94.

11 Young Hun Kim, 'Impeachment and Presidential Politics in New Democracies' (2014) 21 *Democratization* 519–53.

something that exists only in the constitution. It has also been actively used by political actors.

Since a growing number of presidential democracies have been relying on impeachment to remove the incumbent, it is important to ask what impacts impeachment may have on these new democracies. Several studies have examined the effects of presidential impeachment and more broadly, interruptions on several political outcomes. Marsteintredet and Berntzen and Pérez-Liñán, for example, find that presidential interruptions have contributed to the suppression of the (re)emergence of authoritarian regimes in Latin America by making presidentialism more flexible.[12] Ginsburg et al., by examining nine cases of impeachment from 1990 to 2017, report that impeachment does not have a negative effect on democracy.[13] However, the first two studies focus only on Latin American countries. Ginsburg et al. focus on a global sample of countries,[14] but it is less clear what effects the constitutional removal of presidents may have on different aspects of democracy.

Accordingly, this study attempts to address the following questions. What kind of effects does impeachment, which in theory is the most formalized and constitutional presidential exit mode, have on the quality of democracy? Does it strengthen democracy or is it instead a liability for democracy? Or is it the case that the effects are rather dependent on the context of the presidential removal, and as a result, each impeachment is likely to have different effects?

In the next section, I will review the theoretical arguments on why impeachment may have either negative or positive effects on the quality of democracy. Next, I will discuss the data encompassing all Third Wave presidential and semi-presidential democracies from 1974 to 2018 and analyze it. Then, I will discuss the findings. The final section presents the conclusion.

3.2 Effects of Impeachment on Democracy: Theoretical Arguments

For the countries who have experienced impeachment, what effects did it have on their democracy? The literature has been inconclusive on this important question. Some suggest that impeachment is more likely to be a liability for democracy for several reasons. First, presidential impeachment is such a dramatic and explosive political event that may easily paralyze a country's political system for an extended time. In addition to the fact that impeachment removes a chief executive from office, which is already a dramatic outcome,

12 Marsteintredet and Berntzen (n 4) 83–101; Aníbal S. Pérez-Liñán, *Presidential Impeachment and the New Political Instability in Latin America* (CUP 2007).

13 Tom Ginsburg, Aziz Z. Huq and David Landau, 'The Comparative Constitutional Law of Presidential Impeachment' (2021) 88(1) *The University of Chicago Law Review* 81–164.

14 ibid. They focus on presidents with a fixed term in office for all countries. As a result, there are a small number of indirectly elected presidents in the sample such as Indonesian President Wahid. In addition, they include all types of democracies, new and established.

impeachment requires multiple steps to follow involving several institutions and often takes several months to complete.[15] Moreover, a presidential removal inevitably leads to political conflicts, ideological polarization, and social unrest between those who are in favor of the impeachment and those who are against it. In this regard, impeachment may be viewed as a type of political instability[16] and is thus not likely to leave a positive imprint on democracy.

Second, those who do not support impeachment may view it as an effort of the opposition to reap political gains. This may undermine the legitimacy of such a removal and public confidence in democracy.[17] Zhang, for example, notes that the impeachment of South Korean President Roh Moo-hyun in March 2004 was a result of power struggle between Roh and the opposition.[18] Ideologically progressive Roh was a political outsider with no college degree who remained at odds not only with the conservative opposition Grand National Party (GNP) but also with the liberal ruling party turned opposition Millennium Democratic Party (MDP). To the GNP and MDP, Roh was an unpalatable president who needed to be removed no matter what. To do

15 Jody C Baumgartner, 'Introduction: Comparative Presidential Impeachment' in Jody C Baumgartner and Naoko Kada (eds), *Checking Executive Power: Presidential Impeachment in Comparative Perspective* (Praeger 2003) 1–19; Ginsburg, Huq and Landau (n 13) 81–164.

16 Elsayed Ali Abofarha and Ramez Ibrahim Nasreldein, 'Explaining Presidential Instability in Latin America: Evidence from Brazil, Argentina and Ecuador' (2022) 7(1) *Review of Economics and Political Science* 56–70; Martínez (n 4) 683–704. There is no unified understanding of political instability. Examples of political instability observed in both democracies and non-democracies include democratic reversals, state collapse, revolutionary and ethnic wars, genocides/politicides (Jack A Goldstone and others, 'A Global Model for Forecasting Political Instability' (2010) 54(1) *American Journal of Political Science* 190–208), polity changes (Scott Gates and others, 'Institutional Inconsistency and Political Instability: Polity Duration, 1800–2000' (2006) 50(4) *American Journal of Political Science* 893–908), regime changes (Christopher Carothers, 'The Surprising Instability of Competitive Authoritarianism' (2018) 29(4) *Journal of Democracy* 129–35; James R Hollyer and others, 'Transparency, Protest, and Autocratic Instability' (2015)109(4) *The American Political Science Review* 764–84), assassinations, strikes, riots, revolutions, government crises, anti-government demonstrations, purges, and terrorism/guerrilla warfare (Nayef Al-Shammari and John Willoughby, 'Determinants of Political Instability Across Arab Spring Countries' (2019) 24(2) *Mediterranean Politics* 196–217; Arthur S Banks and Kenneth A Wilson, 'Cross-National Time-Series Data Archive (CNTS)' *Databanks International* (2022) <www.cntsdata.com> accessed 6 March 2023. For a good discussion on the measurements of political instability, see Luisa Blanco and Robin Grier, 'Long Live Democracy: The Determinants of Political Instability in Latin America' (2009) 45(1) *Journal of Development Studies* 76–95. For critiques on the measurements of political instability, refer to Jakob de Haan, 'Political Institutions and Economic Growth Reconsidered: Presidential Address for the European Public Choice Society Conference, Turku, April 2006' (2007) 131(3–4) *Public Choice* 281–92.

17 John M Carey and others, 'The Threat of Impeachment Can Push Presidents Out the Door. But There's a Catch: 5 Takeaways from the Departure of Peru's President' *Washington Post – Blogs* (2018) <www.proquest.com/docview/2024335772/citation/BAA8C5D-7C4A84BB9PQ/1> accessed 6 March 2023.

18 Baohui Zhang, 'Improving Democratic Governance in East Asia' (2008) 16(1) *Asian Journal of Political Science* 64–84.

this, these parties cited several controversial grounds for impeachment ranging from violations of the constitution and laws and corruption scandals implicating his aides to mismanagement of the economy.[19] However, the nationwide demonstrations after the passage of the impeachment motion in the National Assembly and the opposition's poor performance in the legislative elections held a month later show that the public did not view the attempt to impeach Roh legitimate and justifiable. In the end, the Constitutional Court reinstated Roh to the office in May.

In a similar vein, Santos and Guarnieri characterize the impeachment of Rousseff Dilma of Brazil in 2016 as a 'parliamentary coup.'[20] In addition to their understanding that there was no legitimate basis for impeachment, they point out a problem involving the sequence of events leading up to the impeachment. That is, the opposition led by the Brazilian Social Democracy Party (PSDB) decided to impeach the president first before coming up with impeachment charges. It may appear that the removal of Dilma enjoyed procedural legitimacy. However, they conclude that it was no different from a military coup because it was an unlawful seizure of power by the opposition.

The impeachment of Paraguayan President Fernando Lugo in 2012 is another contentious case. Although the impeachment motion listed several charges against him such as negligence and ineffectiveness of the government as shown in the Matanza Curuguaty case (a bloody clash between police and landless workers that led to 17 deaths on June 15, 2012), growing insecurity in the country, and a lack of transparency in the government,[21] some view that President Lugo was impeached for the controversial 'poor performance in office' rather than for criminal activities.[22] Moreover, the Senate finalized his impeachment and installed Vice President Federico Franco as the new president just one day after the Chamber of Deputies passed the impeachment motion.[23]

Not all impeachments arise from criminal activities, violations of the constitution, abuses of power, and treason of the president. Some constitutions list incapacity, poor performance, and even 'general dissatisfaction' with the president as the bases for impeachment.[24] The problem with these charges is that they are highly subjective and controversial. There is no clear-cut understanding of what constitutes incapacity of the president, poor performance in office,

19 Youngjae Lee, 'Law, Politics, and Impeachment: The Impeachment of Roh Moo-Hyun from a Comparative Constitutional Perspective' (2005) 53(2) *The American Journal of Comparative Law* 403–32.

20 Fabiano Santos and Fernando Guarnieri, 'From Protest to Parliamentary Coup: An Overview of Brazil's Recent History' (2016) 25(4) *Journal of Latin American Cultural Studies* 485–94.

21 Jatobá and Luciano (n 7) 1–26; Marsteintredet, Llanos and Nolte (n 5) 110–23.

22 Ginsburg, Huq and Landau (n 13) 81–164.

23 Jatobá and Luciano (n 7) 1–26.

24 Ginsburg, Huq and Landau (n 13) 81–164.

and 'general dissatisfaction' and whether all such charges should be subject to impeachment. If charges of presidential impeachment are subject to controversy and understood as a means to reap political gains by the opposition, then impeachment would only deepen political polarization and intensify protests.

Third, impeachment may create a culture of retaliation. Regardless of what the bases and charges of impeachment are, supporters of the removed president, whether they are the political elite or mass public, are not likely to be persuaded that impeachment was inevitable. As a result, once they gain control of the legislature, they may decide to target a president from the party that supported the impeachment of their own earlier. In addition, the requirements for impeachment may get lower after the first impeachment,[25] and political instability and mistrust among political elite and public could become widespread.

Fourth, the debate surrounding dual legitimacy of presidentialism sheds light on the negative effects of impeachment on democracy. As Linz argues, the fact that both the president and legislature are popularly elected in presidentialism is a source of political conflict and instability in new democracies.[26] The already unstable situation under dual legitimacy could get worse if some members of the legislature remove the president from office. This is because successful impeachment, unlike other types of presidential interruptions such as resignation, is an act of nullifying a president's legitimacy by an institution with competing legitimacy.[27] Therefore, impeachment not only is unlikely to gain legitimacy among supporters of the president but also intensifies political polarization, conflict, and instability.

Lastly, although impeachment itself may not be a problem, the immediate aftermath of impeachment can have an adverse effect on democracy. For example, the newly installed interim president may be a source of conflict and instability because he/she does not enjoy the legitimacy and is politically weak. Then, what may follow are other rounds of executive turnover until the new presidential election is held.[28] Relatedly, it is worth noting that an interim president in some countries serves out the rest of the impeached president's term, while in other countries, an interim president plays the role of caretaker for a short period of time until the next presidential election.[29] In the former, political instability is likely to continue because the successor does not enjoy the same kind of popular mandate the predecessor did. In all, the explosive

25 Gi-Wook Shin and Rennie J Moon, 'South Korea After Impeachment' (2017) 28(4) *Journal of Democracy* 117–31 call this a 'trivialization and routinization' of impeachment.

26 Linz, 'The Perils of Presidentialism' (n 1) 51–69.

27 Ginsburg, Huq and Landau (n 13) 81–164.

28 Argentina is a good example of this. Between the departure of Fernando de la Rúa in 2001 and the inauguration of Néstor Kirchner in 2003, there were four interim presidents (Ramón Puerta, Adolfo Rodríguez Saá, Eduardo Camaño, and Eduardo Duhalde), although de la Rúa left office early via resignation, not impeachment.

29 According to Ginsburg, Huq and Landau (n 13) 81–164, 140, 74 percent of presidential and semi-presidential constitutions worldwide belong to the former category.

nature of impeachment, pursuit of partisan goals, controversial impeachment charges, culture of retaliation, revocation of presidential legitimacy, and interim presidents with no popular mandate explain why impeachment is more likely to have adverse effects on democracy.

To the contrary, there are good reasons to believe that successful impeachment may promote a country's democracy. First, the very fact that political actors rely on the constitutional process of impeachment signals that democracy, rule of law, and constitutionalism are broadly institutionalized, recognized, accepted, and practiced.[30] That is, impeachment proves that democracy can correct itself by peacefully removing a beleaguered president.[31] Moreover, a troubled president, once impeached, is expected to leave office peacefully without relying on non-constitutional measures to stay in office. This is a remarkable departure from earlier practices such as military coups, violent overthrow of the government, and foreign intervention observed in some new presidential democracies, and it is clearly a sign of the flexibility of presidentialism.[32]

Second, some impeached presidents are known to be corrupt and incapable, have engaged in criminal activities, and/or have violated the constitution. Removing them from office is, without a doubt, critical to strengthen democracy.[33] In the short run, impeachment may encounter political backlash. However, when these types of presidents stay in office longer, the governability crisis, mass protests, and even the intervention of the military are more likely.[34] Terminating a term of such presidents via a constitutional means may signify the end of political instability and facilitate democratic habituation and consolidation.

Third, impeachment often involves active citizen participation.[35] For example, the massive candlelight vigil of the South Korean public played an important role in sealing the political fate of President Park Geun-hye, while it saved President Roh Moo-hyun from conviction.[36] Although too much participation on the street may indicate that political institutions are not working as intended, it also may be viewed as an effort of civil society to redress violations of the president. Therefore, impeachment involving vigorous participation of the people needs to be viewed as a healthy sign of democracy, not a threat.[37]

30 Hahm Chaihark and Sung Ho Kim, 'Constitutionalism on Trial in South Korea' (2005) 16(2) *Journal of Democracy* 28–42.
31 John Feffer, 'The Future of Korean Democracy' *Hankyoreh* (2012) <https://english.hani.co.kr/arti/english_edition/english_editorials/1072236.html> accessed 6 March 2023.
32 Marsteintredet and Berntzen (n 4) 83–101.
33 Carey and others (n 17).
34 Linz, 'The Perils of Presidentialism' (n 1) 51–69.
35 Hochstetler (n 4) 401–18.
36 Byong-Kuen Jhee and Johann Park, 'How Citizens Reshaped the Path of Presidential Impeachment in Korea' (2019) 50(4) *Korea Observer* 565–86.
37 Shin and Moon (n 25) 117–31.

Lastly, impeachment shows that a president is not guaranteed to serve a fixed term in office.[38] This, in turn, sends a strong warning signal to the next presidents so that they protect the rule of law and the constitution and do not engage in any illegal activities while in office. In this regard, Pérez-Liñán's study needs to be emphasized.[39] He views the increasing reliance on impeachment in Latin America as a corrective mechanism to check hegemonic presidents. He acknowledges that impeachment in some countries has been abused by the legislature to promote their political goals. However, he argues that the main threat to democracy in the region is unchecked powerful presidents who try to stand above other branches of the government. Therefore, impeachment is necessary and good for democratic consolidation. Accordingly, the reliance on constitutional means, removal of a troublesome president, active citizen participation, and learning effect are all likely to contribute to a stronger democracy.

3.3 Data

To analyze the effects of impeachment on democracy, it is crucial to identify democracy. First, I focus on new democracies in the Third Wave from 1974 to 2018. This is because the political dynamics of established and older democracies are likely to be different from new democracies. To identify democracies, I rely on the Polity5 data (Center for Systemic Peace 2022). A country is classified as a democracy if one of the following conditions are met: i) it experienced either 'Major Democratic Transition' (REGTRANS=3) or 'Minor Democratic Transition' (REGTRANS=2)[40] or ii) it has a POLITY score of +1 or greater after state creation, state transformation, or state failure.

Of these new democracies, only popularly elected presidents in presidential and semi-presidential systems who have completed their term or left office by the end of 2018 are included. Indirectly elected presidents by the legislative body and acting/interim presidents are not counted because they do not enjoy the popular mandate and tend to possess limited executive powers. Due to the unique political and social context of small states compared to larger

38 Hochstetler (n 4) 401–18; Kim (n 11) 519–53; Marsteintredet and Berntzen (n 4) 83–101; Pérez-Liñán (n 12).

39 Aníbal S. Pérez-Liñán, 'Impeachment or Backsliding? Threats to Democracy in the Twenty-First Century' (2018) 33(98) *Revista Brasileira de Ciências Sociais* 1–15.

40 'Major Democratic Transition' refers to 'six points or greater increase in POLITY score over a period of three years or less including a shift from an autocratic POLITY value (-10 to 0) to a partial democratic POLITY value (+1 to +6) or full democratic POLITY value (+7 to +10) or a shift from a partial democratic value to a full democratic value'. 'Minor Democratic Transition' refers to 'three to five points increase in POLITY score over a period of three years or less including a shift from autocratic to partial democratic or from partial to full democratic value' (Monty G Marshall and Ted Robert Gurr, 'Polity5 Dataset Users' Manual' (2020) 35–36 <www.systemicpeace.org/inscr/p5manualv2018.pdf> accessed 6 March 2023.

ones,[41] countries with a population of less than one million are not included either. If a president was reelected for a consecutive term, then each term is counted separately.

Next, I identify different modes of presidential interruptions in new democracies. In this study, presidential interruptions are defined as occasions where popularly elected presidents had to leave office early before their term expired.[42] The most common modes include, but are not limited to, impeachment including a declaration of incapacity, resignation, and coup/deposition. A failure to complete a president's term due to assassination, illness, or accident are not interruptions because they are not political by nature.

I identify 289 presidential terms out of 64 Third Wave democracies from 1974 to 2018. Of these cases, 45 presidential terms were interrupted, which account for approximately 16 percent of all cases. Of the different modes of interruptions, resignation and coups are the most common in new democracies. A total of 15 presidents (about 5 percent of all cases and 33 percent of all interruptions) left office early by resigning, and 19 presidents (approximately 7 percent of all cases and 42 percent of all interruptions) were removed from office by coup or forcible deposition, mostly in Africa. Although military coups globally have become less frequent than before, they still remain a significant threat to new African democracies.[43]

In contrast, leaving office early via successful impeachment was less frequent. In this sample, only 8 presidents (less than 3 percent of the total cases and 18 percent of all interruptions) had to leave office early because of successful impeachment or deposition by the legislature (e.g., Abdala Bucaram Ortiz and Lucio Gutierrez of Ecuador and Viktor Yanukovych of Ukraine). Although Kim reports that approximately 45 percent of presidential democracies attempted to impeach the president from 1974 to 2003, the success rate shown in this updated data is not very high.[44]

There are three 'fuzzy' interruptions that do not perfectly fit into the resignation, impeachment, and coup classifications. One is President Antonio Guzmán of the Dominican Republic who committed suicide in July 1982 after learning about scandals involving his closet aides.[45] Another one is President Didier Ratsiraka of Madagascar who fled the country in July 2002 after months-long disputes surrounding the presidential election outcome held in December 2001.[46] The last case is the Philippine President Joseph Estrada. He

41 Timothy J Power and Mark J Gasiorowski, 'Institutional Design and Democratic Consolidation in the Third World' (1997) 30(2) *Comparative Political Studies* 123–55.

42 Kim and Bahry (n 2) 807–22, 811.

43 Of the 16 presidential interruptions in African democracies from 1974 to 2018, 14 (87.5 percent) were due to military coups. For a list of these presidents, see Table 3.1.

44 Kim (n 11) 519–53.

45 'Rulers. Org' *Rulers* (2022) <www.rulers.org/indexg4.html#> accessed 6 March 2023.

46 Rachel L Swarns, 'Longtime Madagascar Leader Flees as Rival Gains' *New York Times, Late Edition (East Coast)* (2002) A.6.

was neither successfully impeached nor tendered his 'resignation.' Initially, the country's House of Representatives passed an impeachment motion against him for corruption charges, but the Senate did not take a vote to convict. In the end, he fled the country in January 2001 after succumbing to the 'people power.'[47] These three interruptions account for about 1 percent of all presidential terms and 7 percent of all interruptions.

Notably, some presidents decided to resign upon imminent impeachment because impeachment is less honorable and possibly deprives the officeholder of perks and future political opportunities. For example, President Fernando Collor de Mello of Brazil was impeached for corruption charges by the Chamber of Deputies in October 1992. Then, he resigned in December a year after the Senate had started an impeachment trial he was certain to lose.[48] Paraguayan President Raul Cubas Grau resigned in March 1999 after Congress impeached him for abuse of power related to the assassination of Vice President Luis María Argaña and conviction in the Senate became almost certain.[49] Similarly, President Pedro Pablo Kuczynski of Peru resigned in March 2018 facing a conviction in the impeachment trial over a vote-buying scandal.[50] Although these presidents technically resigned, there is no denying that a looming successful impeachment was behind their decision to do so. Therefore, I classify these cases as impeachment in this study.[51] Then, the total number of impeachments in the Third Wave democracies increases to 11 (and the number of resignations decreases to 12), which is approximately 4 percent of all presidential terms, 24 percent of all modes of interruptions, and 42 percent of interruptions excluding a coup. Table 3.1 shows the distribution of interruptions in new presidential and semi-presidential democracies from 1974 to 2018.

47 Yuko Kasuya, 'Weak Institutions and Strong Movements: The Case of President Estrada's Impeachment and Removal in the Philippines' in Jody C Baumgartner and Naoko Kada (eds), *Checking Executive Power: Presidential Impeachment in Comparative Perspective* (Praeger 2003) 45–63.

48 Nathaniel C Nash, 'Brazilian Leader Quits as His Trial Starts in Senate' *New York Times, Late Edition (East Coast)* (1992) A.1.

49 Stephen Brown, 'Paraguayans Celebrate After President Resigns: The Departure of Raul Cubas Follows a Week of Conflict in the Small South American Country' *The Vancouver Sun* (1999) A14.

50 Marcelo Rochabrún and Nicholas Casey, 'Peru's President Offers Resignation Over Vote-Buying Scandal' *New York Times (Online)* (2018) <www.proquest.com/central/docview/2019084217/abstract/ED80831075584C38PQ/1> accessed 6 March 2023.

51 Overall, this understanding is consistent with Marsteintredet and Berntzen's definition of impeachment: 'An interruption can be categorized as impeachment, if an impeachment procedure is initiated by the legislature even if the president resigns before the final vote in congress takes place, as was the case with Cubas in Paraguay in 1999' (88). However, they define presidential resignation as 'a situation in which a president, during popular protests, duress, or the loss of congressional support, resigns without a previous impeachment procedure or a congressional vote that unseats the president' (88) (see Marsteintredet and Berntzen (n 4) 83–101).

Table 3.1 Different Modes of Presidential Interruptions in New Democracies from 1974 to 2018

	Country	*President*	*Year*
Resignations	Dominican Republic	Joaquín Balaguer	1996
	Guatemala	Jorge Serrano Elías	1993
	Guatemala	Otto Pérez Molina	2015
	Bolivia	Hernán Siles Zuazo	1985
	Bolivia	Gonzalo Sánchez de Lozada	2003
	Argentina	Raúl Alfonsín	1989
	Argentin	Fernando de la Rúa	2001
	Serbia	Boris Tadic	2012
	Russia	Boris Yeltsin	1999
	Georgia	Eduard Shevardnadze	2003
	Georgia	Mikheil Saakashvili	2007
	Kyrgyzstan	Kurmanbek Bakiyev	2010
	Subtotal	12	
Coups/forcible depositions	Haiti	Jean-Bertrand Aristide	1991
	Honduras	Manuel Zelaya	2009
	Ecuador	Jamil Mahuad	2000
	Georgia	Zviad Gamsakhurdia	1992
	Azerbaijan	Abulfez Elchibey	1993
	Guinea-Bissau	João Bernardo Vieira	1999
	Guinea-Bissau	Kumba Ialá	2003
	Mali	Amadou Toumani Touré	2012
	Mauritania	Sidi Mohamed Ould Cheikh Abdallahi	2008
	Niger	Mahamane Ousmane	1996
	Niger	Mamadou Tandja	2010
	Burkina Faso	Sangoulé Lamizana	1980
	Sierra Leone	Ahmad Tejan Kabbah	1997
	Ghana	Hilla Limann	1981
	Nigeria	Alhaji Shehu Shagari	1983
	Central African Republic	Ange-Félix Patassé	2003
	Republic of the Congo	Pascal Lissouba	1997
	Zimbabwe	Robert Mugabe	2017
	Madagascar	Marc Ravalomanana	2009
	Subtotal	19	
Impeachments/deposition by the legislature	Ecuador	Abdala Bucaram Ortiz	1997
	Ecuador	Lucio Gutierrez	2005
	Peru	Pedro Pablo Kuczynski*	2018
	Brazil	Fernando Collor de Mello*	1992
	Brazil	Dilma Rousseff	2016
	Paraguay	Raul Cubas Grau*	1999
	Paraguay	Fernando Lugo	2012
	Lithuania	Rolandas Paksas	2004
	Ukraine	Viktor Yanukovych	2014
	Madagascar	Albert Zafy	1996

(*Continued*)

Table 3.1 (Continued)

	Country	*President*	*Year*
	South Korea	Park Geun-hye	2017
	Subtotal	11	
Others	Dominican Republic	Antonio Guzman Fernandez	1982
	Madagascar	Didier Ratsiraka	2002
	Philippines	Joseph Estrada	2001
	Subtotal	3	
	Total	45	

* Since an imminent successful impeachment was behind their decision to resign, these cases are classified as successful impeachment.

To detect the impact of impeachment on democracy, I first focus on the overall levels of democracy. To measure these, I rely on two broadly used indicators of democracy: the index of liberal democracy (*v2x_libdem*) from the V-Dem data and the Polity2 scores from Polity5 data.[52] The liberal democracy index is constructed by focusing on electoral competition, equality before the law, civil liberties, and judicial and legislative constraints on the executive.[53] The Polity2 score is a modified version of the Polity scores that is calculated by subtracting the AUTOC score from the DEMOC score.[54] I also examine specific political outcomes that successful impeachment may have impacted. These include horizontal accountability, corruption in the executive branch, executive's respect for the constitution, and mass mobilization. This is because the judicial and legislative branches play important roles during the impeachment process, corruption of the president is one of the most frequently cited charges of impeachment along with violations of the constitution, and civil society often leads the legislature to take action against the chief executive. For these outcomes, I rely on the judicial constraints on the executive (*v2x_jucon*), legislative constraints on the executive (*v2xlg_legcon*), executive branch corruption (*v2x_execorr*), executive's respect for the constitution (*v2exrescon*), and mass mobilization (*v2cagenmob*) from the V-Dem (Varieties of Democracy (V-Dem) Project 2022b).[55] Since the effects of impeachment in a given

52 Ginsburg and others also rely on Polity2 scores to examine the impact of impeachment on democracy. However, they focus on the change in the scores from two years prior to impeachment (not the impeachment year) to two years after (121). Therefore, the Polity2 score changes, if any, may not be a result of impeachment (Ginsburg, Huq and Landau (n 13) 81–164).

53 Varieties of Democracy (V-Dem) Project, 'V-Dem Codebook' (2022) <https://doi.org/10.23696/vdemds22> accessed 6 March 2023.

54 Marshall and Gurr (n 40) 35–36.

55 Questions that measure these variables are as follows: Judicial constraints on the executive (*v2x_jucon*) – 'To what extent does the executive respect the constitution and comply with court rulings, and to what extent is the judiciary able to act in an independent fashion?';

year may not be immediate, I look at the change in the values of these variables from the year of impeachment to the next two years after impeachment.

3.4 Findings and Discussion

Table 3.2 reveals a couple of interesting points regarding the overall levels of democracy. First, the liberal democracy index does not show a meaningful association between impeachment and levels of democracy (Column A). Impeachment has been successful in countries with different levels of democracy. On the one hand, countries such as Peru, Brazil, Lithuania, and South Korea had relatively higher levels of democracy when they experienced impeachment. On the other hand, Paraguay (Raul Cubas Grau in 1999), Ukraine, and Madagascar had lower levels of democracy in the year of impeachment. However, the Polity2 scores reveal less dispersion than the V-Dem index. All countries, except for Ecuador in 2005, had Polity2 scores of six or greater (Column D). Since countries with such values are considered to be full democracies, it can be concluded that most impeachments occurred in full democracies.

Regarding the changes in the levels of democracy, there is no consistent effect of impeachment. In the following year after impeachment, six cases had an increase in the liberal democracy index while the remaining five cases experienced a decrease (Column B). The changes in the level of democracy two years after impeachment are not notably different. Peru and Brazil (Fernando Collor de Mello) had a positive change in the level of democracy after suffering from a drop in the first year after impeachment, but Ecuador (Lucio Gutierrez) had the opposite result (Column C).

However, when I use the Polity2 scores, impeachment does not appear to have negative effects on democracy in the following year. In two cases (Lucio Gutierrez of Ecuador and Fernando Lugo of Paraguay), there was an increase in the score, while in other cases, no change was observed (Column E). The changes are less optimistic two years after impeachment since Ecuador (Lucio Gutierrez) and Madagascar had a decline in the score (Column F).

However, the findings from the Polity2 scores should be interpreted with caution. This is because the DEMOC (institutionalized democracy) and

legislative constraints on the executive (*v2xlg_legcon*) – 'To what extent are the legislature and government agencies, e.g., comptroller general, general prosecutor, or ombudsman, capable of questioning, investigating, and exercising oversight over the executive?'; executive branch corruption (*v2x_execorr*) – 'How routinely do members of the executive or their agents grant favors in exchange for bribes, kickbacks, or other material inducements, and how often do they steal, embezzle, or misappropriate public funds or other state resources for personal or family use?'; executive's respect for the constitution (*v2exrescon*) – 'Do members of the executive (the head of state, the head of government, and cabinet ministers) respect the constitution?'; mass mobilization (*v2cagenmob*) – 'In this year, how frequent and large have events of mass mobilization been?' (Varieties of Democracy (V-Dem) Project (n 53)).

Table 3.2 Impeachment and Overall Levels of Democracy

Country	*President*	*A*	*B*	*C*	*D*	*E*	*F*
		Liberal democracy index in the year of impeachment (t)	*Change in liberal democracy index (t => t +1)*	*Change in liberal democracy index (t => t +2)*	*Polity2 score in the year of impeachment (t)*	*Change in Polity2 score (t => t +1)*	*Change in Polity2 score (t => t +2)*
Ecuador	Abdala Bucaram Ortiz (1997)	.462	.009	.005	9	0	0
Ecuador	Lucio Gutierrez (2005)	.463	.001	–.059	6	1	–1
Peru	Pedro Pablo Kuczynski (2018)	.685	–.011	.007	9	N/A*	N/A*
Brazil	Fernando Collor de Mello (1992)	.732	–.002	.001	8	0	0
Brazil	Dilma Rousseff (2016)	.697	–.058	–.080	8	0	0
Paraguay	Raul Cubas Grau (1999)	.395	.004	.004	7	0	0
Paraguay	Fernando Lugo (2012)	.483	–.074	–.062	8	1	1
Lithuania	Rolandas Paksas (2004)	.769	.003	.002	10	0	0
Ukraine	Viktor Yanukovych (2014)	.211	.012	.021	4	0	0
Madagascar	Albert Zafy (1996)	.347	–.059	–.066	9	0	–2
South Korea	Park Geun-hye (2017)	.775	.029	.010	8	0	N/A*

Sources: The liberal democracy index and Polity score are from the V-Dem and Polity5, respectively (Center for Systemic Peace 2022; Varieties of Democracy (V-Dem) Project 2022b).

* This is because the last data point of Polity5 is 2018.

AUTOC (institutionalized autocracy) variables focus on the competitiveness and openness of executive recruitment, constraints on the chief executive, and the competitiveness and regulation of political participation,[56] which impeachment may not have a direct impact on. Therefore, it might be more reasonable to examine the effects of impeachment on the specific aforementioned political outcomes.

Table 3.3 shows the results. First, there are mixed results regarding the judicial constraints on the executive, one of the indicators of horizontal accountability. In the first year after impeachment, the judicial constraints increased in some cases, while decreasing in other cases (Column A). However, more cases experienced a decrease in the judicial constraints two years after impeachment (Column B). Overall, it is difficult to conclude that impeachment had a meaningful impact on the judicial constraints on the executive. Second, impeachment seems to have a negative effect on another indicator of horizontal accountability, the legislative constraints on the executive, in both years after impeachment (Columns C and D). The only exceptions are Ukraine and South Korea. The results imply that successor president(s) do not become more constrained by the legislature after the successful impeachment. This is somewhat surprising because impeachment has been viewed as a corrective mechanism for hegemonic presidents at least in Latin America (Pérez-Liñán 2018).[57]

Third, impeachment does not seem to affect corruption in the executive branch (Columns E and F) or the executive's respect for the constitution (Columns G and H) in a particular way. Considering that corruption and violations of the constitution are two frequently cited charges of impeachment, these results are somewhat surprising. Successor presidents after impeachment are not any more or less likely to engage in corrupt activities and respect the constitution. This implies that presidential vulnerability to impeachment is not likely to decline in the near future.

Lastly, successful impeachment seems to make mass mobilization such as protests less likely (Columns I and J). It has been shown that civil society has been playing an important role before and/or during the impeachment process.[58] Once impeachment is concluded, protests seem to recede.

However, Peru appears to be one noteworthy exception. The resignation/impeachment of President Kuczynski in 2018 led to higher levels of mass mobilization in both 2019 and 2020. There may be a couple of explanations for this. One is that the First Vice President Martín Vizcarra succeeded the presidency. Although he was elected together with President Kuczynski in 2006, some may have concluded that he did not enjoy the popular mandate as the new president. In addition, the Peruvian Constitution allows the

56 Marshall and Gurr (n 40) 14–16.
57 Pérez-Liñán (n 39) 1–15.
58 Hochstetler (n 4) 401–18; Kim and Bahry (n 2) 807–22; Pérez-Liñán (n 12).

Table 3.3 Impeachment and Horizontal Accountability, Corruption in the Executive Branch, Executive's Respect for the Constitution, and Mass Mobilization

Country	*President*	*A*	*B*	*C*	*D*	*E*	*F*	*G*	*H*	*I*	*J*
		Judicial constraints on the executive (t => t +1)	*Judicial constraints on the executive (t => t +2)*	*Legislative constraints on the executive (t => t +1)*	*Legislative constraints on the executive (t => t +2)*	*Executive branch corruption (t => t +1)*	*Executive branch corruption (t => t +2)*	*Executive's respect for the constitution (t => t +1)*	*Executive's respect for the constitution (t => t +2)*	*Mass mobilization (t => t +1)*	*Mass mobilization (t => t +2)*
Ecuador	Abdala Bucaram Ortiz (1997)	0	−.006	0	0	−.015	.039	0	−.238	−1.649	−.839
Ecuador	Lucio Gutierrez (2005)	.017	−.009	−.052	−.269	−.020	−.035	.100	.147	−1.460	−1.460
Peru	Pedro Pablo Kuczynski (2018)	.018	.020	−.032	0	.020	.018	−.181	−.134	.211	1.915
Brazil	Fernando Collor de Mello (1992)	0	0	−.009	−.024	−.123	−.163	0	0	−2.664	−2.664
Brazil	Dilma Rousseff (2016)	−.050	−.074	−.064	−.064	−.002	−.002	−.020	−.020	−.93	−.749
Paraguay	Raul Cubas Grau (1999)	0	0	0	0	0	0	0	0	0	0
Paraguay	Fernando Lugo (2012)	−.178	−.178	−.196	−.196	.006	.002	−.189	−.189	−.089	−.089
Lithuania	Rolandas Paksas (2004)	0	0	0	−.008	0	0	0	0	−.474	−.974
Ukraine	Viktor Yanukovych (2014)	.010	.010	.066	.066	−.080	−.080	.216	.216	−2.965	−3.257
Madagascar	Albert Zafy (1996)	−.011	−.015	−.290	−.336	.277	.377	0	0	0	0
South Korea	Park Geun-hye (2017)	−.028	−.026	.012	.015	.006	−.013	0	0	−1.989	−2.087

presidential and legislative elections to be held concurrently,[59] which means that the interim president serves out the remaining term of the removed president. Therefore, it can be argued that the resignation/impeachment of Kuczynski did not resolve the political crisis but extended it. This is why Ginsburg et al. prefer a 'reset' model with a new presidential election under the caretaker government after impeachment to allow the successor, be it the vice president, prime minister, or president of congress, to complete the deposed president's term.[60] In the end, President Vizcarra was also impeached for the negligence of his duties, incapacity, and corruption in 2020.[61]

This political instability in Peru may make one wonder if there is evidence for impeachment becoming 'trivialized and routinized' or being used as a weapon of political retaliation in other countries.[62] If I understand these outcomes by the number of successful impeachments, then there seems to be some evidence for this. Out of eight new democracies that have experienced impeachment, four of them including Peru had more than one impeachment (Ecuador, Brazil, and Paraguay) until 2018. However, to answer this question more thoroughly, future research also needs to examine the interplay of unsuccessful impeachment attempts (Kim 2014), charges and timing of impeachment, electoral outcomes after impeachment, and reactions of the mass public on impeachment.

Another notable question is whether there are any differences in the effects of impeachment on democracy by the type of charges. For example, impeachment based on criminal activities of the president compared to 'general dissatisfaction' is more likely to have a positive effect because impeachment is easier to justify and tends to enjoy higher legitimacy in this case. However, testing this empirically does not seem to be straightforward because these charges often turn out to be intertwined. Although I did not examine this question in this chapter, future research can rely on the number of defectors from the ruling party during the impeachment vote to classify the different types of impeachment charges. It is expected that ruling party deputies are more likely to cross the party line if their president turns out to have engaged in criminal activities.

3.5 Conclusion

The experience of new presidential democracies has revealed that several assumptions of presidentialism need to be revisited. First, presidents are not

59 Simeon Tegel, 'Castillo's Ouster Is Not the End of Peru's Political Crisis' *Foreign Policy* (2022) <https://foreignpolicy.com/2022/12/16/peru-president-castillo-impeached-removed-political-crisis-protests/> accessed 6 March 2023.

60 Ginsburg, Huq and Landau (n 13) 81–164.

61 Mark Katkov, 'In Midst of Pandemic Crisis, Peru's Legislature Impeaches the Nation's President' *NPR* (2020) <www.npr.org/2020/11/10/933334195/in-midst-of-pandemic-crisis-perus-legislature-impeaches-the-nations-president> accessed 6 March 2023.

62 Shin and Moon (n 25) 117–31.

necessarily guaranteed to stay in office until the end of their term.[63] Some of them have had to leave office early by either resigning or being removed in constitutional and extraconstitutional manners. Second and related to the first point, the early terminations of a presidential term have contributed to the increased flexibility of presidentialism.[64] Third, the lofty requirements of impeachment did not prevent some countries from experiencing impeachment.[65]

In this chapter, I examined the effects of impeachment on democracy by focusing on new presidentialism from 1974 to 2018. I found that impeachment has not been exclusive to either full or partial democracies. It has been used in countries with diverse levels of democracy. In addition, I found that impeachment did not have a uniform effect on democracy. In some countries, the level of democracy increased after impeachment, while it had the opposite effect in other countries. When it comes to specific political outcomes, successful impeachment does not seem to promote the horizontal accountability between the executive and legislative branches. Quite contrarily, more countries experienced weaker legislative constraints on the executive after impeachment. Lastly, mass mobilization is shown to recede after impeachment. Therefore, it can be concluded that impeachment has been addressing public discontent quite successfully.

Although these findings are informative, future research warrants more sophisticated analyses of the question. For example, it would be necessary to control variables that are known to influence the level of democracy such as economic performance, ideological polarization, ethnic and religious diversity, social unrest, electoral systems, and divided government, to list a few. Moreover, it needs to examine how long the different effects of impeachment will last.

It is most likely that the constitutional removal of presidents will be observed more frequently in the future. Accordingly, it would also be interesting to examine the effects of impeachment on different outcomes such as economic performance.

63 Pérez-Liñán (n 12); Kim and Bahry (n 2) 807–22; Hochstetler (n 4) 401–18.
64 Marsteintredet and Berntzen (n 4) 83–101.
65 Kim (n 11) 519–53.

4 Impeachment and the Rule of Law

It's Complicated

John Ohnesorge

4.1 Introduction

This chapter explores impeachment in light of the Rule of Law. But the Rule of Law is an amorphous and contested concept,[1] and impeachment exists in many different legal systems, with many variations.[2] Definitional boundaries are therefore necessary to keep the inquiry manageable. 'Rule of Law' refers here to a set of characteristics describing the form and operation of a legal system. The term is aspirational and relative in that it refers to a set of objectives for how a legal system should operate that no legal system will ever completely meet. Rule-of-Law values are specific aspirations that fall within the overall concept, such as procedural due process. The discussion here of impeachment focuses primarily on presidential as opposed to parliamentary systems based on the notion that the structural insulation of the president and other members of the executive branch from the legislative branch in a presidential system drives much of the need for impeachment.[3] The need for impeachment of judges, however, is similar in presidential and parliamentary democracies: both kinds of systems aspire to judicial independence, a core Rule-of-Law value.

The analysis that follows also assumes a functioning democracy, following Schumpeter's definition of democracy as 'that institutional arrangement for arriving at political decisions in which individuals acquire the power to decide

1 John Ohnesorge, 'The Rule of Law' (2007) 3 *Annual Review of Law and Social Science*; John Ohnesorge, 'The Rule of Law, Economic Development, and the Developmental States of Northeast Asia' in Christoph Antons (ed), *Law and Economic Development in East and Southeast Asia* (Routledge Curzon 2003).

2 See generally John Ohnesorge, 'Comparing Impeachment Regimes' (2021) 31 *Duke Journal of Comparative and International Law* 259; Tom Ginsburg and others, 'The Comparative Constitutional Law of Presidential Impeachment' (2021) 88 *University of Chicago Law Review* 81. Impeachment is used here to refer to the entire process, both the bringing of charges and their adjudication, unless otherwise noted.

3 In a presidential system in which executive branch officials other than the president are also elected, the need for impeachment against these officials is arguably lessened because they can also be removed by the voters.

DOI: 10.4324/9781003256007-5

by means of a competitive struggle for the people's vote.'[4] Even if impeachment occurs in a non-democracy, it will not be governed by the same dynamics as impeachment in a functioning democracy, where those who carry out the impeachment will themselves be subsequently judged through free and fair elections. In addition, political systems that do not meet even Schumpeter's procedural definition of democracy are not political systems in which the Rule of Law prevails at the highest levels of power, though some Rule-of-Law values may be met. The normal operation of impeachment also relies on the Rule of Law being present, at least to the extent that an impeached official leaves office voluntarily or is removed by law enforcement. The Rule of Law thus serves as a necessary condition to impeachment as discussed here. It also provides standards against which impeachment can be judged and establishes normative aspirations for legal systems that impeachment may help protect.

In framing a discussion of impeachment and the Rule of Law, several possible approaches come to mind. One could connect impeachment and the Rule of Law by asking what role the Rule of Law plays in impeachment actions. This leads naturally to the normative question of what role the Rule of Law should play. One could take the position that impeachment and the Rule of Law are like oil and water and that although impeachment is dressed up in legal language and judicial-like procedures, as a factual matter, impeachment is politics unmediated by the law. This position is held by some political scientists who study impeachment comparatively.[5] From this perspective, references to the Rule of Law when discussing impeachment add an unhelpful layer of legalese obscuring what impeachment is really about, which is politics. Yet with respect to this normative question, impeachment is an official act of government taken against an individual, which is the paradigmatic situation where the Rule of Law should apply. Thus, even if the skeptics are correct as a descriptive matter, as a normative matter, it may still be important to impose Rule-of-Law constraints on the impeachment process.

A second strategy for connecting impeachment and the Rule of Law asks under what circumstances impeachment can be used to help a society achieve, or perhaps maintain, the Rule of Law. Rather than inquiring to what extent impeachment can or should be constrained by the Rule of Law, this approach asks to what extent a society in which the Rule of Law is threatened might use impeachment as a defense against this threat, regardless of whether impeachment would be carried out in a manner consistent with the

4 Joseph A Schumpeter, *Capitalism, Socialism and Democracy* (3rd edn, Harper & Brothers 1950) 269.

5 See, Aníbal S. Pérez-Liñán, *Presidential Impeachment and the New Political Instability in Latin America* (CUP 2007); Jody C Baumgartner and Naoko Kada (eds), *Checking Executive Power: Presidential Impeachment in Comparative Perspective* (Praeger 2003). This literature focuses on presidential impeachment, in which the political stakes are generally high. If this is the right way to understand impeachment, however, then it is not clear why judicial or other impeachments should be analyzed differently.

Rule of Law. A third avenue for approaching impeachment and the Rule of Law draws on the fact that impeachment and the Rule of Law share an important similarity: at an operational level, both can raise substantial tensions between short- and long-term goals and between desires for results in individual cases and concerns for the larger systems within which individual decisions are made.

This chapter proceeds in this outlined order and discusses in Section 4.2 the extent to which the Rule of Law can or should prevail within impeachments. The answers to these questions are complex. Therefore, addressing them here requires breaking down both the impeachment process and the Rule of Law to facilitate a more detailed analysis. Section 4.3 then turns to the question of whether, or under what circumstances, impeachment can be used by a society to maintain the Rule of Law. The primary conclusion is that impeachment can function to help preserve the Rule of Law when it is threatened, but because the Rule of Law is necessary to the functioning of impeachment as this term is used here, impeachment is unlikely to be sufficient for establishing the Rule of Law when it is entirely absent. Finally, Section 4.4 explores the dynamic shared by both impeachment and the Rule of Law, which is that they both can raise tensions between outcomes in individual cases and important long-term concerns.

4.2 The Rule of Law as a Constraint on Impeachment

Turning to the Rule of Law as a possible constraint on impeachment, the relationship turns out to be quite complex, both descriptively and normatively. Descriptively, it is too simple to say that impeachment is an entirely political rather than legal process and that, therefore, the Rule of Law plays no role. As a normative matter, although specific Rule-of-Law values arguably should be pursued as impeachments are carried out, important aspects of impeachment are in fundamental tension with the Rule of Law and should remain that way.

4.2.1 What Role Does *the Rule of Law Play in Impeachment?*

Although important impeachment scholarship frames impeachment as an entirely political rather than legal matter,[6] there are at least three problems with this framing. First, it assumes an overly rigid distinction between law and politics; second, it obscures the distinction across impeachment regimes between legislators and courts as impeachment adjudicators; and third, it does not sufficiently consider the extent to which a society's voters may value the Rule of Law and therefore punish those who violate it through the democratic process.

6 See n 5.

Impeachment clearly is a deeply political process, one prosecuted and often also adjudicated by elected bodies.[7] To expect the individual politicians who make up these bodies to set aside partisan considerations and perform their assigned roles in legally formal ways would be naïve. It is thus unhelpful to over-emphasize the legalistic aspects of impeachment such as legally formulated impeachment standards, procedural or evidentiary rules within the impeachment bodies, or the choice of courts rather than legislative bodies as adjudicators.[8] In contrast, legal scholars of a realist bent have long argued that areas of governance that are highly legalized are also infused with policy preferences and political partisanship; two obvious examples in the United States (U.S.) are the regulation of elections and competition policy. It is true that elected legislators play designated roles in impeachment that they do not play in more legalized areas of governance, but the bureaucrats and judges who play the leading roles in elections and in competition enforcement do not operate within realms of legality distinct from politics.[9] The legal and political spheres are simply not distinct in the way that a political-therefore-not-legal framing assumes.

Framing impeachment as an entirely political rather than a legal process over-emphasizes the difference between law and politics, and it also fails to engage convincingly with the fact that a number of countries align with South Korea in assigning the adjudication of impeachments to their courts, almost certainly with Rule of Law concerns in mind.[10] The effects of this choice are worth investigating empirically, but at the very least, the judges who adjudicate impeachments in such systems are not subject to the same political dynamics as sitting legislators. Sitting legislators who happen to officiate over impeachments as one of their duties do so while embedded within complex ecosystems involving party politics and legislative agendas and will always need to consider how their conduct during an impeachment will affect them within this larger context.[11] Judges are unlikely to be subject to the same concerns.

7 The United States provides an example of an impeachment regime administered entirely within the legislative branch, while the South Korean regime assigns adjudication in impeachment cases to its Constitutional Court. See Ohnesorge (n 2).

8 Additional legalist aspects of impeachment include the quorum and voting requirements of the bodies charged with bringing and adjudicating impeachment actions and the structure of judicial review in impeachment regimes in which this is available.

9 The practice in many U.S. states of electing judges and prosecutors represents an intentional collapsing of the political and legal realms.

10 Rule-of-Law values that might be advanced by a court as the adjudicator would include due process, respect for rules of evidence and evidentiary sufficiency, and respect for the definition of an impeachable offense.

11 Because impeachments in the U.S. federal system are carried out by the two houses of Congress and are not subject to judicial review, the U.S. regime arguably represents an ideal-type of legislature-dominated impeachment. A middle ground might be achieved between the U.S. and Korean approaches by subjecting impeachments conducted within the legislative branch to review by the judiciary.

A final drawback of framing impeachment as entirely political and, therefore, not legal arises from the fact that politicians engaged in impeachment who plan to run for re-election must include in their political calculations their voters' commitment to the Rule of Law. How much this would matter in a specific impeachment would vary, but it is fair to assume that if a country's impeachment regime is highly legalized, and if its electorate values the Rule of Law, a legislator expecting a re-election battle following the impeachment will be motivated to show respect for the Rule of Law.

4.2.2 *What Role* Should *the Rule of Law Play in Impeachment?*

Whether existing impeachment regimes succeed in imposing the Rule of Law on impeachments does not determine the desirability of doing so. This section turns to normative concerns, exploring arguments for and against imposing Rule-of-Law values in impeachment settings.

4.2.2.1 Due Process

Impeachment is adjudicative in nature, with state actors applying legally formulated standards to potentially sanction specific individuals. Even though impeachment is carried out partially or entirely by the legislative branch, it thus raises classic due process concerns. Much like a prosecutor in the criminal process,[12] the body bringing an impeachment charge should have engaged in fact finding concerning the target's conduct and should have concluded that the facts it found constitute an impeachable offense. Each member who votes for or against an impeachment should do so based on findings of fact and principled legal interpretation. Traditional due process norms also require that the targeted official be given notice of the charges, an opportunity to present and respond to evidence, to confront hostile witnesses, and to an unbiased adjudicator. A reasoned explanation would add to the legitimacy of the ultimate decision.

As a normative matter, pursuing most of these goals during impeachments seems desirable. There is no reason that the body bringing the impeachment action cannot specify the factual and legal bases for its decision and allow the targeted official to respond and to confront hostile witnesses. Members of the charging body should honestly believe in the factual and legal merits of the case they are bringing, much as prosecutors in the criminal justice system should believe that cases they pursue can properly result in conviction. Due process concerns also apply to the adjudicating body, whether a part of the legislature or a court, which should find facts and apply the impeachment standard in a proceeding that is fair to the accused.

12 In the U.S. federal system, the closer analogy is to a Grand Jury, which has the power to issue indictments based on factual and legal arguments presented by prosecutors.

The main obstacles to meeting these Rule-of-Law objectives arise from the fact that groups of elected politicians carry out the prosecution and in some cases, the subsequent adjudication. Aspirations of good faith can be difficult to meet in the realm of ordinary criminal justice, where accusations of bias against prosecutors and judges are not rare. Given the partisan nature of impeachment, however, expecting good-faith neutrality and open minds seems fanciful no matter the rules. Two institutional choices that could address this issue involve granting formal roles to courts in impeachments, either as threshold adjudicators of impeachment charges, or as after-the-fact reviewers of legislative judgments.[13] The challenge raised by judicial involvement in impeachment is that it forces the judiciary into the role of policing battles between the executive and legislative branches. In close cases, these battles will be politically charged and turn on political judgments. If a court serves as the adjudicator, then it may have difficulty convincing partisans upset by either a conviction or an acquittal, especially if it is a multi-member court that produces both majority and dissenting opinions. Even empowering the courts to review rather than adjudicate impeachments raises similar risks because of the challenge of maintaining a limited role for courts conducting judicial review when the judges feel strongly about the outcome. A country could try to limit the judiciary to simply reviewing for compliance with procedural requirements, but judges will have their personal views about the merits of impeachments, and procedural review has a way of intensifying when the court disagrees with the substance of the action under review.[14] If a decision is too politically contested, then assigning it to a court may end up politicizing the court more than it legalizes the decision. A society concerned about judicial legitimacy and cultivating the Rule of Law might well decide to follow the U.S. approach and leave impeachments entirely within the legislative branch.

Although this sounds discouraging from a Rule-of-Law perspective, it is important to keep in mind that the primary punishment imposed via impeachment is typically removal from office, not criminal punishment.[15] A president, officer or judge who is impeached and removed from office is injured professionally but is typically not imprisoned. However, injecting the judiciary into the process may prove costly in the long run. When an elected president is impeached, the potential blow to his supporters and to overall political stability is arguably much more important for society than the harm to the individual. Providing due process thus becomes more a matter of political legitimacy than

13 The two options are not mutually exclusive in principle, so an impeachment regime could allow judicial review even if it also assigned impeachment adjudications to its courts.

14 This has certainly been the history of judicial review of administrative action in the U.S. under the Administrative Procedure Act, both when courts review for procedural compliance and when they review the reasoning processes underlying agency decisions.

15 In the U.S. system, the Senate has the option of imposing the additional sanction of banning the official from ever again holding high office, but this is also mild compared to the penalties for serious crimes.

of protecting individuals. The number of unmerited impeachments might be better minimized by high voting thresholds rather than judicial involvement. The voters will then be able to use the electoral process to weigh in on whether Rule-of-Law values were complied with adequately.

4.2.2.2 Defining the Impeachable Offense

In addition to the due process concerns just addressed, Rule-of-Law values also speak to the design of the substantive legal norm against which the actions of the accused official will be judged, that is, the 'impeachable offense.' An important Rule-of-Law value is that legal rules of conduct should be clear and knowable in advance. This provides parties subject to the rules with fair notice so that they can adjust their behavior. It also constrains the discretion of adjudicators so that they do not have the freedom to punish conduct that was not clearly prohibited. The discourse of criminal law invokes these ideas through the Latin maxim *nullum crimen sine lege* ('no crime without law'), but the basic principle also extends to non-criminal sanctions. For example, the presumption against retroactive application of regulations in administrative law can be seen as responding to the same underlying concern. In the U.S. at least, arguments for or against an impeachment will often center on whether the alleged conduct constituted a 'high crime or misdemeanor,' the most important impeachment criterion in the Constitution and also the vaguest.[16]

From a Rule-of-Law perspective, a clear definition of an impeachable offense would seem desirable. But in this area, rigid attention to the Rule of Law is not appropriate. Taking the U.S. as an example, it is well understood that if 'high crimes and misdemeanors' were applied rigidly, it would be both over- and under-inclusive with respect to what impeachment needs to achieve.[17] It would not be a crime or a misdemeanor for an official to simply stop doing her work, and it would not be a crime to be caught in a 'hot mic' moment using racial slurs. Nevertheless, many Americans would think impeachment proper in both situations. By the same token, it is easy to identify crimes or misdemeanors too trivial to justify impeachment. Similar problems are raised by the fact that the Constitution does not address whether an act committed before assuming office constitutes an impeachable offense or whether an act committed while in office but unconnected with official duties is impeachable.

Perhaps reflecting skepticism about the extent to which better drafting could solve these problems or the difficulty of amending the U.S. Constitution,

16 U.S. Constitution, art 2, sec 4. Treason and bribery are listed as additional impeachable offenses, but most impeachment efforts have been based on the more general standard. Judicial impeachments are not covered by this provision, but the provision in art 3, sec 1 that federal judges serve during 'good Behavior' has been interpreted to be equivalent to art 2, sec 4.

17 For a classic presentation, see Charles L Black Jr, *Impeachment: A Handbook* (Yale UP 1974) 33–36.

commentators who appreciate these potential gaps between the Constitution and the role they want impeachment to play typically identify some general principle from which to reason out boundaries on 'high Crimes and Misdemeanors' and answers to the two timing questions.[18] Much of the discussion of these issues proceeds within the criminal justice framing, but this is not necessarily the best approach. First, it is undisputed that the U.S. Congress *can* impeach and remove an official for any reason that it decides is sufficient, regardless of the constitutional text, because ex post judicial review is unavailable.[19] The most compelling arguments for judicial review of impeachments in the U.S. context focus on ensuring due process,[20] but the Supreme Court has rejected any role for judicial review,[21] and Supreme Court Chief Justices have been restrained even in their constitutionally mandated role of presiding over presidential impeachment trials in the Senate.[22] Second, as the previous discussion suggests, the informed consensus seems to be that as a normative matter, Congress should not try to cabin its impeachment discretion within the kind of legal framework one associates with the Rule of Law. This is true with respect not only to the meaning of 'high Crimes and Misdemeanors' but also to impeachability for acts committed prior to taking office or acts committed during tenure but not related to official duties. A president found to have committed murder before being elected should be impeached. A sitting federal judge who attends Ku Klux Klan meetings after leaving the office should be impeached. Extreme cases are easy, but they also lead directly to the slippery slope on which clear rules are often unhelpful. How old should a bad act be to justify impeachment? The answer surely must depend on how bad it was, but how is this decided? If a very bad act committed outside official duties is an impeachable offense, then how bad does it have to be, and how is the scope of official duties defined? The sex life of a sitting President should be a private matter, but was the fact that Bill Clinton was having sex with a subordinate and that it took place in the White House make his actions impeachable?

Congress may face some or all of these issues in an impeachment case, and it seems clear that simple appeals to the Rule of Law are not going to resolve them. If impeachment were frequent, then there would be a body of

18 Black, for example, suggested applying the *eiusdem generis* rule of statutory interpretation to define 'high Crimes and Misdemeanors' because art 2, sec 2 also lists bribery and treason as impeachable offenses, and the interpretive process would render less substantial crimes insufficient. ibid at 36–39.

19 Then-Congressman Gerald Ford was partially correct when he stated, '[a]n impeachable offense is whatever a majority of the House of Representatives considers it to be at a given moment in history', though the Senate's view matters more.

20 See, e.g., Raoul Berger, *Impeachment: The Constitutional Problems* (enlarged edn, Harvard UP 1974) 108–26.

21 *Nixon v United States*, 506 US 224 (1993).

22 Adam Liptak, 'Chief Justice's Impeachment Handbook: Determined Minimalism' *New York Times* (10 February 2020) <www.nytimes.com/2020/02/10/us/john-roberts-trump-impeachment.html>.

precedent, vindicating to some extent the Rule of Law's call for rules knowable in advance. Impeachment cases are too few, however, to draw firm conclusions from practice. Moreover, the lack of judicial review means that there would be no mechanism to hold Congress to its precedent.

There is no easy solution to these challenges, but one way to advance the discussion would be to import the reasoning structure of fiduciary duty law as it has developed in business setting into the impeachment context. Fiduciary jurisprudence is highly flexible and thus displays a somewhat relaxed commitment to Rule-of-Law values, but approaching impeachment at least partly through a fiduciary lens would have significant benefits.[23] The classic situation in which fiduciary duties arise is where one party, the fiduciary, has come to have discretionary authority over something of value – wealth, property or confidential information – belonging to someone else. The existence of discretion held by the fiduciary justifies the imposition of duties to police exercises of this discretion. Fiduciary duty law as it has developed in the business law setting is understood to impose two primary duties, a duty of care and a duty of loyalty. The fiduciary duty of care is similar to the negligence standard in torts, imposing upon the fiduciary a minimum standard of conduct in situations in which the fiduciary is not accused of self-dealing. This duty of care requires the fiduciary to maintain a basic level of diligence in carrying out their tasks. So long as self-dealing is not alleged, the standard tends to be deferential. Courts are rightly reluctant to second-guess decisions that have turned out badly but were not motivated by self-interest. A separate duty of loyalty, which restricts self-interested behavior by fiduciaries, involves a higher level of judicial scrutiny because it is applied in situations in which the fiduciary is charged with self-dealing, not simply poor performance.

The basic outlines of fiduciary jurisprudence were developed by ordinary courts exercising their equitable powers to resolve individual disputes. Even though statutes now often refer to fiduciary duties, defining these duties is still an exercise in parsing cases in which judges apply vague standards to very fact-intensive situations. This resembles the task that Congress faces in many impeachment cases notwithstanding the Constitution's more legalistic framing of the legislative role.

23 The entire relationship between citizens and their governments can be seen through a fiduciary lens if one views governments as existing to exercise discretionary authority over rights belonging to their citizens. At a more concrete level, a growing body of scholarship applies fiduciary thinking to the U.S. Constitution. See, e.g., Gary Lawson and Guy Seidman, *A Great Power of Attorney: Understanding the Fiduciary Constitution* (Kansas UP 2017); Ethan J Leib and Stephen R Galoob, 'Fiduciary Political Theory: A Critique' (2016) 125 *Yale Law Journal* 1820. An explicit connection between impeachment and fiduciary analysis was made in the context of the effort to impeach President Nixon, but it does not appear to have been taken up by other commentators. See, E Mabry Rogers and Stephen B Young, 'Public Office as a Public Trust: A Suggestion That Impeachment for High Crimes and Misdemeanors Implies a Fiduciary Standard' (1975) 63 *Georgetown Law Journal* 1025.

Applying this basic fiduciary duty framework in the impeachment context, Congress should impeach a president, officer or judge whose job performance becomes unacceptably poor, whether from incompetence or from laziness. Because being deeply inattentive or incompetent in one's job is not a crime, a Rule-of-Law approach to 'high Crimes and Misdemeanors' will lead either to a conclusion that impeachment would be improper or to an attempt to stretch the constitutional text to reach behavior that on its face it does not seem to address. Applying instead a fiduciary duty perspective to the same facts calls for a duty of care analysis. Congress would be asked to articulate a minimum level of competency and attentiveness imposed upon officials subject to impeachment and to then decide whether the behavior alleged, if proven, fell below that standard. As in the business law context, there are good reasons for keeping the standard undemanding and judicial review deferential. If Congress were to impose a high standard of care on an official in a constitutionally co-equal branch, then this would risk substituting its judgment for the judgment of someone to whom the Constitution assigned authority, and it would likely encourage more impeachment efforts than it has the capacity to handle. Extending the fiduciary metaphor, an official who puts her own interests or the interests of a third party above the national interest should also be impeached. This corresponds to a fiduciary duty of loyalty, and the task for Congress here would be to determine whether the target acted out of self-interest to obtain improper benefits in the performance of their official duties. In the impeachment context, this loyalty analysis would differ from the duty of care analogy in that some self-interested acts would also fall within 'high Crimes and Misdemeanors' with minimal interpretive gymnastics. Not all would, however, and in any case, Congress is better equipped to engage in quasi-equitable than in quasi-criminal adjudication. Bad acts involving self-dealing that rise to the level of criminal offenses can be prosecuted criminally, but impeachment is not a criminal punishment, and Congress need not be limited to impeaching only self-dealing that can also be prosecuted.

From a Rule-of-Law perspective, shifting impeachment from a criminal justice framing to a fiduciary duty analysis might seem risky, as fiduciary law, based as it is in equity, is not very rule-like. Judges who write fiduciary duty decisions tend to focus very heavily on the facts and to avoid creating clear rules to be applied in future cases. In fact, however, a quasi-fiduciary approach would more accurately reflect both what we want impeachment to do – remove officials who are either unacceptably incompetent or disloyal – and the reality that trying to constrain impeachment within a rule-like frame more compatible with the Rule of Law does not actually work.

4.3 Impeachment as a Protector of the Rule of Law

Having explored the Rule of Law in impeachment, this chapter now asks whether impeachment can be an effective tool to defend the Rule of Law when it is under threat. The judiciary is the primary point of focus, as its functioning is key to whether the Rule of Law prevails in a society. There are two distinct roles that impeachment can play in helping the judiciary maintain the Rule of Law. First, impeachment can be used as a shield to protect judges so that they are able to perform their judicial functions free from improper external pressures. These pressures are most likely to come from the executive branch but could also flow from the higher ranks of a bureaucratically organized judiciary. Second, impeachment can be used as a sword to remove judges who fail to live up to Rule-of-Law ideals in performing their role. In addition, impeachment can be used to protect the Rule of Law against threats from executive branch officials.

4.3.1 Shielding the Judiciary

Definitions of the Rule of Law typically devote significant attention to the function of judges in individual cases and ask that they be unbiased, not prejudge cases, and rule to the best of their abilities based only on the facts and the law as developed through the litigation process. It is unrealistic to think that judges will perform in this way if they are not insulated from external pressures, especially from the executive, but sometimes also from the upper levels of the judicial bureaucracy. Legal systems thus deploy various ways to insulate individual judges, including protections for judicial tenure, guaranteed judicial salaries, etc. In the U.S., for example, presidents have regularly expressed their disagreement with important judicial decisions. It is important for preserving the Rule of Law, however, that the possibility of impeachment create a line (i.e., removal) that a president cannot alone cross.

It is impossible to say in advance where exactly this line is or should be drawn, but it is easy to imagine conduct by a president toward the judiciary that would justify impeachment. Encouraging supporters to demonstrate outside a judge's house or to disrupt a judicial proceeding should be considered grounds for presidential impeachment to preserve the independence of individual judges that is key to the Rule of Law. Although members of a president's own party will have an immediate interest in protecting 'their' president, this interest should be balanced against a larger systemic interest in the Rule of Law. In addition, as noted previously, if the electorate values the Rule of Law and democracy, which is not sustainable if a president is not bound by the law, then a rational politician will have personal reasons to consider impeaching even a president of her own party if the conduct is sufficiently bad. At a more systemic level, because of the intimate relationship between the Rule of Law and constitutional democracy, preservation of the Rule of Law requires impeaching a president who threatens the democratic order even if he has not yet attacked the judiciary. Presidents who attempt to overthrow the democratic orders in which they serve will eventually need to control the judiciary, so an attack on judicial independence will come sooner or later.

In addition to protecting individual judges from presidents, in countries with bureaucratically organized judiciaries, the independence of the individual judge to perform in a manner consistent with the Rule of Law can be threatened by superiors within the judiciary itself. There has been a good deal of research on this issue with respect to Japan and South Korea. Both the motives and the means that would allow this to happen surely exist in other bureaucratically organized judiciaries. Subjecting those at the top of a judicial bureaucracy to the threat of impeachment could deter them from using their positions to interfere with the independence of the judges below, though impeachment of judges is obviously a double-edged sword that could also threaten judicial independence and the Rule of Law.

4.3.2 Disciplining the Judiciary

In addition to using impeachment to constrain those who would endanger the Rule of Law by threatening judicial independence, impeachment can also be a powerful tool to sanction judges whose own conduct violates the Rule of Law. In the U.S. experience, this is by far the most common use of impeachment. Judicial impeachments far outstrip impeachments of presidents or other executive branch officers.

The obvious risk in using impeachment this way is that doing so can also directly threaten the Rule of Law. Although in the U.S. experience, the judicial impeachments that have proceeded very far have not been improperly motivated, efforts such as the movement to impeach Chief Justice Earl Warren for his civil rights jurisprudence have attracted significant scholarly attention. A potential threat to the Rule of Law is posed by judicial impeachment, but it is also important to the Rule of Law that dysfunctional or corrupt judges be removed from the bench. Given the reality that the Rule of Law sometimes requires that judges be removed, the risks that judicial impeachment poses to the Rule of Law must be weighed against the obvious alternatives, such as criminal prosecution or bureaucratic discipline by the judiciary itself. These two alternatives also pose obvious threats to judicial independence, though the threat comes from the executive and judicial branches and not the legislative branch.

4.3.3 Disciplining Lower Executive Officers

The possibility of presidential impeachment to protect judicial independence and the Rule of Law was discussed earlier; so, this section focuses on executive branch officials other than the president whose conduct could threaten the Rule of Law. It is important when considering impeachment in the context of such officials that there may be other ways that they can be disciplined, but impeachment might be important nonetheless if these other mechanisms prove inadequate. Two possible examples are offered here, one from the U.S. federal system and one from state law.

The U.S. Constitution provides that impeachment is available against '[t]he President, Vice President and all civil Officers of the United States.'[24] It is not

24 U.S. Constitution, art II, sec 4.

entirely clear which positions other than the President and Vice President fall within the last category. It is reasonably clear, however, that cabinet positions such as Secretary of State or Attorney General and those who head regulatory agencies are covered. In keeping with the logic of separation of powers in presidential systems, Congress has little or no ability short of impeachment to discipline any of these officials, and even the President has complete freedom to terminate only those who work directly under him, such as cabinet secretaries and the heads of agencies directly under the President.[25] These are generally powerful positions, imbued with a great deal of authority, but Congress has not used its impeachment authority against them. An Attorney General, a head of the FBI or the CIA, or a Federal Trade Commission chair would clearly have opportunities to use their authority in ways inconsistent with the Rule of Law, perhaps most obviously by launching investigations or prosecutions for illegitimate reasons. We should not expect a sitting President to protect us against actions of his chosen subordinates, and although a court might eventually provide relief against their improper actions, this may require the victim to spend years litigating toward an uncertain outcome. A case can be made that Congress should use its impeachment powers more often against officials such as these, if only as a warning to presidents who might be tempted to use their subordinates to take legally questionable actions. The stakes would be lower than in presidential impeachments, and especially with domestic regulatory agencies, it is well-accepted that Congress has a legitimate oversight role.[26]

A somewhat different example arises in states in which executive branch officials other than the chief executives are separately elected. These officials are not subordinate to the state's governor or its cities' mayors in the same way that federal officers are subordinate to the U.S. President, so if their powers allow them to violate the Rule of Law, impeachment by the state legislature may be even more necessary than impeachment of federal officials under presidential oversight. The fact that many state and local governments elect their top prosecutors has brought this issue to the forefront across the U.S. Some prosecutors have declared that their offices will not prosecute certain offenses found in the statutes they are entrusted with enforcing. Prosecutorial discretion is inevitable at the level of individual cases, but one could argue that it violates the Rule of Law for a chief prosecutor to declare preemptively that his or her office will not prosecute whole categories of crimes defined by the legislature. In the U.S. legal tradition at least, this is an aggressive use of prosecutorial discretion that arguably usurps the legislature's constitutional authority.[27]

25 Statutes prohibit the President from removing members of independent regulatory commissions without cause, but there is little precedent defining what constitutes cause.

26 Congressional oversight over officials involved in military or foreign affairs would raise more serious separation of powers issues, but Congress' impeachment power clearly extends to them as well.

27 A variation on this theme has also been playing out at the national level in the context of immigration law. See, Amy Howe, 'In USV Texas, Broad Questions Over Immigration

In the U.S., this movement has been led primarily by local prosecutors on the political left, but prosecutors from the political right could be tempted to do the same thing with acts they do not believe should be criminalized. Some state legal systems allow the impeachment of local officers, and an impeachment action targeting the District Attorney of Philadelphia has been progressing through the Pennsylvania legislature.[28]

4.4 Short-Term Objectives, Long-Term Implications

A final point of contact between impeachment and the Rule of Law arises from the fact that both demand consideration of short-term outcomes and long-term effects. This dynamic was mentioned earlier, but it is worth focusing on the general issue. With respect to both impeachment and the Rule of Law, there exists a larger system or tradition that is worth preserving. Outcomes in individual cases should be judged for their possible effects on this system or tradition and their more immediate outcomes. This dynamic is a core concern of ordinary criminal justice, where respect for the Rule of Law is often in tension with immediate policy demands. If the due process protections afforded to a criminal defendant allow him to be acquitted, then the traditional response of the legal community would be that fealty to due process is more important than convicting any one individual and that one price of maintaining a Rule-of-Law tradition is that sometimes, the guilty go free.

Presidential and other executive branch impeachment presents a similar dynamic, though the short- and long-term concerns are different. The appropriate balance may be more contestable.[29] With respect to such impeachments, the larger system that needs to be protected from possible erosion through individual cases is the power balance between the legislative and executive branches. Even within a single nation there can be quite divergent opinions on what this relationship should be, with some favoring more presidential authority and some less. One could agree with America's Founders, for example, that in a presidential system, impeachment of the president should be difficult to

Enforcement and States' Ability to Challenge Federal Policies' *SCOTUS Blog* (28 November 2022) <www.scotusblog.com/2022/11/in-u-s-v-texas-broad-questions-over-immigration-enforcement-and-states-ability-to-challenge-federal-policies/>.

28 As of this writing, the District Attorney has been impeached by Pennsylvania's lower house and the case has moved to the state senate for trial. 'Larry Krasner Impeachment Process Continues in PA Senate' *CBS Philadelphia* (29 November 2022) <www.cbsnews.com/philadelphia/news/larry-krasner-impeachment-process-continues-in-pennsylvania-senate-philadelphia-district-attorney-progressive/>. Other states allow recall elections of elected prosecutors, and San Francisco's District Attorney was successfully recalled in the Spring of 2022. Thomas Fuller, 'Voters in San Francisco Topple the City's Progressive District Attorney, Chesa Boudin' *New York Times* (8 June 2022) <www.nytimes.com/2022/06/07/us/politics/chesa-boudin-recall-san-francisco.html>.

29 The stakes with respect to judicial impeachments, discussed in sec 3 b, are less contested because like due process, judicial independence is integral to the Rule-of-Law tradition.

ensure that presidents do not become responsible to the legislative branch. In this view, the desire to impeach any particular president should be carefully balanced against a more systemic concern for maintaining a strong presidency as an institution. From this point of view it would be unfortunate if a highly partisan impeachment led to tit-for-tat retaliation against future presidents, resulting in a general lowering of the bar for presidential impeachments and a weakening of the presidency as an institution. For those concerned that U.S. presidents have become too powerful in relation to Congress, the calculus would be different. From this standpoint, perhaps the U.S. Constitution makes presidential impeachment too difficult by requiring a two-thirds supermajority of the Senate for conviction. Given that a constitutional amendment to fix the problem is unlikely, the second-best solution might be if impeachment were normalized as a regular feature of Washington politics. It would not be surprising if countries that have more features from parliamentary models embedded within their presidential systems addressed these balancing concerns quite differently, perhaps to the point of impeachment being a regular tool of the legislature to influence presidential behavior.

4.5 Conclusion

This chapter sought to demonstrate that the quality of our thinking about both impeachment and the Rule of Law can be improved if we think about them in tandem. Despite being deeply political, impeachment is also a legal process in which an arm of the state acts against an individual, ultimately backed by force. The Rule of Law can thus provide a set of aspirations such as procedural due process against which impeachment can profitably be judged. Ultimately, however, Rule-of-Law values should have limited weight in the impeachment context, especially in defining impeachable offenses.

In addition to thinking about how the Rule of Law can improve the quality of an impeachment mechanism, our understanding of the Rule of Law itself can be deepened by turning the inquiry around and asking how impeachment can be used to support the Rule of Law. The analysis here suggests that impeachment will not produce the Rule of Law where it is missing because the functioning of impeachment ultimately depends upon the Rule of Law. Impeachment may be an important tool for preserving the Rule of Law when it is threatened, however, if it is used to remove from office those responsible for these threats. Indeed, this may be the most important function of impeachment, especially when used to remove individuals, such as presidents, who simultaneously threaten the Rule of Law and democracy.

Finally, thinking about impeachment and the Rule of Law together highlights the importance of keeping an eye on long-term, systemic implications while pursuing results in individual cases. Just as criminal convictions obtained by cutting legal corners can undermine the Rule of Law, so, too, a rashly executed impeachment may provide short term satisfaction to political partisans but long-term pain to the political order.

Part II

Core

5 The Role of the Judiciary in the Presidential Impeachment Process in Korea

*Youngjae Lee**

5.1 Introduction

In 1974, Charles Black, writing about impeachment in the United States (U.S.) context as Richard Nixon was facing a potential impeachment, considered the role of the judiciary in the presidential impeachment process.[1] Black imagined a situation in which the House impeaches the president, and the Senate convicts, but then, the Supreme Court steps in, vacates the conviction, and '*puts the impeached and convicted president back in for the rest of his term*,' and 'we all live happily ever after.'[2] Black's take on the scenario was unequivocal. 'I don't think I possess the resources of rhetoric adequate to characterizing the absurdity of that position,'[3] he wrote, calling the result 'preposterous'[4] and asking '[w]ith what aura of legitimacy would a thus-reinstated chief magistrate be surrounded?'[5] Black concluded that when it comes to presidential impeachment, the only rule that 'matter[s]' is that 'the courts have, in this, no part at all to play.'[6]

In the U.S. constitutional thinking, the view that the judiciary's role in the presidential impeachment process should be limited dates back to

* All translations are my own unless translations from the Constitutional Court of Korea are available, which is the case for the Constitution of Korea, the Constitutional Court Act, and the two Constitutional Court opinions discussed extensively in the following. When I depart from the Constitutional Court's translation for reasons of style and substance, I note this accordingly with the notation 'author's translation'. Korean words have been Romanized according to the McCune-Reischauer system, except for proper names of public figures and publications, in which case either their own preferred romanization has been used when it is known, or when preferred romanization of proper names is not known, the romanization most typically used in English-language journalistic accounts is followed. Parts of this chapter draw from Youngjae Lee, 'Law, Politics and Impeachment: The Impeachment of Roh Moo-Hyun from a Comparative Constitutional Perspective' (2005) 53 *American Journal of Comparative Law* 403. Thanks to Joon-Sung Choe, Ju Hyun Park, Katherine Huffman, Chaihark Hahm, and Dohee Kim.

1 Charles L Black Jr, *Impeachment: A Handbook* (Yale UP 1974) 53–64.

2 ibid 54.

3 ibid.

4 ibid 55.

5 ibid 54.

6 ibid 63.

DOI: 10.4324/9781003256007-7

the Founders. Alexander Hamilton argued in the *Federalist Papers* that the Supreme Court should not be endowed with the power to determine impeachments.[7] He doubted 'whether the members of that tribunal would at all times be endowed with so eminent a portion of fortitude, as would be called for in the execution of so difficult a task' and whether 'they would possess the degree of credit and authority, which might, on certain occasions, be indispensable towards reconciling the people to a decision that should happen to clash with an accusation brought by their immediate representatives.'[8] Hamilton added,

> The awful discretion which a court of impeachments must necessarily have, to doom to honor or to infamy the most confidential and the most distinguished characters of the community, forbids the commitment of the trust to a small number of persons.[9]

However, this seemingly natural and necessary nature of presidential impeachments quickly proves illusory once one looks outside the U.S. This chapter is about the role of the judiciary in the impeachment process in South Korea,[10] an important counter-example to the U.S. model. Korea has undergone two presidential impeachments, one in 2004 and one in 2016 and 2017. The first impeached president was reinstated, and the second impeached president was removed. In both instances, the Constitutional Court of Korea had the final say on the fate of the impeached president.

This chapter introduces the basic legal structure governing presidential impeachments in Korea, discusses the political background and the unfolding of each impeachment process, and concludes by drawing some generally applicable observations about the significance of judicial involvement in presidential impeachments.

5.2 The Role of the Constitutional Court of Korea in Presidential Impeachments

The Constitutional Court of Korea is a specialized body that is charged with adjudicating constitutional matters.[11] Largely modeled on the Federal Constitutional Court of Germany,[12] the Court was established in 1987, as part of

7 Alexander Hamilton, James Madison and John Jay, *The Federalist 'No 65'* (Jacob E Cooke ed, Wesleyan UP 1961).
8 ibid.
9 ibid 441–42.
10 In this chapter, both 'South Korea' and 'Korea' refer to the Republic of Korea.
11 Tom Ginsburg, *Judicial Review in New Democracies* (CUP 2003) 213–17; Chaihark Hahm, 'Law, Culture, and the Politics of Confucianism' (2003) 16 *Colum. J. Asian L.* 253, 260–65.
12 For comparisons to the Federal Constitutional Court of Germany, see Ginsburg (n 11) 218; Chaihark Hahm, 'Rule of Law in South Korea: Rhetoric and Implementation' in Randall Peerenboom (eds), *Asian Discourses of Rule of Law* (Routledge 2004).

the constitutional amendments of 1987. The 1987 amendments themselves were ratified by the National Assembly as part of the country's democratization process and emergence from its military dictatorships of the seventies and the eighties.[13] The Court consists of nine justices, three selected by the President, three selected by the National Assembly, and three selected by the Chief Justice of the Supreme Court,[14] and each justice serves a six-year term, which is renewable.[15] The Court has jurisdiction over five areas: 1) review of constitutionality of statutes, 2) impeachments, 3) dissolution of political parties, 4) jurisdictional disputes among governmental bodies, and 5) constitutional petitions.[16]

The Constitution provides that 'in case the President . . . violate[s] the Constitution or other Acts in the performance of official duties, the National Assembly may pass motions for their impeachment.'[17] Other than this requirement of violation of 'the Constitution or other Acts,' the text of the Constitution is silent on grounds for impeachment. Under the Constitution, a motion for impeachment requires the votes of two-thirds or more of the total members of the Assembly to pass.[18] In order for the Court to affirm the National Assembly's vote to impeach and remove the president, six out of the nine justices must vote in favor of removal.[19]

Under this structure, if the Court disagrees with the National Assembly, then it can keep the president in power by voting against removal. Another possibility is for the majority of the Court to vote in favor of removal, but without the requisite six votes for removal, the president will stay in power. In the two Korean impeachments discussed here, the Court's decisions were unanimous.

5.3 2004 Impeachment of Roh Moo-Hyun

On March 12, 2004, for the first time in Korean history, the National Assembly of Korea passed a motion to impeach the president, which led to an immediate suspension of Roh Moo-Hyun's presidency.[20] On May 14, the Constitutional Court of Korea dismissed the impeachment motion and reinstated the President.[21]

13 Ginsburg (n 11) 218; Hahm (n 12) 389.

14 Taehanmin'guk Hŏnbŏp [Hŏnbŏp] [Constitution] art 111.

15 ibid art 112. Although the terms are renewable, Constitutional Court justices have rarely sought renewal and generally serve only one term; 'Yŏktae & Hyŏnjik Chaep'an'gwan Kusŏng' [Composition of Past & Current Judges] *Constitutional Court Library* <https://library.ccourt.go.kr/#/history/court-justices> accessed 20 February 2023.

16 ibid.

17 ibid art 65, sec 1.

18 Hŏnbŏp art 65, sec 2.

19 ibid art 113, sec 1.

20 Samuel Len, 'South Korean Parliament Votes to Strip President of Powers' *The New York Times* (New York, 12 March 2004) 7.

21 James Brooke, 'Constitutional Court Reinstates South Korea's Impeached President' *The New York Times* (New York, 14 May 2004) 6; Anthony Faiola, 'Court Rejects South Korean

5.3.1 Political Context

Roh Moo-Hyun was elected president through a direct popular vote in December 2002. A former human rights lawyer without a college degree, he came to the presidency – which is limited to a single, five-year term under the Constitution[22] – with a compelling personal story and a progressive reformist agenda.[23] However, his presidency faced a difficult political landscape from his inauguration in February 2003. The opposing conservative party, the Grand National Party (GNP), had the majority in the National Assembly,[24] the unicameral legislative branch in Korea,[25] and Roh's own party, the Millennium Democratic Party (MDP), was paralyzed by a generational rift between those who rose to power under the previous President Kim Dae-jung and a younger generation of legislators who identified themselves more with Roh.[26] The division within the MDP meant that Roh was not always able to count on the MDP's support in the Assembly, and his support base became even more fragile when the pro-Roh forces left the MDP to form a new party, the Uri Party, in September.[27]

Once the Uri Party members defected, the MDP turned squarely against Roh, forming an anti-Roh alliance with the GNP. The GNP, holding 149 seats, and the MDP, holding 63 seats, formed a supermajority in the National Assembly of 272 members.[28] Under the Korean Constitution, a vote of two-thirds or more of the National Assembly is sufficient to override the president's vetoes on legislation,[29] expel members of the Assembly,[30] impeach the president,[31] and propose constitutional amendments to be put to national referenda.[32] The upshot of the shifting political landscape meant that Roh had to manage the weak economy, relations with North Korea,

President's Impeachment' *The Washington Post* (Washington, DC, 14 May 2004); Barbara Demick, 'South Korean President Is Reinstated: A Court Rules That His Impeachment Was Unjustified. Meanwhile, New National Assembly Is Set to Take Office' *Los Angeles Times* (Los Angeles, 14 May 2004).

22 Hŏnbŏp art 70.

23 Barbara Demick, 'A "Lincoln" Climbs to Top in Elitist Korea' *Los Angeles Times* (Los Angeles, 20 December 2002) 26.

24 Kim Hyung-Jin, 'Assembly Opens Special Session: Lawmakers to Focus on Confirmation Hearing, Payoff Flap' *Korea Herald* (Seoul, 5 February 2003).

25 Hŏnbŏp chap. III.

26 Hwang Jang-Jin, 'Post-Election Crisis Deepens in Ruling Party: Roh Supporters, Old Guards Face Off Over Creation of New Party' *Korea Herald* (Seoul, 30 April 2003).

27 Lee Joo-Hee, 'Ruling Party Splits Today: About 40 Pro-Roh Lawmakers to Form New Party' *Korea Herald* (Seoul, 20 September 2003); 'New Party Changes Name to "Uri Party"' *Korea Times* (Seoul, 24 October 2003).

28 'GNP Flexes Muscle, MDP Reorganizes' *Korea Herald* (Seoul, 29 September 2003).

29 Hŏnbŏp art 53, sec 4.

30 ibid art 64, sec 3.

31 ibid art 65, sec 2.

32 ibid art 130, sec 1.

and the strained alliance with the U.S. while facing a hostile and powerful legislative body.[33]

In October of 2003, some of Roh's closest aides were arrested for accepting illegal campaign contributions to Roh's 2002 presidential campaign.[34] Finding himself in the middle of a political crisis with few allies in the Assembly and plummeting approval ratings[35] and anticipating the upcoming General Election in April, Roh made a series of moves. First, in October, he proposed a national referendum to ascertain the nation's confidence in his leadership.[36] Second, in response to the campaign contribution scandal, he promised to resign if the amount of illegal contributions his 2002 presidential campaign accepted exceeded one-tenth the amount of illegal contributions the opposing GNP accepted for the same election.[37] Third, he made no secret of his view that his political fortunes were directly aligned with the performance of the Uri Party at the April election. Although he had not formally joined the party, he made his preferences clear and even suggested that he may quit if the Uri Party did not make a strong showing in the election.[38]

The opposing GNP and MDP parties fiercely criticized every one of these moves by Roh and repeatedly made threats to impeach Roh for these steps and others that Roh had taken. In fact, calls for impeachment were made so frequently – starting in April 2003[39] – that at times, it appeared that the opposing parties, realizing that they potentially had the votes needed to remove Roh, did not hesitate before flexing their muscles at every turn. They also appeared

33 'Expecting Trouble?' *Economist* (London, 14 March 2003); John Burton, 'South Korea Caught Between Two-Forces: The President-Elect Is Under Pressure from Both the US and North Korea' *Financial Times* (London, 3 January 2003) 6; Andrew Ward, 'Paralysis Feared as Lawmakers Snub Roh' *Financial Times (Japan edn)* (Tokyo, 27 September 2003) 1.

34 Anthony Faiola, 'Crisis Widens for South Korea Leader: Aides' Arrest in Bribery Scandal Is Latest in Roh's Brief Tenure' *The Washington Post* (Washington, DC, 24 October 2003) A21; 'Roh's Former Top Aide Arrested' *Korea Times* (Seoul, 16 October 2003); Kim Kyung-Ho, 'Roh's Aide Faces Arrest on Bribery Charges' *Korea Herald* (Seoul, 16 October 2003).

35 Barbara Demick, 'Even Supporters Complain About South Korean Leader: Roh Is Criticized for Leaving the Party and Other Erratic Moves, and His Ratings Have Plunged' *Los Angeles Times* (Los Angeles, 5 October 2003) 3.

36 Anthony Faiola, 'South Korean President Calls for Vote: Roh Offers to Quit if Referendum Goes Against Him' *The Washington Post* (Washington, DC, 13 October 2003) A16.

37 Sim Sung-Tae, 'Roh Takes Another Political Gamble: President May Resign if Campaign Spent Over 10% of GNP Funds' *Korea Herald* (Seoul, 15 December 2003).

38 'President's Gamble Aims for Election Jackpot in April' *Korea Times* (Seoul, 9 January 2004).

39 Hwang Jang-Jin, 'NIS Chief Controversy Grows' *Korea Herald* (Seoul, 28 April 2003); 'Opposition Threatens to Impeach President' *Korea Times* (Seoul, 13 June 2003); 'Roh Faces All-Out War with Opposition Party' *Korea Times* (Seoul, 9 September 2003); Joo Sang-Min, 'GNP Threatens Impeachment: Opposition Calls for Thorough Probe of Scandal' *Korea Herald* (Seoul, 15 October 2003); Lee Joo-Hee, 'Politics Rumble and Tumble Over Referendum' *Korea Herald* (Seoul, 20 October 2003); Joo Sang-Min, 'Opposition Threatens Impeachment' *Korea Herald* (Seoul, 25 November 2003).

to be mindful of the fact that the strength of their alliance, based on their common dislike of Roh, was not going to last forever, given the upcoming elections in April.

After a quick turn of events in February and March, the opposition parties successfully passed a motion to impeach Roh. On February 24, 2004, at a press conference, the President urged voters to support the Uri Party at the April elections.[40] He again made clear his intention to tie the fate of his presidency to the election, stating that he 'wanted to do everything that was legally permitted to help the Uri Party.'[41] On February 27, the MDP, alleging that Roh's comments amounted to a violation of election law, filed a complaint with the National Election Commission.[42]

On March 3, the Commission ruled that Roh violated the law requiring the neutrality of public officials in elections.[43] Although the Commission did not impose any formal sanctions on Roh, it warned Roh to refrain from further violations. The opposition parties swiftly demanded an apology from Roh and threatened to impeach him. In response, Roh held a press conference on March 11. Although he apologized for the various scandals involving his close aides, he refused to apologize for the remarks he made in support of the Uri Party. Instead, he stated that he substantively disagreed with the Commission's conclusion that his support for the Uri Party was a violation of law.[44]

The opposition parties responded to Roh's showing of defiance by passing a motion to impeach Roh. The motion listed twenty-one separate counts as grounds for impeachment, ranging from Roh's support of the Uri Party and corruption scandals involving Roh's close aides to Roh's management of the economy.[45] Out of 272 members in the Assembly, 193 voted in favor of the motion, and two voted against it, while all forty-seven Uri Party members in the Assembly protested the vote and did not participate in it.[46]

40 'Roh Calls on Nation to Support Pro-Government Party' *Korea Times* (Seoul, 25 February 2004).

41 2004 Hun-Na 1.

42 Joo Sang-Min, 'MDP Takes Roh and Uri Leader to Election Watchdog' *Korea Herald* (Seoul, 1 March 2004). The Commission is a constitutionally established body that monitors elections and campaign activities and is composed of nine members, three of whom are appointed by the President, three are chosen by the Assembly, and three are chosen by the Chief Justice of the Supreme Court. Hŏnbŏp art 114.

43 Joo Sang-Min, 'Parties Demand Roh Apology for Violating Election Law: Opposition Threatens Impeachment If Demand Is Not Met' *Korea Herald* (Seoul, 5 March 2004).

44 Seo Hyun-Jin, 'Poll Results Will Decide My Fate: Roh; President Rejects Rivals' Demand to Apologize for Violating Elections Law' *Korea Herald* (Seoul, 12 March 2004).

45 Taet'ongnyŏng (Roh Moo-hyun) T'anhaek Soch'uŭikyŏlsŏ [Motion for Impeachment of President Roh Moo-Hyun] (12 March 2004).

46 Park Song-Wu, 'National Assembly Impeaches President Roh' *Korea Times* (Seoul, 12 March 2004).

The impeachment vote threw the country into a state of turmoil. As provided by the Constitution, Roh's presidency was immediately suspended, and the Prime Minster, traditionally powerless, assumed the duties of the office of the presidency. In the meantime, the impeachment was highly unpopular politically, with the polls indicating that seven out of ten Korean citizens were against the impeachment, and there were demonstrations nationwide protesting the National Assembly's actions.[47]

As the Constitutional Court deliberated the question of removal, the impeachment vote became a campaign issue in the General Elections, and in a result that was widely assumed to have been influenced by the unpopularity of the impeachment, the Uri Party gained a majority, with 152 out of the 299 Assembly seats, while the GNP won 121 seats, and the MDP ended up with a mere nine seats.[48] After holding seven bench trial-like hearings starting on March 30 and ending on April 30,[49] the Court announced its decision rejecting the National Assembly's motion and reinstating Roh on May 14.[50]

5.3.2 The Constitutional Court's Decision

The Court's decision had two parts. First, it addressed the question of whether alleged instances of misconduct by Roh, as described in the National Assembly's motion to impeach, violated the Constitution or other laws.[51] Then, the Court considered whether the violations were serious enough to warrant his removal from office. The Court found that Roh was in violation of law in three instances and then ruled that none of these violations were serious enough to justify removing him from office.[52]

47 Samuel Len, 'President's Impeachment Stirs Angry Protests in South Korea' *The New York Times* (New York, 13 March 2004) 2; Ryu Jin, '7 Out of 10 Oppose Impeachment' *Korea Times* (Seoul, 13 March 2004).

48 Anthony Faiola, 'Korean Vote Shifts Power in Assembly: Turnover May Aid Impeached President' *The Washington Post* (Washington, DC, 16 April 2004) A14; James Brooke, 'South Korea's Impeached President Gains Support in Vote' *The New York Times* (New York, 16 April 2004) A6; Barbara Demick, 'Supporters of South Korea's Roh Push Legislature to Left: The Election Results are Seen as Response to Conservative Lawmakers' Vote Last Month to Impeach the President' *Los Angeles Times* (Los Angeles, 16 April 2004) A3; Lee Joo-Hee, 'Crushed MDP on Uncertain Path' *Korea Herald* (Seoul, 17 April 2004).

49 Kim So-Young, 'Court Ends Roh Hearings, to Rule in Mid-May' *Korea Herald* (Seoul, 1 May 2004); Na Jeong-Ju, 'Court Seeks Fast Impeachment Ruling' *Korea Times* (Seoul, 30 March 2004).

50 2004 HunNa 1 (14 May 2004). The Court's opinion was per curiam, and the Court did not disclose the final vote breakdown. Instead, the Court released a statement announcing that it would not reveal individual justices' votes and that no dissenting opinion would be released. Taet'ongnyŏng T'anhaek Sagŏnŭi Kyŏlchŏngmune Hŏnbŏp Chaep'ansoŭi Ŭigyŏnmanŭl Kijaehan Iyu [The Reason the Court Released Only the Court's Opinion in the Presidential Impeachment Decision] (14 May 2004).

51 Hŏnbŏp art 65, sec 1.

52 2004 Hun-Na 1.

5.3.2.1 *What Laws Did Roh Violate?*

POLITICAL NEUTRALITY REQUIREMENT

The National Assembly claimed that Roh's statements in support of the Uri Party were in violation of the president's legal duty to be politically neutral, and the Constitutional Court agreed. The Court pointed out that because Roh actively expressed his support for a particular party and urged the voters to do the same, he improperly used the political weight of his position to influence the outcome of the election. The Court concluded that such conduct by Roh was incompatible with his constitutional duty to be a 'servant[] of the entire people and . . . be responsible for the people'[53] and was in violation of his duty of political neutrality.[54]

RESPECT FOR THE CONSTITUTION AND CONSTITUTIONAL BODIES

The National Assembly alleged that Roh showed contempt for the Constitution and constitutional bodies by questioning the National Election Commission's ruling that he was in violation of the requirement of political neutrality and by seeking an illegal national referendum.[55] The Constitutional Court agreed with the National Assembly and found Roh to be in violation of his constitutional duty to uphold the Constitution.[56]

The Court scrutinized the way in which Roh reacted to the National Election Commission's decision that Roh's comments in support of a specific party were in violation of the election law. Through his press secretary, Roh stated that 'it should be made clear that the National Election Commission's decision

53 Hŏnbŏp art 7, sec 1.

54 2004 Hun-Na 1. The Court's interpretation of the law and the wisdom of applying the law to the president were by no means uncontroversial. Roh himself cited an episode of the popular television drama *West Wing*, in which Martin Sheen's character campaigns for a candidate from his party, to argue that '[t]he President is a politician' and should be allowed to be partisan. 'Roh Likens Crisis to "West Wing"' *Korea Times* (12 March 2004). Scholars in Korea actively debated this issue as the impeachment proceedings took place. See, e.g., Reuben Staines, 'Presidential Political Neutrality Central Issue in Impeachment Trial' *Korea Times* (28 March 2004). Roh's lawyers (ultimately unsuccessfully) argued that the law in question did not apply to the president and that, if it did apply, then it was unconstitutional. Tappyŏnsŏ (3) [Brief for Respondent No 3] at 5–30 (2004 Hun-Na 1).

55 2004 Hun-Na 1.

56 The Constitutional Court derived Roh's duty to uphold the Constitution from two constitutional provisions, articles 66 and 69. 2004 Hun-Na 1. Article 66, section 2 of the Constitution provides, 'The President shall have the responsibility and duty to safeguard the independence, territorial integrity and continuity of the State and the Constitution' Hŏnbŏp art 66, sec 2. Article 69 provides that 'The President, at the time of his inauguration, shall take the following oath: "I do solemnly swear before the people that I will faithfully execute the duties of the President by observing the Constitution, defending the State, pursuing the peaceful unification of the homeland, promoting the freedom and welfare of the people and endeavoring to develop national culture."' Hŏnbŏp art 69.

is difficult to comprehend,' that 'it is time for us to change our system and custom in a way that is more suited to a developed democratic society like ours,' that 'election laws that accompanied our past presidents' authoritarian institutions should be reformed and updated,' and that 'interpretation and enforcement of election laws must be revised to reflect the current changes from the past's authoritarian culture.'[57] In short, the Court concluded that Roh's view was that the election law he was found to have violated was, in his words, 'a relic from our dictatorial past.'[58]

The Court held that the President issuing a public statement that challenges the legality and legitimacy of an existing law cannot be squared with his duty to observe and uphold the Constitution. If the President doubts the constitutionality of a law properly enacted by the National Assembly, the Court stated, then he should attempt to revise the law by introducing a reform bill to the National Assembly instead of questioning the law that he was found to have violated.

The Court also took issue with Roh's proposal for a referendum to determine the country's confidence in his leadership. Article 72 of the Constitution provides that the president 'may submit important policies relating to diplomacy, national defense, unification and other matters relating to the national destiny to a national referendum if he deems it necessary.'[59] The Court observed the risk that the president could use the Article 72 power to call national referenda not as a device to ascertain the will of the people but as a political weapon in partisan conflicts. To prevent such abuses of power, the Court stated that Article 72 should not be read to allow the President to test the public's confidence in him. Therefore, the Court concluded that Roh's referendum proposal amounted to an attempted abuse of the constitutional process to enhance his political standing and was in violation of the Constitution.[60]

5.3.2.2 *Should Roh Be Removed for His Violations?*

After finding that Roh 'violated the Constitution [and an] Act[] in the performance of official duties,' as provided under the impeachment provision of the Constitution,[61] the Court addressed the question of whether he should be removed from office. The Court announced that the appropriate guide for making such determination is the principle of proportionality (*pŏbikhyŏngnyang*) – whether the particular legal violation by the public official is serious enough to justify removal from office. In the impeachment context, the relevant variables

57 2004 Hun-Na 1 (author's translation).
58 ibid.
59 Hŏnbŏp art 72.
60 2004 Hun-Na 1.
61 Hŏnbŏp art 65, sec 1.

consider whether removal is proportionate to, as the Court stated, 'the gravity of the legal violation' and 'the consequences of removal from office.'[62]

The Court noted that there are two main adverse consequences of removing a president from office. The first adverse consequence is that removal results in cutting short the term of a democratically elected leader, thereby thwarting the will of the people. The second adverse consequence is the political turmoil that can occur when the work of an administration is interrupted and the country is left without leadership until a new president is elected. Therefore, the Court concluded that whether a president's conduct in violation of law warrants his removal should be considered in light of the democratic legitimacy of his tenure and the importance of continuity in his administration.[63]

The question then was what type of legal violation is sufficient to justify effecting such adverse consequences of removing the president. Because the purpose of the impeachment process is to protect and preserve the Constitution, the Court explained that the gravity of the legal violation has to be considered from the perspective of protecting the constitutional order, and the relevant question is how much damage to the existing constitutional order has been inflicted by the particular legal violation. The Court concluded that impeachment and removal are appropriate only when 'such steps are necessary to rehabilitate the damaged constitutional order.'[64]

More specifically, the Court equated 'constitutional order' with 'free and democratic basic order' (*chayuminjujŏk kibonjilsŏ*).[65] The 'free and democratic basic order,' the Court explained, consists of respect for fundamental human rights, separation of powers, independence of the judiciary, parliamentary institutions, multi-party system, and electoral institutions. The Court then listed several examples of acts that directly threaten the free and democratic basic order: acceptance of bribery, corruption, embezzlement, abuse of presidential

62 2004 Hun-Na 1 (author's translation).

63 ibid.

64 ibid.

65 ibid. There is some controversy over the proper way to translate the phrase '*chayuminjujŏk kibonjilsŏ*'. Hahm (n 12) 269 ('free and democratic basic order'); Sungmoon Kim, 'From Remonstrance to Impeachment: A Curious Case of "Confucian Constitutionalism" in South Korea' (2019) 44 *Law & Social Inquiry* 586–87 ('liberal democratic basic order'); Justine Guichard, 'South Korea's Multilayered "Basic Order": Uses and Meanings in Constitutional Rulings from 1989 to 2019' in *The Constitutional Court of Korea as a Protector of Constitutionalism: Global Perspectives* (Constitutional Court of Korea, Constitutional Research Institute 2021) ('free democratic basic order'); Hannes B Mosler, 'Decoding the "Free Democratic Basic Order" for the Unification of Korea' (2017) 57 *Korea Journal* 5 ('free democratic basic order'). The word '*chayu*', when used as an adjective, can be translated as either 'free' or 'liberal.' My decision to use 'free and democratic basic order' over some other formulation should not be taken to imply an endorsement of one reading of the Korean Constitution over another. Terms such as 'freedom', 'liberty', and 'liberalism' all are notoriously complex and contestable, and these words by themselves, without further elaboration, do not tell us all that much in any event. In addition, both 'free and democratic' and 'liberal democratic' are capacious enough phrases to be consistent with numerous interpretations that may conflict with one another.

power to attack the authority of other branches of the government, violation of human rights, and oppression of citizens through the use of the coercive power of state institutions, use of public office for illegal campaigning, and manipulation of election results.[66]

In applying this standard, the Court held that none of the violations by Roh justified removing him from office. First, the Court pointed out that the President's support of the Uri Party, while in violation of law, did not involve any 'active, premeditated scheme' to use the governmental authority to undermine the democratic process. Instead, his act was merely a statement of support that was incidental to his answers to reporters regarding his policy outlook.[67] Similarly, the President's defiance in the face of the National Election Commission's ruling that he had violated the election law, while inexcusable, was not serious enough to justify removal, as his conduct did not rise to the level of attempting to thwart the free and democratic basic order or of challenging the idea of the rule of law. Finally, the Court concluded, given the hitherto uncertainty surrounding the proper scope of the president's power under Article 72 to hold a national referendum and considering that he did not pursue his proposal after facing opposition, his misconduct in this instance was not a serious enough violation to justify his removal.[68]

5.3.2.3 Other Grounds for Impeachment: Corruption and Maladministration

The National Assembly also impeached Roh on the grounds of 'Corruption and Abuse of Power' and 'Maladministration.'[69] The Court summarily dismissed both charges. The text of the impeachment provision in the Korean Constitution limits impeachable offenses to violations of 'the Constitution or other Acts in the performance of official duties.'[70] Because most of the allegations of bribery and illegal campaign fundraising involved conduct before Roh assumed office, the Court dismissed the corruption claims as being outside the scope of the impeachment provision and thus improper as a basis for impeachment. As to the maladministration claim, the Court held that because impeachment was a 'legal,' not 'political,' procedure, the National Assembly's accusation that Roh neglected his duties and that his administration lacked direction and created an uncertain political and economic environment were mere policy disagreements, which cannot serve as grounds for impeachment and must await resolution through the electoral process instead.[71]

66 2004 Hun-Na 1.
67 ibid (author's translation).
68 ibid.
69 ibid.
70 Hŏnbŏp art 65, sec 1.
71 2004 Hun-Na 1.

5.4 2016–2017 Impeachment of Park Geun-hye[72]

5.4.1 Political Context

Park Geun-hye was elected president through a direct popular vote in 2012.[73] Park was the first female president of Korea[74] and the daughter of the controversial former President Park Chung-hee.[75] She had been a familiar public figure for a long time because at age 22, she took on the role of first lady following the assassination of her mother in 1974. She served in this role until her father was assassinated several years later.[76]

The first year of her presidency was marked by moderately high approval ratings.[77] However, in April 2014, what is now described as 'South Korea's most traumatic peacetime disaster' struck.[78] A ferry boat carrying around 450 people sank, and over 300 people died. Among the 300 were 250 high school students who were on a field trip.[79] There was plenty of blame to go around

72 The Park impeachment has received some scholarly attention. See Jaime Doucette, 'The Occult of Personality: Korea's Candlelight Protests and the Impeachment of Park Geun-Hye' (2017) 76 *The Journal of Asian Studies* 851; Byong-Kuen Jhee and Johann Park, 'How Citizens Reshaped the Path of Presidential Impeachment in Korea' (2019) 50 *Korea Observer* 565; Kim (n 65); Mark Turner, Seung-Ho Kwon and Michael O'Donnell, 'Making Integrity Institutions Work in South Korea' (2018) 58 *Asian Survey* 898; Hannes B Mosler, 'The Institution of Presidential Impeachment in South Korea 1992–2017' (2017) 50 *Law and Politics in Africa, Asia and Latin America* 111; Hyunjin Seo, *Networked Collective Action: The Making of an Impeachment* (OUP 2021) 73–98; Soomin Seo, 'South Korea's Watergate Moment: How a Media Coalition Brought Down the Park Geun-Hye Government' (2020) 15 *Journalism Practice* 526; Chaihark Hahm, 'Constitutional Court of Korea: Guardian of the Constitution or Mouthpiece of the Government?' in Albert HY Chen and Andrew Harding (eds), *Constitutional Courts in Asia* (CUP 2018); see also Tom Ginsburg, Aziz Z. Huq and David Landau, 'The Comparative Constitutional Law of Presidential Impeachment' (2021) 88 *University of Chicago Law Review* 81.

73 See Choe Sang-Hun, 'Ex-Dictator's Daughter Elected President as South Korea Rejects Sharp Change' *The New York Times* (New York, 20 December 2012) 12.

74 The fact that she would be the first female president of Korea, however, was perceived in the election to be a far less significant factor than the fact that she was Park Chung-Hee's daughter. See Choe Sang-Hun, 'Steely Leader of South Korea Is Battle-Ready' *The New York Times* (New York, 13 April 2013) 1.

75 On Park Chung-Hee's presidency, see generally Byung-Kook Kim and Ezra F Vogel (eds), *The Park Chung-Hee Era: The Transformation of South Korea* (Harvard UP 2013); Carter J Eckert, *Park Chung-Hee and Modern Korea* (Harvard UP 2016).

76 See Martin Fackler, 'In a Rowdy Democracy, a Dictator's Daughter with an Unsoiled Aura' *The New York Times* (New York, 21 April 2012) 10.

77 'Gallup Korea Daily Opinion: No 238' *Gallup* (Seoul, 2 December 2016).

78 Choe Sang-Hun, 'The Country Has Moved on, but Their Grief Has No End' *The New York Times* (New York, 9 June 2022) 4; Martin Fackler, 'A Korean City with 250 Holes in Its Heart' *The New York Times* (New York, 2 May 2014) 6; Martin Fackler, 'A Year After Sewol Ferry Tragedy, Peace Is Elusive for South Korean City' *The New York Times* (New York, 16 April 2015) 10.

79 Su-Hyun Lee and Choe Sang-Hun, 'Students Among Hundreds Missing After South Korean Ferry Sinks' *The New York Times* (New York, 17 April 2014) 6.

for the incident – a lax and corrupt regulatory environment,[80] greedy and criminally neglectful business executives,[81] and a cowardly and selfish captain and crew,[82] to name a few.[83] However, one increasingly intense focal point of the public's anger and grief was Park herself. There were questions about the slowness of her government's response to the emergency, where she was on the day of the incident, what she was doing as the crisis was unfolding over several hours,[84] and whether her administration was being transparent about the incident itself, the rescue efforts, and the investigation afterwards.[85]

In June 2015, another crisis hit with an outbreak of Middle East respiratory syndrome. The Park administration was again widely criticized for its slow response and lack of transparency.[86] One editorial of a widely circulated conservative daily newspaper read, '[t]he government was a super-spreader of mistrust.'[87] An editorial from another major daily newspaper criticized her administration for making South Korea look like 'an underdeveloped country.'[88]

On April 13, 2016, Park's Saenuri Party lost its majority in the National Assembly.[89] By the time the new assembly members were seated, four parties were represented, and none held a majority.[90] The main opposition Minjoo Party won the plurality of seats with 123 members, and the President's Saenuri Party held 122.[91] Perhaps this setback is to be attributed to the public's

80 Choe Sang-Hun, 'South Korea Tightens Rules Against Gifts to Fight Graft' *The New York Times* (New York, 4 March 2015) 4.
81 Choe Sang-Hun and others, 'In Ferry Deaths, a South Korean Tycoon's Downfall' *The New York Times* (New York, 26 July 2014).
82 Christopher Drew and Jad Mouawad, 'Breaking Proud Tradition, Captains Flee and Let Others Go Down with Ship' *The New York Times* (New York, 19 April 2014) 6.
83 Choe Sang-Hun, 'An Overloaded Ferry Flipped and Drowned Hundreds of Schoolchildren: Could It Happen Again?' *The New York Times* (New York, 10 June 2019) 4.
84 Chŏng Nogyong, '"Nollanŭi Taet'ongnyŏng 7Sigan", "Ch'ŏngwadae Kyŏngnaee Issŏtchi Ŏdie Issŏtkenna"' ['The Controversy Over the President's Seven Hours'] *Chosun Ilbo* (Seoul, 8 August 2014) <http://premium.chosun.com/site/data/html_dir/2014/08/08/2014080802213.html> accessed 20 February 2023.
85 See, e.g., Choe Sang-Hun, 'South Korea's Leader and Media Face Scrutiny Over Ferry Disaster' *The New York Times* (New York, 9 May 2014); Choe Sang-Hun, 'Ferry Disaster That United South Korea Now Polarizes It' *The New York Times* (New York, 2 October 2014) 4.
86 Se-Woong Koo, 'Opinion Yet Another Disaster for Seoul' *The New York Times* (New York, 12 June 2015); Choe Sang-Hun, 'Experts Fault South Korean Response to MERS Outbreak' *The New York Times* (New York, 13 June 2015) 11.
87 Choe Sang-Hun, 'South Korean Hamlet, Under MERS Quarantine, Symbolizes Weaknesses in the System' *The New York Times* (New York, 15 June 2015) 4.
88 ibid.
89 Choe Sang-Hun, 'Party of South Korea's President Loses Majority in Parliament' *The New York Times* (New York, 13 April 2016) 4.
90 ibid.
91 Choe Sang-Hun, 'After South Korea Spurns Park Geun-Hye, She May Press Agenda Abroad' *The New York Times* (New York, 14 April 2016); 'Bareun Party's Presidential Nominee Known as Aide-Turned-Critic of Park' *Yonhap News Agency* (Seoul, 28 March 2017) <https://en.yna.

disapproval of the Park administration's work, but whatever the reason, the upshot was that Park was then in a weakened political state.

Park's presidency did not start to unravel past the point of no return, however, until after a series of shocking and bizarre press accounts. On July 26, 2016, a story raised questions about a cultural foundation called 'Mir' that raised almost fifty billion Korean won (equivalent to about forty-five million U.S. dollars at the time) in two months from Samsung, Hyundai, SK, LG, and Lotte.[92] The story noted that the Federation of Korean Industries, an industry group, led the fundraising effort and that Ahn Chong-bum, the Senior Presidential Secretary for Policy Coordination, was deeply involved, perhaps even issuing guidelines for donations from each company.[93] Ahn was interviewed for the story and denied his involvement.[94]

Another story broke in September, this time naming two foundations, Mir and K-Sports.[95] The story noted that the two foundations, which were established extremely quickly with instant approvals by the government, raised nearly 80 billion Korean won combined (about 72 million U.S. dollars) in less than a year. Yet the two foundations appeared not to have done anything, and the donors did not seem to know or to be interested in knowing what the foundations did. The story further indicated that the chair of K-Sports was the head of a massage center frequented by Choi Soon-sil, described as a shadowy and influential figure around Park ('*pisŏnsilsein*'), and that it was Choi who had suggested the appointment.

More stories about Choi followed shortly after; this time, they focused on Choi Soon-sil's daughter's education and career. Stories reported that Ewha University bent its rules to accept Choi's daughter, an equestrian, as a student,[96] that when the daughter faced expulsion for absenteeism, Choi

co.kr/view/AEN20170328014051315> accessed 16 February 2023; Park Sŭngch'ŏl, U Jeyun and Kim Gangrae, '16Nyŏnmane Yŏsoyadae . . . 3Tangch'eje K'aesŭt'ingbot'ŭ Chwin Kungminŭidang' [A Minority Government for the First Time in 16 Years. . .. The People's Party Holds the Deciding Vote] *Maeilgyŏngjae* (Seoul, 14 April 2016) <www.mk.co.kr/news/politics/7301684> accessed 17 February 2023.

92 Chung Dong Kwon, 'Ch'ŏngwadae Anjongbŏm Susŏk, "Munhwajaedan Mirŭ" 500ŏk Mogŭm Chiwŏn' [Blue House's Ahn Chong-Bum Helped Raise 50 Billion Won for 'Cultural Foundation Mir'] *TV Chosun News* (Seoul, 26 July 2016) <http://news.tvchosun.com/site/data/html_dir/2016/07/26/2016072690265.html> accessed 15 February 2023.

93 ibid.

94 ibid.

95 Kim Ui Gyom, Kim Chang Gum and Bang Jun Ho, 'K Sŭp'och'ŭ Isajangŭn Ch'oesunsil Tan'gol Masaji Sent'ŏjan' [K-Sports Chair Is the Head of a Massage Center Frequented by Choi Soon-Sil] *Hankyoreh* (Seoul, 20 September 2016) <www.hani.co.kr/arti/politics/politics_general/761796.html> accessed 15 February 2023.

96 Ha O Young and Bang Jun Ho, 'Ch'oesunsil Tonŏmŭn Kaeip . . . "Sŭngmahanŭn Ttal" Kobimada T'ŭkhye Nollan' [Choi Soon-Sil's Extensive Interventions . . . Controversy Over Preferential Treatment for Her Equestrian Daughter at Crucial Moments] *Hankyoreh* (Seoul, 26 September 2016) <www.hani.co.kr/arti/politics/politics_general/762864.html> accessed 15 February 2023.

showed up at the university and managed to replace her daughter's advisor with another professor,[97] and that the university shortly afterwards changed its rules to enable the daughter to remain enrolled despite her absences.[98] The stories suggested that Choi appeared to have an enormous amount of power that lacked a good explanation.

After these stories, the nature of the relationship between Choi Soon-sil and Park began to attract more attention.[99] In October, Ko Young-tae, someone who was apparently close to Choi, mentioned in the presence of a reporter that Choi's favorite activity was revising the President's speeches.[100] This was vehemently denied by the President's Chief of Staff.[101] A week later, the same news outlet reported that it had come into possession of a computer belonging to Choi that had forty-four speeches and other official remarks by the President, and furthermore, these files had dates that preceded the dates on which the speeches were given by the President.[102]

The next day, Park made a brief public apology.[103] She described Choi as someone who was helpful to her during difficult times in the past and that during the presidential election, Choi advised Park with various speeches. Park admitted that Choi continued to give her advice after Park became the

97 Ryu I-Gŭn, 'Ttal Chidogyosukkaji Pakkun "Ch'oesunsirŭi him"' [Choi Soon-Sil's Power Can Even Change the Daughter's Professor] *Hankyoreh* (Seoul, 26 September 2016) <www.hani.co.kr/arti/politics/politics_general/762866.html> accessed 15 February 2023.

98 Ryu I-Gŭn, 'Sŭngma Hullyŏndo Ch'ulsŏk Injŏng . . . Idae, Ch'oesunsil Ttal Match'umhyŏng Hakch'ik Kaejŏng?' [Equestrian Practices Count as Attendance . . . Did University Change Its Rules for Choi Soon-Sil's Daughter?] *Hankyoreh* (Seoul, 28 September 2016) <www.hani.co.kr/arti/politics/politics_general/763247.html> accessed 15 February 2023.

99 There were other stories about Choi previously, but they never gained the kind of momentum the stories did in 2016, and there are indications that those who tried to speak about the relationship between Choi and Park were paid to remain silent. See Seo, *Networked Collective Action* (n 72).

100 'Ch'oech'ŭkkŭnŭi Chŭngŏn "Ch'oesunsil, Taet'ongnyŏng Yŏnsŏlmun Koch'igido"' [A Person Close to Choi Says 'Choi Soon-Sil Revises President's Speeches"] *JTBC News* (Seoul, 19 October 2016) <https://news.jtbc.co.kr/article/article.aspx?news_id=NB11337111> accessed 15 February 2023. It later came out that Ko was the one who started leaking damaging information about Choi to the media after a personal dispute with Choi about his failure to walk her daughter's dog as she had expected. Choe Sang-Hun, 'Key Figure in South Korean Leader's Troubles: A Puppy' *The New York Times* (New York, 9 December 2016) 10.

101 Kim Jong-Ha and Park Yu-Mi, 'Ponggŏnsidaeedo Issŭl Su Ŏmnŭn Yaegi'kukkam Chŭngŏn Iwŏnjong Pisŏsiljang Konhok' [A Story That Cannot Exist Even in the Middle Ages, Chief of Staff Lee Won-Jong Expresses Bafflement to the National Assembly] *JoongAng Ilbo* (Seoul, 25 October 2016) <www.joongang.co.kr/article/20780117#home> accessed 15 February 2023.

102 'Ch'oesunsil PC P'ail Ipsu . . . Taet'ongnyŏng Yŏnsŏl Chŏn Yŏnsŏlmun Patatta' [Choi Soon-Sil PC File Shows Receipt of Presidential Speeches Before the Speeches Were Given] *JTBC News* (Seoul, 24 October 2016) <https://news.jtbc.co.kr/article/article.aspx?news_id=NB11340632> accessed 15 February 2023.

103 'Pakkŭnhye Taet'ongnyŏng Taegungminsagwa Chŏnmun' [Text of President Park Geun-Hye's Public Apology] *Chosun Ilbo* (Seoul, 25 October 2016) <www.chosun.com/site/data/html_dir/2016/10/25/2016102502058.html> accessed 15 February 2023.

president but that once her official staff was in place, Choi no longer played the role of an advisor.

The apology failed to put an end to the growing crisis, as one damaging story quickly followed another. For instance, as the president-elect, Park had a private, one-on-one meeting with President Lee Myung-bak shortly after the 2012 presidential election, and there was evidence that Choi knew in detail, as early as ten hours before the meeting was to take place, what was to be discussed between Lee and Park. The document revealing the anticipated content of the conversation involved sensitive matters regarding foreign relations, national security, and the economy, none of which were disclosed to the public after the meeting.[104] Another story noted that Choi was in possession of documents detailing assessments of candidates for various posts in the government, including in the Blue House (the Korean equivalent to the White House), during the presidential transition and speculated that Choi was making recommendations and requests for personnel appointments to Park.[105] Yet another story noted that Choi had advance access to documents prepared by Ministry of Foreign Affairs in preparation for President-elect Park's conversation with the Prime Minister of Australia.[106] A document unearthed by another news organization indicated that Choi was given the President's itinerary of her official visits to foreign nations in advance and that Choi handwrote instructions regarding what the President was to wear.[107] In another story featuring a secret video recording, Choi appeared to be ordering around two Blue House staff members, who responded in a highly subservient manner.[108]

So, who was Choi? She was not a government official. She was a private citizen. However, she seemed to have an outsized influence over the President. Choi's involvement in Park's life goes back to Choi's father's relationship

104 'Ch'oesunsil, MBwa "Tangsŏnin Toktae" Sinariodo Pata' [Choi Soon-Sil Received Meeting Notes Between President-Elect and President Lee Myung-Bak in Advance] *JTBC News* (Seoul, 25 October 2016) <https://news.jtbc.co.kr/article/article.aspx?news_id=NB11341539> accessed 15 February 2023.

105 'Ch'oesunsil, Ch'ŏngwadae Insa·Chŏngbu Chojigedo Kaeip Chŏnghwang' [Choi Soon-Sil Intervened in Blue House Personnel and Governmental Organization] *JTBC News* (Seoul, 25 October 2016) <https://news.jtbc.co.kr/article/article.aspx?news_id=NB11341535> accessed 15 February 2023.

106 'Oegyobu Tŭng Chŏngbubuch'ŏ Kongsik Mun'gŏndo Ch'oesunsil Sone' [Choi Soon-Sil Had Official Documents in Possession of Ministry of Foreign Affairs and Other Governmental Bodies'] *JTBC News* (Seoul, 25 October 2016) <https://news.jtbc.co.kr/article/article.aspx?news_id=NB11341519> accessed 16 February 2023.

107 Park Kyŏng-Jun, 'Ch'oesunsil Sone Sunbangiljŏngp'yo, Taet'ongnyŏng Ot Mamdaero Kyŏljŏng' [Choi Soon-Sil Had the President's Itinerary and Decided on the President's Clothes] *TV Chosun* (Seoul, 25 October 2016) <www.chosun.com/site/data/html_dir/2016/10/25/2016102503181.html> accessed 16 February 2023.

108 Kim Jŏngu, 'Ch'ŏngwadae 2pusoksil Haengjŏnggwandŭl Ch'oesunsil Sangjŏn Mosi' [Blue House Staff Submit Like Servants to Choi Soon-Sil] TV Chosun (Seoul, 25 October 2016) <http://news.tvchosun.com/site/data/html_dir/2016/10/25/2016102590214.html> accessed 16 February 2023.

with Park. Choi Soon-sil was a daughter of Choi Tae-min who befriended Park, 40 years his junior, shortly after her mother was assassinated. There were rumors for years about Choi Tae-min's close relationship with Park and about his daughter Choi Soon-sil's relationship with Park.[109] In any event, the picture that began to emerge clearly is that this private citizen was someone that Park turned to for counsel, that Park authorized the sharing of sensitive documents with Choi, and that Choi was using her influence over the President to amass wealth for herself through the establishment of fake cultural foundations and by directing the President to order a collection of donations from conglomerates.

These stories about Park and Choi precipitated a cascade of events that proved unstoppable. Protests,[110] calls for her resignation and impeachment,[111] investigations,[112] arrests,[113] and prosecutions of Choi Soon-sil and presidential aides believed to have been closely involved with Choi and Park's actions in question[114] quickly followed. Park attempted to control the crisis by giving multiple contrite speeches (without giving factual details or admitting any serious wrongdoing),[115] replacing a number of senior officials,[116] and cooperating with opposition parties on appointments,[117] but her approval ratings were at a free fall by this point, dropping from approximately 30% at the beginning

109 Choe Sang-Hun, 'A Presidential Friendship Has Many South Koreans Crying Foul' *The New York Times* (New York, 27 October 2016) 7; Choe Sang-Hun, 'South Koreans "Ashamed" Over Leader's Secretive Adviser' *The New York Times* (New York, 5 November 2016) 4.

110 Choe Sang-Hun, 'South Korean President Dismisses Aides in Bid to Stem Worsening Scandal' *The New York Times* (New York, 30 October 2016) 9 (the number of people at the first protest in October varied between 12,000 and 30,000).

111 Se-Woong Koo, 'South Korea's President Must Go' *The New York Times* (New York, 9 November 2016) 14.

112 Choe Sang-Hun, 'South Korean President Dismisses Aides in Bid to Stem Worsening Scandal' *The New York Times* (New York, 30 October 2016) 9.

113 Choe Sang-Hun, 'Choi Soon-Sil, at Center of Political Scandal in South Korea, Is Jailed' *The New York Times* (New York, 31 October 2016) <www.nytimes.com/2016/11/01/world/asia/south-korea-park-geun-hye-choi-soon-sil.html> accessed 16 February 2023; Choe Sang-Hun, 'Weakened South Korean President Allows Parliament to Pick Prime Minister' *The New York Times* (New York, 7 November 2016) 6.

114 Choe Sang-Hun, 'South Korean Prosecutors Say They Will Bring Charges Against President's Friend' *The New York Times* (New York, 2 November 2016) 13; Choe Sang-Hun, 'Park Geun-Hye Was Accomplice in Extortion, South Korean Prosecutors Say' *The New York Times* (New York, 20 November 2016) 13.

115 Choe Sang-Hun, 'South Korean Leader Says She Will Submit to Scandal Inquiry' *The New York Times* (New York, 4 November 2016) 6; Choe Sang-Hun, 'Park Geun-Hye, Embattled South Korean President, Says She's Willing to Resign' *The New York Times* (New York, 29 November 2016) 4.

116 Choe Sang-Hun, 'Weakened by Scandal, South Korea's President Picks New Premier' *The New York Times* (New York, 2 November 2016) 8.

117 Choe, 'Weakened South Korean President Allows Parliament to Pick Prime Minister' (n 113) 8.

of October down to 5% within a month.[118] Weekly protests against the President kept growing in size,[119] and more stories came out about the ways in which Choi used her close relationship with Park to pressure others to help her enrich herself and her family and friends.[120]

The National Assembly jumped into action. After some back-and-forth between the National Assembly and the Blue House about the choice between impeachment and resignation,[121] the National Assembly appointed a special prosecutor to investigate Park and Choi,[122] and 171 members of the National Assembly filed a motion to impeach the President on December 3, 2016.[123] Then, on December 9, the National Assembly passed the motion by a vote of 234 members of 300, which was over the required two-thirds to pass the motion.[124] Per the Korean Constitution, Park was temporarily removed from office, and the Prime Minister assumed the duties of the office of the presidency.[125] The Constitutional Court held preliminary hearings and the trial in December 2016 and January 2017[126] and delivered its decision ordering the removal of Park from the presidency on March 10, 2017.[127]

5.4.2 The Constitutional Court's Decision

The Court addressed a number of issues in its opinion, but the substantive portion of the ruling followed the same outline as its Roh impeachment

118 'Gallup Korea Daily Opinion: No 238' (n 77).

119 Choe Sang-Hun, 'South Koreans Rally in Largest Protest in Decades to Demand President's Ouster' *The New York Times* (New York, 13 November 2016) 10; Choe Sang-Hun, 'Protest Against South Korean President Estimated to Be Largest Yet' *The New York Times* (New York, 27 November 2016) 6.

120 Choe Sang-Hun, 'South Korean Leader Digs in Against Rising Calls for Impeachment' *The New York Times* (New York, 28 November 2016) 1.

121 ibid 1; Choe, 'Park Geun-Hye, Embattled South Korean President, Says She's Willing to Resign' (n 115) 4.

122 Ju-Min Park and Jack Kim, South Korea to Appoint Special Prosecutor to Probe Park Scandal' *Reuters* (Seoul, 17 November 2016) <www.reuters.com/article/us-southkorea-politics/south-korea-to-appoint-special-prosecutor-to-probe-park-scandal-idUSKBN13C0RR> accessed 20 February 2023.

123 Taet'ongnyŏng (Park Geun-hye) T'anhaek Soch'uan [Motion for Impeachment of President Park Geun-hye] (12 December 2016); Choe Sang-Hun, 'Claims Against South Korean President: Extortion, Abuse of Power and Bribery' *The New York Times* (New York, 8 December 2016).

124 Choe Sang-Hun, 'South Korea Enters Period of Uncertainty with President's Impeachment' *The New York Times* (New York, 10 December 2016) 1.

125 Hŏnbŏp art 65, art 71.

126 Choe Sang-Hun, 'South Korean Court Begins Hearings on Park Geun-Hye's Impeachment' *The New York Times* (New York, 23 December 2016) 12; Choe Sang-Hun, 'Park Geun-Hye, South Korean President, Is a No-Show at Impeachment Trial' *The New York Times* (New York, 4 January 2017) 8; Choe Sang-Hun, 'Impeachment Trial of South Korea President Called Mob Justice' *The New York Times* (New York, 6 January 2017) 3.

127 2016 HunNa 1 (10 March 2017).

decision. The Court first considered whether Park engaged in any misconduct and then considered whether the misconduct was serious enough to warrant her removal from office.

5.4.2.1 What Did Park Do Wrong?

PARK'S ENABLING OF CHOI SOON-SIL'S MISCONDUCT

Most of the opinion detailing Park's misconduct concerned the myriad ways in which Choi influenced Park and used her relationship with Park for personal gain.

The Court first stated that Park continued to meet with Choi after her inauguration in her residence, that Choi was in regular contact with Park's closest presidential aides, and that Choi had free access to presidential compounds.[128] The Court then recounted that through such channels, Choi received a number of documents from the Blue House on a regular basis for years after Park's inauguration and that these documents concerned various state affairs, such as personnel matters, ongoing state and policy matters, speeches or remarks for meetings, and the President's schedules.[129]

The types of personnel matters that Choi reviewed and advised on were not trivial. The Court recounted that Choi received documents regarding appointments of the Chair of the Board of Audit and Inspection, a Deputy Director of the National Intelligence Service, and a number of other senior-level staff members in various government agencies.[130] The Court also pointed out that Choi had access to many Blue House internal documents about Park's foreign visits and that Choi advised Park on what she should wear and what schedule changes ought to take place. The Court inferred from the easy flow of information and the kind of advice brought back to the Blue House that Park had either ordered or at least tacitly approved the practice of seeking Choi's opinions on various matters and giving her access to confidential documents.[131]

The Court then turned to the issue of the ways in which Choi exploited her personal connection to Park to enrich herself. Choi, the Court explained, recommended and ultimately successfully placed a number of people for government posts, especially in the Ministry of Culture, Sport and Tourism, which is significant because much of Choi's self-enriching activities involved obtaining approvals from the Ministry.[132]

The Court next went into detail about the establishment of Mir and K-Sports, which were the focal points of some of the earliest damaging

128 ibid.
129 ibid.
130 ibid.
131 ibid.
132 ibid.

stories in the press about Choi and Park. The Court focused on the curious timeline. In February 2015, an order to form a foundation related to culture and sports was communicated from Park to Ahn, and Park met with chairs of conglomerates such as Samsung, Hyundai Motor Company, SK, and LG to ask for donations to form cultural and sports foundations. In September, Choi devised a list of people to run Mir, and Park used this list when requesting that steps be taken to establish a foundation. The Court noted that no government employee delivered this list to Park, from which the Court inferred that Park received the list directly from Choi. The actual concrete steps to form a foundation were not taken until October 2015, but once steps started to be taken, then the establishment of Mir happened extremely quickly, with an approval from the Ministry of Culture, Sports, and Tourism coming down on October 27. During this month, following Park's order, donations in the amount of 50 billion Korean won (nearly 40 million U.S. dollars) were secured from a handful of conglomerates, though the companies were given little information about the foundation or the expected use of the funds. Mir was structured so that the ratio of restricted funds to unrestricted funds was set at 2:8, not at 9:1 as originally set. The companies were simply given an amount expected to be paid, and they promised to contribute without much inquiry.[133]

The other foundation, K-Sports, was established in much the same way. Choi devised a list of executives to run it, Park received the list from Choi, and Park then ordered an establishment of the foundation and named the total size of funds needed for it. In December 2015 and January 2016, donations from conglomerates in the amount of 30 billion Korean won (almost 24 million U.S. dollars) were secured, and the foundation was approved by the Ministry of Culture, Sports, and Tourism in January.

After the two foundations were established, Choi assumed the position of the de facto chairman of both foundations even though she was neither a donor nor an official executive of either foundation. Choi was able to accomplish all of this, the Court stated, because of her close relationship with Park and everyone's perception that they had to please Choi if they did not want to displease the President.[134]

With Mir and K-Sports successfully put in operation, Choi engaged in a series of self-dealing activities. She started an advertising company called 'Playground,' which then won several projects from Mir worth 138.6 million in Korean won (around 110,000 U.S. dollars). Playground also won projects from KT (formerly known as Korea Telecom) after Choi placed her acquaintances in relevant departments of KT by getting the Blue House to compel KT to hire them. Choi was also able to get the Blue House to introduce

133 ibid.
134 ibid.

Playground to Hyundai and Kia Motors, which then hired Playground despite their existing relationship with other advertising agencies.[135]

Choi also established a company called 'The Blue K,' a sports management company. She then used the Blue House to pressure companies, such as POSCO and Lotte, to start sports teams and hire The Blue K to manage the teams. Choi also ordered people at K-Sports to start working closely with The Blue K and created conditions in which government-sponsored activities of K-Sports would lead to more contracts for The Blue K. Simultaneously, Park ordered K-Sports to take on more active roles nationally to manage sports clubs nationwide.[136]

After this lengthy account of the ways in which Choi took steps to profit from her relationship with Park, the Court delivered its legal conclusions. Again, a president may be impeached for violations of 'the Constitution or other Acts in the performance of official duties' according to the Constitution, and the Court focused on legal violations. First, like in the Roh case, the Court found Park to be in violation of Article 7, Section 1 of the Constitution, which requires public officials to be 'servants of the entire people and . . . be responsible for the people.'[137] The Court also stated that Park was in violation of several statutory provisions that require public officials to serve the public interest.[138]

The Court explained that Park violated these laws because she appointed those recommended by Choi, and Choi was able to use such appointments to pursue personal gain. Park also helped establish Mir and K-Sports by using her position as the president to collect contributions from companies and appointed persons recommended by Choi to leadership positions of the foundations, which enabled Choi to take control of the two foundations. With this influence, Choi was able to pursue personal gain through the establishment of two companies, Playground and The Blue K, both of which were able to enter into business deals through the two foundations or through the Blue House's interference.[139]

135 ibid.
136 ibid.
137 Hŏnbŏp art 7, sec 1.
138 2016 HunNa 1 (describing Article 59 of the State Public Officials Act ('Every public official shall work kindly and impartially as servants of all citizens'); Article 2-2, Section 3 ('No public official shall pursue private interests or grant illegal preferential benefits to any individual, institution or organization in his or her public position'); Article 2 of the Act on Preventing Corruption and the Civil Rights Commission (defining an act of corruption as 'The act of any public official's abusing his or her position or authority or violating statutes in connection with his or her duties to seek gains for himself or herself or any third party'); Article 7 of the same act ('Every public official shall abide by statutes, perform his or her duties fairly and hospitably, and refrain from committing any act of corrupting himself or herself or losing his or her dignity')).
139 ibid. The Court mentioned some other violations, such as infringement of the right to property and freedom of occupation, both guaranteed in the Constitution, and laws governing state secrets.

PARK'S BEHAVIOR ON THE DAY OF THE SEWOL FERRY DISASTER

The Court then addressed the claim that Park should also be impeached for her failure to fulfill her obligations under Article 10 of the Constitution, which says that the State has a duty to protect the basic rights of individuals.[140] The Court briefly described the Sewol ferry disaster and the missed opportunities to save lives on that day and recounted her slow responses in the face of the unfolding emergency. The Court affirmed that the president 'bears the duty to exercise authority and perform duties to enable the state to faithfully fulfill its duty to protect the lives and physical safety of the people.'[141] At the same time, the Court concluded that her 'insufficient and inadequate' response to the emergency did not by itself lead to the conclusion that she was in violation of the Constitution.[142] The Court also considered the claim that Park, during the Sewol ferry disaster, violated Article 69 of the Constitution, which states the oath of the presidency as a promise to 'faithfully execute the duties of the President.'[143] The Court noted that while this provision appears in the Constitution, whether the President is in fact fulfilling her duty under this provision is 'not the kind of thing that can be evaluated under a standard that can be judicially ascertained.'[144] The Court accordingly concluded that Park's response to the Sewol ferry disaster could not serve as the basis for impeaching her.

5.4.2.2 *Should Park Be Removed?*

The remaining question was whether Park's violations were serious enough to justify her removal from presidency. The Court largely echoed its Roh opinion in stating that 'the decision to remove a President from office would deprive the democratic legitimacy delegated to the President by the national constituents through an election' and 'may bring about significant national loss such as an interruption in state affairs and political chaos.'[145] The Court should weigh such costs against 'the benefits of upholding the Constitution . . . on account of the severity of the negative impact on or harm to the constitutional order caused by the President's violation of law,' and the benefits should 'overwhelmingly outweigh' the 'national loss incurred' by the removal.[146] The Court concluded that 'a decision to remove the President from office may be justified only when the President's violation of the law' threatens the Constitution in such a way that the removal is necessary to 'restore the impaired

140 Hŏnbŏp art 10.
141 2016 HunNa 1.
142 ibid (author's translation).
143 Hŏnbŏp art 69.
144 2016 HunNa 1 (author's translation).
145 ibid.
146 ibid.

constitutional order.'[147] More specifically, the Court explained that a president can be removed only when the President, 'by violating the law, has betrayed the public's trust to the extent that such public trust vested in the President should be forfeited before the presidential term ends.'[148]

The Court listed several grounds to justify its decision to remove Park. First, Park shared confidential documents with Choi, a private citizen with no official position in the government. Second, Park abused her office and took a number of steps to use the presidency to benefit Choi, including soliciting contributions to establish Mir and K-Sports, which served no obvious purpose other than enriching Choi. Third, Park allowed Choi to intervene in many official decisions by the government without making Choi's role in governance transparent to the public. Fourth, any time that any member of the press or the National Assembly sought to inquire into Choi's interventions, Park tried to shut down the inquiries, which 'undermined the principle of representative democracy and the rule of law' and 'gravely violated the obligation of the President to serve the public interest.' The Court also faulted Park for her failure to promptly address various questions raised about Choi and observed from Park's inadequate responses that she lacked the will to protect the Constitution.[149] The Court concluded from all of this that Park betrayed the people's confidence by engaging in grave violations of the law, that such violations seriously damaged the constitutional order, and that in order to restore the Constitution, Park must be removed from the presidency.

Compared to Roh, this question was easy to answer in many ways. Not only was Park's misconduct, such as soliciting monetary contributions from conglomerates for personal gain, more obviously serious in this case (in ways that were both recognizable and outlandish) but also the Court's opinion in the Roh impeachment had explicitly named bribery and corruption as the types of presidential misconduct that could justify removal. So, although the facts in this case required a detailed account describing multiple parties working surreptitiously, the legal analysis itself was a straightforward application of the standard articulated in the Roh case.

5.5 Significance of Judicial Involvement in Impeachment: Lessons from Korea

The Korean impeachment examples are theoretically significant because they illustrate the ways in which having the judiciary play an essential role in the impeachment process shapes the nature of presidential impeachment itself. We can note three points, which build on one another. First, if a court is charged with defining the nature of impeachment, it is likely to define what is

147 ibid.
148 ibid.
149 ibid.

impeachable in legal, as opposed to political, terms. Second, when a court is assigned a decisive role in the impeachment process, it is likely the case that an explicitly articulated jurisprudence on presidential impeachment will develop over time. Third, a court involving itself in a political conflict with legal concepts is likely to wield its power carefully in ways that are cognizant of the nation's history and politics, and features of its institutional design can aid and legitimize its use of power.

5.5.1 Constitutional Court and the Law and Politics Distinction

Once the Constitutional Court of Korea faced the question of whether a president impeached by the National Assembly should be removed in the Roh impeachment case, it had an opportunity to set the terms of the debate for years to come. There is no question that presidential impeachment is among the most politically sensitive issues that a court can confront. So, as a body that is charged with enforcing the law as opposed to participating in everyday politics the way that the National Assembly participates, it had to decide how to navigate the distinction between law and politics in the case of impeachment. Furthermore, the Court could either shrink or expand its own significance in the process by characterizing the nature of impeachment as a political or legal issue. The 2004 Court ('Roh Impeachment Court') took the path of embracing an expansive version of its power in the impeachment process by emphasizing the *legal*, as opposed to the political, aspect of presidential impeachment.

As noted earlier, the impeachment provision in the Constitution allows the National Assembly to pass impeachment motions only when the public official in question has 'violated the Constitution or other Acts.'[150] The Roh Impeachment Court inferred from this provision that the purpose of the impeachment process was to protect the Constitution and to prevent the abuse of power by members of the executive and judicial branches. By providing for a mechanism for the impeachment and removal from office of high-ranking public officials for violations of the law, the Court noted that the Constitution makes clear that no one is above the law and that the nation is committed to the rule of law. The Court pointed out that the Constitution limits grounds for impeachment to violations of law and designates the Constitutional Court as the ultimate decisionmaker. The Court concluded from such considerations that the process of impeachment is a *legal*, not political, process and that a president can be impeached only on legal, not political, grounds.[151]

The Roh Impeachment Court's syllogism – that the Constitution limits impeachment to legal violations and that impeachment is therefore a legal, not political, process – seems straightforward, but the apparent simplicity is misleading, as the complexities of the Court's actual position are obscured

150 Hŏnbŏp art 65, sec 1.
151 2004 Hun-Na 1.

by the formulation. First, the Court was not entirely consistent on the question of what is 'legal' and what is 'political.' The scope of the 'law,' and thus 'legal violations' that are potentially grounds for impeachment, are potentially quite broad. The definition of the 'law' that the Court gave in its opinion encompasses anything that may be considered the 'law,' including the Constitution itself, the body of precedents interpreting the Constitution, domestic legal provisions, international treaties, and customary international law.[152] In its own opinion, however, the Court did not sustain such a broad definition of 'law.'

Article 66, Section 2 of the Constitution states that the 'President shall have the responsibility and duty to safeguard the independence, territorial integrity and continuity of the State and the Constitution.'[153] Article 66, Section 3 states that the 'President shall have the duty to pursue sincerely the peaceful unification of the homeland.'[154] Article 69 requires the President to take an oath and swear that he or she 'will faithfully execute the duties of the President by observing the Constitution, defending the State, pursuing the peaceful unification of the homeland, promoting the freedom and welfare of the people and endeavoring to develop national culture.'[155] Although by the Roh Impeachment Court's own definition, these are 'legal' provisions in the sense that they are in the Constitution, the nature of the enumerated duties makes it difficult to see in what sense applying these provisions involves 'legal' as opposed to 'political' judgments and why the Court should be entrusted with determining whether the president has fulfilled these duties of the presidency. At the same time, the Court's own definition of the 'law' and the Court's duty to evaluate the appropriateness of motions to impeach appear to compel the conclusion that the Court must decide whether these presidential duties have been fulfilled satisfactorily.

The Roh Impeachment Court resolved this tension by declaring that some of these provisions are *irrelevant* for the purposes of impeachment. The Court gave its answer in its consideration of the claim that Roh should be removed from office for maladministration. The National Assembly argued that Roh violated not only Article 66, Section 2 but also his oath specified in Article 69 by failing to 'execute the duties of the President' and bringing about economic and political instability.[156] The Court dismissed this claim. The Court stated that although the president's Article 66 and Article 69 duties are

152 ibid. That a president can be impeached for violating customary international law may seem extraordinary, but it is not so far-fetched once one considers that Article 6, Section 1 of the Korean Constitution provides that '[t]reaties duly concluded and promulgated under the Constitution and the generally recognized rules of international law shall have the same effect as the domestic laws of the Republic of Korea.'

153 Hŏnbŏp art 66, sec 2.

154 ibid art 66, sec 3.

155 ibid art 69.

156 2004 Hun-Na 1.

'constitutional duties,' whether they have been fulfilled is not something that can be determined as a matter of law and that the proper forum for such judgment is the political realm. Since Article 65, Section 1 limits the grounds for impeachment to violations of the Constitution or other laws, the Court concluded that the President's failure to fulfill his duties under Article 66, Section 2 and Article 68 could not serve as grounds for impeachment – with one exception. Article 66, Section 2 of the Constitution imposes on the President the duty 'to safeguard . . . the Constitution.' Because whether the President was fulfilling this particular duty was ascertainable through application of the law, the Court asserted that failure to fulfill this duty could serve as a ground for impeachment.[157]

Thus, from the clause providing that a president may be impeached for 'violat[ion] of the Constitution or other Acts,' the Roh Impeachment Court inferred that the impeachment process is a legal, not political, process, and when it faced the provisions of the Constitution that clearly seemed to call for political, not legal, judgments, the Court declared them 'political,' not 'legal,' and, thus, outside scope of the impeachment process. That is, no offense is impeachable *unless* the judiciary can determine that the offense has taken place. If the alleged offense lies outside the scope of offenses that the judiciary can identify, then it might as well not exist for the purposes of impeachment.

An alternative way of drawing the boundaries of impeachable offenses that is consistent with the text of the Korean Constitution is easy to imagine. Instead of limiting the scope of impeachment to what is legally ascertainable, the Court could have gone in the other direction. For instance, because the scope of impeachable offenses is broader than the scope of questions that can be answered by the judiciary by applying legal standards, the Court could have concluded that it should defer to the National Assembly on questions that are not susceptible of resolution through a legal analysis. The Court did not take this path and instead chose to exclude certain reasons from the realm of permitted grounds for impeachment itself.

Although the Roh Impeachment Court's reasoning thus appears simplistic and even arbitrary at times, the motivation is understandable. Given that it is charged under the Constitution to adjudicate impeachments, the Court was likely reluctant to yield its authority to be the final arbiter of impeachment disputes. At the same time, the Court appeared to have recognized the danger of permitting impeachment on the basis of a president's 'failure' to satisfy the constitutional aspiration of 'pursuing the peaceful unification of the homeland, promoting the freedom and welfare of the people and endeavoring to develop national culture'[158] and on the near impossibility of adjudicating the claim that the president's performance falls short of the ideal outlined in the presidential oath. Because the Court sought not to weaken its constitutional

157 ibid.
158 Hŏnbŏp art 69.

status to be the ultimate decisionmaker, the Court narrowed the scope of impeachable offenses only to those that it considered to be within its competence to manage, instead of deciding the proper scope of impeachable offenses first and then narrowing the Court's own role in it. The narrowing of the scope of impeachable offenses, then, may be one consequence of designating a judicial body as the ultimate decisionmaker in the impeachment process.

The complexity of the Court's position on the law-politics distinction does not end here. Even if it is the case that only straightforward 'legal' violations can lead to impeachment, it does not necessarily follow that answering the question whether a democratically elected president should be removed from his office midterm calls for legal judgment. As seen previously, the Roh Impeachment Court's ultimate decision – that Roh was in violation of the law but that the violations were not serious enough to warrant removal – involved judgment that was broader than the narrower question of whether he violated any law. That is, because not every violation of law is considered serious enough to warrant impeachment, the Court had to judge not only whether there had been a legal violation but also whether it was serious enough to justify removal.

The National Assembly recognized this, and it argued in its briefs during the Roh impeachment trial that judging the seriousness of misconduct involved the kind of judgment that the Constitutional Court was not suited to make. The National Assembly thus suggested the following division of labor. The National Assembly, which is the democratically elected body, should be the final arbiter of whether the particular legal violations at issue by the President are grounds for impeachment and removal. The role of the Constitutional Court should be limited to deciding, the National Assembly argued, whether the passage of the impeachment motion followed the correct legal procedure and whether the alleged conduct by the president involved legal violations. Whether particular legal violations justify the National Assembly's attempt to remove the president from his office, the Assembly argued, should be left to the Assembly's discretion.[159]

The Assembly's reading was rejected by the Roh Impeachment Court in favor of a broader reading of the Court's power. As noted previously, the Court inferred from the text and structure of the Constitution that impeachment is strictly a legal, not political, process. From the Court's view that impeachment is a legal proceeding, the Court drew out the following standard of review. The Court stated that in deciding whether the President should be removed, it could consider only those facts alleged by the National Assembly to constitute grounds for impeachment. However, the Court made clear that it was not constrained by the Assembly's judgment in any other way. The Court stated that there is no deference to the Assembly in determining whether there has been such a legal violation. The Court also stated that, given the facts

159 2004 Hun-Na 1.

alleged by the Assembly, the Court may, de novo, find legal grounds other than those identified by the Assembly as grounds for impeachment. Accordingly, the Court confined the Assembly's role at this stage to delimiting the range of conduct by the president that the Court may consider. As to whether such conduct in fact was in violation of law, whether it constituted grounds for impeachment and removal, and which grounds were entirely up to the Court.[160]

The question remained, in what sense is judgment of the seriousness of the president's offense 'legal,' as opposed to 'political,' judgment? The Roh Impeachment Court needed a standard that could serve two purposes. First, the standard had to supply a way of ranking legal violations in terms of their seriousness, from trivial to impeachable. That is, the Court needed a way to discuss a hierarchy of values in order to assess the gravity of the president's legal violations. Second, the standard had to be a 'legal' standard whose application properly belonged, or appeared to belong, to the Constitutional Court.

The Court found its solution in the concept of the 'constitutional order.' As discussed earlier, the Court held that impeachment and removal of a president are appropriate only when 'such steps are necessary to rehabilitate the damaged constitutional order,' and the Court explained that by 'constitutional order,' it meant 'free and democratic basic order.'[161] By invoking the concept of the constitutional order in judging whether a president was impeachable, the Court took the impeachability decision outside the realm of politics. However, in doing so, the Court also had to reach outside the Constitution and appeal to something more fundamental than the Constitution itself – the foundational concepts that underlie the Constitution.

The 2017 Constitutional Court ('Park Impeachment Court') continued to note the same theme when the Court took care to point out the various ways in which Park's behaviors amounted to legal violations; it also held that Park's inadequate handling of the Sewol ferry disaster could not be a basis for impeachment because Park's failures, which in theory, amounted to a 'legal' violation insofar as the failures can be described as failures to fulfill a constitutional duty, were not susceptible to judicial evaluation.[162]

5.5.2 Constitutional Court and Building a Jurisprudence of Impeachment

The Korean Constitutional Court is a reason-giving institution. It issues opinions and explains the reasons underlying its decisions, and such opinions over time have built the country's constitutional jurisprudence and culture. The Roh impeachment opinion for instance arrived at several legal conclusions. The

160 ibid.
161 ibid.
162 2016 Hun-Na 1.

Court decided that the president can be impeached only for violations of law,[163] for conduct only while in office,[164] and only when the damage he has inflicted on the free and democratic basic order is so grave that only his removal from office can repair the damage.[165] Moreover, through the two contrasting cases, the Roh and Park impeachments, South Koreans have undergone a collective process of coming to terms with the idea of impeachable offenses.

Contrast this phenomenon against the American model. What have Americans learned about impeachment in the three presidential impeachments it has had? During the three impeachments and acquittals, the nation witnessed a lot of bickering among politicians and talking heads, but it is not clear if the Americans as a collective have reached a better understanding as to what kind of presidential misconduct is sufficient to impeach and remove the president. If anything, the three impeachments and three acquittals appear to have confirmed the truth of the notorious statement made by Gerald Ford that an impeachable offense is 'whatever a majority of the House of Representatives considers it to be at a given moment in history' and a conviction results from 'whatever offense or offenses two-thirds of the other body considers to be sufficiently serious to require removal of the accused from office.'[166]

Perhaps this type of uncertainty and rough-and-tumble is by design. As Cass Sunstein has proudly noted about the U.S. model, '[I]mpeachment . . . is designed for We the People, not the judges at all. It's not just for specialists. It can't be.'[167] However, as further noted in the next section, the Korean model demonstrates the ways in which a system can draw from the strengths of both judges and 'the people.'

5.5.3 Constitutional Court's Power and Its Use: The Importance of Political and Historical Context

The Constitutional Court of Korea wielded a significant amount of power in the two impeachment cases by deciding whether a president is to be removed or not after the National Assembly's impeachment. One question we might ask is how the Court was able to assume and exercise such powers without a significant backlash. This is of course a complex issue, but the following are some considerations.

First, the history of modern Korea is a history of the authoritarianism of Syngman Rhee, Park Chung Hee, and Chun Doo Hwan from the end of the

163 2004 Hun-Na 1.

164 ibid.

165 ibid.

166 Cong Rec 116, daily edn (15 April 1970) 11,913. This quote is frequently quoted out of context for effect. The full quotation includes the following assessment: 'To remove [the President and Vice President] in midterm . . . would indeed require crimes of the magnitude of treason and bribery.' ibid.

167 Cass R Sunstein, *Impeachment: A Citizen's Guide* (Harvard UP 2017) 13.

Korean War in 1953 to the constitutional amendments in 1987.[168] There was no independent judiciary during this period, and when a judicial body, in a few instances, went against the president's wishes, it was either quickly overruled or dismantled.[169] The 1987 constitutional amendments that gave birth to the current Constitution were a byproduct of a conscious political liberalization effort, backed by popular demand, that sought to repudiate this model of politics.[170] Because the main image of governance that the country rejected in the reform process was that of a lawless, oppressive, all-powerful dictator, one possible way to control the president was through the judiciary. At the time of the amendment, however, very few people anticipated the Constitutional Court to play a strong role in restraining the governmental exercise of power.[171] Yet the Court matured and performed well beyond everyone's expectation in curbing the governmental authority,[172] with the Park impeachment being a recent, dramatic example. It appears then that the Court has been able to draw on the strong sentiment of the population, informed by history, that the executive branch is not always to be trusted and that its power should be restrained by the rule of law.

Second, the institutional structure of the Constitutional Court itself may enable it to be aggressive without being vulnerable to the charge that it is not politically accountable. The composition of the Constitutional Court itself – three by the Chief Justice of the Supreme Court, three by the President, and three by the National Assembly – gives the appearance that the Constitutional Court is designed to be a place where different perspectives of the government are represented.[173] In addition, although the justices of the Constitutional Court are not elected, each justice serves only for a six-year term. The term is renewable, but the norm in the recent past has been for the justices to serve for single terms only. The Korean Constitution itself is much easier to amend than the constitution in, for example, the U.S., as a supermajority in the National Assembly combined with a national referendum can amend the Constitution.[174]

168 For good overviews, see Bruce Cumings, *Korea's Place in the Sun: A Modern History* (Norton 1997) 337–93; David I Steinberg, *The Republic of Korea: Economic Transformation and Social Change* (Avalon Publishing 1989) 48–68; Robert E Bedeski, *The Transformation of South Korea: Reform and Reconstitution in the Sixth Republic Under Roh Tae Woo, 1987–1992* (Routledge 1994); Sunhyuk Kim, *The Politics of Democratization in Korea: The Role of Civil Society* (U of Pittsburgh P 2000).

169 Ginsburg (n 11) 208–13.

170 Steinberg (n 168) 59–66; Kim (n 168) 77–104; Ginsburg (n 11) 218; Hahm (n 12) 389.

171 See, e.g., Hahm (n 12) 395; James J West and Dae-Kyu Yoon, 'The Constitutional Court of the Republic of Korea: Transforming the Jurisprudence of Vortex?' (1992) 40 *American Journal of Comparative Law* 73, 115.

172 See, e.g., Ginsburg (n 11) 221–26; Hahm (n 12) 395; Kyu Ho Youm, 'Press Freedom and Judicial Review in South Korea' (1994) 30 *Stanford Journal of International Law* 1.

173 Hŏnbŏp art 111.

174 ibid art 130.

Third, the impeachment cases have turned out to be perfect vehicles for flexing judicial muscles and enhancing the Court's power and status without offending Korean democratic sensibilities; specifically, the National Assembly's decision to impeach Roh was very unpopular, whereas its decision to impeach Park was overwhelmingly supported nationwide.[175] In the Roh case, it is difficult to imagine the Court invoking the vague concept of 'constitutional order' while ignoring the citizens' strong disapproval of the National Assembly's behavior and the results of the General Election, which gave a majority of the Assembly seats to the very party that Roh was impeached for supporting. Similarly, in the Park case, we cannot ignore the massive anti-Park demonstrations that took place for several weeks in a row. That is, behind the Court's exercises of its power is its confidence that its decisions were strongly supported by the people nationwide.

5.6 Conclusion

The Roh impeachment, as the first case in the world in which a president was impeached by a legislature but was reinstated by a judicial body, was a landmark event not only in modern Korean history but also in the history of modern constitutionalism generally. The Park impeachment was a significant event for the Constitutional Court of Korea in that it gave the Court an opportunity to apply the innovations of the Roh Impeachment Court. The historical importance of these cases is far-reaching and multi-faceted, but this chapter limited its discussion to only the question of the significance of assigning a role to the judiciary in the impeachment process. The Roh and Park impeachment cases should prompt us to ask what difference it makes to let a court, as opposed to more obvious political branches, have the final word on the question of presidential impeachment.

175 On the Roh impeachment, see Brooke (n 21) 6; Faiola (n 21); Demick (n 21). On the Park impeachment, see Jhee and Park (n 72); Turner, Kwon and O'Donnell (n 72); Motoko Rich, 'Defiance and Disillusionment in Heartland of South Korean President's Support' *The New York Times* (New York, 8 December 2016) 14.

6 Latin America

Between Governability Crises and the Impeachment Trap

John Polga-Hecimovich[1]

6.1 Introduction

Upon taking office in July 2021, Peruvian president Pedro Castillo faced almost immediate threats of legislative removal from an intransigent opposition. Indeed, legislators brought a formal motion of impeachment against Castillo on the grounds of 'moral incapacity' by early December of his first year, but the resolution fell six votes short of triggering a full trial. In March 2022, however, Castillo again faced the prospect of impeachment, with the process this time advancing to a full trial in congress in which the president was required to respond to the array of charges laid out against him. As before, he survived the floor vote. However, this was only a temporary reprieve. On December 7, 2022, just hours before he was due to face a third impeachment vote, Castillo announced that he would close congress and form an emergency government until new legislative elections could be held. Lawmakers widely condemned these actions as an *autogolpe* and proceeded with the impeachment vote, approving his removal from office by a sweeping margin after a little more than 16 months in power.

Part of Castillo's experience has become more common in Latin America in recent decades, where impeachment has displaced other forms of presidential instability. Since 1991, there have been 22 impeachment trials in Latin America, with eight removals, four resignations ahead of near-certain removals, nine cases of survival, and one dissolution of congress and the presidency pending removal – in addition to dozens of motions that never garnered sufficient votes to open a formal process. Across the region, impeachment is simultaneously what the editors of this volume refer to as a 'core' process (Argentina, Brazil, Chile, Ecuador, Guatemala, Honduras, Paraguay, and Peru), a 'peripheral' process (Bolivia, Colombia, and Panama), and in other places, a 'satellite' process

1 The views expressed in this chapter are solely those of the author and do not represent the views of or endorsement by the United States Naval Academy, the Department of the Navy, the Department of Defense, or the United States Government.

DOI: 10.4324/9781003256007-8

(Costa Rica, Cuba, the Dominican Republic, El Salvador, Mexico, Nicaragua, and Uruguay). Several of these countries also featured other forms of executive instability, from presidential resignations due to street protests (Argentina, Bolivia, and Guatemala) to military coups d'état (Bolivia, Ecuador, and Honduras).

In the places where impeachment is a core process, its use has skyrocketed. In Peru, both Pedro Pablo Kuczynski (2016–2018) and Martín Vizcarra (2018–2020), like Castillo, survived one impeachment trial only to fall in a second, while Ecuador's Guillermo Lasso survived one impeachment attempt only to constitutionally dissolve his presidency amid a second trial. Likewise, Chile's Sebastián Piñera (2018–2022) survived two impeachment trials, while Brazil's Dilma Rousseff (2010–2016) was ousted in 2016 after facing the threat of impeachment throughout her last two years in office. Honduran president Juan Orlando Hernández (2014–2022) and Paraguay's Mario Abdo Benítez (2018–2023) also faced the possibility of impeachment on at least two occasions, although none of these accusations made it to the trial phase. Curiously, every country with an impeachment or impeachment-like removal has had more than one, except for Venezuela, whose 1999 Constitution eliminated impeachment.

This raises some questions: has impeachment become more prevalent across Latin America in the 2010s and 2020s? If so, why? Existing explanations tend to focus on the conditions under which legislatures remove presidents, such as the presence of a presidential crisis, executive corruption scandals, poor economic performance, anti-government demonstrations, or lack of a 'legislative shield'. Others try to elucidate the factors that led to the rise in impeachment and concurrent decline in coups d'état by focusing on such things as regionwide democratization and the changing role of the military and international actors. Few of these explanations, however, can account for the rise in impeachment attempts across the region since 2019. In this chapter, I propose two complementary explanations: 1) the presence of acute governability crises that have spread across the region, especially since 2019; and 2) the existence of an impeachment trap, by which the presence of one impeachment process is likely to result in the appearance of a subsequent one. Like a 'coup trap', the impeachment trap occurs when a presidential interruption fails to provide relief from underlying political, economic, and social problems, thus resulting in its further use.

The chapter begins with an overview of the historical development and use of impeachment in Latin America, followed by a survey of the contemporary prevalence of impeachment and presidential interruptions in the region. Section three synthesizes the scholarly explanations of impeachment and offers additional interpretations of the uptick in cases since the late 2010s. I develop the concept of the 'impeachment trap' and then examine the empirical evidence of such a phenomenon in Latin America. The last section concludes.

6.2 The Development and Use of Impeachment

Globally, most democratic constitutions provide for removal of the head of state, either for incompetence, criminal actions, or some other basis.[2] In Latin America's presidential systems, constitutions have typically provided for impeachment – the political trial of the president authorized by one legislative body and typically conducted by a separate political institution – as the mechanism of horizontal accountability since the nineteenth century. This model of congressional oversight authority follows the U.S. Constitution, which, in turn, draws from the British experience. However, in Latin American constitutions, legislative oversight mechanisms may also include provisions for presidential removal based on mental, physical, or moral incapacity, or vacancy of office.[3]

Regarding impeachment, constitutions are split between legislature-dominant systems, where only the legislature is involved in the impeachment process, and mixed systems, where both a legislature and the judiciary play a role.[4] Under the so-called 'American model' (adopted by Argentina, Brazil, Chile, Colombia, the Dominican Republic, Mexico, Paraguay, and Uruguay) the accusation is initiated by the lower house of congress, and the trial is conducted by the upper house. By contrast, under the 'Unicameral model' (adopted by Panama, Peru, and Ecuador), both the accusation and trial are carried out by the country's sole legislative body. In the mixed or judiciary-dominant systems (adopted by Bolivia, Costa Rica, El Salvador, Honduras, Nicaragua, and Venezuela from 1961–1999), a unicameral congress initiates proceedings, and the trial is carried out by the country's high court.[5] These different thresholds for removal result in difference patterns of presidential instability: two of the countries in the unicameral model, Ecuador and Peru, are notoriously unstable, while there has only been a single removal in the judiciary-dominant systems (Venezuela in 1993).

Prior to the third wave of democratization, impeachments in Latin America were rare. The region's first recorded trial took place in the Dominican Republican in 1857, when President Buenaventura Báez was removed by a hostile congress for 'usurpation of the presidency' during an open revolt against his government. In 1916, another Dominican president, Juan Isidro Jimenes, was impeached by the House of Deputies and then, the Senate for violations of the constitution and laws, and in 1936, Cuban president Miguel Mariano Gómez

2 Tom Ginsburg, Aziz Z. Huq and David Landau, 'The Comparative Constitutional Law of Presidential Impeachment' (2021) 88 *The University of Chicago Law Review* 81.

3 Gabriel L Negretto, *Making Constitutions: Presidents, Parties, and Institutional Choice in Latin America* (CUP 2013).

4 Naoko Kada, 'Comparative Presidential Impeachment: Conclusions' in Jody C Baumgartner and Naoko Kada (eds), *Checking Executive Power: Presidential Impeachment in Comparative Perspective* (Praeger Publishers 2003).

5 Victor J Hinojosa and Aníbal S Pérez-Liñán, 'Presidential Survival and the Impeachment Process: The United States and Colombia' (2006) 121 *Political Science Quarterly* 653.

was removed by his country's senate. The incidence of impeachment picked up after World War II, with four impeachments taking place in Panama, three in Brazil, and one in Chile, and removals occurring in four of the eight cases (Arnulfo Arias in Panama, 1951; José Ramón Guizado in Panama, 1955; Carlos Luz in Brazil, 1955, and Café Filho in Brazil in 1955). Common across these processes is the fact that legislative assemblies generally removed these presidents under pressure from the military in contexts that were not wholly democratic.

Instead, military coups were typically the mechanism to remove presidents from office during the Cold War period. Militaries directly governed in 12 of 19 Latin American countries at some point in the 1960s and 1970s,[6] and in 1977, only three states in the region (Colombia, Costa Rica, and Venezuela) were democratic. Authoritarian governments are unlikely to be displaced by non-independent congresses or judiciaries or through ordinary institutional channels, and between 1950 and 1990 there were 57 military coups d'état in Latin America. Conversely, constitutional forms of involuntary presidential removal such as impeachment became rare.

6.3 The Ubiquity of Impeachment in Contemporary Latin America

As such, impeachment has only become a central feature of Latin American presidentialism since re-democratization in the 1980s and 1990s.[7] After Panamanian president Guillermo Endara survived an impeachment attempt in 1991, Brazilian President Fernando Collor de Mello and Venezuelan President Carlos Andrés Pérez were accused of corruption and ousted on impeachment charges in successive years. This was only the beginning. Between 1991 and 2023, there were 22 impeachment trials across nine Latin American presidential democracies. As shown in Table 6.1, these resulted in eight removals, four resignations, one government dissolution, and nine cases of presidential survival.[8] Analytically, the category of 'resignation' is the equivalent of 'removal', since the four presidents (Fernando Collor de Mello, Otto Pérez Molina, Raúl Cubas Grau, and Pedro Pablo Kuczynski) only resigned pending their near-certain removal through legislative vote. The same holds true for Guillermo Lasso in Ecuador, who used article 148 of the 2008 Constitution, the so-called figure of *muerte cruzada* ("crossed death"), to dissolve the presidency and congress while facing impeachment in 2023.

6 These 12 countries are Argentina, Bolivia, Brazil, Chile, the Dominican Republic, Ecuador, El Salvador, Guatemala, Honduras, Panama, Peru, and Uruguay.

7 Aníbal S Pérez-Liñán, *Crisis Without Breakdown: Presidential Impeachment and the New Political Instability in Latin America* (CUP 2007)

8 As I explain in the following, some of these votes to remove the presidents in Ecuador and Peru technically deviate from impeachment trials but act as their functional equivalent.

However, impeachment is even more common than the scholarly literature or even the list in Table 6.1 would suggest. With few exceptions, the comparative scholarship on presidential removals in Latin America tends to select successful impeachments or successful removals, while leaving out the myriad resolutions that fail to leave committee or reach a legislative vote, those that fail on the assembly floor, and those that fall short in the trial stage.[9] In this way, the literature undercounts the prevalence of the procedure.

In fact, Latin American legislators, judges, and citizens have filed hundreds of motions against leaders that never reach an assembly vote. Llanos and Pérez-Liñán, for instance, find that impeachment resolutions normally die at the committee stage.[10] They count 87 impeachment resolutions introduced against Argentine presidents between 1983 and 2018, although no impeachment ever took place, and a whopping 193 impeachment resolutions in the Brazilian Congress between 1990 and 2018, although only two were successful (Fernando Collor de Melo in 1992; Dilma Rousseff in 2016). Numbers rose further under the controversial presidency of Jair Bolsonaro (2019–2022). During his four years in office, the President of the Chamber of Deputies received 153 different impeachment requests, largely based on Bolsonaro's response to the COVID-19 pandemic, participation in anti-democratic demonstrations, and 'breach of decorum'.[11] The high number is also a function of law 1079/50, popularly known as the 'Impeachment Law', which allows any Brazilian citizen to file a request to impeach the president, as long as it includes a justification.

Other motions leave the committee stage and fail to reach a trial, but ultimately reveal presidents' weaknesses vis-à-vis their legislatures and/or prove damaging to their survival. These include a failed resolution against Raúl Cubas Grau of Paraguay in February 1999, which came amid a political crisis and presaged his removal in March of that year; a narrow lack of support for a motion to begin impeachment against Lucio Gutiérrez in Ecuador in November 2004, which nonetheless paved the way for his removal in April 2005; and failed votes to begin trials against Peru's Martín Vizcarra (2019) and Pedro Castillo (2021), which preceded their ultimate removals. In Ecuador, Lasso faced down an impeachment motion in December 2021 and then a trial in June 2022 before the trial in 2023 in which he ended up dissolving the government. In all of these cases, the floor votes revealed not only significant legislative opposition to the presidents but also the precariousness of their grip on power. In other instances, the dismissal of charges reflected support from other key state institutions that would guarantee presidents' survival, as with

9 See, e.g., Mariana Llanos and Aníbal S. Pérez-Liñán, 'Oversight or Representation? Public Opinion and Impeachment Resolutions in Argentina and Brazil' (2021) 46 *Legislative Studies Quarterly* 357; Hinojosa and Pérez-Liñán (n 5).

10 ibid.

11 Agência Pública, 'Os Pedidos de Impeachment de Bolsonaro' (*Agência Pública*, 2023) <https://apublica.org/impeachment-bolsonaro/> accessed 23 February 2023.

Table 6.1 Impeachment Trials in Latin America (1991–2022)

Country	*Year*	*Date*	*President*	*Outcome*
Brazil	1992	12/29/92	Fernando Collor de Mello	Resigned
	2016	8/31/16	Dilma Rousseff	Removed
Chile	2019	12/12/19	Sebastián Piñera	Survived
	2021	11/9/21	Sebastián Piñera	Survived
Colombia	1996	6/12/96	Ernesto Samper	Survived
Ecuador	1997	2/6/97	Abdalá Bucaram	Removed
	2005	4/20/05	Lucio Gutiérrez	Removed
	2022	6/28/22	Guillermo Lasso	Survived
	2023	5/17/23	Guillermo Lasso	Dissolution
Guatemala	2015	9/1/15	Otto Pérez Molina	Resigned
Panama	1991	3/12/91	Guillermo Endara	Survived
Paraguay	1999	3/25/99	Raúl Cubas Grau	Resigned
	2003	2/11/03	Luis González Macchi	Survived
	2012	6/21/12	Fernando Lugo	Removed
Peru	2000	11/21/00	Alberto Fujimori	Removed
	2017	12/15/17	Pedro Pablo Kuczynski	Survived
	2018	3/15/18	Pedro Pablo Kuczynski	Resigned
	2020	9/11/20	Martín Vizcarra	Survived
	2020	11/2/20	Martín Vizcarra	Removed
	2022	3/14/22	Pedro Castillo	Survived
	2022	12/1/22	Pedro Castillo	Removed
Venezuela	1993	3/20/93	Carlos Andrés Pérez	Removed

Source: Author

Honduras's Juan Orlando Hernández (2019 and 2021), Argentina's Mauricio Macri (2017), and Brazil's Michel Temer (2017).

Combined with the list of impeachment trials in Table 6.1, these examples reveal a great deal of regional variation in the use (or non-use) of impeachment across the region. In Argentina, Brazil, Chile, Ecuador, Guatemala, Honduras, Paraguay, and Peru, impeachment motions – or the threat of impeachment motions – have become what the editors of this volume define as a 'core process' of legislative-executive relations, a central and visible process of executive control. In other countries, such as Bolivia, Colombia, and Panama, impeachment constitutes more of a 'peripheral process': although it is not often employed, it has been used and remains a tool in legislators' toolkits to confront presidents.[12] In still other countries, such as Costa Rica, the Dominican Republic, El Salvador, Mexico, Nicaragua, and Uruguay, impeachment exists but is not used in contemporary politics. Meanwhile, the current constitutions of Cuba and Venezuela do not permit impeachment.

12 Andrea Paola Buitrago Rojas, Juan Guillermo Miranda Corzo and Juan Sebastián López López, *Juicio político a presidentes en Colombia (1982–2018)* (Ediciones USTA 2020).

The absence of impeachment, however, does not mean that presidents are free of legislative or judicial oversight or can govern free of threats to their power.[13] To the contrary, presidents' terms can be interrupted through democratic means, such as impeachment, declarations of incapacity, resignations, and popular recalls, and non-democratic forms, such as assassinations, military coups d'état, and foreign invasions. As Table 6.2 shows, expanding the range of categories means that 33 Latin American presidencies since 1985 have suffered interruptions, with exits ranging from negotiated resignations to facilitate governance (Raúl Alfonsín, Eduardo Duhalde, Hernán Siles Zuazo, and Joaquín Balaguer) and resignations in the face of popular protest (Fernando de la Rúa, Adolfo Rodríguez Saá, Gonzalo Sánchez de Lozada, Carlos Mesa, Jorge Serrano, and Manuel Merino), to military coups d'état (Jamil Mahuad, Manuel Zelaya, and Evo Morales). There is also another variation: the category of 'impeachment' also contains legislative votes of removal for 'mental incapacity' (Abdalá Bucaram), 'abandonment of post' (Lucio Gutiérrez), and 'moral incapacity' (the Peruvian cases), all of which I consider to be the functional equivalents of impeachment.

Analytically, the combination of impeachments with other types of presidential interruptions or presidential exit, however, has meant that the comparative literature of presidential instability in Latin America has at times been at cross-purposes. Some scholars have specifically focused on impeachment,[14] while others emphasize a wider range of popular presidential removals.[15] For the purposes of this book, it is worth considering that although impeachment may not (yet) be a core process in all countries in the region, presidents in

13 Leiv Marsteintredet and Einar Berntzen, 'Reducing the Perils of Presidentialism through Presidential Interruptions' (2008) 41 *Comparative Politics* 83, Leiv Marsteintredet, Mariana Llanos and Detlef Nolte, 'Paraguay and the Politics of Impeachment' (2013) 24 *Journal of Democracy* 110.

14 See, e.g., Jody C Baumgartner and Naoko Kada (eds), *Checking Executive Power: Presidential Impeachment in Comparative Perspective* (Praeger Publishers 2003), David De Micheli, Jose T Sanchez-Gomez and Kenneth M Roberts, 'Tenuous Pacts and Multiparty Coalitions: The Politics of Presidential Impeachment in Latin America' (2022) 54 *Journal of Latin American Studies* 283; Young Hun Kim, 'Impeachment and Presidential Politics in New Democracies' (2014) 21 *Democratization* 519; Pérez-Liñán (n 7).

15 See, e.g., Kathryn Hochstetler, 'Rethinking Presidentialism: Challenges and Presidential Falls in South America' (2006) 38 *Comparative Politics* 401; Leon Zamosc, 'On Popular Impeachments' [2012] *Latin American Studies Association* 15–18; Christopher A Martínez, 'Presidential Survival in South America: Rethinking the Role of Democracy' (2017) 38 *International Political Science Review* 40; Christopher A Martínez, 'Presidential Instability in Latin America: Why Institutionalized Parties Matter' (2021) 56 *Government and Opposition* 683; Mariana Llanos and Leiv Marsteintredet (eds), *Presidential Breakdowns in Latin America: Causes and Outcomes of Executive Instability in Developing Democracies* (Palgrave Macmillan 2010); Leiv Marsteintredet, 'Explaining Variation of Executive Instability in Presidential Regimes: Presidential Interruptions in Latin America' (2014) 35 *International Political Science Review* 173; Marsteintredet and Berntzen (n 13).

Table 6.2 Early Presidential Exits in Latin America (1985–2022)

Country	*Year*	*Name*	*Interruption*
Argentina	1989	Raúl Alfonsín	Early departure/ Resignation
	2001	Fernando de la Rúa	Resignation
	2001	Adolfo Rodríguez Saá	Resignation
	2003	Eduardo Duhalde	Early elections/ Resignation
Bolivia	1985	Hernán Siles Zuazo	Early elections/ Resignation
	2003	Gonzalo Sánchez de Lozada	Resignation
	2005	Carlos Mesa	Resignation
	2019	Juan Evo Morales	Military coup
Brazil	1992	Fernando Collor de Mello	Impeachment
	2016	Dilma Rousseff	Impeachment
Dominican Republic	1996	Joaquín Balaguer	Early elections/ Resignation
Ecuador	1997	Abdalá Bucaram	Impeachment
	2000	Jamil Mahuad	Military coup
	2005	Lucio Gutiérrez	Impeachment
	2023	Guillermo Lasso	Government dissolution
Guatemala	1993	Jorge Serrano	Resignation
	2015	Otto Pérez Molina	Impeachment
Honduras	2009	Manuel Zelaya	Military coup
Paraguay	1999	Raúl Cubas Grau	Impeachment
	2012	Fernando Lugo	Impeachment
Peru	2000	Alberto Fujimori	Impeachment
	2018	Pedro Pablo Kuczynski	Resignation
	2020	Martín Vizcarra	Impeachment
	2020	Manuel Merino	Resignation
	2022	Pedro Castillo	Impeachment
Venezuela	1993	Carlos Andrés Pérez	Impeachment

Note: Does not include exits of disputed interim presidents Gustavo Espina (Guatemala 1993), Rosalía Arteaga (Ecuador 1997), or Pedro Carmona (Venezuela 2002), or president de jure Eric Delvalle (Panama 1988).
Source: Author

places such as Bolivia, Colombia, and others may still face legislative, judicial, or popular threats to their rule.

6.4 Crisis, Social Unrest, and Impeachment Traps

These data seem to indicate that impeachment has become more prevalent across Latin America in the 2010s and 2020s. The academic literature, however, offers limited interpretations of why. Macro explanations view impeachment in the post-Cold War era as a natural response to presidentialism and its Linzian attributes, such as the rigidity of the fixed term and lack of confidence mechanisms.[16] Others suggest that the coalitional aspect of presidentialism is to blame. Specifically, as the president's legislative coalition erodes, presidents are more likely to fall regardless of other factors.[17] Different scholars have also tried to elucidate the factors that led to the rise in impeachment and concurrent decline in coups d'état by focusing on elements such as democratization and the changing role of the military and international actors[18] or a country's underlying democratic 'stock'.[19] Although useful, these explanations nonetheless do a poor job of explaining variation in the use of impeachment within democratic periods.

More useful are explanations that focus on the conditions under which legislatures remove presidents. These include the presence of executive corruption scandals,[20] and reasons such as poor economic performance,[21] low public opinion of the president,[22] elite radicalism,[23] weak political party system institutionalization,[24] social protest or anti-government demonstrations,[25] and perhaps most importantly, the presence or absence of a 'legislative shield' to protect the president during the impeachment trial.[26] Importantly, these explanations help link Latin America's acute social, political, and economic crises with the region's executive instability. Specifically, during times of economic stagnation and citizen discontent, presidents are more likely to confront low approval ratings, legislative opposition, and challenges to their leadership on the streets. In this context, impeachment becomes more likely.

Latin America's post-commodity boom era of the mid- to late-2010s is the perfect example of how global economic and political conditions can cause a regional wave of instability. Incumbents were re-elected at record rates during the commodity boom of the 2000s and early 2010s, but they suddenly faced threats to their survival as conditions changed. During this time, the region was beset by low economic growth, myriad high-level corruption scandals,

16 Arturo Valenzuela, 'Latin American Presidencies Interrupted' (2004) 15 *Journal of Democracy* 5; Hochstetler (n 15).
17 Andrés Mejía Acosta and John Polga-Hecimovich, 'Coalition Erosion and Presidential Instability in Ecuador' (2011) 53 *Latin American Politics and Society* 87; De Micheli, Sanchez-Gomez and Roberts (n 14).
18 Pérez-Liñán (n 7); Martínez, 'Presidential Survival in South America' (n 15); Aníbal S. Pérez-Liñán and John Polga-Hecimovich, 'Explaining Military Coups and Impeachments in Latin America' (2017) 24 *Democratization* 839.
19 Martínez, 'Presidential Survival in South America' (n 15).
20 Pérez-Liñán (n 7); Kathryn Hochstetler and Margaret E Edwards, 'Failed Presidencies: Identifying and Explaining a South American Anomaly' (2009) 1 *Journal of Politics in Latin America* 31; Kim (n 14).
21 Hochstetler and Edwards (n 20).
22 Ginsburg, Huq and Landau (n 2); Hinojosa and Pérez-Liñán (n 5).
23 Pérez-Liñán and Polga-Hecimovich (n 18).
24 Martínez, 'Presidential Instability in Latin America' (n 15).
25 Hochstetler (n 15); Pérez-Liñán (n 7); Young Hun Kim and Donna Bahry, 'Interrupted Presidencies in Third Wave Democracies' (2008) 70 *The Journal of Politics* 807, and Kim (n 14).
26 Hochstetler (n 15); Pérez-Liñán (n 7); Kim and Bahry (n 25); Kim (n 14).

and in many places, a return to austerity, all of which conspired to produce an unprecedented wave of social unrest. In 2017, anti-government demonstrations took place in Brazil, Honduras, and Venezuela, while even larger anti-Ortega protests followed in 2018 in Nicaragua in which police and militia repression led to the deaths of an estimated 500 protestors.[27] In 2019, a benchmark year, anti-government protests took place first in Venezuela, Nicaragua, and Guatemala and then in Ecuador, Peru, Chile, Colombia, and Bolivia – almost all of which threatened the survival of the president.[28] The COVID-19 pandemic, supply chain disruptions, and the subsequent rise in the cost of living have only exacerbated discontent with the status quo.[29] Although protests subsided during the global pandemic, they returned in force in 2022.

A complementary explanation is that some countries have also fallen victim to an 'impeachment trap', a cycle of instability in which one impeachment process is likely to result in a subsequent one. This concept is inspired by and represents a democratic version of what Finer and Putnam called a 'coup trap'.[30] They hypothesized that a single coup could cause the erosion of a society's political culture and lead to a greater risk of future interventions, as recurrent disruptions embolden coup-mongers and weaken civilian institutions. Furthermore, since the underlying social, economic, or political disfunction that contributed to the initial coup is likely to remain, the baseline probability of a subsequent coup rises. This proposal has been borne out in repeated empirical analyses that find that military rebellions are more likely to occur in countries with a previous history of coups.[31]

Like a coup trap, an impeachment trap also has both psychological and structural explanations. Psychologically, a first impeachment trial 'breaks the seal' for politicians, lays out a roadmap for how the process works, and helps them establish norms around how it will be used. This familiarity may also

27 Graig R Klein, José Cuesta and Cristian Chagalj, 'The Nicaragua Protest Crisis in 2018–2019: Assessing the Logic of Government Responses to Protests' (2022) 14 *Journal of Politics in Latin America* 55.

28 Anthony Faiola and Rachelle Krygier, 'How to Make Sense of the Many Protests Raging Across South America' *The Washington Post* (Washington, D.C., 14 November 2019) <www.washingtonpost.com/world/the_americas/a-government-chased-from-its-capital-a-president-forced-into-exile-a-storm-of-protest-rages-in-south-america/2019/11/14/897f85ba-0651-11ea-9118-25d6bd37dfb1_story.html>.

29 Ryan Dube and Juan Forero, 'Turmoil and Protests Shake Latin America as Region Sours on Democracy' *The Wall Street Journal* (New York, 16 January 2023) <www.wsj.com/articles/turmoil-and-protests-shake-latin-america-as-region-sours-on-democracy-11673886497>.

30 Samuel E Finer, *The Man on Horseback* (Pall Mall 1962); Robert D Putnam, 'Toward Explaining Military Intervention in Latin American Politics' (1967) 20 *World Politics* 83.

31 Rosemary HT O'Kane, 'A Probabilistic Approach to the Causes of Coups d'Etat' (1981) 11 *British Journal of Political Science* 287; John B Londregan and Keith T Poole, 'Poverty, the Coup Trap, and the Seizure of Executive Power' (1990) 42 *World Politics* 151; Fabrice Lehoucq and Aníbal S. Pérez-Liñán, 'Breaking Out of the Coup Trap: Political Competition and Military Coups in Latin America' (2014) 47 *Comparative Political Studies* 1105; Naunihal Singh, *Seizing Power: The Strategic Logic of Military Coups* (Johns Hopkins UP 2014).

lead formerly hesitant lawmakers to incorporate it into their legislative toolkit, allowing them to wield it not only as a mechanism of accountability but also as a political weapon – potentially leading to further use (or misuse). There are also structural reasons for why one impeachment may presage another. As with the coup trap, there are no guarantees that removing one president will either resolve the core social, political, or economic crisis that tends to accompany a chief executive's removal or meaningfully change other underlying structural debilities (e.g., a fragmented and weakly institutionalized party system) that contributed to the president's fall. Moreover, the presidential successor generally lacks legitimacy. As Llanos and Marsteintredet point out, although an impeachment may successfully remove a president, it does not necessarily provide the successor with a broad mandate or political backing to lead the country out of the crisis.[32] On the contrary, it may reduce rather than enhance the executive's legitimacy and governance capacity.

Many scholars have recognized the possibility of an impeachment trap in Latin America without calling it by that name. Helmke, for example, points out that 'countries [in the region] tend to experience multiple [constitutional] crises or none at all',[33] while Marsteintredet argues that a presidential interruption does not create further turmoil if the president is removed for violating the law but may lead to more crisis when the removal is due to policy or economic issues.[34] For their part, Hochstetler and Samuels find that a presidential ouster tends to lead to a climate of political instability that usually lasts about one year.[35] Despite the fact that Pérez-Liñán and Polga-Hecimovich find little statistical evidence of an impeachment trap in Latin America, they also acknowledge that they were working with a rare event; since their data cut-off of 2010, there have been eight additional presidential interruptions, many in countries with previous experiences of executive instability.[36]

6.5 Evidence

Data on Latin America instability lends credence to both the governability crisis and impeachment trap interpretations, at least anecdotally. Figure 6.1 uses a stacked bar chart to overlay the outcomes of presidential impeachment trials in Latin America dating from 1990 to June 2023. It shows eleven such events from 1990 to 2014, with only 2005 featuring more than one impeachment.

32 Mariana Llanos and Leiv Marsteintredet, *The Political Limits of Presidential Impeachment: Lessons from Latin America* (German Institute for Global and Area Studies (GIGA) 2021).

33 Gretchen Helmke, 'The Origins of Institutional Crisis in Latin America' (2010) 54 *American Journal of Political Science* 737, 742.

34 Marsteintredet (n 15).

35 Kathryn Hochstetler and David J Samuels, 'Crisis and Rapid Re-Equilibration: The Consequences of Presidential Challenge and Failure In Latin America' (2011) 43 *Comparative Politics* 127.

36 Pérez-Liñán and Polga-Hecimovich (n 18).

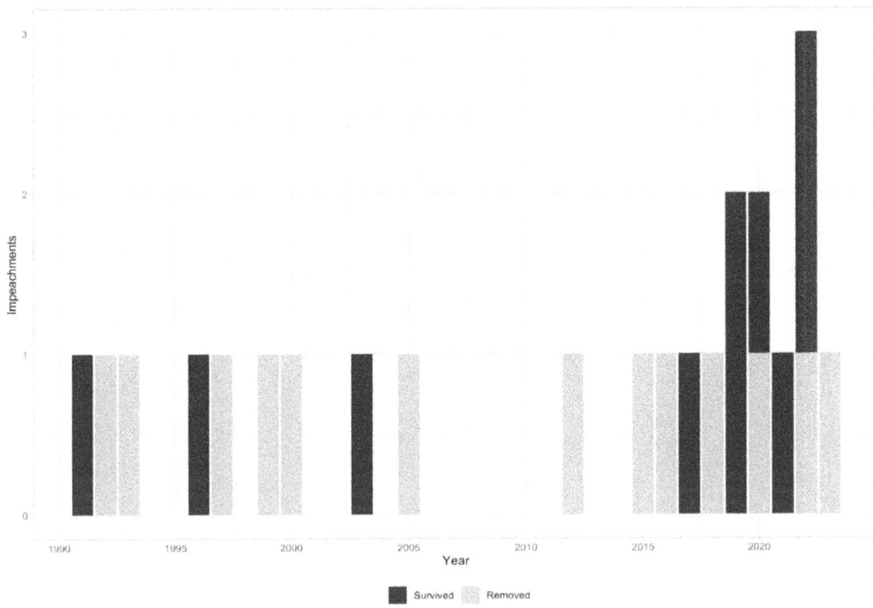

Figure 6.1 Presidential Impeachments Trials in Latin America (1990–October 2023)

However, beginning in 2015, there has been an impeachment trial every year. The bunching of cases in this latter period suggests that the region's multiple crises influenced legislators' demands of presidents in a systematic way. The disaggregation of presidential removals (including resignations) and survivals also reveals that although the total number of presidents forced from office has not varied considerably over time, there are far more cases of unsuccessful impeachment trials since 2017. This may indicate that recent impeachment processes were sparked more by social demands against beleaguered presidents rather than by inter-branch conflict, since the presidents were able to count on legislative majorities to survive.

Data on the geography of impeachment trials and presidential interruptions from 1990–2023 show another, possibly complimentary pattern. As the left-hand plot of Figure 6.2 indicates, countries tend to either never experience presidential impeachment trials or they endure multiple cases. This is especially true of Peru (seven trials), Paraguay (three trials), and Ecuador (four trials), all of which display signs of having fallen into an impeachment trap. The right-hand side of the figure combines removals via impeachment with negotiated resignations, forced resignations, and coups d'état, showing a sort of 'presidential instability trap' not only in Peru, Paraguay, and Ecuador but also in Bolivia (three removals) and Argentina (three removals). As with impeachments, presidential interruptions either are foreign to countries' political systems or tend to occur repeatedly.

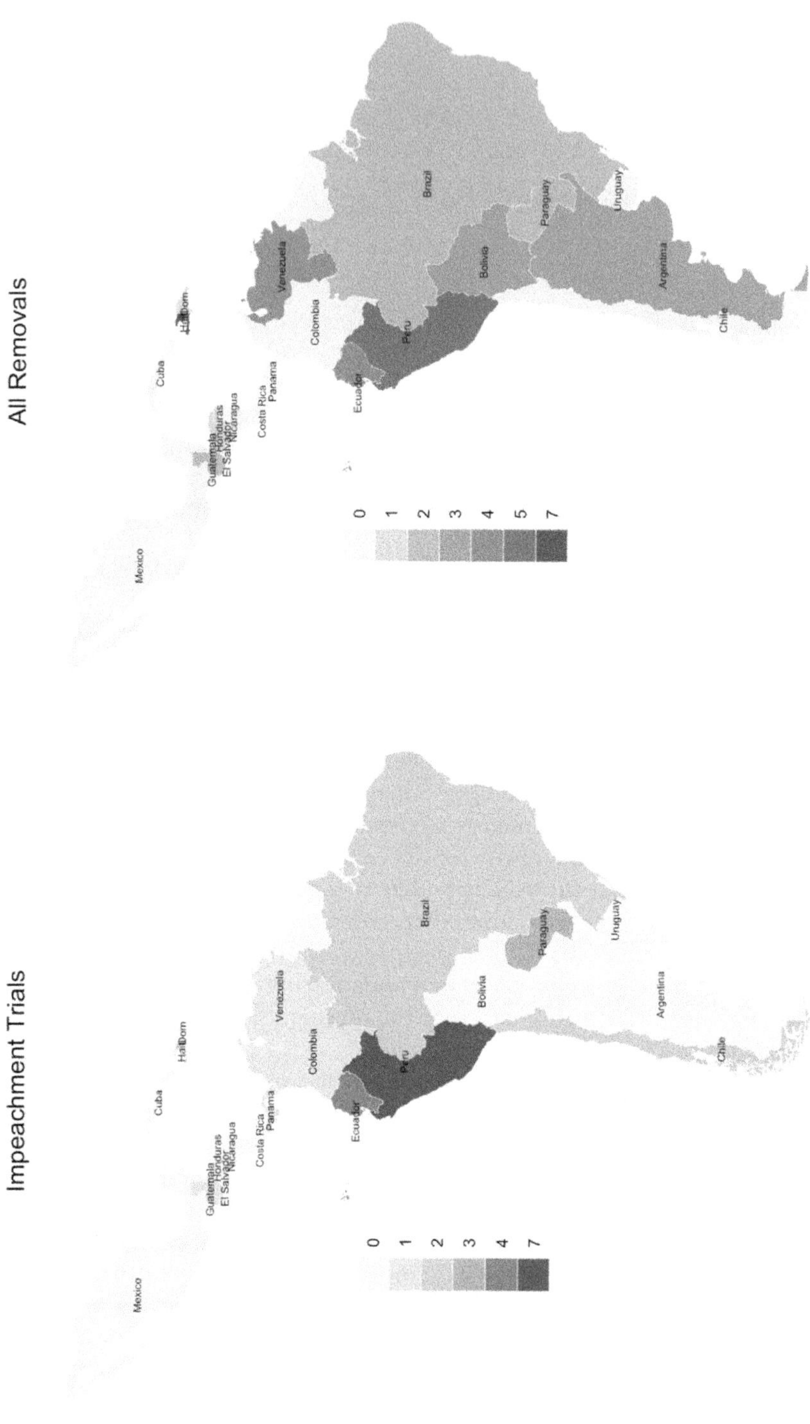

Figure 6.2 Impeachment Trials and Removals by Country (1990–2022)

Nonetheless, if underlying structural deficiencies enable presidential crisis and impeachment votes, then it follows that impeachment – or interruptions in general – should be bunched temporally. The evidence from Latin America fits when examining impeachment trials over shorter periods of time. For instance, in the five years from 2018–2022, there were ten impeachments in the region: with two in Chile and a whopping five in Peru (and a sixth if extending the period back an additional year). Ecuador's Guillermo Lasso survived an impeachment vote in June 2021 after having survived an impeachment motion in December 2021 and then faced another impeachment trial in May 2023.[37] No other country in the region experienced an impeachment trial during this time, putting into stark terms the difference between places where impeachment is a core process and those where it is not.

The same holds true of presidential interruptions more generally, as instability events have also been concentrated in a short period of time and tended to feature similar underlying causes. In Ecuador, the legislative removal of two presidents and a coup d'état against a third between 1997 and 2005 followed a pattern of presidential scandal, anti-government protests, and the erosion of the president's legislative partners.[38] Similarly, three of Argentina's presidential resignations took place in the short period from 2001–2003 during that country's unprecedented economic breakdown and resulting social and political crisis,[39] while the Bolivian presidential resignations in 2003 and 2005 were in response to massive social uprisings and related anti-neoliberal protests.[40] In all three countries, successors to fallen presidents failed to resolve the social or economic problems that drove the removal of their predecessors.

Of course, the paradigmatic illustration of a country beset by crises and social unrest and caught in the throes of an impeachment trap is contemporary Peru. As of this writing, four of the previous five presidents have been forced from office before their terms ended: Pedro Pablo Kuczynski (2016–2018), who resigned in the face of certain impeachment; his replacement, Martin Vizcarra (2018–2020), who was impeached; Vizcarra's successor, Manuel Merino (2020), who resigned after only five days in office facing credible threats of impeachment; and Pedro Castillo (2021–2022), who was impeached after he attempted an autogolpe. The only president in the last three decades who has not faced accusations of corruption is interim leader Valentin Paniagua

37 Haiti is not included in this analysis because it does not have a presidential system. However, it experienced an impeachment vote in 2019 against Jovenel Moïse, followed by another episode of instability when the president was assassinated in 2021 – providing evidence not of a trap of impeachment but one of instability.

38 Mejía Acosta and Polga-Hecimovich (n 17).

39 Steven Levitsky and María Victoria Murillo, 'Argentina Weathers the Storm' (2003) 14 *Journal of Democracy* 152.

40 Jeffery R Webber, 'Carlos Mesa, Evo Morales, and a Divided Bolivia (2003–2005)' (2010) 37 *Latin American Perspectives* 51.

(2000–2001), with the others facing indictments, house arrest, and imprisonment.[41] Moreover, both Vizcarra and Castillo survived one motion of impeachment, and Kuczynski, Vizcarra, and Castillo all survived an initial impeachment trial before they were forced from power in a second. By any reasonable standard, this is the definition of an impeachment trap.

The geographical concentration of impeachment trials in Latin America also converges with some of the region's most noteworthy governability crises. In this sense, Peru is also emblematic. At least some of these leaders committed impeachable acts, to be sure, but a multiplicity of structural difficulties also plagued their rule. These include many of the micro-conditions the impeachment literature argues can lead to removals, such as a poorly institutionalized and nearly non-existent party system, numerous corruption scandals that weaken the executive, elite radicalism, and poor public approval of nearly all politicians, all of which facilitate broad social protest and rejection of the status quo.

The destruction of the party system and resulting legislative fragmentation are particularly important, and they contribute to presidential instability in at least three ways. First, they incentivize the candidacy of outsiders and populists, which hampers governance. Specifically, the paucity of programmatic parties means less vetting of presidential candidates and fewer institutional checks to filter out unprepared outsiders and populists. Second, a weak party system means Peruvian presidents have to engage in costly negotiations to govern. Excessive fragmentation and a deficit of programmatic parties means that presidents must constantly forge and maintain floor voting coalitions in the National Congress. This makes them more likely to purchase votes in illicit ways and leaves them open to public accusations of corruption. Lastly, a multiplicity of parties makes building a legislative shield difficult at the time of the impeachment motion or vote.

Accordingly, Peru's extreme presidential instability suggests the compatibility of several factors highlighted in the literature along with an impeachment trap. Unfortunately for the country, these phenomena also seem to reinforce one another: underlying problems give way to a crisis, which leads to an impeachment; the removal of the president then fails to resolve the underlying problems, and the cycle continues.

6.6 Dangers of the Impeachment Trap

Impeachment has long existed in Latin American constitutions. However, for most of the region's history, it was used only sparingly and often as legal cover for a presidential removal orchestrated by elites or the military. This changed

41 In addition, ex-president Alan García (1985–1990; 2006–2011) committed suicide in April 2019 when Peruvian police arrived to arrest him over participation in the Odebrecht bribery scheme.

with the third wave of democratization. Freed from the vicissitudes of the Cold War, impeachment replaced the military coup d'état as Latin America's modal form of presidential removal. Between 1991 and October 2023, there were 22 impeachment trials across nine Latin American presidential democracies. These resulted in eight removals, four resignations, one government dissolution, and nine cases of survival. Furthermore, Latin American legislators, judges, and citizens have filed hundreds of motions against leaders that never left committee or reached an assembly vote.

The use of this tool, however, is not uniform. In some countries, impeachment is an instrument that the legislature wields as a 'core' part of the executive control process, and without exception, these political systems have experienced multiple impeachment trials or multiple presidential interruptions. Where impeachment or other types of presidential interruptions have become core processes, they are invoked quite often. In other countries, impeachment is a 'peripheral' process; it is rarely invoked, and motions or resolutions related to the process fail to reach the trial phase. In a third group of countries in Latin America, impeachment is considered a 'satellite' process where impeachment exists on paper but is not invoked by legislators as a mechanism of accountability or as a political weapon.

The temporal evolution of impeachment across Latin America, including the rise in impeachments since 2016, indicates not only a relationship between socio-economic conditions and presidential stability but also the existence of an 'impeachment trap'. During the commodity boom of the late 2000s and early 2010s, incumbents were often re-elected and rarely faced threats to their survival. However, as this period of prosperity ended and economic conditions worsened, the depth of popular grievance and popular protest increased along with the number of impeachment trials. In places where presidents have fallen, many of their successors have also faced challenges to their rule.

An impeachment trap and a high level of presidential instability are probably not healthy for Latin American democracy. Some scholars initially welcomed impeachment as a needed 'flexibilization' mechanism of presidentialism, allowing the removal of presidents but survival of the regime.[42] However, multiple, repeated challenges to presidential rule do not necessarily resolve political crises and may instead contribute to them by raising citizen disenchantment, increasing polarization, and undermining the legitimacy and governing capacity of politicians. In these places, impeachment is no longer used as a mechanism of accountability but almost exclusively as a political weapon, undermining trust in the political system, politicians, and political parties.

42 Marsteintredet and Berntzen (n 13).

7 Contemporary Impeachment in Brazil

Political Time and Aporias

Carina Barbosa Gouvêa and Pedro H. Villas Bôas Castelo Branco

7.1 Introduction

The institutional safeguard mechanism foreseen mostly in western liberal democratic systems called impeachment is an extraordinary measure with effects in the uncertain field that unfolds in political time. This chapter discusses the relationship between impeachment and political time through an analysis of the Brazilian case.

The impeachment political process in Brazil is hybrid in the sense that it involves both political and judicial bodies. It is detailed in several provisions of the Constitution of Brazil promulgated in 1988.[1] The constitution was the outcome of a re-democratization process following 20 years of military dictatorship. In the Brazilian political system, the President, the State Ministers, the Supreme Court Ministers, and the Prosecutor General can be impeached for a responsibility crime.[2] Strictly speaking, it is not a crime, but the conduct or behavior of the entire political content is only typified and named a crime without having this nature. The sanctions in this case are substantially political: loss of office or eventually, disqualification from holding public office and ineligibility for political office. The Constitutional Amendment N° 25 of 2000 added to the Constitution the 'crimes of responsibility' of the Municipal Mayor and the President of the Municipal Chamber. State governors answer for crimes of responsibility as defined in federal law.

In the case of presidential impeachment, the responsibility crimes defined in the constitution are considered fixed. All of them relate to the harmful effects of certain presidential actions to the fundamental democratic principle.[3]

1 Constitution of Brazil 1988, art 29ª§2°; art 29ª§3°; art 50; art 50§2°; art 52, I; art 52, II; art 85.

2 The process and judgment of crimes of responsibility in Brazil are regulated by the federal constitution and by Law 1079 of 10 April 1950.

3 They are grouped in eight different categories: against the federative system; against the free exercise of legislative and judiciary powers, of the Public Prosecution and of the constitutional powers of the units of the federation; against the exercise of political, individual, and social rights; against the internal security of the country; against the administrative probity against the budgetary law; and, against the fulfillment of the laws and judicial decisions that are defined in

DOI: 10.4324/9781003256007-9

A finding that someone has committed one of these crimes of responsibility will lead to the loss of office. It can also lead to disqualification of up to eight years for the exercise of any public function that is imposed by the Federal Senate. The voting procedures are distinct: first, the vote is for removal from office and then, for disqualification. In the event of conviction, the Senate, on the initiative of its President, shall fix the period of disqualification of the convict for the exercise of any public function; in the event of a common crime, the President of the Senate shall also decide whether the President shall be submitted to ordinary justice, irrespective of the action of any interested party.

Any citizen is allowed to report the commission of a responsibility crime by the President, the Vice President, or State Ministers to the Chamber of Deputies. Such a complaint must be signed with a notarized signature. It should also be accompanied by proving documents or by a declaration explaining why it is impossible to present such supporting evidence. Such a report must be channeled through the Chamber of Deputies. It is then forwarded to its President of the Chamber of Deputies who will decide to receive the complaint or not. The procedure is the same for an accusation against the President of the Republic or a Minister of State.

7.2 Impeachment in Brazil: The Historical Experience

The impeachment process in the current Brazilian constitution is an institutional safeguarding tool that is rarely used. When it has been applied, it has involved an attempt to control the exercise of federal executive power in ways that threaten to entrench the power of the highest representative. In Brazil, two Presidents have suffered what in effect were parliamentary coups, and another two Presidents suffered impeachments in compliance with formal and constitutional rules – these last processes occurred under the present constitution.

The parliamentary coups occurred in 1955 while the 1946 Constitution was in effect: Café Filho – the 18th President of Brazil, whose mandate lasted one year and 76 days (August 24, 1954–November 8, 1955); and Carlos Luz – the 19th President of Brazil who occupied the presidency for the least amount of time, whose mandate lasted three days (November 8, 1955–November 11, 1955). Both were prosecuted and accused of conspiracy to prevent the presidential inauguration of Juscelino Kubitschek.

The impeachment processes of these two presidents happened extremely quickly, and the impeachments processes caused tension with the 1946 Constitution.[4] Their trials started and ended in a few hours. The procedures determined by Law 1.070/1950, which regulates the impeachment process, were

special laws. Crimes of Responsibility, Process and Judgment Act, 1950; Penalties applicable to Public Agents Act, 1992.

4 Wagner William, *O soldado absoluto: Uma biografia do marechal Henrique Lott* (1 st supp, Editora Record 2020).

not followed in either case. Deputies and Senators justified this derogation at the time by stating that the political situation was extremely fragile and pointed to the risk of civil war.

According to William,[5] this extralegal dismissal of two presidents in turn was the most critical point of the turbulent period between the suicide of Getúlio Vargas in August 1954 and the inauguration of President Juscelino Kubitschek in January 1956.[6]

Since neither of these presidential removals followed the constitution or the statutory framework for regulating the adjudication of a responsibility crime, they cannot be treated as instances of successful use of the impeachment process.

Two further impeachment trials occurred under the current 1988 Constitution. One resulted in the impeachment of former President Fernando Collor de Melo – the 32nd President of Brazil – in 1992 based on accusations of corruption. After the report drawn up by the Parliamentary Commission of Inquiry (CPMI) was approved, the President was accused of receiving money from Paulo César (PC) Farias (the 'PC Farias' scheme).[7]

The second impeachment involved the trial of former President Dilma Rousseff – the 36th President of Brazil – which occurred in 2016, 28 years after the 1988 Constitution was created.[8] Rouseff was accused of disrespecting the Budget Law and the Administrative Improbity Law. The President of the Republic, according to the judgment, committed a responsibility crime by taking loans from the financial institution controlled by the Union and by opening supplementary credits without authorization from the National Congress.

7.2.1 President Fernando Collor de Mello

President Fernando Collor de Mello was the first civilian elected directly by popular vote after the military coup of 1964. His presidential mandate was short-lived, running from March 15, 1990 to October 2, 1992, when he was

5 ibid.

6 In November 1955, Brazilians witnessed a wave of political and military conspiracies that culminated in two successful coups. Rio de Janeiro, then the capital of the country, was the stage for scenes of war, with tanks in the streets and cannon fire on the beach. In a single week, Brazil had two presidents, Café Filho and Carlos Luz, who suffered parliamentary coups.

7 The report found that Collor's personal expenses were paid for by 'ghosts' who supplied the President's accounts. Also according to the text, these phantom accounts were a creation of the PC scheme. The CPMI also concluded that Paulo César (PC) Farias was speaking on behalf of the President of the Republic, who received undue economic advantages.

8 Historical references were fully obtained from the Federal Senate's official website to ensure reliability of the historical context. Federal Senate, 'Impeachment of Dilma Rousseff Marks 2016 in Congress and Brazil' *Senate News* (28 December 2016) <https://www12.senado.leg.br/noticias/materias/2016/12/28/impeachment-de-dilma-rousseff-marca-ano-de-2016-no-congresso-e-no-brasil> accessed 30 May 2023.

Table 7.1

President	*Political Party*	*Term of Office*	*Impeachment Requests*	*Political Effects*
Fernando Collor de Melo	Partido Trabalhista Cristão (PRN)	1990–2002	24 requests	Loss of office and disqualification for eight years to hold public office
Dilma Rousseff	Partido dos Trabalhadores (PT)	2011–2016	68 requests	Loss of office without disqualification to hold public office

removed from the presidency to face the impeachment process. He was thus the first president to be judged and condemned for a responsibility crime and hence became the first object of impeachment under the 1988 Constitution. As a result of the trial, Collor received the penalty of suspension of political rights for eight years. This meant that he was ineligible for any public function of office (at the federal, state and municipal levels) during this period.

In May 1992, Fernando Collor's brother, Pedro Collor, accused PC Farias of being the 'figurehead' or the President's representative. After the accusation, a Joint CPMI[9] was opened to investigate not only PC Farias's business[10] interests in relation to the federal government but also the existence of an influence trade network in the government with the connivance of the President. Marvelo Lavenère presented the impeachment request to the Chamber of Deputies.[11]

News of these accusations led to a wave of popular protest across the country. Around 40,000 students, called out by the National Student Union (UNE), took to the streets and demanded the removal of the President. The President of the Chamber of Deputies at the time, Ibsen Pinheiro (RS), accepted the impeachment request made by citizens Barbosa Lima Sobrinho,

9 Federal Senate, 'Application (CN) No 52, of 1992' <https://www2.camara.leg.br/atividade-legislativa/plenario/discursos/escrevendohistoria/20-anos-do-impeachment/cpmi-pc-farias> accessed 30 May 2023.

10 According to the complaint, Treasurer of Collor's election campaign in 1989, PC Farias, transited in the business environment and brokered business, favors and appointments through the collection of bribes. In these contacts, he said that he spoke on behalf of the President. The CPMI confirmed the existence of the scheme and the interference of PC Farias at all levels of the government and found that the personal expenses of the President of the Republic and his wife, Rosane, were paid for by the businessman with account checks in the name of ghosts. The scheme headed by the former treasurer moved approximately $1 billion between funds raised from businessmen in the form of bribes and embezzled public funds.

11 Marcello Lavenère Machado was former president of the Federal Council of the Brazilian Bar Association and author of the impeachment request for Collor.

President of the Brazilian Press Association, and Marcelo Lavenère, President of the Federal Council of the Brazilian Bar Association.

The impeachment process took seven months, from June 1 to December 29, 1992. As a result of the interference by the National Congress party, the CPMI investigated the allegations made by Mr. Pedro Collor de Mello in his complaints concerning Farias's activities, which came to be known as the 'CPMI – PC Farias Scheme.' The Chamber of Deputies established a Special Commission to give its opinion on the accusation against the President on responsibility crime.[12] It included the Chamber's President, Deputy Gastone Righi, and Rapporteur, Deputy Nesoln Jobim. The Chamber voted in favor of opening Collor's impeachment process. There were 441 votes cast in favor, 38 against, 1 abstention and 23 absent. In 1992, 18 of the 28 deputies from the then-president's party, Partido da Reconstrucão Nacional (PRN), voted for impeachment. The vote of the PRN deputies was a faithful reflection of the absolute loneliness with which Collor faced the process. His political ruin, strictly speaking, began with an interview with his brother, condemning the President's behavior and practices.

An impeachment process was then instituted in the Federal Senate.[13] As a consequence, President Collor had to withdraw from the presidency while the Federal Senate undertook the impeachment process. As a result, Vice President Itamar Franco took office. Collor de Melo's trial began in the Federal Senate on December 29, 1992. To avoid impeachment, however, he resigned from his mandate in a letter read by attorney José Moura Rocha. Nevertheless, Collor de Melo was disqualified from exercising public functions for eight years, without prejudice to other legal sanctions applicable according to Resolution N° 101, 1992.[14] Here, there were 76 votes in favor of the penalty and two against.

7.2.2 President Dilma Rousseff

President Dilma Rousseff's impeachment started on December 2, 2015, when the former President of the Chamber of Deputies, Eduardo Cunha, accepted a submission made by jurists Hélio Biculo, Miguel Reale Júnior and Janaína Paschoal. Hélio Pereira Bicudo, Miguel Reale Júnior and Janaína Paschoal are Brazilian jurists who based their denunciation on three pillars: the petrolão scandal, revealed by the investigations of Operation Lava Jato, the so-called 'pedaladas fiscais,' and the issue of Supplementary Credit Decrees without the authorization of Congress. The ensuing process lasted 273 days. The case was

12 Chamber of Deputies, 'P.C5/1992 CESP, Parecer CD' <www.camara.leg.br/proposicoesWeb/fichadetramitacao?idProposicao=165335> accessed 30 May 2023.

13 Federal Senate, 'Federal Senate Resolution No 101 of 30 December 1992' <https://www25.senado.leg.br/web/atividade/materias/-/materia/2390> accessed 30 May 2023.

14 Federal Senate, 'Federal Senate Resolution No 101 of 30 December 1992' <https://legis.senado.leg.br/norma/564156> accessed 30 July 2022.

closed on August 31, 2016. It resulted in Rousseff's impeachment and her loss of the presidential mandate but with no deprivation of political rights.

As a justification for the impeachment process, the jurists argued that President Rousseff had committed a responsibility crime by practicing the so-called 'pedaladas fiscais'[15] (accounting trickery in order to disguise the true size of the budget deficit) and by editing decrees to open credit without Congress's approval. The accusation argued that Rousseff had issued decrees authorizing the supplementation of the budget by more than R$95 billion. This contributed to Brazil exceeding the 2015 fiscal targets set by Congress. The jurists also alleged that Rousseff had tampered with the federal budget to mask the government's widening fiscal deficit. It asserted not merely operational delays respecting payments. Treasury debt often accumulates in public banks for an extended period of time. However, the delay in debt repayment in effect expanded the fiscal basis for government action by an unauthorized channel. According to the jurists, Rousseff allowed debt to accumulate in ways that in effect manufactured a fiscal surplus that did not exist and that created a positive balance in public accounts that was not true. The goal of these 'pedaladas fiscais,' as the jurists labeled them, was to intentionally hide the real fiscal situation of the country.

Rousseff's defense, to the contrary, affirmed that the Supplementary Credit Decrees were based on the ordinary and proper reallocation of resources with an excess of collection or a financial surplus. The decrees, however, did not lead to or allow an increase in expenses. According to Rousseff's defenders, delays in payments of the equalization of the interest rates of the Safra Plan could not be considered borrowing because this borrowing was made to agriculturists and not to the government.[16]

15 'Pedaladas Fiscais' is a nickname given to a type of accounting maneuver used by the Executive Branch to meet fiscal goals, which makes it seem that there is a balance between spending and expenses in public accounts. In the case of the Dilma Rousseff government, the Federal Court of Auditors understood that the National Treasury voluntarily delayed the transfer of resources to Caixa Econômica Federal, Banco do Brasil, the National Bank for Economic and Social Development (BNDES) and the Guarantee Fund for Length of Service (FGTS) for the payment of social programs such as Bolsa Família and Minha Casa Minha Vida, which are social benefits such as salary allowance, unemployment insurance and agricultural subsidies. These institutions made the payment with their own resources, ensuring that the beneficiaries received the benefits on time. At the same time, the government omitted these liabilities in the public debt statistics and postponed their accounting until the following month. With this, the public accounts presented good results that, however, were not real. See Senado Federal <https://www12.senado.leg.br/noticias/entenda-o-assunto/pedalada-fiscal>.

16 The former Minister of Finance, Nelson Henrique Barbosa Filho, explained in the Joint Parliamentary Commission of Inquiry that the six decrees of supplementary credit cited in the request for impeachment of President Rousseff, totaling R$95.9 billion, were based on a reallocation of resources with an excess collection or a financial surplus. According to him, 'these additional credits, at no time, authorize the increase of financial expenses,' and he used the example of a shopping list that would be the equivalent of a budget, while the financial limit would be the volume of money that the citizen would have in his pocket. If you change an

Unlike the impeachment process for Collor de Melo, the impeachment process for Rousseff was marked by great controversies. On December 8, 2015, the Chamber Plenary elected through secret vote a single slate of opposition politicians to make up the Special Commission that would analyze the impeachment request. Prosecutor General Rodrigo Janot and Attorney General of the Union Luís Inácio Adams advocated for the annulment of the secret vote to elect the Special Commission. They challenged its composition before the Federal Supreme Court (STF). On December 17, 2015, the STF held that the impeachment proceedings used by the Chamber were invalid and annulled the Special Commission's election. The Court held that the votes of the impeachment process have to be open, including votes to elect the Commission's members. In February 2016, the Chamber filed an appeal against the STF's decision. However, the court rejected it and insisted on the procedures it had previously mandated.

The President of the Chamber at the time, Eduardo Cunha, installed a new Special Commission. Deputies Rogério Rosso (PSD-DF) and Jovair Arantes (PTB-GO) were elected its President and Rapporteur, respectively. With an impeachment process now moving forward in the Chamber, President Rousseff began to lose the support of all major parties. In March 2016, the Brazilian Democratic Movement Party (PMDB) officially broke ties with the government after a meeting of the National Directorate.

According to political scientist Rolf Rauschenbach,[17] some key factors led to the fall of Rousseff and the loss of support from major parties. Firstly, these factors included errors in economic management, as she proved unable to approve reforms to reverse the situation. Secondly, Rousseff lacked political skill – she delegated little, and when she did, she often chose aides who were not popular with Congress. Thirdly, becoming isolated from her largest grassroots political partner. Fourthly, Rousseff had political myopia in the face of problems related to her administration. Fifthly, Rousseff did not orchestrate a decisive offensive to stop the impeachment process while it was still in the House. Sixthly, Rousseff made the mistake of appointing Lula as minister while he faced ongoing investigations without realizing the impact of this measure on public opinion. Seventhly, Rousseff wasted energy by speaking regularly

item, then 'you change the list, but the value you can use is still what you have in your pocket.' The Minister insisted that in what became known as 'pedaladas fiscais' (late payments to public banks, referring to the equalization of interest rates on agricultural credits), there was no act of the President of the Republic, and he denied that there had been a delay. Equalization is performed when a resource is made available to a farmer, for example, at a rate of 6%, but with the payment of 8% to the banks that operate the credit. The difference in this rate is funded by the government. Nelson Barbosa stated that this grant is approved by the National Congress and authorized and regulated by the National Monetary Council and the Ministry of Finance. See Agência Brasil <https://agenciabrasil.ebc.com.br/politica/noticia/2016-04/ministro-da-fazenda-defende-dilma-ao-falar-no-senado>.

17 Jean-Philip Struck, 'Os fatores que levaram à queda de Dilma' <www.dw.com/pt-br/os-fatores-que-levaram-%C3%A0-queda-de-dilma/a-19514830>.

to audiences who lacked the influence to help her. Eighthly, the corruption scandals eroded the image of Rousseff's government, as investigators began to reveal the involvement of ministers, her campaign treasurer and influential PT (Worker's Party) figures. Finally, several opposition politicians did not sympathize with the impeachment, but the pressure of street protests and the government's permanent deterioration in popularity made the decision to impeach Rousseff more acceptable.

On April 11, 2016, the Special Commission approved the opening of an impeachment process against Rousseff by a vote of 38 to 27. On April 17, after a six-hour session and by nominal vote, the Chamber Plenary also authorized the opening of the process against Rousseff, with 367 votes in favor, 137 votes against and seven abstentions.

The day following the deputies' decision, the President of the Senate, Renan Calheiros, received the charges against Rousseff from Eduardo Cunha. Towards the end of April 2016, the leaders of the parties appointed members to the Special Commission that would analyze the admissibility of the accusation received in the Chamber. Senator Raimundo Lira (PMDB-PB) was elected president of a new Special Commission, and Antonio Anastasia (PSDB-MG) was elected its Rapporteur.

On May 6, 2016, this Commission approved Antonio Anastasia's report favorable to the opening of the impeachment process with 15 votes in favor and 5 against. On May 12, the Senate decided to open the process. It removed Dilma Rousseff from office. From this moment, the President of the STF, Ricardo Lewandovski, assumed control of the impeachment process.[18]

By June 2016, the Special Impeachment Commission had held close to 100 hours of hearings including many tense moments. At the end of this step, the Commission debated investigative reports according to the terms of the complaint. These were drafted by a board of Senate advisers and expert assistants to the prosecution and defense.

In the beginning of August 2016, the Commission debated a Final Report drafted by Senator Antonio Anastasia that defended the accusation as being well-founded. The senators who defended the impeachment praised Anastasia's work; Rousseff's allies responded by saying that the document amounted to a 'coup.' On August 4, the Report was approved by the Commission and

18 According to Article 86 of the Constitution, in admitting the accusation against the President of the Republic by two-thirds vote of the Chamber of Deputies, the President will submit to trial before the STF for common criminal offenses or before the Federal Senate for crimes of responsibility. The President will be suspended from his/her duties as follows: in common criminal offenses, if the complaint or criminal complaint is received by the STF; in crimes of responsibility, after the initiation of the process by the Federal Senate. If after a period of 180 days the judgment has not concluded, the removal of the President will cease, without prejudice to the regular continuation of the process. If a condemnatory sentence does not occur, then in common infractions, the President will not be subject to arrest. The President, during his/her term, cannot be held responsible for acts outside the exercise of his/her functions.

proceeded to the Plenary Senate. In the session that begun on the morning of August 9 and ended in the early hours of August 10, the Plenary decided, with 59 votes in favor and 21 against, that Rousseff would go to trial. Rouseff was accused of a responsibility crime against the Budget Law and against the custody and legal use of public resources in the form of three Supplementary Credit Decrees and operations with public banks. After six days of trial, the Senate finally decided the impeachment of Rouseff on August 31. It revoked the President's mandate but did not deprive her of political rights. The trial, which was the longest in the history of the National Congress and of Brazil, resulted in senators voting 61 in favor and 20 against Rousseff's impeachment.

Both the Collor de Melo and the Rousseff impeachments can be considered in light of how the 1988 Constitution envisages impeachment as a process. They also demonstrate the way in which Law 1079 of 1950, which defines in more detail the substance of responsibility crimes and regulates the impeachment process in Brazil, interacts with the constitutional framework. Analyses of these cases point to several key conclusions about the role of different factors and institutions.

The Role of the STF. The STF was involved countless times during both processes. After the judgement of admissibility by both houses of the National Congress and after being temporarily stripped of his functions, President Collor de Mello filed several requests for a writ of mandamus to the STF.[19,20] During Rousseff's trial, the STF was asked to intervene again. Legal controversies arose regarding the use of secret voting for the Special Commission and the possibility of single candidatures[21] to form the Commission. The role that the STF played in both processes was one of conforming the process to current constitutional rules but not interfering in the 'interna corporis' matters of the political process made in parliament.

19 From the judgment of these writs, specifically 21.564, 21.623 and 21.689, the STF elaborated the new discipline of the impeachment process. In MS 21.564/DF, the decision confirmed that the House of Representatives would have the competence to make the prior judgment of admissibility and acceptance of the accusation and that the vote would have to be public and not secret. Writ 21.623/DF was filed against the acts of Minister Sydney Sanches, then-President of the STF and of the impeachment process conducted in the Senate, who denied the request for suspicions made against the senators. The writ was known but dismissed by a majority vote. As for the impeachment of the senators, the STF held that it makes no sense to apply the rules of suspicion to the legislative branch, especially since impeachment is a political trial. The act challenged by Mandado de Segurança 21.689/DF was the resolution of the Federal Senate that imposed on Fernando Collor soon after the impeachment trial the sanction of disqualification from holding public office for eight years. By majority vote, the writ of mandamus was granted, but the injunction was denied (MS 21.564/DF, rel. p/ acórdão min. Carlos Velloso, DJ (25 September 1992); MS 21.623/DF, rel. min. Carlos Velloso, DJ (28 May 1993); MS 21.689/DF, rel. min. Carlos Velloso, DJ (7 April 1995).

20 Marcus Vinicius Furtado Coêlho, 'O protagonismo do Supremo no processo de impeachment de presidentes' (*Consultor Jurídico*, 5 June 2016) <www.conjur.com.br/2016-jun-05/constituicao-protagonismo-stf-processo-impeachment-presidentes> accessed 30 May 2023.

21 Single candidacies are those that are disconnected from political parties.

The political context and social and popular participation movements. According to the Federal Senate, at the time that the impeachment process began in each case, both presidents found themselves facing economic crises and low popularity. Rousseff's process led to sharp public controversy and a divergence of opinions in both Parliament and society, which differentiates it from what happened to Fernando Collor in 1992. Rousseff, at least initially, was able to count on broad support, but this diminished over time. She was also strongly supported by social movements and union organizations, such as the Workers Unique Central Office (CUT), which organized protests opposed to the impeachment process. Collor, in contrast, governed with little parliamentary support. Moreover, during his impeachment, larger social and civil society forces were generally favorable to his removal. The Special Commission in Rousseff's trial conducted four public hearings and received 13 guest speakers in four debates, which did not occur in Collor's political process.

Presidents' reactions to impeachment. Collor resigned his term through a letter read by his attorney, Moura Rocha, before the Federal Senate to avoid impeachment. His resignation request was an attempt to forestall the impeachment process, which applies only to a president in office at the time of the legislative action. After he presented his resignation request, the Federal Senate considered whether this foreclosed their process or not. The Senate decided to continue its work, with 73 senators voting in favor. In Rousseff's case, on the third day of trial, the President insisted on appearing before Congress to defend herself. In her presentation, she denied having committed the responsibility crimes of which she was accused. She also described the impeachment approval as a 'coup' and accused then-Vice President, Michel Temer, and the former President of the Chamber, Eduardo Cunha, of a conspiracy.

7.3 Impeachment in Brazil: A Political Process in Political Time

Impeachment in Brazil is considered a hybrid judgment because it has both legal and political elements. Experience suggests, however, that it primarily plays out on the political field, not on the legal field. The process from a legal standpoint has formal trappings that legitimize the process and bring it under a constitutional aegis, but they do not alter its fundamentally political nature. To see this, consider the identity of the key guardian of the impeachment process in Brazil, that is, the only official who can consider whether a complaint meets constitutional requirements and is therefore valid: this is the President of the Chamber of Deputies. He has a type of absolute and unreviewable power. His exclusive possession of this power in practice makes impeachment a fragile instrument and subject to political oscillations. From this conjecture, two paths open: impeachment can become either the Achilles heel of the democratic system or its guardian. Because of the primacy of a politician (over a judge) in determining when and how the process will be used, its results are uncertain.

The legal-political instrument of impeachment, which is typically understood in western liberal democratic systems as a tool for safeguarding institutional stability and integrity, operates in Brazil on *political time*. That is, impeachment unfolds as a process that is shifted and changed in meaning and effect because of pervasive political themes and currents that operate over time. Unless impeachment is situated in political time, it is difficult to understand or predict its effects. Although it is possible to observe the evolution of the concept of 'political time,' both in political science and in contemporary constitutionalism, it contains aporias that have not yet been settled. Reflection on impeachment helps reveal these gaps.

The importance of political timing can be perceived in at least four ways: (1) the strength of impeachment as an instrument for discipling the executive is diluted as the periodic democratic elections approach; (2) the use of impeachment tends to cause a certain political paralysis because it necessarily produces friction in ordinary political activity, for example, the suspension of parliamentary activities unrelated to the impeachment process; (3) impeachment exponentially increases political polarization and social tensions; and (4) when the prospect of impeachment materializes, it tends to provoke democratic destabilization not only via the switching of seats across partisan divides but also through more widespread effects in the economic, social and political fields.

According to Juan Linz,[22] the degradation of the democratic system occurs in the political context in which it arises. The declining state of the present democratic regime and the availability of alternatives offered by more unfair and disloyal political oppositions can together stimulate the process of collapse. Writing in the same vein, Richard Pildes argues that the most fundamental challenges that democracies face today include democratic setbacks, coups and the rise of populism.[23] Pildes considers that the greatest challenge to western democratic government currently is what he calls 'political fragmentation.' When the political power of making and influencing public decisions and policies is dispersed over many different hands and centers of power, it becomes difficult to organize and maintain an effective government response. Given the centrality of political parties to democratic rule, some political fragmentation is inevitable. An excess of this fragmentation manifests itself differently depending on the political system in the democracy.

Brazil considers multipartyism to be a fundamental principle of democracy. It employs a system of proportional representation for federal deputies and a majoritarian system for the national senate. Because of multipartyism, this institutional design fractures power among many smaller parties. This makes

22 Juan J Linz, Wallace Sayre and Alfred Stepan (eds), *The Breakdown of Democratic Regimes* (Johns Hopkins UP 1978) 55.

23 Richard H Pildes, 'The Age of Political Fragmentation' (2021) 32(4) *Journal of Democracy* 146–59.

not only uniting coalitions initially more difficult but also the resulting coalitions more volatile. This can lead to substantial popular dissatisfaction with the incapacity of the government and the main parties to provide effective policy solutions to social and economic questions.

According to Piles, the historical record demonstrates that after financial crises, votes for right-wing populist parties tend to increase.[24] In the cultural sphere, the spectrum of accelerating social change associated with rising rates of immigration can also lead voters to choose xenophobic political parties. Such tectonic changes to the political landscape place new pressures on large parties and related coalitions as they struggle to respond to voters' concerns and adopt ideological positions adequate for the new political climate.[25] For Piles, political fragmentation generates a great paradox: it arises out of the difficulty that governments have in responding effectively to certain policy challenges but simultaneously makes it more difficult for them to address these problems.

The decline of dominant parties and the rise of other smaller parties also ends up making coalitions more unstable. The democratic institutions must restructure themselves to resist party fragmentation and excessive pressure from interest groups. If divisions between political parties cannot be overcome such that government cannot persistently respond effectively, then we should expect to see increasing levels of popular distrust, alienation, and even parliamentary coups or the ascension of populists. This can lead to a situation in which the violation of laws and fundamental democratic principles and political violence are tolerated by leaders or parties and not resisted by broad sectors of society or by intermediate institutions. This can prove fatal to democracy.

Discussion of impeachment under current conditions cannot be separated from debates about the parliamentary coup. The two are sometimes confused with each other. Impeachment is a heteroclite instrument because it has both a political character and a legal appearance. The decision is unmistakably political, but it employs a legal form and gains legitimacy through the use of legal procedures. However, its political nature is evident because it generates fierce party disputes that are accentuated by moments of polarization. In the Brazilian political system, which is marked by excessive party fragmentation and the difficulty of the elected executive leader to form a majority in Congress, the fragility of the coalitions, which are stitched together by tenuous agreements and political opportunism without a minimal common project, make impeachment more likely.

However, because impeachment is not used as an *ultima ratio* of the democratic system but rather as a common expediency of a party or political dispute, the meaning of impeachment changes. Rather than working as an instrument for safeguarding democracy from responsibility crimes perpetrated by the

24 ibid.
25 ibid.

president, it becomes an operation of politicized criminalization. In this way, it reveals itself to be a potential instrument for the downfall of liberal democracy. That is, the effort to respond to the dissatisfaction expressed by movements in civil society clears the path (via impeachment) for the ascension of populists who present themselves as the panacea for all evils.

In Brazil, a broad scholarly consensus affirms that the post-1988 Constitutional impeachment processes have been, in effect, parliamentary coups.[26] Former President Dilma Rousseff, for example, governed a broad ally base in Congress, with PT having the second largest participation in the Chamber of Deputies. On December 2, 2015, the same day that PT declared support for the process of revoking the term of the then-President of the Chamber, Eduardo Cunha, in the Ethics Committee, the former President of the Chamber announced the initiation of the impeachment process against President Dilma Rousseff.

There have been countless draft bills and proposed constitutional amendments in the Chamber of Deputies that aim to reduce the power of the President of the Chamber specifically in relation to impeachment. At least eight proposals have been presented since 2015 to this end. These have been debated for years but have not gained sufficient support to move forward. Indeed, they all remain as 'proposition[s] subject to the appreciation of the plenary,' whose handling is left to the President of the Chamber himself. In 2021, new parliamentary proposals aimed at reducing the power of the President of the Chamber were again pressed. These were intended to jumpstart the process on the countless severe complaints of responsibility crimes against President Jair Messias Bolsonaro. To date, these have not been considered by the President of the Chamber, and no explanation or justification has been offered for this lack of consideration.

In Brazil, 139 impeachment-related complaints have been filed against President Jair Messias Bolsonaro; this number has no precedent in Brazilian history.

In all, over 1,550 people and over 500 organizations signed these 139 requests.[27] The complaints document potentially illegal actions in many areas, including public health, policing, and administration. Specific allegations against Bolsonaro include illegalities in the acquisition of the vaccines and supplies for combating the pandemic; scientific denialism; attacks on democratic institutions; actions that have led to an increase in hate speech; a failure to safeguard the health of the population through the failure to address the COVID-19 pandemic; actions that escalated the public health crisis, such

26 See Wanderley Guilherme dos Santos, *A Democracia Impedida: O Brasil no século XXI* (Editora FGV 2017).

27 This is according to research carried out by Pública, which was founded in 2011 by female reporters and is the first non-profit investigative journalism agency in Brazil. See <https://apublica.org/impeachment-bolsonaro/page/2/> accessed 23 May 2021.

Table 7.2

President	*Political Party*	*Period in Office*	*Impeachment Requests*
Fernando Henrique Cardoso	Brazilian Social Democracy Party (PSDB)	1995–2002	24 requests
Luís Inácio Lula da Silva	Workers' Party (PT)	2003–2010	37 requests
Dilma Rousseff	Workers' Party (PT)	2011–2016	68 requests
Michel Temer	Brazilian Democratic Movement (PMDB)	2016–2018	31 requests
Jair Messias Bolsonaro	Social Liberal Party (PSL)/No Party	2018–2020	139 requests

as delays in vaccination, fake information on COVID-19, vaccines and early treatment, the purchase of medication without proven effectiveness, the lack of a federal vaccination plan, disrespect towards scientific guidelines, vaccine-related fraud, sabotage of state initiatives on COVID-19 and data blackouts on COVID-19 deaths; financial corruption; prevarication; crimes against the Union; crimes against political, individual and social rights; dismantling of institutional structures to fight corruption; attempts to interfere with the federal police; militarization of health and politics; attacks on the press; incitement of actions that could lead to a military dictatorship; abuse of power and the abuse of state institutions through self-dealing; tolerance of political militarism; systematic violation of human and fundamental rights, including freedoms of the press, speech and access to information; and threats to democracy. According to Deputy Ivan Valente (PSOL/SP), over 136 documents were forwarded to the President of the Chamber documenting an immense list of responsibility crimes committed by President Bolsonaro. According to Valente, none were accepted.

The Federal Senate on March 27, 2021 responded to the serious accusations levelled at the President by creating a Parliamentary Committee of Investigation called the 'Pandemic CPI.'[28] This had the aim of investigating the actions, inactions and omissions of the federal government in dealing with the COVID-19 pandemic in Brazil, particularly the worsening health crisis in Amazonas State, where there was a shortage of oxygen for hospitalized patients and possible irregularities in contracts, bid rigging, overbilling, diversion of public resources and signing contracts with shell companies to provide generic or fictitious services.

28 Federal Senate <https://www12.senado.leg.br/noticias/materias/2021/10/20/cpi-da-pandemia-principais-pontos-do-relatorio> accessed 30 May 2023.

The CPI's 1,180-page Final Report presented by Senator Renan Calheiros (MDB-AL) recommended the formal accusation of 66 people and two legal entities. These accusations are related to a more general pattern of denialism about the virus and the vaccines; suspicions of corruption in the negotiations for the purchase of vaccines by the Ministry of Health; and deaths caused by the use of treatments without scientific support. President Bolsonaro was the first person mentioned on the list and was accused of the following: prevarication; quackery;[29] epidemic with resulting death; violation of preventive health measures; irregular use of the public budget; incitement of crime; falsification of private documents; violations of social rights, human dignity, honor and decorum; and crimes against humanity.

Bills in Congress have proposed constitutional amendments to Law 1.079 of 1950 and have aimed to establish time limits for the processing of charges against the President of the Republic or a Minister of State by the President of the Chamber of Deputies. The accompanying explanatory memorandum explains that the constitution does not vest an absolute power in any single parliamentarian. It points out that there is no absolute prerogative to refrain from expressing an opinion on an impeachment request and then failing to offer reasons for not doing so. Such action, it explains, would be authoritarian, arbitrary and unconstitutional.[30]

There is no information as to whether these 139 complaints will ever even be considered. This inertia has arisen due to a gap in the law for the investigation of responsibility crimes omitted by the President or State Ministers. The gap concentrates absolute power in the hands of the President of the Chamber, allowing him to secure a zone of impunity in which the President of the Republic can violate the law or Constitution. The gap compromises the stability of the country and as recent history suggests, even puts lives at risk. The gap thus creates a situation at odds with the Rule of Law.

7.4 Conclusion

Impeachment in Brazil plays out over uncertain political terrain. Improvements to democratic systems cannot occur without trauma and institutional scars. The primacy of the political realm creates contingencies that undermine

29 The crime of quackery in Brazil occurs when someone, acting in bad faith, indicates or propagates by secret and infallible means a cure of any disease but in general, of incurable diseases or difficult treatments, through the distribution of pamphlets, publication of advertisements or any other form of promotion. The conduct is typified in Article 283 of the Penal Code. It is fraud and deception through which the person usually seeks to achieve some type of economic advantage (but this is not necessary for the characterization of the crime) by undermining public health. The penalty for the offense is imprisonment from three months to one year in addition to a fine. See <https://legis.senado.leg.br/comissoes/comissao?codcol=2441>.

30 Camara of Deputies, 'Law Project No 3134/21, Author Hildo Roca, MDB/MA' <www.camara.leg.br/proposicoesWeb/fichadetramitacao?idProposicao=2298512> accessed 30 May 2023.

the operation of law. Brazil is facing challenges that might call for impeachment in the future. Its difficulties and democratic crises also reflect global trends. An interpretation and analysis of impeachment that is decoupled from politics and limited to a normative concept will not advance the goals of the democratic system.

8 Impeachment in the United States

Frank O. Bowman, III

8.1 Introduction

Since the ratification of the United States Constitution in 1788, impeachment has served two functions at the national level – as a legislative check on the President, the nation's chief executive officer, and to remove grievously incompetent or misbehaving federal judges.[1] Impeachment has been employed against presidents only rarely and, as a rule, only against extraordinarily deviant characters or in periods of particular national turmoil. Impeachments of judges have been far more common and have customarily been matters of governmental housekeeping – evicting gravely deficient judicial officers otherwise unremovable because of their constitutional tenure of service 'during good behavior.' Both of these functions are inheritances of British constitutional history or at least of the American founders' interpretation of this history.

This chapter describes the origins and later application of the impeachment provisions of the American constitution. It first addresses the history of the constitution's provisions for the impeachment of presidents and other executive officers. It then turns to the history and practice of the more common but less controversial impeachments of federal judges. The chapter concludes with a brief survey of the five actual or near-impeachments of U.S. presidents and finally some reflections on the continued value of impeachment in America.

1 This chapter considers only impeachment of officers of the American federal government. Virtually every state in the American federal union has a constitutional process for impeaching executive branch officials. National Governors Association, 'Governors: Powers and Authorities' <www.nga.org/governors/powers-and-authority/> accessed 23 January 2023. At this writing, Oregon appears to be the sole exception, although efforts have been made to add impeachment to the state constitution. See, 'Oregon Impeachment of Elected State Executives Amendment' (*Ballotpedia*, 2018) <https://ballotpedia.org/Oregon_Impeachment_of_Elected_State_Executives_Amendment_(2018)>. However, state impeachments after 1788 are not discussed here.

DOI: 10.4324/9781003256007-10

8.2 Impeachment of Presidents and Other Executive Branch Officials

Impeachment was a British invention. In the 14th century, the English Parliament was slowly developing into a recognizable legislature representing the interests of the power centers in society other than the monarch – the hereditary aristocracy and landed gentry; the merchants, artisans, and traders of the towns; the clergy; and the men of law.[2] As British society became more complex and the requirements of managing a national government with international ambitions and obligations became correspondingly more onerous and expensive, the interests represented in Parliament acquired a variety of mechanisms for cabining or constraining royal authority, notably the ability to withhold 'supplies,' that is, money, to pay for the royal establishment and the monarch's particular projects. However, these modes of resistance were not always successful, particularly if the monarch was a forceful character determined to assert royal prerogative. Parliament needed other more potent tools to resist royal overreach.

With the monarchy being both hereditary and for life, Parliament could not *legally* remove a king or queen with whom it was at loggerheads. Removal was also impossible *in practice* absent assassination or war.[3] But Parliament realized that even kings can do nothing alone. They require others to act on their behalf. If the king's critical servants – his most active royal ministers and favorites – could be removed, then the king could be restrained without the dangerous inconvenience of regicide or rebellion. Largely with this object in mind, in 1376, Parliament invented impeachment as a procedurally novel mode of charging, convicting, punishing, and thus disempowering unpopular favorites of King Edward III.[4]

In the ensuing four centuries, impeachment was sometimes employed against lesser targets, including judges, relatively low-level officials, and even ordinary citizens. But its most notable uses, the ones from which the American founders drew particular lessons, were the cases brought by Parliament against senior servants of the Crown in order to constrain royal authority, modify royal policy, or alter the unwritten constitutional framework of the kingdom.

2 See generally Clyve Jones (ed), *A Short History of Parliament: England, Britain, the United Kingdom and Scotland* (Boydell & Brewer 2012) 16–28, 75–85; Frederic William Maitland, *The Constitutional History of England* (CUP 1908) 85–90, 165–90.

3 One might argue that the abdication of James II and ascension to the throne of King William III and Queen Mary by invitation of Parliament that culminated in the 'Glorious Revolution of 1688' involved an assertion of parliamentary authority over royal tenure, but although bloodshed was minimal, James II surrendered his crown only after William invaded England and James' supporters abandoned him. See Will Durant and Ariel Durant, *The Story of Civilization: The Age of Louis XIV* (Simon and Schuster 1963) 294–99; Peter Akroyd, *Rebellion: The History of England from James I to the Glorious Revolution* (Pan Macmillan 2014) 453–70.

4 Frank O. Bowman III, *High Crimes & Misdemeanors: A History of Impeachment for the Age of Trump* (CUP 2019) 26–27 (hereinafter Bowman, *High Crimes & Misdemeanors*).

Fairly quickly, at least in historical terms, impeachment assumed the procedural form we immediately recognize today. The lower house of the legislature (in England, the House of Commons) 'impeached' by voting to approve charges. A select group of members of the lower house became 'Managers' who presented the charges to the upper house (in England, the House of Lords) in a trial.[5]

As noted, impeachment from its beginnings was always a political tool. However, the British impeachment process also had aspects of what we would consider a criminal proceeding. It employed certain forms of a criminal prosecution, such as formal charges of specified misconduct, the presentation at a trial of evidence supporting those charges, and a verdict on whether the charges had been proven. Moreover, conviction could result in the same punishments available upon conviction of a serious crime. If the Lords convicted in an impeachment, the accused could not only be removed from office but also possibly imprisoned, banished, fined, disinherited, or executed (all of these punishments were imposed over the centuries).[6]

In addition to impeachment, Parliament also created other tools to deal with its political enemies or in some cases, those perceived to be enemies of both the monarch and a legislative majority. The most notable was the 'bill of attainder,' which allowed the legislature to pass a bill imposing on the person attainted the same sort of grievous punishments that could follow impeachment (or a conviction in the criminal courts) without the prerequisite of any trial proving specific wrongdoing.[7]

This condensed account of the British origins of impeachment and attainder is included here because the drafters of the American constitution were inheritors of Britain's constitutional tradition, familiar with its most notable incidents, and acutely conscious of what they took to be its strengths and weaknesses. They recognized both impeachment and attainders as historically important legislative instruments in the struggle with executive ambition but were also conscious of their potential for excess and injustice in individual cases.[8]

5 TFT Plucknett, 'The Impeachments of 1376' (1951) 1 *Transactions of the Royal Historical Society* 153, 164. See also, MV Clarke, *Fourteenth Century Studies* (OUP 1968) 243, 268–69.

6 See Bowman, *High Crimes & Misdemeanors* (n 4) 22–42 (describing British impeachments from 1376–1787 and the variety of punishments imposed upon conviction). For example, William Latimer and Richard Lyons, the subjects of the first impeachment in 1376 were both imprisoned after conviction, Laura Tompkins, 'The Good Parliament of 1376' (*The National Archives*, 29 April 2016) <https://blog.nationalarchives.gov.uk/good-parliament>. The Earl of Suffolk was also imprisoned following his impeachment and conviction in 1386 (Bowman, *High Crimes & Misdemeanors* (n 4) 27). During the reign of Richard II (1377–1399), persons convicted following impeachment were executed, banished, or imprisoned (ibid 28). Sir Francis Bacon and the earl of Middlesex were impeached, convicted, and imprisoned or impoverished in the reign of James I (1603–1625) (ibid 32–33).

7 ibid 29–30.

8 ibid 99–103 (describing the familiarity of the American constitutional framers with British history and practice regarding impeachment and attainder).

The American framers were also conscious of their own history as inhabitants of the former colonies of British North America. In the century before the American Revolution, the Maryland, Pennsylvania, and Massachusetts colonies employed impeachment against colonial officers, sometimes by virtue of specific grants of impeachment authority in colonial charters and sometimes by simple assumption on the part of colonial assemblies that impeachment was an implied power of legislatures. By 1776, impeachment had come to seem so natural a feature of Anglo-American constitutional practice that 10 of the 13 new states that declared independence from Great Britain that year wrote impeachment into their state constitutions. All ten made judges impeachable, and nine states made their chief executive officers amenable to impeachment.[9]

Given this history, it is unsurprising that impeachment in some form would make its way into the national constitution of the United States drafted in 1787 and ratified the following year. Even so, inclusion of impeachment was sharply debated at the Constitutional Convention, and the particular contours of the impeachment mechanism we now have were shaped not only by British, colonial, and early state practice, but more importantly, by the delegates' decisions about the fundamental architecture of the new government they were imagining.

When the Framers wrote the American constitution, they made a series of choices and assumptions. First, they chose a federal model of nationhood, a union of states under a national government of limited powers. Second, they created a national government of three separate but mutually checking branches: executive, legislative, and judicial. In this, they melded contemporary enthusiasm for the French philosopher Montesquieu's doctrine of separation of powers[10] with a web of provisions that made the effective operation of any one branch dependent on cooperation or restraint by the others. Third, they rejected monarchy of any kind but realized the need for an active executive, who they called the President. Fourth, they assumed the legislature would naturally be the strongest branch and that the presidency would be relatively weak. Fifth, they nonetheless recognized that their assumptions about the weakness of the presidency might prove wrong as the country evolved and, therefore, that a manifestly incompetent, corrupt, or autocratic president could pose a serious risk to the nation.

Finally, they were particularly afraid of a personality type they recognized from their study of classical antiquity – demagogues: men who craved power

9 ibid 50–79. In addition, Maryland had a special procedure akin to impeachment for removing sitting judges (ibid 79).

10 The American founding generation was heavily influenced by the writings of Charles Louis de Secondat, Baron de La Brède et de Montesquieu, particularly his conception of the separation of powers among executive, legislative, and judicial branches of government. See, e.g., Montesquieu, 'Book XI: On the Laws That Form Political Liberty in Its Relation with the Constitution' in Anne M Cohler and others (eds and trans) *Montesquieu: The Spirit of the Laws* (CUP 1989).

for its own sake and who gained and kept it by dishonest appeals to popular passions.[11] To protect the new Republic against demagogic, would-be-dictator presidents specifically and corrupt or dangerously incompetent presidents generally, the Framers erected three basic protections.

The first was presidential elections, which the Framers envisioned not only as screening out unworthy candidates from ever assuming office but also as evicting poorly performing incumbents. However, although there were advocates for selecting the president by national popular vote, the majority of the Framers did not trust the masses to elect presidents directly.[12] Some of them were generally suspicious of democracy in its most inclusive forms because they did not believe that ordinary, largely uneducated laborers, farmers, artisans, and backwoodsmen possessed either the knowledge or political acumen to pick leaders wisely. Others were concerned that in a country as large as the new United States and one lacking rapid, reliable means of disseminating news nationally, ordinary citizens would rarely be able to garner enough information about competing presidential candidates from around the continent to make an intelligent choice among them.

Moreover, the Framers were struggling to negotiate the terms of a closer national union among representatives of fractious states leery of surrendering too much authority to a redesigned national center. One result of this contentious negotiation was an effort to confer on the states and their governments an intermediary role in the selection of the national chief executive. Thus, the Framers decided that the president would be selected by a vote of electors chosen by the states, and the number for each state would match the number of its members of the House and Senate. This 'Electoral College' was thus designed to place the presidential choice in the hands of a body of sober public figures chosen by the leadership class in each state. Such a body, it was thought, would both reflect state interests better than might a general vote of the whole population of the nation and would naturally reject any obviously dangerous or unfit aspirant to the presidency. If the Electoral College failed to produce a majority for one candidate – as some framers anticipated would happen routinely – then the constitution cast the choice to the House of Representatives, yet another body of ostensibly sober statesmen who would surely reject any obvious misfit.[13]

11 See Frank O. Bowman III, 'What the Founders Would Have Done with Trump' (*Washington Monthly*, 18 January 2021) <https://washingtonmonthly.com/2021/01/18/what-the-founders-would-have-done-with-trump/> (discussing, *inter alia*, the American founding generation's focus on demagogues).

12 James Wilson was a particularly strong advocate of selecting the president by national popular vote. James Madison also favored the idea in principle, though he ultimately retreated in the face of the perceived political difficulties in implementing it (see Alexander Keyssar, *Why Do We Still Have the Electoral College?* (Harvard UP 2020) 19–21.

13 US Constitution, art II, §. 1, cl. 3. This basic design was retained in the Twelfth Amendment, which revised the mode of voting for President and Vice President. US Constitution, amend. XII. For the history of the so-called 'Electoral College', see Keyssar (n 12) 15–55.

Second, if a really bad apple should nonetheless become President, then the Framers undoubtedly thought that the most effective protections against misbehavior by such a person would be the institutional checks and balances on the office of the presidency written into the Constitution. Ambassadors, senior administration officials, and federal judges cannot be appointed without Senate approval.[14] War cannot be declared and treaties cannot be ratified without congressional action.[15] Indeed, in the American system, a president can, *in theory*, do very little without the acquiescence of Congress. Even after the 20th Century engorgement of the executive branch into a massive regulatory and administrative behemoth, Congress retains the plain constitutional authority to stop, start, or restrain virtually all of it and in this way, constrain the president. For example, just as was true during the centuries of struggle between Parliament and the British crown over 'supplies,' the American Congress can, in principle, simply refuse to fund any executive branch activity of which it disapproves.[16] The Framers assumed that members of Congress would, as a matter of course, act in their institutional self-interest and fight ferociously any effort by presidents to siphon away the institutional power of Congress and, thus, the members' personal power over government.

Finally, the Framers, although they were a hard-headed bunch with considerable hard-won skepticism about political man, also assumed an irreducible minimum of public virtue in at least the majority of those would serve in Congress. They assumed that solid majorities of Congress would turn against any president whose corruption, incompetence, or autocratic urges posed real danger to the national welfare. Accordingly, the Framers bestowed on Congress a final, break-the-glass-in-case-of-emergency tool for use if all else failed and a truly bad president assumed office and began acting in ways that genuinely threatened national security, the rule of law, or the constitutional order. This tool, inherited from Britain[17] and employed in early American practice, was impeachment.

It is essential to understand that, although the American Framers adopted important aspects of Great Britain's impeachment practice, they modified it significantly.

The Framers copied the British in leaving the impeachment process in the hands of the national legislature. They did not, as some suggested at the time,

14 US Constitution, art II, §. 2, cl 2.

15 US Constitution, art I, § 8, sec 11 (power to declare war); US Constitution, art II, §.2, cl 2 (treaty power).

16 See, e.g., US Constitution, art I, § 8, cl 1 (granting Congress the taxing power); US Constitution, art I, § 7, cl 1 (providing that all bills for raising revenue must originate in the House of Representatives).

17 Although the British origins of the Framers' design of American impeachment are obvious enough, Alexander Hamilton made the point explicit in *Federalist 65* by saying that impeachment in the British parliament was '[t]he model from which the idea of this institution has been borrowed'. Alexander Hamilton, 'The Federalist No 65' in Clinton Rossiter (ed), *The Federalist Papers* (New American Library 1961) 397.

confer the power to try impeachments on the judiciary, some hybrid body, or a group wholly distinct from the three constitutional branches.[18] Instead, just as was true in Great Britain, the lower house (the House of Representatives) impeaches.[19] The upper house (the Senate) conducts the impeachment trial.[20] The reasons for arriving at this division were more complicated than simple imitation of a familiar model. For example, during a significant portion of the Constitutional Convention, the preferred method of selecting the president was by a vote of Congress. Hence, early opponents of placing impeachment trials in the Senate worried that doing so would make this body too powerful by giving it a role in both hiring and firing the president. Critics of senatorial impeachment trials were mollified when the Convention rejected the idea of having presidents elected by Congress in favor of selection by the Electoral College.[21]

Accordingly, the Framers' assignment of the whole impeachment process to Congress was based not just on a mechanistic distribution of elements of constitutional power among branches. It seems clear that the Constitution's grant of the 'sole' power of impeachment to the House and the 'sole' power of trying impeachments to the Senate expresses the Framers' judgment that impeachment is a political remedy delegated to a political body empowered to use political judgment to address political dangers.[22]

The most significant American deviation from British historical practice was to make impeachment applicable to the Chief Executive, not just his or her subordinates.[23] Presidents, unlike kings, can be impeached. In Great Britain after American independence, impeachment became increasingly superfluous as the unwritten constitution evolved toward a system of parliamentary sovereignty in which the crown's role shrank and the majority legislative party controlled both the increasingly dominant House of Commons and the ministerial offices of the executive branch. Although it still cannot depose the monarch, a majority of the Commons can now sack either the prime minister or any subordinate government minister without employing the cumbrous

18 Bowman, *High Crimes & Misdemeanors* (n 4) 90–91. For Alexander Hamilton's discussion of proposals that the Supreme Court or some other body ought to have been the venue of impeachment trials, see Hamilton (n 17) 398–401.

19 US Constitution, art I, § 2, cl 5.

20 ibid § 3, cl 6.

21 Bowman, *High Crimes & Misdemeanors* (n 4) 87.

22 See, for example, Alexander Hamilton's famous observation that impeachable offenses 'are of a nature which may with peculiar propriety be denominated POLTICAL, as they relate chiefly to injuries done immediately to the society itself'. Hamilton, (n 17) 397 (capitalization in original).

23 Senior executive branch officers such as cabinet secretaries are 'civil officers' theoretically subject to impeachment. However, only one such person, Secretary of War William Belknap, has ever been impeached, and this was done, despite his hasty resignation before the House could act, primarily to embarrass his boss, President Ulysses S. Grant. See Bowman, *High Crimes & Misdemeanors* (n 4) 122–23 (describing the Belknap impeachment).

antique mechanism of impeachment. In the American system in which presidential tenure is unconnected to congressional majorities and is instead regulated by the inflexible calendar of quadrennial elections, impeachment remains the only mode of removing a misbehaving chief executive between elections.[24]

Although the Framers expanded the category of government officers subject to impeachment, they dramatically limited the possible consequences of conviction. Unlike in Britain where the House of Lords could impose all the penalties available under the criminal law on a subject convicted in an impeachment, in the United States, conviction by the Senate produces only mandatory removal from current office and a possible permanent ban on future office.[25]

Relatedly, at same time that the Framers embraced impeachment, their constitution barred *ex post facto* laws, by which a legislature could retrospectively criminalize conduct, and bills of attainder, with which Parliament sometimes condemned a subject to prison, impoverishment, or death by simply passing a bill.[26] As a result, an American official who is impeached and convicted can in theory be convicted of crimes and sentenced to criminal penalties for the behavior that led to his impeachment, but this can only happen after an entirely separate proceeding in a regular court of law.[27]

Regarding penalties, the British Parliament sometimes authorized the severe penalties of imprisonment, impoverishment, and even death for impeachment not simply because they were bloody-minded. Rather, the men that they impeached were often rich, powerful, landed, and in favor with the Crown and sometimes possessed their own military resources. Just throwing them out of office did not necessarily neuter them politically or eliminate the danger that they would return to power and strike, perhaps fatally, at those in Parliament who condemned them. Imprisonment, exile, impoverishment, or execution were sometimes considered necessary means of taking them off the political board.

24 A president found to be 'unable to discharge the powers and duties of his office' can be removed pursuant to the complex procedures of the Twenty-Fifth Amendment. US Constitution, amend. XXV. However, this amendment was designed to address the contingency of a president who dies or becomes physically or mentally disabled during his or her term of office. It probably does not apply to a president who can perform the duties of office but nonetheless abuses its powers. See Bowman, *High Crimes & Misdemeanors* (n 4) 286–95.

25 The constitution makes removal from office mandatory upon conviction by the Senate. US Constitution, art II, §. 4. It also provides for the possible additional penalty of future 'disqualification to hold and enjoy any Office of honor, Trust or Profit under the United States'. US Constitution, art I, § 3, cl 7. Since early in the 20th century, Senate precedent has provided for separate votes on conviction, with its automatic penalty of removal, and disqualification.

26 US Constitution, art I, § 9, cl 3.

27 ibid §3, cl 7 ('Judgement in Cases of Impeachment shall not extend further than to removal from Office, and disqualification to hold and enjoy any Office of honor, Trust or Profit under the United States: but the Party convicted shall nevertheless be liable and subject to Indictment, Trial, Judgement and Punishment, according to Law').

The American Framers wanted to eliminate this sort of savage legislative pre-emptive strike. But they were acutely aware of the possibility that some public figures – most importantly the demagogues that they feared so much – could pose a continuing danger unless barred from ever holding office again. Thus, it is critical to see the disqualification penalty not as a type of casual aside in the impeachment clauses of the United States Constitution but as a key to understanding what the Framers most feared and as a critical component of the remedy they crafted.

Finally, the Framers decided to include a definition of impeachable conduct in the constitutional text. Doing this may seem an obvious step, but Parliament had impeached people for centuries without ever expressly defining the parameters of impeachable behavior. After some debate, the Framers settled on impeachment for 'Treason, Bribery, or other high Crimes and Misdemeanors.'[28]

The commission of 'treason' seems an obvious ground for removing a government official. Nonetheless, the American Framers were troubled by the sometimes expansive uses of the term in the state trials of Great Britain and thus carefully constrained its reach by including in the Constitution itself a limiting definition: 'Treason against the United States shall consist only in levying War against them, or in adhering to their Enemies, giving them aid and comfort.'[29] 'Bribery' also seems an obvious ground for impeachment. It had long been a serious ordinary crime in Great Britain and America, and in impeachment cases, it arguably embraced varieties of official corruption beyond the strictly indictable sort.[30] As for 'high crimes and misdemeanors,' oceans of ink have been spilled in analyzing this enigmatic phrase.[31] Here, we emphasize only that the choice to adopt 'high crimes and misdemeanors' signaled three things, two about substance and one about process.

28 'The President, Vice President and all Civil Officers of the United States, shall be removed from Office on Impeachment for, and Conviction of, Treason, Bribery, or other high Crimes and Misdemeanors'. US Constitution, art II, § 4.

29 US Constitution, art II, § 3, cl 2.

30 Defining 'bribery' in impeachments turns out to be rather tricky. Doing so necessarily raises multiple questions: (1) should 'bribery' for impeachment purposes be limited to the indictable crime of bribery, or does it in impeachments signify a wider array of official corruption? (2) If 'bribery' in impeachments is limited to the technically criminal sort, then should the crime be defined as it was in common law in 1787, or should it instead be defined using modern criminal statutes? In 2019, the House of Representatives considered charging then-President Donald Trump with bribery for his machinations with Ukraine. Aaron Blake, 'Why "Bribery" Is the Democrats' New Impeachment Focus' *Washington Post* (14 November 2019) <www.washingtonpost.com/politics/2019/11/02/impeachable-offense-trump-may-have-committed-democrats-arent-really-talking-about/>. However, upon closer examination of the definitional complexities of doing so, the House opted for a charge of 'abuse of power' instead.

31 See Bowman, *High Crimes & Misdemeanors* (n 4) 99–111.

First, the phrase was drawn directly and consciously from British parliamentary practice. It was first used in an impeachment in 1386[32] and over time became a catch-all term of art for any sort of conduct Parliament found to be impeachable. For this reason, the phrase invites, perhaps even commands, Congress to consider its pre-1787 historical usage and meaning when trying to decide the proper constitutional scope of American impeachment.

Second, any study of British and American impeachments before the ratification of the constitution in 1788 reveals that 'high crimes and misdemeanors' embraced a wide array of public misconduct, some of it technically criminal, but much of it not criminal at all. The unifying feature of the charges in the great British impeachments was that they were political in the sense of offending dangerously against the constitutional order or at least Parliament's view of a proper constitutional order.[33]

Third, at least in the great cases, Parliament's decisions about what constituted a 'high crime or misdemeanor' meriting impeachment were driven by political judgments *coupled with* a constant reexamination of its precedents that amounted to a kind of common law constitutional judging. By giving the impeachment job to Congress, a political entity, and defining its scope by reference to the old malleable Parliamentary phrase 'high crimes and misdemeanors,' the American Framers conferred on Congress the same mantle taken up by Parliament in its great impeachments – that of defender of the constitutional order – and imposed on Congress an obligation to consider constitutional text, its own developing body of precedents, contemporary circumstances, and the facts of particular cases to develop its own common law of impeachment.

The final point about the American constitution's impeachment clauses is that the Framers also inserted a towering barrier to action – the requirement of a two-thirds majority for conviction in the Senate.[34] This, too, was a deviation not only from British practice, in which a mere majority of the House of Lords sufficed to convict, but also from the constitutional structures of all but two of the new American states.[35] It seems fair to conclude that the adoption of this super-majority requirement flowed from the interplay of two considerations: first, the obvious concern that removing a president, in particular, is a matter

32 ibid 103; TB Howell, *A Complete Collection of State Trials and Proceedings for High Treason and Other Crimes and Misdemeanors: From the Earliest Period to the Year 1783, with Notes and Other Illustrations* (TC Hansard for Longman, Hurst, Rees, Orme, and Brown 1816) 89, 91.

33 Bowman, *High Crimes & Misdemeanors* (n 4) 45–49.

34 US Constitution, art I, § 3, cl 6 ('And no Person shall be convicted without the Concurrence of two thirds of the Members [senators] present').

35 As of 1787, of the ten states with impeachment provisions in their constitutions, only New York required a supermajority for conviction. In addition, Maryland's special provision for dismissed judges allowed the governor to remove a judge upon an 'address' of the General Assembly joined by two-thirds of its members. Bowman, *High Crimes & Misdemeanors* (n 4) 75–79.

of great consequence to the nation and ought not be undertaken on a legislative whim, and second, a perhaps unjustified faith that, in a case of truly grave presidential wrongdoing, considerations of factional loyalty or even personal political advantage would be easily subordinated to the national good. We consider presently whether this faith was misplaced.

8.3 Impeachments as Precedents

Before considering the limited universe of actual American impeachments, we should note that 'precedent' in impeachment cases does not operate as it does (at least theoretically) in the courts to create rules (or at least powerful presumptions) constraining future decisions. No impeachment decision by one Congress can bind a later one. Still, impeachment history is important because, in practice, Congress has treated impeachment precedents as having at least persuasive power in arguments about how it should proceed in the case before it.

8.4 Judicial Impeachment

Impeachments of federal judges have been far more common, and less controversial, than those of presidents. Just as was true of the presidency, the Framers' decisions about the selection and removal of judges were shaped by old constitutional debates in Great Britain and its North American colonies.

A consistent thread in the story of Britain's evolution from royal absolutism to constitutional monarchy was the struggle over the source of law and the power to interpret and administer it. Monarchs are naturally apt to favor the view that the will of the king is the source of the law and that the role of judges is to divine and enforce this will. In early modern England, judges and parliamentarians increasingly resisted the idea that law is an emanation of royal prerogative, arguing instead that law is properly created by legislative enactments and judicial decisions.

A struggle for control over the law necessarily implies a struggle over the appointment and removal of judges. Whatever the theoretical source of law, judges who serve at the king's pleasure could be corrupted or at least bent to the will of the monarch who could summarily remove them. Accordingly, one front in the fight over the 'rule of law' was judicial independence. The issue was particularly salient in the era of the Stuart kings (1603–1714). When William and Mary assumed the throne after the enforced abdication of James II, the 1701 Act of Settlement upon which their reign was conditioned provided that henceforth, royal judges would be appointed *quamdiu se bene gesserint* – during good behavior.[36] They could be removed but only by a majority vote in both houses of parliament.[37]

36 12 and 13 Will. III, c. 2.
37 Maitland (n 2) 313.

However, across the Atlantic, the judges in the colonies who administered the laws passed by Parliament did not enjoy the protection of appointment during good behavior granted to royal judges sitting in England. Instead, colonial judges were appointed by the crown and served at pleasure. Hence, they could be removed by the crown or its appointed colonial officials for issuing rulings thought unduly favorable to colonial persons or interests. This was, understandably, a sore point among the colonists.

Another method of controlling or at least influencing judicial action is through pay. For a long time, even royal judges in the colonies were paid by local appropriations from colonial legislatures. Thus, colonists retained a degree of crude, but effective, influence over their judges. In 1773, Parliament decided to remove this leverage by dictating that henceforward royal judges in the colonies would be paid salaries by the crown, not by colonial legislatures. This seemingly commonsense provision (commonsense at least from the perspective of Parliament and colonial administrators in England) excited virulent opposition in America: so much so that the only Massachusetts judge who agreed to accept the royal salary, Peter Oliver, was impeached by the Massachusetts colonial assembly for the 'high crime and misdemeanor' of taking what the assembly characterized as a 'bribe.'[38]

Oliver's impeachment was unsuccessful in the sense that no trial of the case was ever convened by the colonial governor and council. But threats of mob violence and the refusal of grand jurors to sit in any court presided over by Oliver effectively drove him from office and eventually from North America once the American revolution got into full swing in 1775.[39] Indeed, his case and the controversy over judicial tenure and salaries became the basis for one of the allegations of tyranny by King George III enumerated in the American Declaration of Independence.[40]

The new Americans' passion for judicial independence manifested itself in the otherwise sparse provisions of Article III of the U.S Constitution, which created the judicial branch of government. Section 1 decrees that 'The Judges, both of the supreme and inferior Courts, shall hold their Offices during good Behaviour, and shall, at stated Times, receive for their Services, a Compensation, which shall not be diminished during their Continuance in Office.'[41]

In short, the American Framers sought to secure the independence of the new federal judiciary both by adopting the English practice of appointment during 'good behavior' and shielding judges from any legislative arm-twisting

38 Bowman, *High Crimes & Misdemeanors* (n 4) 61–64.

39 ibid 63–64.

40 The Declaration charged that King George 'has made Judges dependent on his Will alone, for the tenure of their offices, and the amount and payment of their salaries'. Declaration of Independence (US 1776).

41 US Constitution, art III, § 1.

through salary manipulation.[42] But having written the inherited 'good behavior' provision into the federal constitution, the Framers were obliged to provide some mechanism for removing a federal judge whose behavior was disqualifyingly bad. Curiously, they did not specify in the constitutional text that impeachment would be this mechanism. Rather, they said in Article II (governing the executive branch) that 'all civil officers' would be subject to impeachment and removal for 'Treason, Bribery, or other high Crimes and Misdemeanors.'[43] Since then, everyone has simply assumed that, for impeachment purposes at least, judges are 'civil officers' subject to impeachment.

In the early years of the Republic when everything was new and untested, some thought that impeachment might be employed against judges whose rulings displeased either the executive or dominant factions in Congress. This proposition was tested in the 1804 case of Supreme Court Justice Samuel Chase. Chase was impeached by the House of Representatives nominally for misconduct while serving as a trial judge in several politically sensitive cases and for making politically charged statements during his opening charge to a federal grand jury. However, the generally conceded motive behind the impeachment was that Chase came to the bench as a committed partisan of the Federalist party, then in opposition to President Thomas Jefferson and a majority of congress, and that he remained indelicately outspoken while on the bench.

Chase was acquitted in the Senate, a verdict that has ever since been interpreted as standing for the proposition that judges ought not be impeached for their political leanings. However, the fact that Chase was impeached in the first place served as a warning to federal judges to maintain rigorous political neutrality once on the bench; this warning is manifested in both rules and norms that have, in general, produced an admirable standard of political impartiality among federal jurists.[44]

In addition to Chase, thirteen judges have been impeached. Ten were convicted and removed (or resigned to forestall removal). Three other judges resigned to avoid impeachment or trial.[45] None of these cases were observably partisan-political in character, with perhaps the exception of District Judge West Humphreys, who was impeached at the outset of the Civil War when he abandoned his federal judgeship for a similar post under the seceding

42 A number of the original thirteen states in their first constitutions provided for judicial appointments during good behavior. These included Massachusetts, New York, Delaware, Virginia, North Carolina, and South Carolina. The Constitutions of the Several Independent States of America (1783). However, no American state retains this practice. Robert Dudley, 'Turnover and Tenure on State High Courts: Does Method of Selection Make a Difference' (1997) 19 *The Justice System Journal* 1.

43 US Constitution, art II, § 4.

44 For discussions of the Chase impeachment, see Bowman, *High Crimes & Misdemeanors* (n 4) 128–36; William H Rehnquist, *Grand Inquests: The Historic Impeachments of Justice Samuel Chase and President Andrew* Johnson (William Morrow 1992) 15–134.

45 Bowman, *High Crimes & Misdemeanors* (n 4) 316–41.

Confederacy.[46] In any case, Humphreys' offense may best be characterized as outright treason. Otherwise, American judicial impeachments have targeted corrupt, or in a few cases, egregiously incompetent jurists. It has generally worked well as a mode of dealing with renegade occupants of the federal bench.

8.5 Presidential Impeachments and Near-Impeachments

Only three American presidents have been impeached: Andrew Johnson (1868), Bill Clinton (1998), and Donald Trump (who has the discreditable distinction of being impeached twice, in 2019 and again in 2021). None of the three was convicted. Richard Nixon was nearly impeached in 1974. The House Judiciary Committee approved articles of impeachment against him, but he resigned before a vote on these articles could be taken by the full House of Representatives.

Impeachment of Andrew Johnson: The first impeachment of an American president, that of Andrew Johnson, exemplified the proposition that great impeachments of great officers of state tend to coincide with eras of national turmoil, in Johnson's case the aftermath of the American Civil War (1861–1865).[47]

Johnson was an accidental president. Abraham Lincoln chose Johnson as his vice presidential running mate during his reelection campaign of 1864. The Civil War was still raging, and its outcome was very much in doubt. Lincoln's Republican Party backers wanted a running mate who could appeal to northern Democrats who nonetheless supported fighting the war until the southern rebellion was crushed and the nation reunited. Johnson fit the bill as a staunchly pro-Union Democrat – a former governor, then senator, then military governor of the contested border state of Tennessee. The Lincoln-Johnson ticket won, and so did the Union armies. But in April 1865, Lincoln was assassinated, making Johnson the president.

Johnson's elevation was deeply unfortunate. The nation not only lost perhaps its greatest president at a moment when Lincoln's unique combination of empathy, eloquence, and steely determination was most needed, but the office fell instead to a man singularly unsuited to that moment. Johnson was resolutely determined to defeat the Confederacy, but once this was accomplished, he was equally determined that the United States should revert as nearly as possible to its pre-war condition. Johnson was himself a former slave owner, and his attitude toward the new class of black freeman created by the Thirteenth Amendment abolishing slavery was immovably hostile. In his view, although chattel slavery was properly abolished, the basic social hierarchy of the South and the basic racial hierarchy of the country as a

46 ibid 320.
47 For a description of the Johnson impeachment, see ibid 146–79.

whole – with whites indisputably superior and black Americans a permanent underclass – should remain fundamentally unaltered.

In short, Johnson's view of post-war 'reconstruction' was largely limited to the physical rebuilding of the war-ravaged southern states. So long as the ex-Confederate leadership class swore allegiance to the United States and made pro forma gestures such as ratifying the Thirteenth Amendment, repudiating Confederate debt, and repealing secession ordinances, southern states should be readmitted to the Union and their representatives readmitted to Congress.[48] No fundamental reordering of southern political institutions would be required. And elevation of freedmen into anything approximating political or social equality need not even be contemplated.

Johnson's vision of post-Civil War America was starkly at odds with that of Congress; both houses were held by Republican supermajorities that were determined that the south would be reconstructed not only physically but also politically and along the lines that would improve (at least somewhat) the economic, social, and political lot of freed blacks while disempowering the people and institutions that had produced the late war. The particulars of the conflict between Johnson and congressional Republicans over their incompatible visions of the nation's future are beyond the scope of this chapter. Suffice it to say that Congress repeatedly passed reconstruction and civil rights legislation over Johnson's veto and that he nonetheless sought to employ his executive authority to undercut the effects of such legislation. The battle came to a head when Johnson fired Secretary of War William Stanton in violation of the Tenure of Office Act. The firing was, by the terms of the Act, a 'high misdemeanor' (a term undoubtedly chosen by the statute's drafters with impeachment in mind) and a calculated defiance of Congress's efforts to shape post-War reconstruction policy.

The House impeached Johnson within days of Stanton's dismissal, but after a lengthy trial, the Senate acquitted the president. The guilty votes, although a majority, fell one short of the required two-thirds. The accepted wisdom that developed in the 1870s as Reconstruction failed and yielded to nearly a century of black repression under the so-called 'Jim Crow' regime of anti-black laws and customs was that Johnson's impeachment was a mistake, an example of legislative overreach on a matter of legitimate constitutional disagreement between President and Congress. This view persisted well into the 20th century.[49] However, in the last several decades it has been increasingly questioned.[50]

48 ibid 156.

49 Figures as otherwise disparate as John F Kennedy and William H Rehnquist wrote expressing disapproval of the Johnson impeachment. Compare John F Kennedy, *Profiles in Courage* (Harper & Brothers 1956) 107 with Rehnquist (n 44) 248, 261.

50 See, e.g., Brenda Wineapple, *The Impeachers: The Trial of Andrew Johnson and the Dream of a Just Nation* (Random House 2019); Robert S Levine, *The Failed Promise: Reconstruction, Frederick Douglas, and the Impeachment of Andrew Johnson* (WW Norton & Company 2021).

One can fairly argue either that the Tenure of Office Act that Johnson defied was an unconstitutional infringement on the presidential appointment power or that Secretary of War Stanton did not, for technical reasons, fall within the scope of the Act.[51] However, the eleventh article charged Johnson with violation of his constitutional obligation 'to take care that the laws be faithfully executed' by attempting to thwart the execution of the reconstruction acts.[52] Of this, he was certainly guilty. As I have written elsewhere,

> In the impeachment clauses, the constitution confers on Congress the power, in the last extremity, to choose its fundamental vision of America over the idiosyncratic view entertained by the individual person occupying the presidency. Johnson's conduct merited impeachment because he abused his executive power in the service of a vision that was morally wrong (even if he and many of his contemporaries could not yet see it to be so) and, entirely predictably, endangered the long-term tranquility of the constitutional order. Congress could, entirely constitutionally, have removed him and in doing so charted a different course for the Republic.[53]

The Near-Impeachment and Resignation of Richard Nixon: Over a century would pass before the next presidential impeachment crisis.[54] Richard Nixon was first elected to the presidency in 1968. He was in many ways a gifted and even far-sighted president. However, his character was fatally marred by a dark streak of paranoia and insecurity. Before and after his reelection campaign of 1972, he sponsored or tolerated a plethora of abuses of government power designed to undercut his perceived enemies and promote his own retention in the White House. One such escapade was the June 1972 burglary by operatives connected to the Nixon White House of the headquarters of the Democratic National Committee in the Watergate apartment complex in Washington, D.C. The burglars' apprehension triggered a cascading series of investigations, revelations, and scandals.

The press, a Justice Department special prosecutor, a specially appointed Senate Watergate Committee, and ultimately the House Judiciary Committee all launched investigations. Their collective conclusion was that Nixon had indeed abused the powers of his office in myriad ways. As for the Watergate burglary, although Nixon did not know of it in advance, he was informed almost immediately afterwards and actively conspired to obstruct investigations of the case. In July 1974, the House Judiciary Committee approved three articles of impeachment, one charging obstruction of the Watergate

51 Bowman, *High Crimes & Misdemeanors* (n 4) 167–68.

52 Cong Globe Supp, 40th Cong 2d Session, The Trial of Andrew Johnson (1868) 3–5.

53 Bowman, *High Crimes & Misdemeanors* (n 4) 179.

54 For a more detailed description of the Watergate scandals and the impeachment of Richard Nixon, see ibid 180–209.

investigation, a second charging an array of abuses of power, and a third alleging obstruction of the congressional impeachment investigation by defying House subpoenas.[55]

The question famously raised by Senator Howard Baker of what the president knew about the skullduggery of his aides and associates and when he knew it was settled definitively when the Supreme Court ordered disclosure of tapes of White House meetings involving the President.[56] Once Nixon complied with the court's order and the nation listened to the tapes, his guilt could no longer be denied, even by his staunchest supporters. On August 6, 1974, senior Republican members of Congress went to the White House and told Nixon that he would surely be impeached by the full House and convicted by the Senate. Nixon resigned three days later.[57]

The Nixon case established a number of important points. First, it demonstrated that, in the modern era, effective investigation of serious presidential wrongdoing is most likely through a combination of efforts by the press, Justice Department prosecutors operating with significant insulation from presidential pressure, and Congress itself.

Second, it has generally been conceded that Nixon's conduct was properly impeachable. Hence, the articles of impeachment adopted by the House Judiciary Committee are commonly treated as precedent for the proposition that 'high crimes and misdemeanors' embrace obstruction of justice, criminal and non-criminal abuses of power, and obstruction of a congressional impeachment investigation.

Third, although Nixon was never formally impeached or tried, his forced resignation should be considered a success of the impeachment mechanism. Without the likelihood of impeachment and removal, Nixon would surely have remained in office to the end of his term.

Fourth, and critically, the success of the Senate and House investigations and the political pressure that induced Nixon's resignation depended upon two conditions that are now largely extinct: a media environment in which the public looked to the press as relatively neutral arbiters of fact and a political culture in which members of the president's own party were willing to participate in serious inquiries into possible presidential wrongdoing and once the facts were clear, were also willing to condemn such wrongdoing.

The impeachment of Bill Clinton: In 1998, Democrat Bill Clinton became the second president to be formally impeached.[58] His case could not have been more

55 HR Rep No 93–1305, at 1–3 (Judiciary Committee Report on the Impeachment of Richard M Nixon, President of the United States).

56 *United States v Nixon*, 418 US 683 (1974). The Supreme Court handed down its decision on 24 July 1974, three days before the House Judiciary Committee began voting on articles of impeachment. Nixon released the tapes shortly after the Committee votes, but their contents destroyed any hope that Nixon might survive an impeachment contest. Bowman, *High Crimes & Misdemeanors* (n 4) 189–90.

57 ibid 189–90.

58 For a more detailed description of the impeachment of Bill Clinton, see ibid 210–34.

different than either Johnson or Nixon. The effort to remove Johnson was, at bottom, a fight about the social and constitutional future of the nation. Nixon grievously abused the powers of his office both to maintain himself in office and to injure his perceived political enemies. Bill Clinton had a grubby, adulterous sexual dalliance with a White House intern. He lied about it in a civil deposition and later before a grand jury called by an Independent Counsel with established ties to Clinton's political opponents who, despite a years-long investigation, had failed to find evidence of any other prosecutable wrongdoing by the president. The House of Representatives, then controlled by Republicans, impeached Clinton for perjury and obstruction of justice. The Senate, also in Republican control, acquitted him, with neither article receiving even a majority of votes.

Such lessons as there are in the Clinton impeachment debacle flow from the relative triviality of the charges. Clinton's behavior was execrable, technically criminal, and arguably within the outer boundaries of 'high crimes and misdemeanors.' But his offense was at its core a personal moral failing, did not involve performance of his official duties, and was not the kind of conduct for which presidential impeachment would previously have been contemplated.

The Clinton impeachment is generally thought to have established the propositions that not all criminal conduct is necessarily a proper subject of impeachment and that impeachment is generally reserved for misbehavior involving abuse of official power or demonstrating profound unfitness for office. Of course, it may well be that had the Clinton case arisen today, evolved standards regarding sexual relations in the workplace might have cast the president's conduct in a far more negative light and resulted in his conviction. The definition of impeachable conduct is inescapably tied to the mores of the period in which a particular impeachment occurs.

In addition, the Clinton case highlights the dangers of overly exuberant legal reforms. In the famous 'Saturday Night Massacre,' President Nixon fired the first of the special prosecutors assigned to investigate Watergate, thus graphically demonstrating the vulnerability of ordinary prosecutors on the track of presidential wrongdoing.[59] Following Nixon's downfall, Congress responded by creating the Office of Independent Counsel. Independent Counsels were appointed by a panel of federal judges, were effectively free to pursue their investigations without routine oversight from the Attorney General, were removable by the Attorney General only for cause, and could appeal removal to the judiciary.[60] It is clear that Clinton would never have been impeached had it not been for the obsessive determination of Ken Starr, who served as Independent Counsel during Clinton's term, to pursue the president on any available charge. Starr's excesses largely contributed to the abolition of the Office of Independent Counsel and the reversion of presidential investigations to the Justice Department.

59 ibid 187–88.
60 ibid 203–4.

In any event, the fact that Clinton was impeached in the first place was an early harbinger of a continuing trend in American political culture away from a norm of relative seriousness and dedication to accomplishing useful ends to one of increasingly belligerent partisanship and decreasing commitment to conducting the public's business.

The Two Impeachments of Donald Trump: The presidency of Donald Trump tested all the guardrails erected by the framers of America's constitution against the ascension of a manifestly unfit person to the presidency and his subsequent misuse of the powers of that office.

Trump was plainly unqualified to be president. He was unique among American presidents in having no prior governmental or military experience. He entered the 2016 campaign with a decades-long track record of business failure, personal improprieties, and ceaseless prevarication. Nonetheless, he bested a large field of Republican primary opponents and prevailed in the general election against Democrat Hillary Clinton by winning the electoral vote (while losing the popular vote by nearly 3 million ballots).[61]

Space precludes a full accounting of Trump's manifold failings as a president and his numerous offenses against constitutional propriety while in office. He was first impeached in 2019 because he employed the powers of the presidency to extort personal political favors from Ukraine, an ally in desperate need of U.S. help to resist the expansionist ambitions of Russia.[62] He was impeached again in 2021 because he schemed for months to nullify the results of a properly conducted election that he lost in both the popular and electoral vote count in order remain in office as an unelected autocrat.[63] His conduct in both cases plainly fit within any reasonable historical construction of the phrase 'high crimes and misdemeanors.'[64]

It is no exaggeration to say that Donald Trump was the demagogue the Framers feared, the figure against whom they imagined that the Electoral College would in some measure protect and for whom they inserted impeachment into the constitution, thus arming Congress with the power both to remove a manifestly dangerous president and to disqualify him from ever again holding national office. Yet the Senate acquitted Trump twice. Even though one senatorial

61 Kenneth T Walsh, 'Clinton Wins Popular Vote by Nearly 3 Million Ballots' *US News & World Report* (21 December 2016) <www.usnews.com/news/ken-walshs-washington/articles/2016-12-21/hillary-clinton-wins-popular-vote-by-nearly-3-million-ballots>.

62 House Resolution 755, 116th Cong (18 December 2019).

63 House Resolution 24, 117th Cong, 1st Session (article of impeachment); 167 Cong Rec H191 (13 January 2021) (recording House approval of article of impeachment).

64 See Frank O. Bowman III, 'Trump's Extortion of Ukraine Is an Impeachable Abuse of Power' *Just Security* (3 October 2019) <www.justsecurity.org/66407/trumps-extortion-of-ukraine-is-an-impeachable-abuse-of-power/>; Frank O. Bowman III, 'The Constitutional Case for Impeaching Donald Trump (Again)' *Just Security* (9 January 2021) <www.justsecurity.org/74127/the-constitutional-case-for-impeaching-donald-trump-again/>.

member of Trump's party voted to convict in the first case[65] and seven did so in the second,[66] the two-thirds rule saved Trump, just as it had Andrew Johnson.

One can argue that the constitutional system's other constraints on presidential misconduct and illegitimate ambition nonetheless prevailed. Although Trump served out his term, Congress did, after all, confirm the election of Joe Biden as Trump's successor (albeit only after months of national turmoil and a deadly riot). Moreover, Trump did, although unwillingly, vacate the White House in January 2021 (albeit harboring a fierce determination to return).

Moreover, it may be that, at least in Trump's first case, impeachment served a useful purpose as a vehicle for investigating, exposing, and publicizing the particulars of the president's misconduct. But this is fairly small beer compared to impeachment's primary objectives of removing a dangerous chief executive and disqualifying him from future office. On this score, impeachment failed. This requires some explanation. It also provokes some troubling reflections on the state of American constitutionalism.

8.6 Reflections on the Trump Acquittals and the Utility of Impeachment

The essential lesson of the foregoing survey is that impeachment, like any other constitutional mechanism, can function properly only when the political system of which it is a part is healthy. Impeachment of an American president, in particular, will be supremely difficult in any era because the political stakes of such a step are so high. Nonetheless, as the Nixon case proved, if Congress is functional and the political ecosystem in which it moves is reasonably sound, even majorities of the president's own party can be moved to support impeachment of a sufficiently deviant chief executive.

The acquittals of Donald Trump, a man whose official misdeeds unquestionably equaled or exceeded those of Richard Nixon, cannot be explained by comparative analysis of the two men's conduct. The key lies in comparing the political cultures of the two eras. As turbulent as the political life of the 1970s undoubtedly was, Congress remained a functional legislative body, and the two parties from which its members were elected were reasonably cohesive but not ideologically homogenous coalitions; both parties were committed to the inevitable give-and-take, compromise, and coalition formation necessary to accomplish policy goals in a pluralistic democracy.

These conditions no longer prevail. Both parties have devolved in the direction of becoming ideological monocultures that are increasingly visceral, increasingly emotional, and increasingly tribal. This tendency is further

65 166 Cong Rec No 24 S897 (5 February 2020) (Statement of Senator Mitt Romney explaining his vote to convict Donald Trump in his first impeachment).
66 167 Cong Rec No 28 S733 (February 2013).

advanced among Republicans, but Democrats have been by no means immune. The tribalization of the parties is reflected in a Congress characterized by policy rigidity and reflexive intransigence. Simultaneously and somewhat paradoxically, changes in the way that congressmen and senators fund their campaigns are fostering an increasing obsession among individual members with self-promotion rather than collective accomplishment. These and other developments have produced a broken Congress, one that can barely perform the basic functions of governance, let alone agree on a genuinely wrenching decision such as a presidential impeachment.

The information and media revolution of the past quarter-century has also largely contributed to this distressing political decay. In Nixon's 1970s, and even into Clinton's 1990s, the media was composed of a discrete set of national, regional, and local entities, most of which at least aspired to reasonably robust quality control standards. In the current era, sources of information have proliferated to a dizzying extent and in the process, have become decreasingly professional and increasingly partisan. The result is that, although the voting public of the Nixon and Clinton eras arrived at political judgments based on reasonably broadly shared understandings about the relevant facts, today's American voters are apt to form political views, and even to experience reality, from the inside of separate, non-intersecting, heavily partisan, informational silos.

Given the two-thirds threshold for conviction, a successful presidential impeachment will almost invariably require convincing a significant number of senators to join with their normal political opponents to condemn the leader of their own party. This will always be excruciatingly difficult since senators of the president's party need the support of the same voters who put the presidential defendant in office to keep their own positions. Today, the committed political bases upon whom members of congress largely depend are daily immersed in an information torrent, most of which will reinforce allegiance to the party's leader and disparage any allegations against him. Under these conditions, the Senate's inability to assemble a two-thirds majority even for obvious cases of impeachable misbehavior not only becomes understandable but also seems likely to remain an insuperable barrier to a robust use of impeachment.

In other words, the flaws in the contemporary American political system that made the election of a man like Trump possible in the first place have also, at least for the present, disabled impeachment as a dispositive remedy for presidential misconduct. Judicial impeachments will continue to perform their quotidian function. As for presidents (or other executive branch officials), we may well see new impeachments, but until America's politics are restored to health, these will be, at best, honest investigations of suspected presidential misbehavior and at worst, mere exercises in performative political propaganda.

Part III

Periphery

9 Impeachment in Iceland

Ragnhildur Helgadóttir

9.1 Introduction

Impeachment is very rare in Iceland. It is neither an important nor ordinary part of constitutional or public life. It does exist on the books and has been utilized both in the case of a judge and of a Cabinet minister but never in the case of the president. It is likely that the very existence of such measures – even if seldom used – has a deterring effect. However, the status of the institution of impeachment is very different for the different groups of officials largely due to a recent painful experience with the impeachment of a Cabinet minister that left the impeachment of ministers a very debated and criticized phenomenon.

The legal basis for all impeachment rules is found in the Constitution, no. 44/1933. Regarding the President, the relevant article is no. 11.[1] As is stated in the article itself, Althingi needs to adopt a resolution calling for a plebiscite to remove the President. If the voters do not agree with Althingi, then Althingi will be dissolved, and new elections will be called. This has never come to pass. It would take serious deviations from the usual political processes for it to occur, as the President of Iceland exercises his power for the most part through ministers and cannot be held accountable for executive acts, according to this same article's paragraph 1. This constitutional safety valve is not discussed further here, but there is no reason to doubt that it is a living part of the constitutional order.

Concerning judges, the Constitution's Article 61 states that 'judges . . . cannot be discharged from office except by a judicial decision, nor may they be transferred to another office against their will, except in the event of re-organization of the judiciary.' Such a judicial decision has been made only once – in 1989

1 The article reads in pertinent part as follows: 'The President may be removed from office before his term expires if approved by a majority in a plebiscite called pursuant to a resolution adopted by three-fourths of the Members of Althingi. This plebiscite shall be held within two months from the date of adoption by Althingi of the resolution. The President shall not perform his duties from the time the resolution is adopted by Althingi until the results of the plebiscite are known. If the resolution by Althingi is not approved in the plebiscite, Althingi shall be immediately dissolved and new elections called'.

DOI: 10.4324/9781003256007-12

when a judge was determined to have lost his fitness for office for having bought inordinate amounts of tax-free alcohol.[2] In contrast to the situation regarding cabinet ministers (discussed later), the removal of judges through a judicial decision remains the only way to remove judges except on their own initiative or when they reach the legally mandated retirement age.[3] However, the rules on the impeachment of judges are not discussed further here.

The rules on impeachment that have received the most attention in the last 10–20 years relate to cabinet ministers. These are the focus of the discussion that follows.

9.2 The Constitutional and Legal Framework of the Impeachment of Cabinet Ministers

The Constitution's Article 14 states that 'Ministers are accountable for all executive acts. The accountability of the Ministers is established by law. Althingi may impeach Ministers on account of their official acts. The Court of Impeachment has competence in such cases.' This article – or an article with a similar effect – has been in force since the ministry was founded in Reykjavík in 1904.[4] This chapter focuses on this type of impeachment.

Since 1904, Iceland has, however, had a parliamentary system of government.[5] This means that the cabinet ministers sit at the discretion of Parliament and that they are legally required to resign if Parliament passes a no-confidence vote. In practice, this means that the government coalition has to have the majority (or neutrality) of Parliament in order to be able to govern. Motions of no confidence against individual ministers are generally not put forth, but they could indeed be a less cumbersome way of ousting a cabinet minister who has committed (or is suspected of) an impeachable offense.[6]

Cabinet ministers' responsibility is therefore (like in Denmark and Norway) viewed as being of two different natures: should they make mistakes or commit illegal acts, they can be required to shoulder political responsibility (which can encompass everything from criticism in public debate to formal criticism in Parliament and a motion of no confidence).[7] By contrast, the impeachment process is a criminal process by nature and can result in a conviction of illegal activity and penalties of losing office, fines or a prison sentence.

2 H 1989.1627.

3 See Articles 49–52 of Act 50/2016 on the Judiciary.

4 *Eftirlit Alþingis með framkvæmdarvaldinu, skýrsla starfshóps sem forsætisnefnd fól að fara yfir núgildandi lagareglur um eftirlit þingsins með framkvæmdarvaldinu og leggja mat á hvort breytinga sé þörf* (2009) hereinafter *Eftirlit*, 40 <www.althingi.is/pdf/eftirlit_althingis_med_framkvaemdavaldinu_skyrsla.pdf>.

5 This is variously based on constitutional custom or Article 2 of the Constitution.

6 R Helgadóttir, HS Kjartansson and Þ Magnússon (eds), *Þingræði á Íslandi – samtíð og saga* (Forlagið 2011) 199–202, 188.

7 ibid.

It is clear from Article 14 of the Constitution, cited previously, that the impeachment of cabinet ministers takes place under special rules: it is Parliament that impeaches and a special court – the Court of Impeachment – that adjudicates. No further details are provided in the Constitution.

The Constitution also provides a guarantee of fair trial, based on Article 6 of the European Convention on Human Rights (Article 70), and stipulates (in Article 59) that the organization of the judiciary can only be established by law. Article 61 is intended (along with Article 70 on a fair trial) to guarantee the independence of judges and notes inter alia that 'In the performance of their official duties, judges shall be guided solely by the law.'

These provisions on the judiciary and judicial process in general (Articles 59, 61 and 70), Article 14 on impeachment in particular and the principle of parliamentarism inherent in Article 2 are thus the main constitutional provisions that touch on the impeachment of cabinet ministers.

The process and conditions for the impeachment of cabinet ministers are further set out in the Court of Impeachment Act no 3/1964 and the Ministerial Accountability Act no 4/1964.

The Act on Ministerial Accountability reiterates that 'Ministers are accountable for all executive acts as provided for in the Constitution and this Act' and notes that 'the provisions of the General Penal Code on breaches in a public office also apply to ministers as appropriate.' Materially, it provides (in Article 2) that

> A minister may be held accountable as further provided for in this Act, for any measures or negligence of measures for which he is guilty if the matter is of such a nature that he has either intentionally or through gross negligence breached the Constitution of the Republic, other national law or in other respects foreseeably jeopardized the State's interests.

In Article 8, it is provided that a minister is accountable according to the Act if he a) oversteps the limits of his office by issuing instructions on matters that must be determined by the other branches of government under the Constitution, b) does not seek the consent of Parliament when obliged to do so under the Constitution, c) otherwise breaches the Constitution or d) does anything to reduce the freedom or sovereignty of the country.[8]

8 The description of violations a-d in the article itself is as follows '(a) if he personally issues instructions or sees to the issuance of instructions by the President on matters which, according to the Constitution, can only be determined by law or fall under the auspices of the courts;
(b) if he does not seek the consent of Parliament when obligated to do so according to the Constitution;
(c) if he by other means personally implements, orders the implementation of or allows the implementation of any such measure that contravenes the Constitution of the Republic,

Article 9 criminalizes breaches of laws other than the Constitution, either by recommending to the President that something be done that contravenes statutes or by otherwise violating them by any act or omission. The final substantive penal provision in the Act, Article 10, states the following:

Finally, a minister will be deemed guilty according to this Act:

(a) if he severely misuses his power, although he may not have directly exceeded his executive boundaries;
(b) if he carries out something or causes something to be carried out that foreseeably jeopardizes the State's fortunes although its execution is not specifically forbidden by law, as well as if he fails to carry out something that could avert such danger or causes such execution to fail.

These are thus the main penal provisions, and they criminalize breaches of the constitution and separation of powers (Article 8), violations of other laws (Article 9), misuse of power and jeopardizing the state's fortunes (Article 10). As mentioned earlier, offenses against the Act are subject to a loss of office, fines or up to 2 years of imprisonment, and breaches of the General Penal Code can add to these penalties (Article 11).

As mandated by the Constitution, a special Court adjudicates such cases. The Act on the Impeachment Court provides in Article 2 that the Court of Impeachment shall be composed of the following 15 judges:

(a) The five judges of the Supreme Court who have held seats on the court the longest, the judge presiding in the District Court of Reykjavík and a professor of constitutional law at the University of Iceland. The Supreme Court appoints alternate judges for the Supreme Court judges from amongst the group of other Supreme Court judges and thereafter, teachers of law at the university, Supreme Court attorneys or District Court judges who meet the conditions for being appointed as judges of the Supreme Court. The alternate judge for the judge presiding at the District Court of Reykjavík is the District Court judge in Reykjavík who has held his office the longest. The Law Faculty of the university elects the alternate for the professor of constitutional law.
(b) 8 persons as elected by the United Parliament in proportional voting for a term of 6 years. Parallel to and by the same method, an equal number of alternate members shall be elected. Judges who hold a seat on the Court

---

or omits implementing any such measure as ordered therein or causes an implementation to not take place;

(d) if he causes any decision or implementation that could reduce the freedom or sovereignty of the country'.

> of Impeachment when Parliament has decided to impeach a minister and their alternates shall complete the case procedure even if their term has ended.

The Act is very brief on the impeachment process and the process before the Court. Article 13 states that

> A decision by Parliament to impeach a minister shall be initiated by means of a parliamentary resolution in the United Parliament, and the parliamentary resolution shall precisely state the impeachment items as the prosecution of the case shall be based upon them. Parliament furthermore elects a person to represent the prosecution on its behalf, as well as an alternate if the first-mentioned is unable to attend. The United Parliament also elects in proportional voting a parliamentary committee comprising five persons to monitor the case and to assist the Parliament prosecutor.

Article 12 states that the procedure shall be public. Other articles set out the procedure (quite briefly) including the appointment and role of the Counsel for the Defense, the convening of the Court and the time that shall be given to the accused and his counsel to prepare the defense. The rules of procedure for the judicial proceedings are established in the articles that follow and in the rules on possible searches and seizures and evidence. The Act's final section, Article 51, states that 'If not otherwise stipulated in this Act, the provisions of the Criminal Procedure Act . . . shall apply as appropriate regarding the procedure of a case by the Court of Impeachment.'

There are also some specific rules of procedure particularly for the Court of Impeachment, but they date for the most part from 1963 and are hence vaguer than most current rules on criminal procedure. The catch-all provision of Article 51 modernizes the procedure to a certain degree. It entered into force on January 1, 2009 – at the same time as the sections that had the most characteristics of civil procedure were removed from the Act[9] – but it does not apply unless there is a gap in the Act itself. However, there are many gaps in the Act.

9.3 Criticism and Concerns Before 2010

Already before 2010, there had been considerable criticism and concerns about this system of ministerial responsibility. When new provisions were introduced in 1963, they greatly modernized the laws on this matter (the earlier laws were from 1904), but by the late 2000s, serious concerns had emerged. Some of them were remedied by the changes of 2009 (mentioned previously) that

9 *Eftirlit* (n 4) 235.

moved the impeachment procedure away from civil procedure towards criminal procedure and added the catch-all provision in Article 51.

Nonetheless, there were concerns.[10] Already in 1999, a public committee argued that the Act on Ministerial Responsibility should be revised, firstly, because it viewed Article 10 (misuse of power and jeopardizing the fortunes of the state) as too vague to criminalize conduct and more or less moot after certain changes to Icelandic administrative law.[11] Secondly, the lack of provisions concerning the investigation of possible criminal conduct by ministers was forcefully criticized. This was based on the fact that a premise for the efficacity and relevance of impeachment was that Parliament could determine based on established facts whether to impeach.[12] Thirdly, the lack of a provision making ministers responsible for not giving information or giving false information to Parliament was discussed repeatedly.[13] Fourthly, there were doubts about the wisdom of impeachment in a parliamentary system, the necessity of a special Court of Impeachment and special legislation on ministerial responsibility. Finally, many argued that the independence and impartiality of the Court of Impeachment were doubtful since the prosecuting party (Parliament) elects the majority of the members of the court.[14]

In 2008, Parliament tasked a committee of experts (including this author) with writing a report on parliamentary oversight of the executive branch. Impeachment of cabinet ministers was obviously part of this mandate.[15] The expert committee summed its conclusions in the following points. Firstly, not only which standing parliamentary committee should address and follow up on suspicions of illegal actions by a minister but also the rules on the procedure to follow in the investigation needed to be clear.[16] Secondly, in referring to its suggestions on amending the rules related to the investigative process in Parliament and the procedure before investigating committees, the expert committee stated that it did not – at that point – see any particular reason to abandon the system of having a special Court of Impeachment. That is, the committee felt that the rules relating to the investigative stage and the mechanisms that Parliament could use had to be amended and that only once this was done would it be appropriate to consider moving away from having a special court adjudicate criminal cases against cabinet ministers. It reiterated

10 For an overview of the criticism before 2009, see *Eftirlit* (n 4) 236–41.

11 'Starfsskilyrði stjórnvalda' (*Forsætisráðuneytið*, 1999) 140 <https://www.stjornarradid.is/media/forsaetisraduneyti-media/media/Skyrslur/F0033_Oll_skor.pdf>.

12 E Tómasson, 'Íslensk lög um ráðherraábyrgð og samanburður á þeim og dönskum lögum um sama efni' [2005] *Rannsóknir í félagsvísindum VI: lagadeild* 117, 141; *Eftirlit* (n 4) 238.

13 ibid 139–41.

14 *Eftirlit* (n 4) 240.

15 Even though the work started well ahead of the banking collapse of 2008, the work took place (to a great extent) in the shadow of these events and the legal questions regarding inter alia impeachment that followed.

16 *Eftirlit* (n 4) 254–55. The second and third points concerned possible constitutional amendments concerning parliamentarism and votes of non-confidence and the committee's conclusions concerning the political responsibility of ministers, motions of censure etc. ibid 255.

the rationale behind having a special law on ministerial responsibility and a special court for such matters.[17] The expert committee recommended revising the composition of the Impeachment Court and the rules of procedure. It similarly concluded that there was no reason to abolish the special law on ministerial responsibility, even though it is not constitutionally mandated like the special court. But it suggested revising its substantive provisions to clarify both them and the relationship between the Act on ministerial responsibility and the general penal code.[18]

Later that same year, Andri Árnason, a member of the expert committee, wrote an article on ministerial responsibility and mentioned that criticism had fallen into 4 categories: vague substantive criminal provisions; the lack of provisions concerning the duty to provide Parliament with correct and sufficient information; the Act's

> not providing for any investigation into putative criminal acts committed by ministers – comparable to a police investigation in criminal cases. This may be in breach of the criminal law principle that matters must be investigated fully before anyone is prosecuted;[19]

and that ministers' responsibility for the actions of their subordinates was unclear.

9.4 The Case of the Financial Collapse

The only impeachment of a cabinet minister that occurred in Iceland rose out of the Financial Collapse of 2008.

9.4.1 The Facts Leading Up to the Case

Three of Iceland's largest banks collapsed in September and October 2008. They had to be taken over by the state and wound up. These banks had a combined size of approximately 10 times the national gross domestic product (GDP). The ensuing crisis had immediate and drastic effects; unemployment doubled from 2008 to 2010, and the percentage of households having problems with housing payments and having financial problems rose sharply. The International Monetary Fund (IMF) stated that the Iceland Krona (ISK) depreciated by more than 70% in the month of October 2008 and that the equity market in Iceland fell by over 80%.[20] The European Free Trade Association (EFTA) Surveillance Authority described the situation in the first weeks after the banking

17 ibid 255–56.

18 ibid 256.

19 A Árnason, 'Ráðherraábyrgð' [2009] *Tímarit lögfræðinga* 3.h 59, árg 239, 259.

20 EFTA Surveillance Authority Decision of 15 December 2010 to close seven cases against Iceland commenced following the receipt of complaints against Iceland in the field of capital

collapse (because it had to assess the legality of certain decisions of the Icelandic authorities) and noted that external payment systems were severely disrupted, hampering the repatriation of proceeds from export. The real economy was threatened with severe disruptions, and according to the IMF, the crisis was 'of huge proportions'. The IMF added in a later publication (Nov. 2008) that the Icelandic economy was in the midst of a banking crisis of extraordinary proportions expected to lead to a deep recession, a sharp rise in the fiscal deficit and a dramatic increase in public sector debt. In November 2008, there was a serious and immediate risk to the economy considering its dependence on imports.[21] The EFTA Surveillance Authority later found this risk to have been such that it would have permitted the use of emergency derogations from, for example, the principles of European Economic Area (EEA) law.[22]

In December 2008, a Special Investigative Commission (SIC) was established by Althingi. In January 2009, the government resigned after mass protests in Reykjavík and elsewhere. A minority government led the country until elections that spring. In April 2010, the SIC released a black report that cited the following as contributing factors to the crash: lack of supervision by the state; 'abnormally easy' access to credit for bank owners; banks that went 'beyond normal practices' in supporting their owners; weak equity and cross-financing of banks and, therefore, a dangerously high concentrated risk; a budget policy by the state that increased the imbalance; some 'highly reproachable' decisions; lack of activity by the government when things started to go bad and unfocused activity and general lethargy later; incorrect prioritization by supervising bodies; and plain negligence by a number of public officials, including three cabinet ministers.

A Parliamentary Review Committee (PRC) was set up to address the issues set out in the SIC's report.[23] On its suggestion, Althingi passed a resolution stating among other things that the report was a heavy judgment of government, politicians, the administration and especially their mode of work and lack of formal procedures; that those running and owning financial institutions were mainly responsible for the collapse; that supervisory authorities had disappointed; and that important legislation, including the Constitution and laws regarding government ministries, parliamentary and administrative procedures, should be revised.[24] The PRC, however, was not only to make recommendations to Parliament based on the SIC's report but also to adopt a position on ministerial accountability and assess whether there were grounds for impeachment proceedings.

movements and financial services (Dec No 501/10/COL) (2010) [22] <www.eftasurv.int/media/decisions/571071.pdf>.

21 ibid [30].

22 ibid [87] (citing Case E-10/04 Piazza [2005] EFTA Ct Rep 76 [42]; Case E-3l98 Rainford-Towning 1998 1EFTA Ct. Rep 205 [42].

23 This author was one of the experts assisting the PRC.

24 Þingsályktun um viðbrögð Alþingis við skýrslu rannsóknarnefndar Alþingis 2010. Þskj. 1537, 138. löggj.þing <www.althingi.is/altext/138/s/1537.html> accessed 29 December 2022.

Because a lack of provisions on the investigation and preparation of such cases had been a keystone of the criticism levied against the impeachment system, the process leading to the impeachment in 2012 is described in some detail here. The European Court of Human Rights, when adjudicating an Article 6 claim by the former Prime Minister in 2017,[25] described this process as follows:

> 14. The PRC examined the SIC report, held 54 meetings and multiple informal working meetings. It received several expert opinions on ministerial liability from professors as well as the former state prosecutor and Ms Sigríður J. Friðjónsdóttir, then deputy state prosecutor. . .. The PRC further collected original documents relating to the ministers' duties which were mentioned in the SIC report, inter alia letters, notes, minutes, emails from the Government Offices and the Central Bank of Iceland and minutes from meetings of the consultative group on financial stability and contingency planning. On 18 May 2010 the PRC sent letters to 16 individuals, including the applicant, who had held office as ministers during the period covered by the SIC report, asking them to submit comments and information regarding the report's conclusions. The committee received replies from 14 individuals, including the applicant who submitted his reply by letter of 7 June 2010.
>
> On 11 September 2010 the PRC submitted a proposal for a parliamentary resolution to commence impeachment proceedings against four cabinet members: the three mentioned above (including the applicant) and Ms Ingibjörg Sólrún Gísladóttir, who was the former Minister of Foreign Affairs and the head of the Social Democratic Alliance. The proposal listed six points of alleged negligent behaviour, corresponding to the counts in the eventual indictment issued against the applicant (see paragraph 23 below). The applicant was considered to have been negligent in all six respects, whereas the other three ministers were deemed responsible only in respect of five of the points (excluding what was to become count 1.3 in the applicant's indictment). The proposal was presented as a whole but Parliament decided to vote on each former minister separately. In a resolution of 28 September 2010, by 33 votes to 30, it approved the PRC's proposal to commence impeachment proceedings against the applicant. With similar small majorities, the votes concerning the other former ministers led to the conclusion that they should not be indicted.
>
> . . .
>
> 17. On 12 October 2010 Parliament appointed Ms Friðjónsdóttir to prosecute the case on its behalf. It also appointed a parliamentary committee to assist her and to monitor the case.[26]

25 *Haarde v Iceland*, App No 66847/12 (ECHR, 23 November 2017).
26 ibid [13]–[16].

Substantively, the indictment was firstly, for a breach of section 10.b. of the Act on Ministerial Responsibility by 'having shown serious neglect of his duties as Prime Minister in the face of major danger looming over Icelandic financial institutions and the State Treasury' and not having taken certain measures to avert the risk and secondly,

> [f]or having, [in February – October 2008] failed to implement what is directed in Article 17 of the Constitution of the Republic on the duty to hold ministerial meetings on important government matters. During this period there was little discussion at ministerial meetings of the imminent danger; there was no formal discussion of it at ministerial meetings, and nothing was recorded about these matters at the meetings. There was nevertheless specific reason to do so . . . The Prime Minister did not initiate a formal ministerial meeting on the situation nor did he provide the Government with a separate report on the problem of the banks or its possible effect on the Icelandic State.[27]

This was deemed to fall under Article 8c of the Act on Ministerial Responsibility as described earlier (a violation of provisions of the Constitution).

9.4.2 The Case in the Impeachment Court

The Impeachment Court was therefore constituted according to the Act. While the proceedings were ongoing, questionable and criticized aspects of the system were debated, both in public and before the Court:

> The applicant challenged the impartiality and independence of the eight judges appointed by Parliament, mainly on the ground that Parliament had extended their term. . . . By its ruling on 10 June 2011, the Court of Impeachment rejected the petition, finding that the legislator had pursued a legitimate aim and that the measure had been proportionate vis-à-vis the applicant.
>
> On 5 September 2011 the applicant lodged a request to have the case dismissed, relying, among other things, on Article 6 of the European Convention on Human Rights. He claimed that the investigation in the case had been manifestly defective, inter alia as the investigation conducted by the SIC had not been criminal in nature, the SIC having no such mandate, and as no real investigative measures had been undertaken by the PRC or the prosecutor. He had not been questioned or invited to respond to the accusations, neither before Parliament's resolution nor before the prosecutor issued her indictment. He also challenged the impartiality of the prosecutor due to her involvement in Parliament's

27 This quote was taken from *Haarde v Iceland*.

> preparation of the decision to indict him, during which she had been repeatedly consulted by the PRC and had allegedly expressed her opinion on his potential responsibility under the Ministerial Accountability Act. The applicant further maintained that his chance of preparing a proper defence was compromised as the counts of the indictment were undefined and only described in general terms his alleged criminal conduct and the criminal provisions under which that conduct was subsumed were unclear and discretionary. Also the rules governing the impeachment proceedings and the penal provisions of the Ministerial Accountability Act and other invoked legislation were, in his view, so unclear that due process could not be ensured. Finally, he asserted that the decision by Parliament to bring proceedings against him alone had been taken on purely arbitrary and political grounds and thus did not treat him equally with other ministers originally subject to the investigation in the case.[28]

The Court of Impeachment upheld the motion for dismissal in so far as it concerned counts 1.1 and 1.2 of the indictment but rejected the remainder of the request:

> It noted that Parliament held the authority to bring cases against a minister and that its review committee, the PRC, had obtained, inter alia, various evidence referred to in the SIC report and written statements from several ministers, including the applicant, before finding that there was enough evidence for a parliamentary resolution to commence proceedings against the applicant.[29]

The judgment of the Court of Impeachment was handed down in April 2012. The former Prime Minister was unanimously acquitted of counts 1.3, 1.4 and 1.5 of the indictment, and the court found that it had not been established that 'the actions which he was accused of having neglected could or would have averted the danger facing the Icelandic financial institutions and the State treasury or reduced it considerably.'[30]

The majority of the nine judges (five professional judges and four lay judges) found the former Prime Minister guilty with respect to count 2 of the indictment. They found that

> major danger had been threatening the Icelandic commercial banks and the State Treasury as early as February 2008 and that the applicant had to have been aware of that danger [but] that this matter had not been

28 *Haarde v Iceland* [26]–[27].
29 ibid [29].
30 ibid [32].

> discussed during the meetings, apart from the last four meetings, on 30 September and on 3, 5 and 6 October.

It therefore concluded that the applicant had failed to comply with the duty set out in Article 17 of the Constitution to hold ministerial meetings on 'important government matters.'[31]

During the entire proceedings before the Court of Impeachment, the voices arguing that this was an unacceptable political trial or at the very least, the criminalizing of normal if unsuccessful political activity were legion. It seems reasonable to state that Althingi's vote on the indictment (which split according to party lines with some coalition partners protecting their own) created a deep sense of unease among politicians and the general public, and the laws on ministerial responsibility and the Court of Impeachment were generally thought to be flawed.[32]

9.4.3 The Case Before the ECHR

In October 2012, former Prime Minister (PM) Geir Haarde filed a complaint with the European Court of Human Rights (ECtHR), alleging a violation of Article 6 of the European Convention on Human Rights, which guarantees a fair trial. The Court issued a substantive judgment on November 23, 2017. It held unanimously that there had been no violation of Article 6 and with one dissenting judge, that there had been no violation of Article 7 of the Convention.

Before the Court, the former PM argued that

> his rights to be presumed innocent, to be informed in detail of the nature and cause of the accusations against him and to have adequate time and facilities for the preparation of his defence had been breached and that the Court of Impeachment's appointment of defence counsel for him had been made too late.[33]

Regarding the pre-trial phase of the proceedings, the Court noted that the Member States had taken different approaches to questions concerning the criminal liability of members of government concerning inter alia

> the manner in which the relevant penal provisions are structured and formulated, the applicable sanctions as well as the jurisdictional and

31 ibid.

32 Examples of contemporary media discussion are <www.visir.is/g/2011706169983> (2011) <www.mbl.is/greinasafn/grein/1419347/?item_num=8&searchid=10b44128941c37417ee4af99d5b7dfcdbab80bc3> (2012) and later, <www.midjan.is/althingi-akaerur-og-landsdomur/> (2017).

33 *Haarde v Iceland* [59].

> procedural arrangements for dealing with investigations and trials in cases concerning alleged or suspected criminal conduct by members of government.[34]

The Court noted

> that these issues involve important and sensitive questions about how to strike an appropriate balance between political accountability and criminal liability for persons holding and exercising the highest executive offices in each state, and that the solutions adopted are linked with complex matters of checks and balances in each constitutional order.[35]

The key paragraphs of the Court's judgment on the pre-trial phase read as follows:

> The Court is mindful of the fact that while the purpose of the relevant constitutional, legislative and procedural frameworks on this subject should be to seek a balance between political accountability and criminal liability, and to avoid both the risk of impunity and the risk of ill-founded recourse to criminal proceedings, there may be risks of abuse or dysfunctionalities involved, which must be avoided. The Court is aware of the importance of ensuring that criminal proceedings are not misused for the purpose of harming political opponents or as instruments in political conflict. The Court must therefore bear in mind, when reviewing and assessing the circumstances of each case and the conduct of the proceedings complained of under Article 6, the need to ensure that the necessary standards of fairness are upheld regardless of the special features of those proceedings.
>
> 86. Turning to the present case, the Court notes that the impeachment proceedings were based on a decision of Parliament. As the authority to prosecute a former cabinet member, under the Icelandic Constitution and the relevant legislation, rests with Parliament, the matter may, to some extent, involve considerations of a political nature. In this respect, the Court observes that, in a comparative perspective, parliamentary involvement is a feature which is not uncommon in the context of decisions as to whether criminal proceedings should be brought against a member of government for acts undertaken in the exercise of ministerial functions. The Court does not consider that this fact in itself is sufficient to raise an issue under Article 6. It must be borne in mind that the charges brought by Parliament are examined and adjudicated upon by a court of law. Furthermore, in the present case, the conduct of

34 ibid [84].
35 ibid.

> which the applicant eventually was found guilty was his failure to hold ministerial meetings on 'important government matters', as required by Article 17 of the Constitution in conjunction with section 8(c) of the Ministerial Accountability Act. The negligence imputed to him thus concerned an objective legal obligation. Parliament's indictment contained examples of the failure to hold ministerial meetings and further evidence on this issue was later presented to the Court of Impeachment. Moreover, having regard to what has been mentioned above regarding the PRC's collection of evidence, there is no indication that Parliament's decision to bring charges against the applicant was based on insufficient information.[36]

Regarding the procedural aspects of the case in particular, the Court noted that it was

> clear that the few provisions of the Court of Impeachment Act operated as lex specialis and therefore took precedence over the general rules in the Criminal Procedure Act, which regulated all issues not covered by the first-mentioned act. The Court cannot find any indication that the procedural rules applicable in the case were applied incorrectly or generally to the disadvantage of the applicant.[37]

Regarding the independence and impartiality of the Court of Impeachment, the Court found, given the Act on the Court of Impeachment, that there was 'nothing to show that the Court of Impeachment failed to meet the requirements of independence and impartiality under Article 6 § 1.'[38] The same was true of the proceedings before the Court of Impeachment and its judgment; the Court found 'that neither the trial before the Court of Impeachment nor the reasoning given in its judgment breached the guarantees set out in Article 6.'[39]

Accordingly, the Court found that the trial that had taken place before the Court of Impeachment had been fair. However, there were no celebrations, either in Parliament or elsewhere in the Icelandic government, when the ECtHR judgment was published.[40] Geir Haarde, the applicant, was by then, Iceland's Ambassador to the United States. Reaction from the public and news organizations was similarly ill at ease. The debate was not on whether he had been wrongly convicted but instead, whether impeachment – with criminal sanctions to follow – had been justified for such an offense and given the

36 ibid [85]–[86].
37 ibid [92].
38 ibid [108].
39 ibid [119].
40 This is clear from the media coverage at the time; see, for example, <www.ruv.is/frett/geir-tapar-malinu-fyrir-mannrettindadomstolnum> (2017) and <www.visir.is/g/2017412792d> (2017).

procedure in Parliament. The Acts in question were widely criticized. Indeed, the national radio made an overview of criticisms of the legislation (much of which was described earlier) and amendment attempts, all of which had come to nothing.[41] In the years since, there have been repeated motions in Althingi (never yet adopted) for an apology to be issued to former Prime Minister Geir Haarde. Individual politicians who took part in the vote in 2010 have apologized.[42]

9.5 Criticism and Attempts at Changes

The criticism of the current system that was expressed prior to 2009 was described previously. It was also mentioned earlier how many, if not most, observers viewed Althingi's decision-making in the financial collapse case as the worst-case scenario as a vindication of all doubts about a system of impeachment that leaves the decision to impeach – indeed prosecute – in the hands of politicians.

In 2011, Althingi amended its Standing orders (þingskapalög) and passed a new act on investigative committees to strengthen parliamentary control of the executive, including investigative functions.[43] The legal situation is thus not the same as it was 2009 or when the impeachment of Geir Haarde was decided.

In early 2017, the President of Iceland stated in an interview that in his view, it was a mistake to use old legal provisions to prosecute a minister – that it had divided rather than united the country after the financial crash.[44] He also stated the opinion, as many others have done, that there is no need for a special Court of Impeachment. Instead, the regular courts (which regularly find cabinet ministers in breach of various laws, both procedural and, for example, concerning equal protection) should handle such cases. The then-Chair of the Committee on Constitutional Matters and Control of Government Actions agreed and so have many commentators.[45]

Less academic attention has been given to impeachment since 2017 (except for students' final theses, there have been few new writings on the topic).

However, there has been work on amendments, both constitutional and statutory, and this author has worked on a number of these. Firstly, preparatory work for such revisions has taken place as part of the revision of the Constitution, which has been in progress since 2009. In January 2020, the government, led by the Prime Minister and Justice Minister, requested

41 BÞ Guðmundsson, *Deilt á lögin í áratugi en ekkert gert* (RÚV 22 November 2017).

42 Magnús Orri Schram, 'Facebook Post' <www.facebook.com/magnus.schram/posts/10227847532554513> accessed 29 December 2022. See also News Item (2022) <www.ruv.is/frett/2022/09/19/bidst-afsokunar-a-sinum-hlut-i-landsdomsmalinu>.

43 Acts 84/2011 and 68/2011.

44 ÁB Ingvarsdóttir, *Feigðarflan að nýta ákvæði um landsdóm* (RÚV 6 March 2017).

45 E Þorsteinsson, *Vill að Alþingi endurskoði Landsdóm* (RÚV 6 March 2017).

suggestions for revisions of the Act on the Court of Impeachment and the Act on Ministerial Responsibility. These suggestions put forth inter alia possible scenarios should the Court of Impeachment be abandoned (by constitutional amendment), but none of the attempts to revise the system have found favour with either the people or politicians.

I argue that the financial collapse case was very difficult on Althingi, all involved and the system (keeping in mind that Iceland is a tiny society and that political circles are even more so) that there is now a general acknowledgment of the fact that the system must be improved, but no one wants to debate the financial collapse case or the pros and cons of the current system. This is borne out by the lack of academic writing, published reports and motions on the subject and the repeated failures of attempts at improvement (be they great or small) to get off the ground.

9.6 What Lies Ahead?

The impeachment of a president has never taken place in Iceland, but the constitutional provision thereon is mostly seen as a reasonable safety valve.[46] There has been one case where a judge (of the Supreme Court) was impeached, and the provisions concerning the impeachment of judges have been updated regularly and seem to be a living part of the law and the judicial system.

By far the most complicated part of impeachment in Iceland involves cabinet ministers. As in other parliamentary states, Parliament can request the cabinet (or individual members thereof) to step down. That has happened only very rarely, mostly because individual members are generally asked to step down by their party leadership before it comes to that.[47] Similarly, governments who lose the majority resign without waiting for motions of no confidence.

The real issue related to impeachment in contemporary Icelandic law and politics is therefore the adjudication of criminal charges against cabinet ministers – which can lead to them losing their jobs or to criminal sanctions. The Constitution requires a special court to adjudicate such claims that Parliament decides to impeach. There is only one example of such a process – the financial crisis case. Despite the ECtHR finding (as it had before in the Ninn-Hansen case in Chapter 10) that the former Prime Minister's trial before the Court of Impeachment had fulfilled the fair trial requirements of Article 6 of the Convention, the case, its prequel, the decision-making and aftermath left a bitter taste in the mouth of many politicians and much of the public.

Right now, it can be argued that there is total paralysis regarding impeachment. Any putative crimes committed by cabinet ministers would have to be

46 See, e.g., 'Skýrsla stjórnlaganefndar – síðara bindi' (*Stjórnlaganefnd*, 2011) 41–44 <https://www.stjornarradid.is/media/forsaetisraduneyti-media/media/stjornarskra/Skyrsla_stjornlaganefndar_fyrra_bindi.pdf>.

47 See, e.g., GH Kristinsson, 'Ráðherraáhætta' [2006] *Rannsóknir í félagsvísindum VII: félagsvísindadeild* 661.

immensely grave for Althingi to impeach under the same rules. Repeated starts on the work of changing the institution have not come to pass, irrespective of whether the changes proposed are major or minor.

What is then the current status? There are certainly provisions on the books that provide for the impeachment of ministers; we know that the ECtHR finds no fault with these and that their existence probably has an impact on the behaviour of politicians. However, we also know that despite the Court of Impeachment having fulfilled the legal and constitutional minimum requirements for a fair trial, there is immense political fear of utilizing impeachment again. I would say that unless there is a case that is by Icelandic standards thankfully unrealistic and unimaginable (e.g., torture of political opponents), the impeachment of Cabinet ministers is *de facto* a dead letter.

This is – from a legal perspective – not a bad conclusion. The regular courts have shown that they can fully well be trusted to adjudicate cases to which a cabinet minister is part and whose conclusion is a serious slap on the wrist of said minister. Some provisions on criminal responsibility of cabinet ministers are needed, however (if only the substantive penal rules), and it would clearly be to everyone's benefit to address the issues with the current system, recognizing its flaws and virtues, and make the legal and constitutional changes that need to be made.

10 Impeachment in Denmark

Law and Practice*

Henrik Skovgaard-Petersen

10.1 Introduction

Until recently, impeachment was generally considered not just a peripheral but almost exotic phenomenon in Denmark, and there has been relatively little research on the subject in modern legal scholarship.[1] Although a former Minister of Justice was impeached in 1993 – and convicted by the Court of Impeachment in 1995 – this was generally perceived as an outlier or the exception that proved the rule. However, interest in the subject has recently been sparked following the conviction in December 2021 of a former Minister of Immigration, Integration and Housing in a case involving mandatory separate accommodation for couples, one of whom was a minor, in the asylum system. Moreover, impeachment and the conditions for bringing impeachment proceedings came to the fore of public debate, including the recent electoral campaign, following a critical commission of scrutiny report from June 2022 on the culling of all mink in Denmark during the COVID-19 pandemic – particularly because the incumbent Prime Minister was among the ministers subject to the inquiry. This renewed interest in the subject means that it is timely to examine the rules and practice regarding impeachment in Denmark.

In Denmark, impeachment is a strictly judicial process (criminal law proceedings) once impeachment proceedings have been brought; however, the system can best be described as a hybrid legal and political one, as the decision on whether to initiate impeachment proceedings is purely political. In general, the Danish parliament holds a comparatively strong position in the Danish form of government, given that Denmark has an electoral system with a high degree of proportionate

* The views expressed within this chapter are solely those of the author and do not represent the views of his employer.

1 The most notable exception is the doctoral thesis by current Supreme Court President Jens Peter Christensen, *Ministeransvar* (Jurist-og Økonomforbundets Forlag 1997). The thesis has recently been revised by the same author; Jens Peter Christensen, *Ministre og Embedsmænd: Pligter og Ansvar* (DJØF Forlag 2022).

DOI: 10.4324/9781003256007-13

representation and typically minority governments and given that Danish courts generally take a relatively deferent approach to judicial control of the legislature.[2]

This chapter aims to give an historical overview of the development of the rules and practice of impeachment in Denmark. Particular emphasis is placed on an analysis of the present rules on legal (criminal) responsibility for ministers, the rules governing impeachment, and the interaction between impeachment and political forms of ministerial responsibility. The analysis suggests that although political and legal ministerial responsibility (impeachment) are legally separate and distinct, there is a tendency towards their convergence, making it arguable that, for practical purposes, they can be perceived as being on a broad continuum.

10.2 Historical Overview

To understand the current system of impeachment in Denmark, it is necessary to give a brief historical account of the main developments since its introduction in 1849.

The Constitutional Act of Denmark was originally adopted in 1849, marking the transition from absolutist rule to democracy. However, in practice, the transition did not happen instantaneously, and the remnants of absolutist rule were only gradually diluted as the democratic political system developed. Among the traces of the previous regime were the rules and practices governing the appointment of the government and individual ministers; such appointments were not subject to the present-day constraints inherent in the parliamentary form of government. The Prime Minister and other ministers were appointed by the king, ultimately according to his personal preference,[3] and parliament could not table a vote of no confidence in the Prime Minister (the government) or any individual minister.[4] As a result, the distinction between two forms of ministerial responsibility – legal and political/parliamentary (on these, see a later discussion) – enshrined in the current Constitutional Act had not yet been introduced. If parliament wished to hold a minister responsible for his

2 Marlene Wind, drawing on a distinction by Ronald Dworkin, characterises Denmark as a majoritarian (as opposed to constitutional) democracy; Marlene Wind, 'When Parliament Comes First – the Danish Concept of Democracy Meets the European Union' (2009) 27(2) *Nordisk Tidsskrift for Menneskerettigheder* 272, 280.

3 Tim Knudsen, *Statsministeren*, vol 1 (Samfundslitteratur 2020) 128. The Prime Minister's current title (*statsminister*) was not introduced until 1918. Until then, the Prime Minister had borne the title *konseilspræsident* (literally meaning council president, that is, president of the king's council). The change of title in 1918 was a symbolic marker that the Prime Minister was no longer formally viewed as the king's most prominent counsellor but as an official serving the unpersonal state; see Tim Knudsen, *Statsministeren*, vol 4 (Samfundslitteratur 2021) 19.

4 Since 1953, the Danish parliament has been unicameral, consisting only of the *Folketing*, and when present-day conditions are described, reference is simply made to 'parliament'. Prior to 1953, Denmark had a bicameral parliament consisting of an upper house (*Landstinget*) and a lower house (*Folketinget*).

(needless to say, in those days, a minister could always be referred to as 'he') actions, then impeachment was the only formal instrument available.[5]

In the absence of a parliamentary mechanism such as a vote of no confidence, the lower house of parliament attempted to instrumentalise impeachment to assert its rights and competences vis-à-vis the government, particularly in the first quarter of the century following the introduction of the 1849 Constitutional Act. Between 1849 and 1901, the latter being the year in which a system of parliamentary democracy was de facto introduced, three impeachment cases were brought before the Court of Impeachment by majority votes in the lower house of parliament, all of which concerned the limits of ministers' spending powers.[6] In all three cases, the Court of Impeachment decided, by a majority, to acquit the ministers in question.

The final two of the three Court of Impeachment cases in the era prior to the introduction of parliamentary democracy were decided in 1877. At least retrospectively, the failure to obtain a conviction in these cases also marked a point in time when the lower house of parliament gave up its attempts to instrumentalise impeachment proceedings to assert its rights and ultimately achieve a parliamentary form of government.[7] In fact, 1877 marked the beginning of the period when the Danish administration was carried out under provisional Finance Acts not voted on by the lower house (the so-called *provisorietid*, the most important and heated period of which lasted from 1885 to 1894) in an attempt to pave the way for the appointment of a government in harmony with the majority of the lower house that was by far more representative of the general population than the upper house. The lower house attempted this strategy until 1894 without immediate success. The king did not appoint a government in line with the principles of parliamentarism until 1901.

This could have been the end of the history of impeachment proceedings, leaving the relevant provisions of the Constitutional Act a dead letter, of interest primarily to legal historians. However, the fate of impeachment was not sealed by parliamentary democracy. Since 1901, three cases have been brought before the Court of Impeachment, and all of them have resulted in convictions.[8] The cases, decided in 1910, 1995 and 2021, respectively, did not have the added element of an institutional power struggle that the first three cases

5 The preparatory works that aid the interpretation of the Constitutional Act consist primarily of the records of the debates of the 1848–49 Constitutional Assembly. The records show that the distinction between political and legal responsibility for ministers was already applied at the time; however, the Constitutional Act did not introduce any formal instruments of political responsibility. Parliament's right to hold a vote of no confidence was only introduced into the Constitutional Act during the most recent amendment in 1953.

6 A detailed discussion of these cases can be found in Christensen, *Ministeransvar* (n 1) ch 4. Court of Impeachment cases are reported in the Court of Impeachment Reports (*Rigsretstidende*).

7 Contrary to the Danish experience, in Norway, impeachment proceedings were instrumental to introducing parliamentary democracy in 1884; Frede Castberg, *Juridiske stridsspørsmål i Norges politiske historie* (Universitetsforlaget 1961) 40.

8 In the impeachment proceedings decided in 1910, only one of the two former ministers charged was convicted.

had but were primarily intended to sanction alleged breaches of norms applicable to actions or omissions by ministers during their term of office.

Given that impeachment was not consigned to oblivion, one might wonder why there have been so relatively few cases in the span of more than a century. One likely reason – which is further discussed later – is that the introduction of the parliamentary form of government also entailed the introduction of another type of responsibility. We now turn to this type of responsibility.

10.2.1 Parliamentary Democracy and Political Responsibility

As mentioned previously, the Danish system of parliamentary government was established in 1901 when the king finally yielded to the increasing pressure exerted by the lower house of parliament and appointed a government that commanded the support of a majority in this chamber. The upper house of parliament was dominated primarily by the elites, particularly the landowning elite,[9] which meant that the lower house was the only chamber somewhat representative of the will of the people.[10]

Despite the introduction of parliamentary democracy, Denmark did not follow the trajectory of states such as the UK in which impeachment became obsolete.[11] Accordingly, less than a decade later, in 1910, the fourth ever Court of Impeachment case was decided. The judgment, which concerned a fraud scandal of considerable proportions committed by the former Minister of Justice in his capacity as president of a rural savings bank, resulted in the first conviction ever, and former Interior Minister Sigurd Berg was fined DKK 1,000, which was a significant amount at the time.[12] Former Prime Minister J.C. Christensen was acquitted of the charges against him, but the Court of Impeachment effectively reprimanded him for irresponsible conduct because he had not ensured that an inquiry was carried out into the matter.

10.2.2 Codification of Parliamentary Democracy and Instruments of Parliamentary Control

Although parliamentary democracy was introduced in 1901, the Constitutional Act was not amended to codify this form of government until the most

9 During the period between 1866 and 1915, the upper house of parliament was composed of 66 members in total, 12 of whom were appointed by the king, and the remainder were elected by a privileged electorate; see Poul Andersen, *Dansk Statsforfatningsret* (Gyldendal 1954) 56–57.

10 However, universal suffrage had by no means been introduced at the beginning of the 20th century – specifically, women did not become eligible to vote until 1915, at which time the voting age for the lower house was set at 25 years (35 with respect to upper house elections); see, e.g., ibid 64–65.

11 Jack Simson Caird, 'Impeachment' (House of Commons Library Briefing Paper No CBP7612, 6 June 2016), according to which the last recorded impeachment in the UK Parliament was in 1806.

12 Christensen, *Ministre og Embedsmænd* (n 1) 297–98. According to Christensen, the fine roughly corresponded to the annual wages of a skilled worker. Moreover, the costs that the former Interior Minister had to pay amounted to double the amount of the fine (DKK 2,000).

recent revision of the Constitutional Act in 1953.[13] The relevant provision of the Constitutional Act reads as follows:[14]

Section 15

1. A Minister shall not remain in office after the Folketing has passed a vote of no confidence in him.
2. When the Folketing passes a vote of no confidence in the Prime Minister, he shall ask for the dismissal of the Ministry unless writs are to be issued for a general election. When a vote of no confidence has been passed on a Ministry, or it has asked for its dismissal, it shall continue in office until a new Cabinet has been appointed. Ministers who remain in office as aforesaid shall perform only what may be necessary to ensure the uninterrupted conduct of official business.

Section 15 is rarely applied in practice.[15] This is not, however, the result of an exceptionally harmonious political landscape; in fact, Danish governments are almost always minority governments (although a rare example of a government that in practice commands a majority in parliament took office in December 2022) and hence constantly dependent on more or less stable alliances with parties outside government. The main reason why section 15 remains largely dormant is that ministers and governments are acutely aware of the consequences if there is a risk that political parties representing a parliamentary majority publicly express dissatisfaction or a lack of confidence in a minister or the government (the Prime Minister). Ministers who face a vote of no confidence will normally choose to tender their resignation more or less 'voluntarily' not only for their own sake but also to avoid risking the political life of the entire government in case the vote of no confidence should pass. Although the entire government is not legally obliged to resign if a vote of no confidence in an individual minister is passed, it may be difficult to resist the political pressure to do so, particularly if the Prime Minister decides to back rather than sack the minister in question prior to the vote.

13 Whether the parliamentary system of government had obtained a legal basis (in customary law) prior to 1953 is a question that has been subject to debate among constitutional law scholars. For an overview of this debate, see, e.g., Henning Koch, 'Retssædvane eller statsskik – Kampen om parlamentarismen siden 1901' [1990] *Juristen* 64.

14 There is no official translation of the Constitutional Act of Denmark. In the present contribution all quotes in English are from a 2013 publication by the Danish Parliament; Folketinget, *The Constitutional Act of Denmark* (Grafisk Rådgivning 2019).

15 A vote of no confidence in an individual minister (subsection 1) has never been passed in parliament. Only once since the 1953 amendment of the Constitutional Act has a vote of no confidence in the Prime Minister (subsection 2) been passed. See Jørgen Albæk Jensen, *Parlamentarismens statsretlige betydning* (2nd edn, Jurist-og Økonomforbundets Forlag 1997) ch III; Jørgen Albæk Jensen, '§ 15' in Jens Peter Christensen and others (eds), *Grundloven* (Jurist-og Økonomforbundets Forlag 2015).

Moreover, there are numerous less severe measures of parliamentary control or scrutiny that typically come into play prior to the stage at which a vote of no confidence would normally be considered. In particular, the Standing Orders of Parliament provide for a number of such measures, including written or oral questions to ministers.[16] Although ministers are not legally obliged to answer such questions,[17] for obvious political reasons, ministers only decline to do so in very special circumstances. Accordingly, the principle of parliamentary government is at the forefront of everyday parliamentary practice in Denmark even though the provision in section 15 of the Constitutional Act is rarely needed to enforce or assert the principle and therefore remains in the background. As is discussed in further detail in the following, this aspect of parliamentary practice is an essential backdrop for understanding the role and relevance of impeachment proceedings.

10.3 Legal Ministerial Responsibility

In Denmark, impeachment constitutes the means of enforcing ministers' legal responsibility. The fundamental rule on ministerial responsibility is laid down in section 13 of the Constitutional Act, according to which 'The King shall not be answerable for his actions; his person shall be sacrosanct. The Ministers shall be responsible for the conduct of government; their responsibility shall be defined by statute.'

The provision reflects what is stated in section 2 of the Constitutional Act, that is, that the form of government shall be a constitutional monarchy. It follows that ministers, not the monarch, exercise the powers of government that the Constitutional Act nominally confers on the King and that the ministers are legally responsible for the exercise of such powers. It is an important aspect of the organisation of the Danish government that section 13 of the Constitutional Act refers to individual ministers rather than the government as a whole. Under the so-called ministerial system,[18] which applies in Danish

16 For an overview of such measures, see the 2018 report by the committee on commissions of inquiry and parliamentary forms of inquiry (the committee was established by the Ministry of Justice); Justitsministeriet, *Betænkning 1571/2018 om undersøgelseskommissioner og parlamentariske undersøgelsesformer* (Rosendahls A/S 2018) 61–76. Oral questions submitted by a parliamentary committee are a particularly thorough kind of parliamentary control. Such questions are answered by the minister during a committee meeting – typically open to the public and live-streamed and recorded on the website of the Danish parliament – that allows for follow-up questions relating to the subject matter of the question(s) posed in advance.

17 As an exception, it follows from section 53 of the Constitutional Act that, '[A]ny Member of Parliament may, with the consent of Parliament, submit for discussion any matter of public interest and request a statement thereon from the ministers'. There is general agreement that ministers are legally obliged to answer such calls (so-called interpellations).

18 The ministerial system can be contrasted with a so-called collegiate system. On the transition from a pre-constitutional collegiate system to the current ministerial system in 1848, see e.g., Tim Knudsen, 'Ministerialsystemet' in Leon Jespersen, E Ladwig Petersen and Ditlev Tamm (eds), *Dansk Forvaltningshistorie*, vol I (Jurist-og Økonomforbundets Forlag 2000) 465 ff.

constitutional law, each individual minister is ultimately responsible for the administration of his or her field of responsibility, including the relevant legislation, budget, subordinate authorities, etc. In the sphere of political responsibility, there is one particular example of collective responsibility, as section 15(2) of the Constitutional Act entails that a vote of no confidence in the Prime Minister has implications for the government as a whole, leading to either the resignation of the government or a general election. However, the rules on legal ministerial responsibility are ultimately rules of criminal law that require any breach to be individually attributable to one or more ministers.[19]

According to the preparatory documents, the provision on legal ministerial responsibility in the Constitutional Act was not expected to be of great practical significance because an impeachment case was expected to be a rare occurrence. Nevertheless, it was deemed right to have rules in place for such extraordinary cases, but how to define and delimit the exact scope of ministers' responsibility was subject to some debate and disagreement. On the one hand, it was acknowledged that the provision should not be too broad and vague as this might entail the risk that ministers would refrain from acting in the interest of the public good for fear of being held responsible at a later point in time (especially when public opinion and political majority might have shifted). On the other hand, it was also acknowledged that both acts and omissions carried out in the conduct of ministerial duties should be encompassed.[20] The resulting provision, which has been left essentially unaltered since 1849,[21] is of a very general nature, referring merely to 'the conduct of government' and leaving the details to be fleshed out by statute.

Although section 13 of the Constitutional Act has its origins in the original 1849 Constitutional Act, the Ministerial Responsibility Act was not enacted until 1964.[22] Prior to 1964, there was no coherent and specific set of legal provisions governing ministerial responsibility. A number of provisions of the Penal Code were considered applicable, but the Court of Impeachment case law – which consisted of only four judgments – had not provided a great measure of legal certainty.[23]

19 The Ministerial Responsibility Act does in fact provide for ministerial responsibility under civil law in the form of liability to pay damages, given that section 9 of the Act refers to the ordinary rules on liability for damages caused by persons in the service of the state; on this subject, see Rasmus Grønved Nielsen, 'Ministeransvaret i erstatningsretlig belysning' [2021] *Juristen* 159. However, this form of responsibility no longer plays any role in practice.

20 Constitutional Assembly, *Beretning om Forhandlingerne paa Rigsdagen*, vol II (Bianco Luno 1849) cols 1650, 2803–4, 2811.

21 The current provision combines the original section 18 and the last sentence of the original section 21(2) with only a slight adjustment of the language.

22 Act no 117 of 15 April 1964, as amended by Act no 433 of 31 May 2000.

23 See the 1962 report on ministerial responsibility and whether a specific act on ministerial responsibility should be adopted that was produced by an expert committee appointed by the Prime Minister's Office; Statsministeriet, *Betænkning 312/1962 om ministrenes ansvar for*

The centrepiece of the 1964 Ministerial Responsibility Act is section 5 that establishes the substantive rules on criminal responsibility for actions or omissions performed by ministers in the 'conduct of government', as section 13 of the Constitutional Act puts it. Under section 5(1), a minister is criminally liable if the minister wilfully or by gross negligence disregards the duties that fall on him or her under the Constitutional Act or under other laws or due to the nature of his or her office. The provision is somewhat vague and broad, particularly because of the reference to duties that flow from 'the nature of the office'.[24] Section 5(2) specifically defines one such obligation, providing that section 5(1) applies to a minister who provides parliament with untrue or misleading information or who withholds from parliament information that is important to parliament's assessment of a matter that is the subject of parliamentary business.

Sections 3 and 4 of the Ministerial Responsibility Act contain rules on complicity. The former concerns the actions of the minister's subordinates, which means that a minister cannot avoid legal responsibility solely by reference to the fact that the action or omission itself was performed by or attributable to a subordinate. If, for instance, the minister was aware that the action in question would be taken by the subordinate but did not seek to prevent it, then the minister can be held liable. Section 4 concerns complicity in the actions of other ministers. It provides that responsibility for decisions signed by the King is attributable not only to the minister or ministers who have signed the decision but also to other ministers who have taken part in the decision.[25]

Under section 6(1) of the Act, a minister who has breached section 5 of the Act can be punished with a fine or imprisonment not exceeding two years. In cases that do not involve wilful conduct but only gross negligence, section 6(2) provides for a reduced maximum term of imprisonment of four months. The most recent impeachment case, decided on 13 December 2021, resulted in a sentence of 60 days of unconditional imprisonment (the sentence was served by the former minister at home using an electronic tag).

---

regeringens førelse samt om, hvorvidt en særlig ministeransvarlighedslov bør gennemføres (SL Møllers Bogtrykkeri 1962) ch III.

24 Max Sørensen, *Statsforfatningsret* (Peter Germer ed, 2nd edn, Juristforbundets Forlag 1973) 143, in a somewhat critical appraisal of the provision, stated that section 5 did not in fact solve the problem of *nullum crimen sine lege* because the reference to the duties incumbent on the minister due to the nature of his or her office simply constitutes a flexible reference to the generally accepted perception of and practice regarding the duties that fall upon a minister.

25 This rule corresponds to what flows from the generally applicable rules on complicity in the Penal Code; however, in the first Court of Impeachment judgment, handed down in 1856, four of the ministers charged were acquitted because they had not signed the decisions in question. Nevertheless, this element of the judgment has been almost universally rejected by legal scholarship, and the express provision in section 4 now unequivocally states the law on this point; see Christensen, *Ministeransvar* (n 1) 67.

Finally, section 8 contains a special rule on limitation periods. Given that general elections must be held at least every four years,[26] section 8 provides that the limitation period (which is in principle, set by the general statute of limitations in the Penal Code) shall be no less than five years. In practice, this means that a five-year limitation period applies. The five-year limitation period has recently given rise to debate in light of the process leading up to the Danish parliament's most recent decision to initiate impeachment proceedings against a former Minister of Immigration, Integration and Housing. The decision was adopted on 2 February 2021, just eight days before the expiry of the limitation period with respect to the most important event relevant to the case. This prompted a debate in parliament on a proposal for a resolution, which eventually resulted in a majority of the relevant parliamentary committee issuing a statement calling for an amendment of the Ministerial Responsibility Act regarding the statute of limitations.[27] The process that ultimately led to the 2021 Court of Impeachment judgment is illustrative of the fact that a five-year limitation period may no longer be sufficient to serve the purpose originally intended. The main events central to the case took place in February and March 2016, and a general election was held in June 2019, following which a new majority coalition decided to launch a commission of inquiry to examine the case. Although the commission worked at an impressive pace compared with most previous commissions of inquiry,[28] the relevant parts of the inquiry were published on 14 December 2020, leaving less than two months for parliament to form an opinion on whether to initiate impeachment proceedings or not. Furthermore, as discussed in more detail later, it seems that parliament will generally want to consult external lawyers before deciding on whether to initiate impeachment proceedings, adding another step to the process that needs to be completed before the expiry of the limitation period.

This sequence of events illustrates that it is likely that the five-year limitation period can pose a real challenge, given the extensive and thorough preparatory process that will normally take place prior to parliament deciding on whether to resort to impeachment. Although it may be argued that the fact that a thorough inquiry has effectively been made a prerequisite for any serious debate about impeachment proceedings constitutes a positive development from a rule of law and legal certainty perspective, it may give rise to criticism and to questions concerning the legitimacy of the political system if the

26 Section 32(1) and (3) of the Constitutional Act.

27 Report of 11 May 2022 of the Standing Orders Committee on proposal no B 33; Folketingets Udvalg for Forretningsordenen, 'Beretning over Forslag til folketingsbeslutning om at sikre, at der ikke indtræder forældelse for ministre eller embedsmænd i den såkaldte minksag, før sagen er undersøgt til bunds' (Folketingstidende 2021–22, tillæg B, betænkning over B 33).

28 See the 2018 report by the committee on commissions of inquiry and parliamentary forms of inquiry, Justitsministeriet (n 16) ch 4, for an overview of the duration of inquiries established since 1999 (the duration has typically been more than two years even regarding the less complex cases examined).

possibility of initiating impeachment proceedings runs out due to a combination of thorough processes and reluctant parliamentary majorities that must first be replaced at a general election. As to parliamentary majorities, it has typically – though not without exceptions – been the former opposition that, following a general election, has decided to appoint a commission of inquiry to look into supposed 'scandalous' affairs taking place while the previous government was in power.[29]

10.4 Impeachment

In Denmark, impeachment proceedings are of a hybrid legal and political nature in the sense that impeachment involves a number of steps, some of which are taken by parliament, while others are strictly judicial. The Court of Impeachment is a permanent court that functions essentially as a criminal court,[30] but the decision whether to initiate impeachment proceedings is made by parliament, which also performs the role of prosecutor.[31] The hybrid nature of impeachment is also evident from the fact that the Court of Impeachment is composed of an equal number of Supreme Court judges and lay judges elected by parliament.

The basic rules governing impeachment are established in section 16 and sections 59–60 of the Constitutional Act, whose relevant passages read as follows:

> **Section 16**
>
> Ministers may be impeached by the King or the Folketing for maladministration of office. The Court of Impeachment shall try cases of impeachment brought against Ministers for maladministration of office.

29 Under the Commissions of Inquiry and Commissions of Scrutiny Act, Act No 357 of 2 June 1999, as most recently amended by Act No 671 of 19 April 2021, only the Minister of Justice or a parliament majority can establish commissions of inquiry. Commissions of scrutiny may in principle be established with the support of as little as one-third of parliament; however, if at least another one-third is opposed to the establishment of the commission, then the matter can be brought before a plenary session (which means that a majority is once more required).

30 As previously noted, impeachment may in principle involve civil claims for damages; however, in practice, such claims are not brought by the state (parliament) against ministers. Individuals or legal entities can bring claims for damages against the relevant ministry or authority in proceedings before the ordinary courts; see, e.g., Grønved Nielsen (n 19); Jens Peter Christensen, Jørgen Albæk Jensen and Michael Hansen Jensen, *Dansk Statsret* (3rd edn, Jurist- og Økonomforbundets Forlag 2020) 96–98.

31 As mentioned later, the government has never exercised its competence under section 16 of the Constitutional Act to initiate impeachment proceedings.

Section 59

1. The Court of Impeachment shall consist of up to fifteen of the senior ordinary members of the highest court of justice in the Realm (according to length of office) and an equal number of members elected for six years by the Folketing according to proportional representation. One or more substitutes shall be elected for each elected member. No Member of the Folketing shall be elected a member of the Court of Impeachment, nor shall a Member of the Folketing act as a member of the Court of Impeachment. When, in a particular instance, some of the members of the highest court of justice in the Realm are prevented from taking part in the trial of a case, an equal number of the members of the Court of Impeachment most recently elected by the Folketing shall resign their seats.
2. The Court of Impeachment shall elect a president from among its members.

. . .

4. Rules on the Court of Impeachment shall be provided by statute.

Section 60

1. The Court of Impeachment shall try such actions as may be brought by the King or the Folketing against Ministers.

10.4.1 Initiation of Impeachment Proceedings

Under section 16 of the Constitutional Act, both parliament and the King (i.e., the government) are competent to impeach a minister; however, in practice, the decision on impeachment has always been made by parliament. Apart from the six impeachment proceedings that have been brought since the introduction of the 1849 Constitutional Act, parliament has on many occasions debated proposals to impeach an incumbent or former minister without there having been a majority in favour of doing so.[32]

In strictly legal terms, the only requirement for an impeachment decision is a parliamentary majority in favour of initiating proceedings. The Constitutional Act does not institute any restrictions or constraints on parliament's decision in this regard; the decision is of a purely political nature.[33] In practice, however, such decision will be preceded by a special inquiry established under the Commissions of Inquiry and Commissions of Scrutiny Act.[34] Such

32 See Christensen, *Ministeransvar* (n 1) ch 22; Christensen, *Ministre og Embedsmænd* (n 1) 24.

33 See Christensen, *Ministre og Embedsmænd* (n 1) 128.

34 In the spring of 2021, the opposition parties voted in favour of a proposal, based on a citizens' initiative, to impeach the incumbent Prime Minister for her conduct in relation to the culling of all mink in Denmark in November 2020 in connection with the COVID-19 pandemic. The vote in parliament took place before the commission of scrutiny established to investigate the case (with the support of all parties) had even begun its inquiry. Although the opposition did not command enough votes for the proposal to pass, the move was heavily criticised for

commissions typically comprise three members, one of whom (the president) is normally a High Court judge. A commission of inquiry or scrutiny essentially replaces the police and the prosecution service with respect to the investigation of a case involving potential legal ministerial responsibility. If, based on the conclusions of the commission, there are sufficient grounds for parliament to consider the question of impeachment,[35] then the relevant parliamentary committee will seek the advice of external lawyers. Only if the lawyers consider that impeachment proceedings can be expected to lead to a conviction will parliament propose and approve an impeachment decision.

In terms of personal scope, the rules on impeachment apply only to 'ministers'.[36] The term 'ministers' applies not only to incumbent ministers but also to former ministers; in fact, impeachment has exclusively been initiated against former ministers. From a political point of view, this makes sense; if a parliamentary majority can be mobilised to refer a case to the Court of Impeachment against an incumbent minister, s/he is unlikely to continue to enjoy the confidence of his or her own party or party leader.

In terms of substance, ministers may be tried for 'maladministration of office', which means that the actions or omissions with which the minister can be charged have to be linked to the duties that fall on the minister in his or her capacity as a minister. Purely private offences – such as traffic offences or shoplifting – are not impeachable, which means that such matters must be investigated by the police and prosecuted and decided by the ordinary prosecution service and courts.[37] Conversely, the Court of Impeachment is the exclusive forum for charges of maladministration of office for current or former ministers.[38]

10.4.2 The Court of Impeachment

As mentioned previously, section 59(4) of the Constitutional Act provides that rules on the Court of Impeachment shall be provided by statute. The

breaking with convention, and since then, the main opposition parties have on numerous occasions conceded that it would have been proper and in line with convention to await the conclusions of the commission before deciding on the question of impeachment.

35 Again, there are no legal criteria governing this decision; however, based on the relatively few relevant cases, it seems that such grounds typically relate to whether ministers involved have willfully or knowingly misinformed parliament or whether there are indications that they willfully or knowingly performed actions or omissions contrary to the law.

36 The provision in section 60(2) of the Constitutional Act, which provides for other persons to be tried before the Court of Impeachment for crimes that are deemed to be particularly dangerous to the state, lies dormant.

37 Ministers who are also Members of Parliament enjoy parliamentary immunity under section 57 of the Constitutional Act, which means that, for example, criminal indictment cannot take place until parliament has given its consent (unless the minister has been caught *in flagrante delicto*).

38 See, e.g., Christensen, Jensen and Jensen (n 30) 99–102. But see Peter Germer, *Statsforfatningsret* (5th edn, Jurist- og Økonomforbundets Forlag 2012) 58–59.

Court of Impeachment Act[39] establishes the details concerning the composition, functioning and procedure of the Court of Impeachment. Although there are some procedural rules specific to impeachment proceedings, criminal proceedings before the Court of Impeachment are essentially conducted in accordance with the ordinary rules of criminal procedure. Hence, the following discussion focuses on the composition of the Court of Impeachment.

The main principles concerning the composition of the Court of Impeachment are enumerated directly by section 59(1) of the Constitutional Act (quoted earlier). The Court of Impeachment is of a hybrid nature, consisting of an equal number of Supreme Court judges and lay judges elected by parliament. Section 2 of the Court of Impeachment Act entails that the court is composed of the maximum number of Supreme Court judges (fifteen) allowed by the Constitutional Act, resulting in a total of 30 judges on the court. Given that there are currently eighteen Supreme Court judges, the initiation of an impeachment case involves a significant strain on the capacity of the Supreme Court.[40]

The hybrid composition of the Court of Impeachment that combines Supreme Court justices and lay judges elected by parliament (sometimes called 'political expert judges'[41]) is a result of the special nature of impeachment cases: although they are legal trials conducted according to judicial procedural rules, the substance typically has one or more political aspects and relates to the hybrid nature of a minister's duties as both a politically elected official and the top civil servant within the field of his or her responsibilities. According to the preparatory works to the Constitutional Act, the composition of the Court of Impeachment was also originally perceived as a guarantee against any arbitrariness (abuse of powers) on the part of the lower house, which, at the advent of Danish democracy and during the time of a bicameral system (1849–1953), was the chamber of parliament competent to bring impeachment proceedings.[42]

39 Act No 100 of 31 March 1954, as amended by Act No 385 of 4 December 1963.

40 See, e.g., former Supreme Court and Court of Impeachment president Thomas Rørdam in an interview with Danish newspaper *Information*; Anton Geist and Ulrik Dahlin, 'Afgået højesteretspræsident: Folketinget skal gøre sig klart, at en rigsret er et kæmpe apparat' *Information* (Copenhagen, 5 December 2022) <www.information.dk/indland/2022/12/afgaaet-hoejesteretspraesident-folketinget-goere-klart-rigsret-kaempe-apparat> accessed 23 February 2023.

41 See, e.g., the interview by Danish newspaper *Politiken* with former minister Pia Gjellerup who serves on the Court of Impeachment; Kristian Corfixen, 'Som vidne fik hun "et mærkeligt spørgsmål." Derfor ved hun, hvor vigtige politisk valgte dommere er i rigsretssager' *Politiken* (Copenhagen, 1 September 2021) <https://politiken.dk/indland/art8346135/Som-vidne-fik-hun-%C2%BBet-m%C3%A6rkeligt-sp%C3%B8rgsm%C3%A5l%C2%AB.-Derfor-ved-hun-hvor-vigtige-politisk-valgte-dommere-er-i-rigsretssager> accessed 23 February 2023.

42 Constitutional Assembly (n 20) col 1648. Arguably, the fact that section 68 of the Court of Impeachment Act entails that the judgment must not reveal the names of the judges supporting a given vote or opinion may also act as a guarantee against politically motivated voting. However, it can be argued that the secrecy regarding individual votes may compound the suspicion that voting takes place in accordance with the individual judge's political opinion. The

The composition of the Court of Impeachment, particularly the participation of lay judges elected by parliament, has been a controversial subject in recent years. From a legal perspective, the main issue has been whether the composition of the court is compatible with the right to a fair trial enshrined in Article 6 of the European Convention on Human Rights. The question was answered in 1999 by the European Court of Human Rights in a case brought by former Minister of Justice Erik Ninn-Hansen following his conviction in 1995.[43] The applicant cited a number of arguments in support of a violation of Article 6 of the Convention, one of which related generally to the composition of the Court of Impeachment. Specifically, it was argued that the participation of lay judges elected by parliament constituted a violation of the requirements of independence and impartiality. On 18 May 1999, the Court of Human Rights handed down a decision declaring the complaint manifestly inadmissible. Regarding the participation of lay judges elected by parliament, the Court of Human Rights emphasised that the reason for the participation of said judges is that the cases that the Court of Impeachment is intended to adjudicate require a certain insight in political matters. Moreover, the Court of Human Rights pointed to the fact that the lay judges had been appointed for a fixed term of six years during which time it was not possible for parliament or any other authority to influence the composition of the Court of Impeachment.

10.5 Impeachment in Practice

Having examined the rules and procedures governing impeachment, we now turn to some observations on the role, function and significance of impeachment in practice in present-day conditions. Given that only six impeachment cases have been brought since the 1849 Constitutional Act – half of which were brought in the 19th century – one may legitimately wonder whether impeachment has any practical significance in the practice of Danish democracy. However, it is also part of the picture that two of the cases were decided within the past 30 years, and the most recent was decided in December 2021. Although it is difficult to empirically establish whether and the extent to which the mere existence of the rules on legal ministerial responsibility and the possibility (risk) of impeachment proceedings may serve to make impeachment a general preventive measure – as was originally intended – the fact that there have been relatively recent cases, both of which resulted in convictions,

question was subject to debate in the summer of 2021 when a Member of Parliament – who was at the time, subject to impeachment proceedings that ultimately led to her conviction in December 2021 – rather unusually submitted a private bill before parliament with a view to changing (removing) the rule on secret voting; Folketingstidende 2020–21, tillæg A, L 188 som fremsat.

43 *Ninn-Hansen v Denmark* (ECHR, 1999-V) 321.

certainly serves as a reminder to ministers and the ministries (civil servants) working for them.

Indeed, from the outset, impeachment proceedings, which put significant strain on the accused, the public purse and the resources of the Supreme Court, were never intended to be a frequent occurrence but only a last resort. In general, disputes relating to the conduct of government business and political disagreements are intended to be resolved through political means, and, as indicated previously, particularly since the codification of parliamentary democracy in 1953, the day-to-day business of parliamentary control is conducted through the broad range of political measures at the disposal of parliament, parliament committees and individual members of parliament. Moreover, unlike in some countries, it is not necessary to resort to impeachment in order to remove a minister (or government) from office because the instrument of a vote of no confidence is available to a majority in parliament. As mentioned earlier, there is a clear legal divide between legal and political ministerial responsibility in Danish constitutional law.

Despite this clear legal distinction, however, it is interesting to note that a certain degree of 'cross-fertilization' between the two forms of ministerial responsibility can be identified in practice. It has already been noted that legal ministerial responsibility – impeachment – can be characterised as a hybrid given that it is inherent in the system governing the impeachment process that the decision whether to bring a case before the Court of Impeachment is essentially subject to political discretion. Nevertheless, recent experience has shown that in practice, the decision on whether to initiate impeachment proceedings hinges decisively on legal arguments and processes. As mentioned earlier, cases involving alleged misconduct within government can be investigated by an *ad hoc* commission of inquiry/commission of scrutiny. However, because such commissions may not, under the terms of the Commissions of Inquiry and Commissions of Scrutiny Act, draw any conclusions as to ministerial responsibility (as opposed to the disciplinary or criminal responsibility of civil servants), parliament has chosen to add another layer of legal assessment before deciding whether to initiate impeachment proceedings. Thus, prior to the initiation of the 1993–95 impeachment proceedings against a former Minister of Justice, parliament consulted two external lawyers before deciding to initiate proceedings.[44] Similarly, in December 2020, two external lawyers were requested by parliament to advise parliament on whether, based on the commission of inquiry report, it could be expected that the former Minister of Immigration, Integration and Housing would be convicted by the Court of

44 See the Standing Orders Committee report of 2 June 1993 and the proposal (no B 100) to indict former Minister of Justice Erik Ninn-Hansen before the Court of Impeachment, which was contained in the report (and subsequently adopted on 11 June 1993); Folketingstidende 1992–93, tillæg B, col 1607 ff. The lawyers who counselled parliament were chosen by parliament to act as prosecutors in the subsequent impeachment proceedings.

Impeachment.[45] Having received an affirmative answer, parliament proceeded to launch impeachment proceedings. Regarding the recent commission of scrutiny report on the culling of all mink in Denmark, published in June 2022, there has been a lengthy and heated debate about whether Court of Impeachment proceedings should be initiated against the Prime Minister; however, even opposition parties have eventually accepted that such proceedings should only be initiated following (positive) advice by impartial external lawyers.[46]

A similar tendency to apply legal or quasi-legal standards to political decisions can be traced within the field of political ministerial responsibility. As mentioned previously, such responsibility may take numerous forms. If one focuses on the more serious reactions, particularly ministers resigning and formalised criticism levelled at ministers, then the overwhelming majority of such reactions is justified by reference to legal criteria.[47] Most frequently, ministers facing such reactions are either alleged to have misinformed parliament or to have withheld information that parliament deems relevant, both of which constitute potential breaches of section 5(2) of the Ministerial Responsibility Act. Other alleged breaches of legal duties are also sometimes cited, while purely political disagreement or dissatisfaction is rarely invoked by political parties to justify a demand that a minister resign or in support of a formalised statement of criticism.

This discussion suggests a degree of convergence between the two types of ministerial responsibility because of the focus on legal or quasi-legal arguments to support what is ultimately (in the case of political responsibility) or initially (regarding legal responsibility) a discretionary political decision. This

45 See the Standing Orders Committee report of 27 January 2021 and the proposal (no B 134) to indict former Minister of Immigration, Integration and Housing Inger Støjberg before the Court of Impeachment, which was contained in the report (and subsequently adopted on 2 February 2021); Folketingstidende 2020–21, tillæg A, B 134 som fremsat. Once again, the lawyers in question were appointed prosecutors in the impeachment proceedings that followed. The Commissions of Inquiry Act (which in 2021, became the Commissions of Inquiry and Commissions of Scrutiny Act) was passed in 1999, and since then, 10 commissions established pursuant to the Act have completed their investigations. Impeachment proceedings have only been initiated with respect to one of them, and then only following the advice of external lawyers, based on the commission of inquiry's report.

46 As mentioned in n 34, the opposition parties had originally taken a different approach, supporting a citizens' initiative in favour of initiating impeachment proceedings. Most recently, on 13 December 2022, a motion was debated on whether to consult independent lawyers with a view to obtaining their assessment of whether it could be expected, based on the commission of scrutiny report from June 2022, that the Prime Minister (or other ministers involved) would be convicted by the Court of Impeachment in case an indictment were brought (motion No B 5 in the parliamentary year 2022–23(2)). The debate did not reveal a majority in favour of the proposal.

47 Christensen, *Ministeransvar* (n 1) 29–30 pointed to this tendency in his 1997 doctoral thesis. Regarding formalised statements of criticism, an overview of such statements since 1992 has been compiled by the online medium *Altinget*; Laura Bejder Jensen, '58 næser på 30 år: Se listen over minister, der har fået kritik' *Altinget* (5 July 2022) <www.altinget.dk/artikel/50-naeser-paa-30-aar-se-listen-over-ministre-der-har-faaet-kritik> accessed 23 February 2023.

convergence, in turn, points to some important observations for the purposes of assessing the role of impeachment in practice. Rather than a clear divide, the relationship between political and legal responsibility can arguably be seen as points on a continuum with the milder forms of political responsibility at one end and impeachment proceedings at the other end. Viewed in this way, both types of responsibility (and the various subtypes of political responsibility) constitute different means of enforcing perceived breaches of legal duties incumbent on ministers in the performance of their ministerial tasks.

This perspective may also help explain why impeachment has sometimes been taken off the table in situations where it might have been a plausible step. In a number of situations, it seems that a political reaction has been deemed sufficient and that parliament has accordingly stopped short of bringing impeachment proceedings.[48] In particular, the 1993 impeachment proceedings against a former Minister of Justice did not involve the former Prime Minister who had handed in his own and the government's resignation as soon as the special court of inquiry (which was an instrument used prior to the introduction of commissions of inquiry) published its report in January 1993.[49] By contrast, the former Minister of Justice who was in fact impeached based on the results of the inquiry had only reluctantly left his post and had publicly continued to defend his actions after the affair had come to light. A similar picture emerges with respect to the recent episode concerning the culling of all mink in Denmark during the COVID-19 pandemic. The former Minister of Agriculture, who was subject to more serious criticism than any other minister by the 2022 commission of scrutiny report, stepped down from his post in the immediate aftermath of the affair (in November 2020). Although there have been some calls for an assessment as to whether he should be impeached,[50] the debate has primarily concentrated on the Prime Minister (who remains in office). Further down the continuum of sanctions or reactions, similar dynamics may help explain why a case is sometimes settled using, for example, a formalised statement of parliamentary criticism instead of launching an inquiry into the affair.

Arguably, the interaction between the political and legal aspects of ministerial responsibility may serve to add some potency to the general system of

48 However, when parliament has decided to bring impeachment proceedings before the Court of Impeachment, it is not for that court to decide whether a political reaction would have sufficed; see the Court of Impeachment majority judgment (25 out of 26 judges) of 13 December 2021, Rigsretstidende, *Rigsretssag nr 6 mod forhenværende minister Inger Støjberg*, vol 3 (Prinfo Denmark A/S 2022) 1866.

49 On parliament's reasons for choosing not to bring impeachment proceedings against the former Prime Minister, see Folketingstidende 1992–93 (proposal no B 100) (n 44). Similarly, another former Minister of Justice – like the former Prime Minister – was found to have breached section 5(2) of the Ministerial Responsibility Act, but the committee did not recommend that parliament initiate impeachment proceedings against him, and the committee explicitly mentioned the fact that he had stepped down from his post (as Speaker) when the court of inquiry's report was published.

50 See particularly the motion mentioned (n 46).

parliamentary control and scrutiny, given that the exercise of political control is both rhetorically and institutionally supported by the legal aspect. In rhetorical terms, it may be more powerful to accuse a minister of breaching, for example, an obligation to state the (full) truth to parliament, and in institutional terms, the threat that an inquiry may be launched is aggravated by the potential for subsequent discussion of possible impeachment. In contrast, it remains the case that all the steps in the elaborate process that may ultimately lead to a decision on impeachment proceedings are (majority) political decisions, and it may be argued that the use of (quasi-)legal arguments and processes can also serve as a way of glossing over this fact. Moreover, the political and public confidence in the legal system of ministerial responsibility may be undermined if (quasi-)legal arguments (and even threats) are too often presented while reality remains that impeachment proceedings are a very rare occurrence.

Another problem related to the close interaction between the political and legal aspects of ministerial responsibility and accountability is that accusations that are couched in legal terms can only be refuted authoritatively in the Court of Impeachment (which a minister can only gain access to if parliament decides to bring a case). However, this problem should probably not be overstated; the general picture is that it is perfectly possible for ministers who are sanctioned by political means for alleged breaches of legal duties (or ministers who resign as a result of such allegations) to make a comeback.[51]

A final yet important point in explanatory terms is that much of what has been stated previously concerning the convergence between the two forms of ministerial responsibility comes down to the majoritarian nature of Danish parliamentary democracy, which was highlighted as an important general characteristic of Danish democracy in the introduction. Whether it be a formalised political reaction or a decision to take one of the steps that may ultimately lead to impeachment, a parliamentary majority is key. Ultimately, there are no legal or other criteria that dictate that a given matter will or must lead to a given (if any) reaction against a minister, as this decision is always the result of political processes.

10.6 Conclusions and Perspectives

The fundamental rules governing impeachment in Denmark have remained essentially unaltered since the adoption of the 1849 Constitutional Act, which marked the birth of Danish democracy. However, although the basic legal architecture might suggest that not much has changed, the role and significance of impeachment have undergone important developments, and the

51 Indeed, even former ministers convicted by the Court of Impeachment can stage a comeback. Thus, the former Minister of Immigration, Integration and Housing who was sentenced to prison for 60 days in December 2021 was re-elected to parliament at the general election held on 1 November 2022 as leader of a new party that obtained 8.1 per cent of the popular vote.

recent reappearance of impeachment on the legal and political agenda highlights some important questions for the future of impeachment in Denmark.

Only a few years ago, it might legitimately have been asked whether impeachment had been rendered redundant or insignificant. Just as impeachment seemed to disappear from the parliamentary toolbox in the latter part of the 19th century, as impeachment failed to serve as the instrument that ushered in parliamentary democracy, until recently, it might have been argued that parliamentary and political forms of responsibility had effectively absorbed impeachment and legal responsibility. However, although impeachment cases remain rare, the fact that two cases have been brought (and led to convictions) within the past 30 years militates against consigning impeachment to history. Moreover, it was argued previously that political and legal forms of ministerial responsibility can to a certain extent be mutually supportive, adding to the general potency of parliamentary measures of control.

Another aspect of the increased focus on impeachment in recent years concerns the legitimacy of and public confidence in politicians and the political system as a whole. The recent Court of Impeachment case from 2021 and the extensive debate on possible impeachment in the wake of the 2022 commission of scrutiny report on the culling of all mink during the COVID-19 pandemic may contribute to a reduction in public confidence. To the contrary, the mere existence of Court of Impeachment cases and potential cases will not necessarily lead to a challenge to the legitimacy of or trust in democracy. Indeed, more cases can support legitimacy, as they show that potential breaches are dealt with. Moreover, Denmark is generally recognised as a high-performer in terms of the rule of law, including the absence of corruption.[52]

Another aspect of the question concerning public trust and legitimacy relates to the hybrid nature of impeachment in Denmark, particularly the fact that the decision whether to initiate impeachment proceedings is a political one. Recent years have shown that parliament's role as prosecutor before the Court of Impeachment has become an arena for sometimes quite intense and polarised public and political debate; this was especially true in the run-up to and during the 2022 general election campaign. Furthermore, the fact that there are no clear legal or other criteria defining when a case must (or may not) be brought before the Court of Impeachment makes the political class and the political system vulnerable to accusations of opportunistic behaviour in the exercise of parliamentary control with the government. It is somewhat paradoxical that this debate has attained such political salience at the same time as parliament has increased the means at its disposal to carry out parliamentary control.

52 Although there are a number of methodological difficulties involved in compiling such lists, reference can be made to the World Justice Project Rule of Law Index 2022 <https://worldjusticeproject.org/rule-of-law-index/> accessed 23 February 2023.

Impeachment in Denmark has been described as a peripheral phenomenon, meaning that it is less used but appears to be growing in significance. Recent developments seem to confirm this broad categorisation. Impeachment has recently resurfaced not only as a result of the 2021 Court of Impeachment judgment but also as a subject of political and public debate. Moreover, given the introduction of new and more potent instruments for parliament to take initial steps in the process that may lead to impeachment, particularly the possibility of establishing commissions of scrutiny, increased public debate about possible impeachable cases are to be expected. As of now, however, these developments are insufficient to suggest a move towards the 'core' category of countries, and it is unlikely that there would be such a far-reaching break with tradition, even if one were to imagine that impeachable behaviour will occur regularly in future. In any event, significant changes in this direction would at the very least require a fundamental modification of the majoritarian tradition of Danish parliamentary democracy, enabling a minority in parliament to take one or more steps, such as establishing commissions of scrutiny, without the possibility of being outvoted by the majority. Such fundamental changes to the traditional workings of Danish democracy would ultimately depend on political decisions.

11 The Impeachment of the Chief Justice of Sri Lanka, Dr. Shirani Bandaranayake

Geoffrey Robertson KC

11.1 Introduction

The Chief Justice of Sri Lanka, Dr. Shirani Bandaranayake, was impeached by the vote of government members of that nation's Parliament (MPs) on 10 January 2013, after a report from a Select Committee of seven government ministers declared her guilty of misconduct. This decision involved the rejection of a ruling by the Supreme Court that the process was in breach of the Constitution. The impeachment was widely condemned both by a large majority of local lawyers and by international organisations concerned with human rights and judicial independence. The Sri Lankan government at the time claimed that the actions of its ministers and MPs did nothing to threaten judicial independence but merely demonstrated the sovereignty of its Parliament. The Human Rights Committee of the English bar, concerned that judicial independence had been imperilled, asked me to investigate and provide an expert report. This chapter is based on the findings of that report, which was completed on 27 February 2013.

It was a regrettable fact that close scrutiny of the impeachment by independent observers was not welcomed by the Sri Lankan government. It refused to grant visas for an International Bar Association fact-finding mission, which would have been led by the former Chief Justice of India, J.S. Verma. The then-Sri Lankan Media Minister explained that

> The impeachment was done in accordance with the Sri Lankan Constitution. Outsiders cannot criticize the Constitution. This is an infringement of the sovereignty of Sri Lanka, which the government is bound to protect.[1]

On the contrary, the independence of the judiciary is a requirement of every human rights treaty and a requisite for membership in the Commonwealth:

1 Xinhua/Agencies, 'Sri Lanka to Reject Visa for Delegation to Probe Controversial Impeachment' *Xinhua/Agencies* (8 February 2013).

DOI: 10.4324/9781003256007-14

when a Chief Justice is removed from office, whether in accordance with the Constitution or not, the question for both outsiders and insiders is (and was at the time) whether it has been done in a manner that comports with the judicial independence guarantee in international law. A mission of distinguished lawyers seeking to elucidate the facts cannot possibly infringe on the sovereignty of the nation.

Nonetheless, this meant that I was unable to travel to interview the various parties, but fortunately, this was not an obstacle to the establishment of such facts for the original 2013 report. This was because I was in possession of all relevant documents – court judgments, 'Hansard' of the parliamentary impeachment process, the 14 charges against the judge, and two volumes (some 1,600 pages) published by Parliament that contained the evidence. I had statements by the four members who walked out of the Select Committee, its Minutes of evidence, and the findings of guilt on three of the charges. I had also read some press coverage of what happened in papers such as the *Colombo Telegraph*, *The Sunday Times*, and *The Island online* and overseas reporting in journals such as *The Economist* and a collection of documents relevant to the impeachment published by the Asian Human Rights Commission. As will be seen in this chapter, the facts upon which I based my conclusions in the original 2013 report were either on record or incapable of significant challenge.

The question that I was tasked to answer is whether the removal of the Chief Justice was a breach of the guarantee of judicial independence that Sri Lanka is bound to uphold, both by international law and by its membership in the Commonwealth. This required an analysis of firstly, the reasons for the impeachment. Were the motives 'political', for example, as a reprisal for some judgment against the government, or was the impeachment process begun out of genuine concern for the public interest because there was prima facie evidence that Dr. Bandaranayake had committed some crime or serious misconduct? Secondly, an analysis of the nature of the charges was required. Did they relate to the political inconvenience of her judgments or to allegations of serious misbehaviour? Thirdly, the fairness of the method used for proving the charges was examined. Did the Select Committee give her a fair hearing and adopt a proper standard of proof? Finally, the question of political pressure was investigated. Was Parliament prejudiced or placed under pressure, for example, by demonstrations against the judge orchestrated by the government?

Much of the public debate had been over the use of the impeachment process, which takes place in Parliament rather than in the courts, but this was not the key issue: it was whether the impeachment process as used by the then-government in this case was used fairly. Another side-issue was the correctness of the Supreme Court decision to intervene in a parliamentary process. Again, the real question for judicial independence was whether this process was fair, not whether the courts were right to intervene – an interesting question, but one pertaining to a different subject regarding the separation of powers. A different consideration, raised by the United Nation (UN)'s Human Rights Commission, was the fitness of Mrs. Bandaranayake's successor, Mohan Peiris, who had been Attorney General and had led delegations to Geneva to 'vigorously defend' the government over its mass-murder of Tamil civilians. Lawyers briefed to vigorously defend a client do not necessarily believe in the client or the defence: barristers who act for governments sometimes turn out to be remarkably independent of that government when appointed to the bench. The criticism of Mr. Peiris must come from the fact – if it is a fact – that he accepted the office with the knowledge that his predecessor had been unlawfully or improperly removed.

11.2 Judicial Independence

Every international human rights treaty, and every constitutional bill of rights, requires judges to possess 'independence and impartiality'. These are disparate concepts. 'Impartiality' is well-defined, and the tests for real or apparent judicial bias are well established. 'Independence' however, has not been litigated much: I would define it as a duty of the state to put judges in a position to act according to their conscience and the justice of the case, free from pressures from governments, funding bodies, the military, or any other source of influence that can possibly bear upon them. Security of tenure is fundamental to independence, and subject to a mandatory retirement age, it can only be lost by proven mental incapacity or by serious misconduct, proved beyond a reasonable doubt, preferably by a criminal conviction or at least by a trial proceeding that is fair.

That an independent judiciary is a prerequisite for any society based on the rule of law cannot be doubted, and the definition of this independence is uncontroversially set out in the International Bar Association's Minimum Standards of Judicial Independence (1982) and in the Basic Principles of the Independence of the Judiciary adopted by the General Assembly of the UN in 1985.[2] These instruments establish guidelines for appointment and removal and for tenure, conduct, and discipline, which are generally designed to ensure that 'judges are not subject to executive control' (personal independence) and that in the discharge of judicial functions, 'a judge is subject to nothing but the law and the commands of his conscience'(substantive independence). This latter formulation strikes me as inadequate: a judge is additionally subject to certain public expectations arising from the constitutional importance of the office. These should be spelled out in a code of judicial conduct, requiring justice to be done efficiently and decently, without fear or favour and discrimination or discourtesy. Complaints about breaches of the code should be decided by a tribunal that includes senior judges and is itself free from political influence. Most misconduct complaints, if upheld, will result in guidance or a reprimand: if serious enough, in the tribunal's estimation, to warrant removal, this power (which in many countries constitutionally resides in the Parliament)

2 Resolution 40/146, December 1985.

can be exercised after a vote has been taken on whether to adopt the tribunal's recommendation.

Although this is the case with the UN's own justice system[3] and in many countries with Westminster-style constitutions, other countries such as Sri Lanka – and the UK itself – still rely on an archaic system of an 'address' in Parliament to remove a senior judge, the last step in a process known as 'impeachment'. Although in some respects this address is unsatisfactory, it does at least ensure judicial accountability to an outside body – the democratically elected legislature – and this provides an ultimate safeguard against judicial guardians becoming too improperly connected or perceived as too self-interested to guard themselves. The impeachment process per se is therefore unobjectionable – so long as it is conducted fairly, in a way that fully protects the judge's rights and in circumstances where it cannot be credibly suggested that it has been instituted or carried out as a reprisal, for example, if the government does not like the judge's decision in a particular case. Almost all cases of serious misbehaviour will involve allegations of crime: the judge should normally be tried fairly in court and only impeached if convicted.

It is generally accepted, and may now be considered an imperative rule of international law, that judges cannot be removed except for proven incapacity or misbehaviour. 'Incapacity' is clear enough, and was not relevant in this case. 'Misbehaviour' is a broad term and should be limited to serious misbehaviour. Criminal offences would normally qualify, although even here, there are lines to be drawn: in England a circuit judge was sacked after his conviction for smuggling whisky, but senior appellate judges have escaped impeachment for drunk-driving offences. Criminal offences can at least be 'proven' – namely – by the verdict of a judge and/or jury, and subsequent impeachment by Parliament is scrupulously fair to a judge given the opportunity (however unlikely it is to succeed) to claim that his or her conviction was wrongful.

Where for some reason a criminal charge has not been proffered, Parliament has the difficult task of replicating court procedures to prove – necessarily to the criminal standard of beyond a reasonable doubt – that the judge is in fact guilty. Where the 'misbehaviour' alleged does not constitute a criminal offence at all, the question of whether it is serious enough to warrant dismissal becomes acute. Why should a judge be dismissed for conduct that is lawful? There are dangers of judges being impeached because governments dislike what they lawfully say or do. For example, Republican politicians in the U.S. attempted to impeach William O. Douglas because he gave an interview to *Playboy*. In addition, the calculating Dr. Mahartir, fearing that his honest Chief Justice would rule against him in a forthcoming case, had him dismissed

3 The Code of Conduct for UN judges was drawn up by the Internal Justice Council (Chaired by Justice Kate O'Regan – the author was a member), which recommends that complaints be investigated by three distinguished jurists: any recommendation that they make for dismissal would be put before the General Assembly.

because at a University book launch, he spoke up for the independence of the Malaysian judiciary. In every case where it is alleged that non-criminal conduct amounts to 'misbehaviour' sufficient to disentitle a judge to sit, special care must be taken to ensure that the conduct really does reflect so badly on the individual that he or she can no longer be considered fit to judge others – because, in a sense, they cannot even judge themselves.

Some assistance as to the kind and degree of misbehaviour that disqualifies a judge is found in the 'Latimer House Principles' agreed to by Law Ministers of the Commonwealth and by the Commonwealth Heads of Government. A specific rule provides that 'Judges should be subject to suspension or removal only for reasons of incapacity or misbehaviour that clearly renders them unfit to discharge their duties.'[4] This requires clear proof of misconduct that renders them unfit, at least in the eyes of reasonable people, to occupy their seat. This finds an echo in the Beijing Statement of Principles of the Independence of the Judiciary in the ASEAN Region, which is subscribed to by 32 Chief Justices, including Mrs. Bandaranayake's predecessor. Article 22 provides that 'Judges should be subject to removal from office only for proved incapacity, conviction of a crime, or conduct that makes the judge unfit to be a judge.'

This international approach to what is required to secure judicial tenure is fully endorsed by the Constitution of Sri Lanka. It has a special Article – 107 – titled 'Independence of the Judiciary' as if to underline its constitutional importance. Article 107(2) provides that

> Every judge shall hold office during good behaviour and shall not be removed except by an order of the President made after an address of Parliament supported by a majority of the total number of members of Parliament (including those not present) has been presented to the President for such removal on the ground of proved misbehaviour or incapacity.

It is essential that the misbehaviour or incapacity be proved. But how? By what procedures and according to what standards? Article107 is deficient in this respect – it requires at least one-third of the MPs to sign the motion for an address – but it goes on to state that 'the investigation and proof of the alleged misbehaviour or incapacity and the right of such judge to appear and be heard in person or by a representative' is left to Parliament to provide 'by law or by Standing Orders'.[5] The President's powers to appoint (Article 122) and dismiss (Article 107) judges were, of course, based on the presidency as a ceremonial position under a Westminster-style constitution. Subsequently, the

4 Commonwealth Principles on the Accountability of and the Relationship between the three branches of Government, Abuja, 2003. Section IV (Independence of the Judiciary).

5 S107(3).

President became the political leader of the country, with executive power and majority support from his party in Parliament.

Quite clearly, the standards and procedures for trying allegations of judicial misconduct, particularly if a judge has not been convicted in the courts of any offence, must comply with the minimum standards set out in Article 14 of the International Covenant on Civil and Political Rights (ICCPR) to which Sri Lanka is a state party, namely,

> a fair and public hearing by a competent, independent and impartial tribunal, with the presumption of innocence (14(2)) and rights to have adequate time to prepare a defence, (14(3)(6)) to examine and cross-examine witnesses and to call witnesses on his behalf.[6]

These are fundamental safeguards that must apply to quasi-criminal 'misconduct' charges that, if they result in an impeachment address by MPs, will destroy the judge's reputation and deprive him or her of status, job, and pension rights. For this reason, the common law insists on scrupulous fairness, as the Privy Council made clear in the leading Commonwealth case of *Rees v Crane*,[7] where the rules of natural justice were held to require a judge to be given, even at a preliminary stage, all the evidence against him and an opportunity to refute the charges. The Beijing Rules insist that 'Removal by Parliamentary procedure . . . should be rarely, if ever, used' because 'its use other than for the most serious reasons is apt to lead to misuse.'[8] When it is used, 'the judge who is sought to be removed must have the right to a fair hearing.'[9] The Latimer House principles are similarly emphatic: Principle VII requires that 'any disciplinary procedures should be fairly and objectively administered . . . with . . . appropriate safeguards to ensure fairness.' The Latimer House Guidelines go further:

> In cases where a judge is at risk of removal, the judge must have the right to be fully informed of the charges, to be represented at a hearing, to make a full defence and to be judged by an independent and impartial Tribunal.[10]

These principles must be stringently applied to any attempt to remove a Chief Justice, who is the representative of the judiciary as a whole and because he or she has achieved this exalted status, will normally have a high degree of peer approval and possess a recognised judicial distinction. Indeed, many

6 Article 14(3)(e).

7 *Evan Rees v Richard Alfred Crane* (1994) 1 AC 173.

8 Rule 23.

9 Rule 26.

10 Guideline VI(1)(9).

'Westminster model' constitutions give the Chief Justice, through chairmanship of a Legal Services Commission, a leading role in the disciplining and removal of other judges. This makes the removal of a Chief Justice particularly problematic. Some Commonwealth countries provide in their constitution for a tribunal of overseas Commonwealth judges to investigate misconduct charges against the Chief Justice, a recognition of both the momentous political character of such a move and the need to eliminate any suggestion of bias in the membership of the tribunal. The cases are, fortunately, very few, but the tribunal in Trinidad and Tobago called in 2006 to hear charges of misconduct against Chief Justice Sharma provides a procedural exemplar. The tribunal was chaired by Lord Mustill, sitting with distinguished jurists from Jamaica and St. Vincent. The allegation was that Sharma had attempted to pervert the course of justice by pressuring the Chief Magistrate to acquit the leader of the opposition of an imprisonable offence. This is, of course, a serious crime, and it should always be 'proved' in court before removal proceedings are undertaken. The Chief Justice had been charged, but bizarrely, the Chief Magistrate refused to testify when called into court to give evidence against him, so the criminal proceedings were discontinued, and an impeachment process commenced instead. Lord Mustill insisted, after lengthy argument, on scrupulously fair procedures: the Chief Magistrate was cross-examined at length; the rules of evidence at a criminal trial were applied; and the burden of proof (following in *re A Solicitor*)[11] was held to be the criminal standard, that is, proof beyond reasonable doubt. The procedures adopted by Lord Mustill in Sharma's Case provide the best precedents for the first stage of any impeachment of a Chief Justice in a Commonwealth country. Regrettably, the Commission's report has not been properly published by the Trinidad government.

Article 107(3) of the Sri Lankan Constitution must therefore be read consistently with these international and commonwealth requirements. The 'law or standing orders' that it provides for the procedures leading up to the address, such as 'the investigation and proof of the alleged behaviour', must be scrupulously fair. It is unfortunate that Sri Lanka has not passed a law similar to that of Trinidad and some other Commonwealth countries, which provides (usually in their Constitution) for an independent tribunal to hear removal allegations against a judge. An amendment to the Constitution proposed in 2000 would have done exactly that, but it was dropped. As for Standing Orders, which do not have the force of law, those made by the Speaker in Sri Lanka (on the recommendation of a committee that he chairs) do not provide any kind of independent tribunal. The procedure for establishing judicial misconduct is merely set out in Standing Order 78A, which is confusingly titled 'Rules of Debate'. It states that

11 In *re A Solicitor* [1993] QB 69.

1. Where notice of a resolution for the presentation of an address to the President for the removal of a Judge from office is given to the Speaker in accordance with Article 107 of the Constitution, the Speaker shall entertain such resolution and place it on the Order Paper of Parliament but such resolution shall not be proceeded with until after the expiration of a period of one month from the date on which the Select Committee appointed under paragraph (2) of this Order has reported to Parliament.
2. Where a resolution referred to the paragraph (1) of this Order is placed on the Order Paper of Parliament, the Speaker shall appoint a Select Committee of Parliament consisting of not less than seven members to investigate and report to Parliament on the allegations of misbehavior or incapacity set out in such resolution.
3. A Select Committee appointed under paragraph (2) of this Order shall transmit to the Judge whose alleged misbehavior or incapacity is the subject of its investigation, a copy of the allegations of misbehavior or incapacity made against such Judge and set out in the resolution in pursuance of which such Select Committee was appointed, and shall require such Judge to make a written statement of defense within such period as maybe specified by it.
4. The Select Committee appointed under paragraph (2) of this Order shall have power to send for persons, papers and records and not less than half the number of members of the Select Committee shall form the quorum.
5. The Judge whose alleged misbehavior or incapacity is the subject of the investigation by a Select Committee appointed under paragraph (2) of this Order shall have the right to appear before it and to be heard by, such Committee, in person or by representative and to adduce evidence, oral or documentary, in disproof of the allegations made against him.
6. At the conclusion of the investigation made by it, a Select Committee appointed under paragraph (2) of this Order shall within one month from the commencement of the sittings of such Select Committee, report its findings together with the minutes of evidence taken before it to Parliament and may make a special report of any matters which it may think fit to bring to the notice of Parliament.
7. Where a resolution for the presentation of an address to the President for the removal of a Judge from office on the ground of proved misbehavior or incapacity is passed by Parliament, the Speaker shall present such address to the President on behalf of Parliament.
8. All proceedings connected with the investigation by the Select Committee appointed under paragraph (3) of this Order shall not be made public unless and until a finding of guilt on any of the charges against such Judge is reported to Parliament by such Select Committee.

The impeachment procedure is arcane, the Order is elliptically drafted, and at no point does it envisage the involvement of persons other than politicians.

Article 107 requires impeachment to begin with a petition signed by at least one-third of all members of Parliament, setting out the 'full particulars' of the alleged misbehaviour. This is the cue under 78A(2) for the Speaker to appoint a Select Committee of at least seven MPs to investigate and report. It must give the accused judge a copy of the allegations (but not necessarily the evidence), and the judge must provide it with a written defence statement. Then, the judge has the right to be heard and to call evidence (but not, apparently, to question or cross-examine any hostile witnesses). The Select Committee has only a month to investigate, and most importantly (and most unfairly), it must clothe its work in secrecy 'until a finding of guilt on any of the charges against such judge is reported to Parliament by such Select Committee.' After the report has been sent to Parliament, a month must elapse before the impeachment debate, at the end of which, if more than half the MPs favour the motion, the speaker will present the 'address' to the President who may then remove the judge.

These rules, which were broadly followed in Dr. Bandaranayake's case, are highly objectionable. In the first place, the Select Committee members must all be MPs, and the Speaker may (as he did in this case) appoint a majority of government ministers. Secondly, the committee hearings must necessarily be in secret and remain so until reasons for a 'guilty' verdict are presented to Parliament. This is a plain breach of Article 106 of the Constitution that provides that every 'tribunal or other institution established under the Constitution or by Parliament' (which would include a Select Committee established to try a judge and report on whether he or she is guilty) 'shall be held in public and all persons shall be entitled freely to attend such sittings.' The Rules are therefore contrary to the Constitution, which plainly requires open justice, as do the Latimer Rules, the Beijing principles, and the common law. The Standing Order gives the judge a few rights, but the basic protection of openness and the rights to have time to prepare a defence and to cross-examine adverse witnesses are not mentioned. The most important protection of all is also not mentioned: the burden and standard of proof. The burden must fall on the prosecution, and conviction must only come after 'proof beyond reasonable doubt'. In all of these respects, the Standing Orders of Parliament are gravely deficient in fairness.

Other aspects to the protection of judicial independence should be observed when a judge – especially a Chief Justice – is put through the demeaning ordeal of an impeachment. There must be some respected and responsible trigger for this draconian process, but Article 107 provides that merely one-third of the number of MPs can commence it by signing a request to the Speaker. As this number of supportive members will necessarily be commanded by the party or coalition in power, it is a frail reed indeed to protect a judge from reprisals by the government if his or her rulings discomfort its ministers. As for the President, who has the supreme and absolute power to accept or reject the address, this is not the ceremonial President envisaged by Westminster model institutions. Sri Lanka's head of state is not an apolitical figure like the King in the UK but a street-fighting politician who is head of the government and has wide-ranging constitutional powers at his discretion. His party or its supporters will command over half of the MPs and can therefore easily round up one-third of them to initiate the process to remove a judge. In Sri Lanka, in 2012–13, President Rajapakse and his United People's Freedom Alliance, with supporting parties, had a large majority in Parliament – more than two-thirds of its total of 225 members. The President's elder brother, Chamal Rajapakse, was the Speaker of the House who oversaw Dr. Bandaranayake's impeachment. In this situation, the terms of the Constitution afford no real protection to a judge whose rulings incur the enmity of the ruling President, his family, or his party.

It is important to note several non-legal ways in which a government can imperil judicial independence while making attempts to remove a judge. In Sri Lanka, as in many other countries, the government controls and heavily influences the state media, which endorses its campaigns. Tame journalists may wage a propaganda war against disfavoured judges, thereby placing intolerable psychological pressure on them and their families. A government will, by definition, have a political party with control over large swathes of supporters and an ability, for example, to organise demonstrations against judicial targets. The large-scale public protests against Dr. Bandaranayake were of particular concern in this respect: the public at large does not know or much care about fine points of constitutional law, and it is difficult to believe that they took to the streets against her without government manipulation. This was widely alleged in Sri Lanka's free press and requires serious investigation: there is television footage that seems to show demonstrators being paid after chanting slogans against her and against the Supreme Court. Orchestrated protests against a particular judge are a particularly objectionable form of retaliation, and any government political party behind such demonstrations deserves the strongest condemnation. The government, of course, will have control of the police and armed forces, and I note how the authorities later effected the physical removal of Mrs. Bandaranayake from her Supreme Court chambers.

11.3 Background to the Impeachment

11.3.1 The Chief Justice

Sri Lanka is a long-standing democracy that was granted independence from Britain in 1948 and endowed with a Westminster model constitution that has been substantially amended since. The Privy Council was its final Court of Appeal for many years, and its common law and its legal profession reflect their English models. 'King's Counsel' is now styled 'President's Counsel', (somewhat unfortunately when the President is no longer ceremonial but a powerful political figure). The country was plunged for many years into a violent civil war against the secessionist Tamil Tigers, which ended in 2009 when government forces captured their base in the island's north, killing up to

40,000 civilians in the process. A UN Human Rights Committee investigation was highly critical of both sides and particularly of the government, and some commentators have sought to draw connections between the government's lawlessness in the civil war and the disrespect for law it showed when removing the Chief Justice. I saw no such connection other than that the result of the war – the ending of Tamil Tiger terrorism – had the consequence of making President Rajapaske so popular that the next election gave him an overwhelming majority. There were long-standing tensions between the executive and the judiciary, as noted in IBA reports in 2001 and 2009,[12] and two previous impeachment attempts. (The simmering discontent among politicians about judges getting 'too big for their boots' was undoubtedly a background factor in their contemptuous behaviour toward the Chief Justice.) However, in other respects, Sri Lanka was a state in good standing in the Commonwealth: so much so that criticism of its conduct in the 2009 hostilities was removed from the Commonwealth Heads of Government (CHOGM) agenda at the 2012 meeting, and Sri Lanka was paid the compliment of being chosen to host the CHOGM meeting in November 2013.

Dr. Shirini Bandaranayake has had a most impressive career culminating in her appointment in May 2011, at age 53, as Chief Justice – the first woman to achieve this rank. She would later be very briefly reappointed as the Chief Justice in January 2015. She attended a state school in the countryside before obtaining a law degree and winning a Commonwealth scholarship to earn her doctorate at the University of London. She went straight into academic work, rising to become Dean of Colombo's excellent law school and acting as Vice-Chancellor of the university. In 1996, at age 38, she was made a Justice of the Supreme Court by President Kumaratunge, achieving a double first – first woman and first academic on that bench. There were petitions by several barristers objecting to her appointment on the grounds that the President had not consulted the judicial network,[13] but no one suggested that she lacked integrity or intellectual calibre. Her record refutes any suggestion that she was anti-establishment (or, anti-Rajapaske) – on the contrary, her juristic writing in over 300 court decisions is conventional and her approach is quite conservative. Indeed, her appointment as Chief Justice met with criticism from some human rights non-governmental organisations (NGOs) as she was seen as an ally of the President after a ruling in 2010 that upheld controversial legislation extending his powers. She was respected by her colleagues and became one of the two Supreme Court judges sitting with the former Chief Justice on the Judicial Service Commission. During her impeachment tribulation, she had the support of all high court judges and the majority of lawyers and magistrates in Sri Lanka.

12 IBA, *Justice in Retreat: A Report on the Independence of the Legal Institutions and the Rule of Law in Sri Lanka* (IBA Human Rights Institute 2009).

13 Sri Lankan Law Reports (1997) 9 December 1996, *Silva v Bandaranayake & ors.*

On becoming Chief Justice, Mrs. Bandaranayake, under Article III of the Constitution, automatically became chair of the Judicial Service Committee, which comprised herself and two other Supreme Court Justices nominated by the President. The three were required to choose the committee's secretary 'from among senior judicial officers of the Courts of First Instance', and they chose a judge who was not the most senior of possible candidates but was 'senior' nonetheless. The Commission is empowered to transfer, promote, discipline, and dismiss judicial officers and public servants working in the courts.

11.3.2 The Judicial Services Commission (JSC) Under Attack

The power of the Chief Justice, as chair of the JSC, came under political attack in September 2012 shortly before her impeachment. It began with a telephone call from the Secretary to the President on 13 September indicating that the President had directed the three JSC members to meet him at his residence on 17 September. No reason for the meeting was given. This direction was put in writing at the Chief Justice's request, again giving no reason, and the JSC wrote back saying that a meeting would be open to misinterpretation and harmful to public confidence in the independence of the judiciary. This was prudent, as the Chief Justice and another JSC judge were members of the bench that was about to deliver a very controversial decision on the Devineguma Bill (see later). It is a fundamental Latimer House principle that 'While dialogue between the judiciary and the government may be desirable or appropriate, in no circumstance should such dialogue compromise judicial independence.'[14] Summoning two of the three judges who were about to deliver a politically important decision and giving no reason for the summons was unsatisfactory behaviour on the part of the President, and I have no doubt that the judges genuinely feared that a meeting with him would compromise them.

On 17 September, the *Divineguma* Bill decision was handed down, and it went against Minister Basil Rajapaske. A large crowd of governmental supporters suddenly materialized outside Parliament and shouted slogans against the Supreme Court and against the Chief Justice. Whether this demonstration was orchestrated by the government or not, it was clearly not spontaneous (the judgement at this point was delivered to the Speaker, the President's brother, who was reporting it to Parliament.)

As far as the President's action in summoning the judges to a meeting was concerned, the JSC drew the inference – not unreasonably – that he was attempting to exert undue influence over them. On 18 September, the JSC issued a press release that spoke of other threats from government quarters after it had disciplined a particular judicial officer and said that there were 'forces' (unspecified) that were using the electronic and print media to

14 Guideline I, point 5.

make baseless criticism of the JSC and attempting to undermine the judiciary. The press statement was being issued 'to keep the public informed of the threat'.

It was a surprisingly powerful statement, perhaps issued by a Commission rattled by the demonstrations of the previous day, but it threw down the gauntlet to the government. A week went by before President Rajapakse responded by telling the media that he had summoned the JSC members not in his capacity as President but in his role as Minister of Finance merely to discuss their budget. If this had been the case, then it was very surprising that his secretary failed to mention this purpose at the time. Although the President denied any intention of interfering with the judiciary, I have seen no evidence that either he or his law officers ever condemned the public demonstration against it. The following day (28 September), the JSC secretary claimed that there was a security threat to the Chief Justice and her fellow judges, although it turned out that the most immediate threat was to himself. President Rajapaksa told national newspaper publishers at a breakfast meeting on 4 October that he had instructed the Criminal Investigation Department to look into an allegation of sexual harassment that had been made against the Secretary. This man, a district judge, was assaulted three days later, after dropping his wife and son at school, by unidentified men and suffered serious injuries to his face and head. On the following day, judges and magistrates refused to attend their courts in protest against this attack that they said was incited by the government. Its perpetrators have still not been arrested.

These incidents show the pressures that were building up in the weeks before the impeachment, partly as a result of the Supreme Court's decision to strike down the Divineguma Bill. Before explaining its significance, I should mention one other vulnerability of the Chief Justice at this time, namely, her husband. Pradeep Kariyawasam had been appointed by the President as Chairman of the National Savings Bank shortly before his wife was made Chief Justice. Although he was not a politician or a backer of the President's party, the President then appointed him as director of a public company chaired by another one of his brothers (Gotabhyaya Rajapaksa, the Defence Secretary). Some commentators expressed concern that his appointment might incline his wife to repay the favours through more pro-government judgements. However, the bank made a bad investment decision and lost public money, and Kariyawasam tendered his resignation in May 2012. In August, at the very time that the argument about the constitutionality of the Divineguma Bill was being heard by the Supreme Court, he was summoned by the Bribery Commission to give evidence about the share transaction. This might well have been because the share transaction was dubious, although some thought that it was a means by which the government could put further pressure on the Chief Justice. There was media comment at the time about why he alone had been summonsed and not others who were more involved in the decisions to make the bad investment.

11.3.3 The Devineguma Bill

It is difficult for those who do not live in a federal system to understand the political importance of the Divineguma Bill or the government's anxiety to have it declared constitutional. It was the brainchild of another brother of the President, Basil Rajapaksa, the Minister of Economic Development, who presented it to Parliament on 10 August 2012. Sri Lanka, unlike the UK, has a system of preventive overruling, which permits speedy constitutional challenge to government bills as soon as they are placed on the order paper of Parliament, and there were a number of challenges to the Divineguma Bill. This was because it breached the constitution, which required the minister to consult with all Sri Lanka's nine provincial councils before it could be tabled. It was a centralising bill that brought devolved power back to Colombo, in this case, power that would henceforth be wielded by Basil Rajapaska, the President's brother. It also gave his departmental officials new powers to invade privacy and obtain information about citizens.

In deciding constitutional cases, judges must usually choose between arguments that are good and arguments that are better. The decision of the three Supreme Court judges, with the Chief Justice presiding, in the first Divineguma Bill case clearly and logically applied Section 154 of the Constitution requiring such bills to be submitted 'to every provincial council for the expression of its views thereon' before being placed on the order paper. As the bill had been placed on the order paper without any such consultation, it could go no further. It was a straightforward issue, and the decision was in my view, an obviously correct application of Section 154. However, the Solicitor General on behalf of the government had taken a preliminary and highly technical point that Article 12(1) of the Constitution allowed citizens to challenge a bill

> by a petition in writing addressed to the Supreme Court . . . within one week of the Bill being placed on the Order Paper of the Parliament and a copy thereof shall at the same time be delivered to the Speaker.

The bill was placed on the Order Paper on 10 April, and the petition was filed in the Supreme Court Registry on 17 August – just before the deadline. At the same time, it was sent to the Speaker by registered post and arrived in the Speaker's hands only on 20 August, which was obviously not at the same time as it was addressed to the Supreme Court. So, what did the word 'deliver' mean in the context of the constitutional right of citizens to petition against a proposed law – did it mean the act of conveying the document, which was performed when it was sent on 17 August, or did it mean the point at which it came into the Speaker's hands, that is, 20 August? If the latter, then the objectors to the bill would be knocked out – on the merest of technicalities.

This is exactly the kind of problem that lawyers are born to solve. It is their bread and butter, from their first day at law school, when they are asked whether a law against bringing a 'vehicle' into the park should exclude a perambulator or a bicycle or a crashing aeroplane. It is meat and drink to the judges of any country called upon to decide the meaning of words and phrases in a Constitution applying 'literal rules', 'golden rules', and rules of 'purposive interpretation' to the language of sloppy parliamentary draftspersons. The Chief Justice and her two colleagues did what judges in other English-speaking countries usually do when faced with a question of the meaning of a word – they consulted the *Oxford English Dictionary*. It defined 'delivery' as 'the act of conveying into the hands of another, especially the action of a courier in delivering letters entrusted to him for conveyance to a person at a distance.' They reasoned that such an act could be carried out by posting, so the commencement of the delivery by posting on 17 August satisfied the precondition for bringing a petition about the bill's constitutionality. They made reference to a previous 1991 case (the *Sri Lankan Telecommunications case*) but distinguished it on the facts of that case (there had been no posting of the petition simultaneously with its Court filing but instead, an out-of-time hand delivery to the speaker). I have addressed the issue at some length to point out that the court dealt with and distinguished the 1991 precedent and reached a perfectly sensible, logical, and legal conclusion. It must be emphasized that this is a perfectly normal and indeed commonplace example of judicial reasoning because the Chief Justice's accusers later outrageously claimed that it amounted to misbehaviour justifying the impeachment.

The impeachment would soon come. The *Divineguma* decision against the government was handed down on 17 September, which angered the government by invalidating legislation that was important to its agenda, followed by the protest of the JSC and the assault on its Secretary. The press on 26 September and again on 4 October reported that the President and a committee of cabinet members were discussing 'strong measures' against the judiciary. It may be that at this point that the drafting of impeachment charges began, although Basil Rajapaske was prepared to give the Supreme Court one last chance. On 10 October he tabled the Bill again and reported that it had now been approved by eight out of nine elected Provincial Councils and by the Governor who had been imposed on the largely Tamil and war-torn Northern Province. Challenges were made again to the same Supreme Court bench headed by the Chief Justice, this time on the grounds that the governor was not authorised to approve the bill in the absence of an elected council.

Given all of this existing pressure on the Chief Justice, it did not help when on 25 October, the Bribery Commission charged her husband with unlawfully causing a substantial loss to the public. Nonetheless, the Chief Justice and her colleagues reported on 1 November that the bill was even more flawed than they had ruled the first time – the Governor could not usurp the role of an elected council, and other provisions of the Bill would need to be approved through a public referendum. Once again, their decision was properly reasoned, but it tipped the government over the brink. A few hours after the judgment was delivered, 117 MPs signed an impeachment resolution calling on the Speaker to present an 'address' to the President seeking the removal of the Chief Justice. In all of these circumstances, it is impossible to resist the inference that the impeachment was the government's direct response to the unfavourable decision by the Supreme Court in the *Divineguma* Bill cases.

11.4 The Impeachment Charges

11.4.1 The Three Divineguma Counts

The evidence for this proposition is not only circumstantial – it came from the terms of the impeachment charges. There were 14 of them, in not particularly coherent English, appended to the motion. Did any of them charge, as misbehaviour, conduct that on any reasonable view amounted to the exercise of a proper and conscientious professional judgement? This would be proof of a blatant assault on judicial independence: the ousting by the government of a judge who did her duty and arrived at a result that the government did not like. The Rajapaske government did not like the first *Divineguma* decision, and it probably liked the second even less, because the impeachment resolution was tabled on the same day it was handed down. What those 117 MPs did, fatally to their case, was to accuse the Chief Justice of misbehaviour for rendering an utterly professional judgement – shared by her two colleagues – in *Divineguma No.* 1.

Count 8 in the Bill of impeachment read as follows:

> Whereas Article 121(i) of the Constitution has been violated by the said Dr. Bandaranayake despite the fact that it had been decided that the mandatory procedure set out in the said Article of the Constitution must be followed in accordance with the interpretation given by the Supreme Court in the 1991 *Sri Lanka Telecommunications Case.*

This was not an allegation of misbehaviour. It was an allegation that the Chief Justice should be sacked because she (and her two colleagues) had not accepted the Solicitor General's technical argument based on the 1991 case. As I have explained, the judges distinguished the facts of the *Telecommunications Bill* case, which did not therefore bind them, and reached their interpretation on the word 'deliver' by reference to the *Oxford English Dictionary.* They did what judges in all common law countries do and reached a decision that many other judges would have reached. This did not, of course, matter – the important thing is that they reached it honestly and professionally. The only reason that this could appear on an impeachment charge was that the government and the 117 MP's who had all taken to the government whip disliked the consequences of the decision, and it is this motivation that strikes at the heart of judicial independence. No honest lawyer, with any respect for the principles of his or her profession, could support such an impeachment, and those of the 117 who were lawyers deliberately made a false accusation of misconduct against a judge for doing her judicial duty. I can think of no behaviour more likely to bring the profession into disrepute, although in fact it brings these individual MPs into disrepute. As far as Sri Lanka's membership in the Commonwealth was concerned, there can hardly be a more blatant breach of the Latimer House principles.

The Count 8 accusation against a judge for misbehaviour for doing her duty did not stand alone. It was no accidental inclusion overlooked by MPs when they signed up for the impeachment. There was another charge related to the court's dismissal of the Solicitor General's unattractive technical argument for adopting a literal interpretation to dismiss one of the petitions,[15] which had been 'delivered' on time but was addressed to the 'Secretary General of Parliament' rather than to the 'Speaker of Parliament'. As the petitioner's counsel pointed out to the court, the Solicitor General's argument was tantamount to saying that a rule requiring delivery to the Chief Justice could not be satisfied by delivering it to the Registrar of his court. Moreover, it would be hopelessly impractical because the Speaker was a grand figure (especially grand when he was the elder brother of the President), and petitioners, process servers, and lawyers cannot barge into Parliament or serve him personally in his limousine or when he is surrounded by security guards. Citizens usually approached him through the Secretary General of the Parliament, who was, in effect, the Speaker's gatekeeper and Parliament's administrator. The Solicitor General's reliance on the literal rule of construction was absurd and impractical, which is one reason why the literal rule has fallen out of fashion. As Lord Steyn has pointed out,

> The tyrant Temures promised the garrison of Lebastia that no blood would be shed if they surrendered to him. They surrendered. He shed no blood. He buried them all alive. This is literalism. If possible it should be avoided in the interpretative process.[16]

The Chief Justice and her colleagues dealt patiently and correctly with the submission of the Solicitor General, the government's lawyer. They quoted all of Article 121, which showed that the purpose of requiring an urgent delivery to the Speaker was so that parliamentary proceedings on a challenged bill could be suspended as soon as possible while the Supreme Court decided on its constitutionality – and this purpose would be as well-served by delivery to the Secretary General of Parliament as to the Speaker. This 'purposive construction' is one way of ensuring that the law conforms to common sense, and many judges would have rejected the Solicitor General's literal construction, which would have made the right to citizen petition depend on whether the

15 The petition was No 03/2012.

16 The example is from William Paley. See *Sirius Insurance v FAI* (2004) 1 WLR 3251, per Lord Steyn.

citizen could get close enough to the Speaker in time to thrust the petition into his hands. Any court prepared to take this pettifogging approach to protect the government from having its unconstitutional plans overruled would be open to serious rebuke.

Nevertheless, Count 7 of the impeachment accused the Chief Justice of misbehaviour for not upholding the Solicitor-General's argument:

> Whereas with respect to Supreme Court Special ruling no's 2/2012 and 3/2012, Dr. Bandaranayake has disregarded and/or violated Article 121(1) of the Constitution by making a special ruling of the Supreme Court to the effect that provisions set out in the Constitution are met by the handing over of a copy of the petition filed at the court to the Secretary General of Parliament despite the fact that it has been mentioned that a copy of a petition filed under Article 121(1) of the Constitution shall at the same time be delivered to the Speaker of Parliament.

This charge was clumsily worded and incompetently drafted – the court's ruling was in fact confined to petition 3/2012. It was a shameless attempt to re-run the unrealistic argument of the Solicitor General. The same objection applies to Count 7 as to Count 8: the MPs were alleging misbehaviour against a judge for delivering an exemplary judgment on the purposive interpretation of a constitutional provision.

Moreover, they were taking issue with the legal basis of a decision that not only was correct and most courts would have reached but also only the Supreme Court had the right to reach. This is clear from section 125(i) of the Constitution: 'The Supreme Court shall have sole and exclusive jurisdiction to hear and determine any question relating to the interpretation of the Constitution'. It was the duty of the Chief Justice to preside over such a question, and even if she and her colleagues came to what other courts might think an incorrect decision – if they preferred a good argument to a better one (although in truth, both of the Solicitor General's arguments were not very good) – then the decision must stand as the correct interpretation until such time as the Supreme Court itself reconsiders the issue. It is monstrous to charge a judge with misbehaviour for doing her duty. Charges 7 and 8 did exactly that, and their inclusion proved beyond any doubt that this impeachment constituted a blatant attack on the independence of the judiciary and on the Latimer House principles. This country's government and this country's Parliament were out to remove a judge because they disliked her honest and expert decisions. The fact that, in the end, the Select Committee did not need to consider these two charges does not matter. The very fact that they were made mattered a great deal.

The third impeachment charge related to the Divineguma Bill was risible. So furious were the 117 MPs about the Supreme Court's decision that in Count 10, they accused the Chief Justice of bias because one of the petitioners in the case (the Centre for Policy Alternatives) had, twenty years before, published an academic article she had written when she was a law lecturer at the University of Colombo. No rational person would consider this a ground for removal of a judge for misbehaviour or indeed for any suggestion that she might be biased on an issue of statutory interpretation (from which she could obtain no possible benefit) because one of the petitioners happened to be a public interest NGO that had once published an article she had written. This was obviously not 'serious misbehaviour' or misbehaviour of any sort.

11.4.2 The JSC Charges

No less than six charges related to the decisions taken by the Judicial Services Commission in pursuance of its disciplinary functions under the Constitution. None of these could be described as 'misbehaviour'. Count 11, for example, alleged that a magistrate's brother claimed that he had been 'harassed' by a JSC decision – with no details whatsoever of the decision or the 'harassment'. Count 12 is nonsensical: the JSC was accused of acting ultra vires because it 'ordered the magistrate's right to obtain legal protection for lodging a complaint in police against the harassment meted out to her by the Secretary of the JSC.' What did this mean? Did the 117 MPs even read the charges? (Perhaps, as it was widely rumoured, they signed blank sheets of paper). Did they not realise that the Chief Justice's decisions were all supported by her fellow commissioners who were both Supreme Court judges?

Counts 13 and 14 accused the Chief Justice of misbehaviour because the JSC discouraged magistrates from going directly to police to seek protection but directed them to route such requests through the Commission. This seems an eminently sensible policy, given that the JSC was in charge overall of maintaining security for judges. Several of the charges made accusations against the Secretary of the JSC, Manjula Thilakaratne, who had angered the government – and certainly the President – by his September press releases. Count 6, for example, accused the Chief Justice (it did not mention her judicial colleagues) who had joined in the decision of appointing Thilakaratne and 'disregarding the seniority of judicial officers' – as if the JSC was somehow debarred from appointing someone on what it considered to be merit. Article 111G of the Constitution simply says that the Secretary shall be selected 'from among senior judicial officers', and Thilakaratne was one such senior judicial officers. He was more senior, in fact, than some previous Secretaries to the Commission had been at the time of their appointment. In none of these cases could 'serious misbehaviour' be a reasonable description of the work undertaken by the Chief Justice, with the agreement of her other judicial colleagues, in administering the courts and the judges. They were all trivial and unparticularised and accused her of no criminal offence or of any behaviour that could have been described as corrupt or of a type that would make a reasonable person think her unfit to judge.

11.5 Trial by Select Committee

On the subject of the fairness of removal procedures, international law is adamant: extirpating a judge from his or her office determines their rights and obligations, and since 'serious misbehaviour' usually means a criminal offence, it attracts the full force of protections in Article 14 of the ICCPR. This means

- a fair and public hearing
- by a competent, independent, and impartial Tribunal;
- the presumption of innocence;
- adequate time and facilities to prepare a defence; and
- the right to cross-examine any hostile witnesses and to call witnesses.

Each one of these safeguards was blatantly ignored by the 11-person Select Committee (seven government ministers, plus four opposition MPs who soon resigned) appointed by Speaker of the House Rajapaske on 14 November to investigate and report to Parliament. Just three weeks later, on 8 December, the seven government ministers reported her guilty of three charges. The Select Committee's breach of fairness standards can be summarized as follows.

11.5.1 Public Hearing

The Select Committee sat in secret. This was a consequence of Standing Order 78A (8), which required secrecy until a 'finding of guilt' is reported to Parliament. But Standing Orders are not laws – they can be altered or suspended – and the Chief Justice and her counsel repeatedly requested this protection. It was refused, and both her counsel and the opposition MP's spoke of the insulting and demeaning treatment she received, out of public sight, from several ministers. 'At various stages of the proceedings' said one of her counsel, 'two members of the Select Committee hurled abuse and obscene demands at the Chief Justice and her lawyers and addressed the Chief Justice in a humiliating and insulting manner.' This is to some extent corroborated by the four MP's in their resignation letter: 'the treatment meted out to the Chief Justice was insulting and intimidatory and the records made were clearly indicative of preconceived findings of guilt.' Had the proceedings been open to the public, this kind of behaviour might not have occurred.

As I have pointed out earlier, Standing Order 78A(8), which requires secrecy until a 'finding of guilt' is made, appears to be *ultra vires* of Section 106 of the Constitution, which requires such committee proceedings to be open to the public. In any case, the Standing Order is an order ostensibly made for the protection of the accused judge, and the Chief Justice's leading counsel explained to the committee that she wished to waive this protection and have the trial in public or at least to have international observers present. This was supported by opposition MPs, but the Chairman ruled that the committee was bound by the Standing Order. It could, of course, have asked the Speaker to amend or suspend it – the request was made on 4 December before the 'trial' began on 6 December – but the government Ministers apparently had no wish to let the public observe their own behaviour or that of their witnesses, and the request was refused[17] on the basis that it was not possible. It was possible, of course, because the Speaker could immediately have called the Standing Orders Committee (which he chairs) to advise the House to amend or suspend 78A(8). It need hardly be said – Jeremy Bentham said it, and it still holds true – that 'publicity is the very soul of justice. It keeps the judge, while trying, under trial'. These proceedings, particularly the evidence given on 7 December, would have come under public scrutiny, and the prejudice of the committee would have been palpable. It is essential, in cases of this type, for the public to hear the witnesses, because if they tell lies, others will come forward to confound them. The Chairman of the committee, by refusing to suspend the Standing Order after its protection had been waived, ensured that justice was not going to be done.

11.5.2 Competent Independent and Impartial Tribunal

A tribunal that is independent means 'independent of government'. Yet Speaker Rajapaske deliberately chose seven senior government ministers. At the very least he might have scoured the Parliament for government-supporting MP's who had a reputation for independence or had some form of pubic and legal distinction. Instead, he chose six members of the cabinet and a junior minister, all of whom were angry about the government's defeat by the Chief Justice's rulings over the Divineguma Bill.

There were also issues as to impartiality. Not only was the Select Committee majority made up of government ministers but also two of them had recently suffered judgements against their personal interests by Supreme Court benches chaired by Mrs. Bandaranayake. On 23 November, she appeared before the committee and requested recusal particularly of Dr. Senaratne, whose wife's employment claim she had dismissed earlier in 2012 and whom she believed to harbour a grudge against her, and Mr. Weerawansa, whose appeal over a personal matter she had dismissed in 2010. The ministers allegedly replied that the rule against bias did not apply to MPs – which is an absurd proposition, although it accurately reflected the position taken by the Speaker in appointing them. The Chairman rejected the application.[18] He and the other six were government ministers who had signed the impeachment charges and were now embarking on a quasi-judicial inquiry into the charges that they themselves had brought. The judges and magistrates of Sri Lanka (below the Supreme Court rank) all issued a statement that pointed out that

17 See record, Parliamentary Series No 187, 190.
18 ibid 191.

'in no country does the party that makes the charges themselves inquire into the same charges.'[19]

The competency of the tribunal was questionable. None of the committee members had law degrees or had professional experience as adjudicators. They were party politicians and cabinet ministers whose first loyalty was to the government they had sworn to serve, which had been caused great problems by the *Divineguma* decision. The angry tone of the Select Committee's judgement and its frequent foray into rhetoric, far-fetched, or unsubstantiated inference and abuse of the Chief Justice was compelling evidence of their unfitness for the task. The very fact that they produced a 15-page judgement the day after hearing testimony about complex matters by 17 witnesses suggests that part of the judgement had been drafted before they heard the evidence and certainly before they had time to analyse it properly.

11.5.3 The Presumption of Innocence

This involves, at the very least, the rule that a prosecution must prove guilt – in criminal charges – beyond any reasonable doubt. This 'golden thread' that runs through the criminal law is not mentioned at all in 78A. The committee was asked by the Chief Justice to adopt this criminal standard, and the four opposition members supported her request and wanted a prima facie case to be made in relation to each charge, but these requests were refused. The findings of guilt were made on some inarticulate standard – whether on a hunch, a presumption of guilt, pure prejudice, or on a balance of probabilities. This flies in the face of fairness. As the Privy Council said in 2008 in *Campbell v Hamlet*, 'That the criminal standard of proof is the correct standard to be applied in all disciplinary proceedings concerning the legal profession their Lordships entertain no doubt.'[20] Lord Mustill, in his report to the Parliament of Trinidad and Tobago on the impeachment of Chief Justice Sharma firmly rejected arguments that a lesser or more 'flexible' procedure would suffice: 'The allegations against the Chief Justice are so grave, and the effect of an adverse finding so destructive, that the requirement of proof must be at the extreme end of the scale.'[21] The failure to adopt this – or any – burden and standard of proof was the clearest breach of the presumption of innocence.

The presumption also requires restraint in making prejudicial statements about guilt while a trial is underway. Members of the government's parliamentary group made public attacks on the Chief Justice while the so-called 'trial' progressed in secret, and (quite disgracefully) certain members of the Select Committee appeared on television claiming that they were uncovering large sums of undeclared money. But the most serious breach of the presumption

19 ibid.
20 (2006) 66 WLR 346, per Lord Brown of Eaton-Under-Heywood.
21 Report of Chief Justice Sharma Impeachment Tribunal; Lord Mustill, Sir Vincent Eloissac, Mr. Morrison QC (14 December 2007) para [82].

related to public demonstrations against the Chief Justice. On the first day of the trial, a large crowd demonstrated against her outside Parliament; they shouted insulting slogans and waved abusive placards. There were allegations at the time that their transport was organized by members of the government's parliamentary group. I certainly do not believe that the demonstration was spontaneous – the *Divineguma* judgment had been delivered some time before, and the Supreme Court's interpretation of the Constitution was not an obvious spark for public protest. If the demonstrations were organised by government supporters (and they certainly were not stopped or dispersed by any government orders while there is some evidence that they were paid), then this would be further proof of the denial of a fair trial by putting psychological pressure on the committee to convict and on the Chief Justice to give in or give up.

11.5.4 Details of the Charge and Time to Prepare a Defence

The entitlement to be given details of the charge and time to prepare and present a defence are fundamental to the fairness of any 'trial' and are guaranteed by Article 14(3)(a) and (b) of the ICCPR, by the Latimer House Guidelines,[22] and the Beijing Principles that emphasise that the right to a fair hearing remains intact even when removal by parliamentary procedures is required.[23] But Standing Order 78A(3) merely provides the following:

i. that a copy of 'allegations of misbehaviour' should be transmitted to the judge but not any particulars of those allegations;
ii. that the committee shall require such judge to make a written statement of defence, within a period specified by the committee; and
iii. The judge shall have 'a right to be heard . . . and to adduce evidence'.

These provisions were woefully inadequate to protect the judge. There was no requirement that the allegations be particularised, and charge 1, for example, on which she was convicted, was vague to the point of incoherence. Sri Lankan criminal law stipulates that any criminal charge shall be fully particularised (times, places, dates, persons, things, etc.) and not merely a vehicle for broad allegations.[24]

The mandatory rule that the committee 'shall require the judge to make a written statement' is a breach of the right not to incriminate oneself: accused judges, like everyone else, should in principle have the right to remain silent. Of course, normally, judges will wish to speak out, to assert their innocence, or to explain away allegations. But there may be occasions where the charges

22 Guideline VI.1 para [a] [i].
23 Beijing Principles, para [26].
24 Section 165(1) Code of Criminal Procedure Act No 15 of 1979.

are so nebulous, or the evidence non-existent, or the proceedings so unfair that they would be fully justified in refusing to make any statement or else having their lawyer make a legal submission of 'no case to answer'. The requirement that they must answer is grossly unfair. There is no rule in the Standing Orders that the judge should be given reasonable time or facilities to prepare a defence: the timing is left to the Select Committee. Since it is under an international law duty to provide a fair trial, the committee itself should have ensured that the judge was given ample opportunity to contest the charges.

This did not happen. The committee was selected and met on 14 November 2012. That evening, it caused the charge sheet to be delivered to the Chief Justice, with a direction that her written statement be received no later than 22 November 2012. This was a ridiculously short time in which to refute any detail of the 14 charges, which ranged from transactions by relatives in Australia to decisions taken by the JSC. The Chief Justice's lawyer asked on several occasions that the deadline be extended, but the committee Chairman refused. On 20 November 2012, the judge asked for further information and some particulars of the charges – this was also refused. On 23 November 2012, she appeared with counsel in front of the committee and asked to know the procedure that the committee intended to follow – whether it was calling witnesses and if so, who, what standard of proof would it apply, and so on – but no answers were provided. The committee merely told her to present her defence statement by 30 November: there would be a hearing on 4 December, and the trial would start on 6 December. It rejected her application that two of its members should stand down because they had a personal bias against her. On 4 December (the day of the big demonstration against her), counsel for the Chief Justice requested a list of witnesses and relevant documents, but they were not provided. On 6 December, the Chairman announced that no witnesses would be called. At 4 pm on that day, a bundle of 80 documents, totalling over 1,000 pages, was given to the Chief Justice, and she was told that the inquiry would begin to consider charges 1 and 2 at 1:30 pm the next day, 7 December. Her request that independent observers from local and international bar associations attend the hearing was rejected.

In my opinion, these facts demonstrated a clear breach of the fair trial rules relating to particularised charges and to adequate time to prepare defences. It was possible that the Chairman was misinforming the Chief Justice when he said that no witnesses would be called – it would be surprising if the committee simply decided overnight to summon 16 persons who were all available to testify the next day. Even if he believed on 6 December that there would be no live testimony, to deliver 1,000 pages of evidence to the defence at 4 pm and tell them to be ready for trial in less than 24 hours is preposterously unfair. This demonstrates the committee's contempt for justice and its refusal to provide the Chief Justice with even a semblance of fairness. The four committee members from the opposition said they had not been consulted about the Chairman's decisions, and they resigned on the afternoon of 6 December in a letter that protested the lack of time given to the Chief Justice and her lawyers to study the evidence. I am forced to conclude that the Select Committee Chair and his fellow ministers, all of whom took the government whip, were determined to convict the Chief Justice, come what may.

11.5.5 Calling and Cross-Examining Witnesses

Lawyers should not, by virtue of their presence, give credibility to a proceeding that they know to be a sham. After the chairman rejected their application to have the proceedings heard in public, their further application to have independent observers attend, and having heard him insist that there would be no live witnesses, the Chief Justice and her counsel withdrew, announcing that they would no longer accept the legality of a body steeped in such hostility towards the head of the judiciary. Later that day, four opposition members resigned, pointing out that they also had not been given sufficient time to study the documents and that it was clear to them that the seven ministers had already made 'preconceived findings of guilt'. There had been no decision about procedures or the standard of proof. 'We requested a direction that the Chief Justice and her lawyers be given an opportunity to cross-examine the several complainants who had made the charges against her', the four MPs said, but this was not accepted.

The right to cross-examine accusers is fundamental to fairness. Article 14(3)(e) of the ICCPR guarantees, as a minimum, the right of an accused 'to examine, or have examined, the witnesses again him and to obtain the attendance and examination of witnesses on his behalf under the same conditions as witnesses against him.' The Chief Justice and her counsel withdrew on the afternoon of 6 December after having been assured that the committee would allow no live witnesses to be called and would rely only on the documents, albeit documents that the Chief Justice and her team would not be given sufficient time to absorb and deal with. The four opposition MPs withdrew shortly afterwards, and the committee reconvened on 7 December without them. It was then and in secret that the 7 members summoned no less than 16 witnesses and heard their testimony! Just 24 hours later they issued a 15-page 'judgement' finding the Chief Justice guilty of charges 1, 4, and 5.

It might be – indeed, it was – said that by withdrawing, the Chief Justice forfeited her right to confront her accusers or – more realistically in this case – to extract from them by cross-examination the information that would demonstrate her innocence. In my view, having been firmly told that no evidence would be allowed from either side, she had been led to withdraw under false pretences.[25] The committee's conduct involved a breach of faith – it should have at the very least told her lawyers on the morning of 7 December that it

25 The Chief Justice, in a subsequent petition to the Supreme Court, stated that she was specifically informed that that no witnesses would be called and that the burden was on her to disprove the charges. See Petition, *Dr Bandaranayake v Chamal Rajapakse & ors*, filed 19 December 2012 [59–61] (Asian Human Rights Committee, Collected Documents, 10).

had changed its mind and was summoning witnesses. The Chief Justice should have been invited back to cross-examine and to call her own witnesses, including the Chief Justice herself, whose right to be heard in her own defence was one of the very few rights granted by the Standing Order. The Chief Justice had attended the proceeding voluntarily, and despite all the unfairness, she would certainly have decided to testify and might well have taken the opportunity to cross-examine. It would, as will become clear, have been illuminating had she been allowed to question Justice Thilakawardene, whose recollection of the circumstances of being removed from the 'Trillium' case was later challenged with court documents that were unavailable at the time of her testimony. This opportunity was not afforded to the Chief Justice, because of either the misleading behaviour of the committee Chairman or (at best) his change of mind about calling witnesses once she had withdrawn. His failure to invite her back to question them was a serious breach of the ICCPR. Standing Order 78A at the very least envisaged an adversary procedure in which she would have some evidential rights, and the committee's conduct denied her the opportunity to cross examine, to give evidence in her own right, and to call her own witnesses.

The Select Committee, under the aegis of Speaker Rajapakse, blatantly denied due process and natural justice. These are fundamental for any procedure that leads to the removal of a judge. They are required not only by the ICCPR, the Latimer House Guidelines, and the Beijing Principles but also by decisions of international courts and tribunals. The UN's Human Rights Committee had previously pointed out in relation to Sri Lanka that 'the procedure for the removal of judges from the Supreme Court is incompatible with Article 14 of the ICCPR, in that it allows Parliament to exercise considerable control over the procedure', and it recommended that the country strengthen the independence of the judiciary by providing for judicial rather than parliamentary supervision and discipline.[26] This was actually attempted through a constitutional amendment in 2000, which would have set up a Mustill-type tribunal of overseas judges, but the initiative lapsed. The Inter-American Court of Human Rights, like the European Court of Human Rights, has insisted that 'the authority in charge of the impeachment procedure to remove a judge must behave impartially in the procedure established to this end and allow the latter to exercise the right of defence.' That court decided that three judges must be re-instated because their impeachment procedure 'did not ensure their guarantees of due legal process.' This was, most assuredly, the case with Dr. Bandaranayake.

What Standing order 78A(8) terms 'a finding of guilt' was reported to the Speaker by the Select Committee on 8 December – the day after hearing the witnesses. It was a document of 35 pages, which must have been finalised, if not written, the previous evening: a rushed judgement that serves to

26 Concluding Observations on Sri Lanka, UN Doc CCPR/CO/79/Add.86 para [16].

emphasise the injustice of the proceedings. Standing Order 78A(1) requires a month to elapse between the committee request and impeachment resolution, so on 9 January – the first possible date – such a resolution was presented to Parliament. A two-day debate ended with its passage – the government MPs and their supporters, under the party whip, voted that the speaker 'address' his brother the President and request the removal of the Chief Justice.

By this time, the independence of the Sri Lankan judiciary had ended, and the Beijing and Latimer House principles had been abandoned. The Chief Justice had been impeached by the government and its supporters, firstly, by the charges brought in November that had accused her of misconduct for doing her conscientious duty in Divineguma and as Chief Justice at the JSC and secondly, by putting her through a grotesquely unfair secret trial at which she was abused and denied her rights, while outside Parliament demonstrators brought on government buses called for her blood.[27] On any view, this constitutes a shameful abuse of judicial independence. The President had power, of course, to stop it but had fanned the flames and may have authorised the rejoicing when the impeachment motion was passed at 7 pm on Friday 10 January. Celebratory fireworks were set off outside Parliament, without intervention from the police or military, and according to the press reports, four of the brothers Rajapaske – President, Speaker, Environment Minster Basil, and Defence Secretary Gotabaya – along with other ministers, appeared on a balcony to watch a special fireworks display put on by the Sri Lankan navy. For four hours, a jubilant crowd surrounded the Chief Justice's home, with the knowledge that Dr. Bandaranayake and her family were inside. A 'milk rice celebration' took place, a free meal was served, fireworks were lit (presumably at government expense), and later, the mob (said by some reporters to be members of the civil defence force in plain clothes) was addressed by members of the Select Committee and told to urge Dr. Bandaranayake to resign. They did so – when not singing and dancing to loud music.

A nation whose leaders treat the head of the judiciary as if she was a public enemy, abuse the democratic process to put her through an unfair trial as punishment for doing her constitutional duty, and then celebrate her unjust impeachment with feasting and fireworks deserves to have those leaders treated by the international community in ways that I shall suggest at the end of this chapter

11.6 Conclusion

The denouement was as unseemly as the procedures used to bring it about. On 12 January, two days after receiving the 'address' from his brother, the

27 Much of the contemporary press coverage collected by the Asian Human Rights Commission reports on a government publicity campaign against the Chief Justice by posters and leaflets (p. 303), bussing in demonstrators, and state media bans against her (230–31). See, AHRC, *Collection of Documents* (revised edn, AHRC 21 December 2012).

President summoned the remaining 10 Supreme Court judges to his office for a 90-minute meeting. It is not known what he said – the meeting was highly improper – although it seems that he asked them to pass on one threatening message to the Chief Justice, namely, that if she resigned without further fuss, she could then keep her full pension entitlements. The Chief Justice, who appears to have behaved throughout with great dignity, remained with her family at her official residence. The following day, she received a Presidential order removing her from office, and (in a despicably petty gesture) her security guards were withdrawn while threatening demonstrators remained outside. On the next day, a holiday Monday, police ordered the Registrar to pack up all her belongings in her chambers to make way for the next incumbent. A large phalanx of military police occupied the court building overnight, and a riot squad (with a water cannon) arrived the next morning along with a government rent-a-crowd who shouted slogans in praise of the new Chief Justice. He was Mohan Peiris, a man without judicial experience, who served as the legal advisor to the cabinet and was Chairman of a bank and of an arms procurement firm established by Defence Secretary Rajapanske. He was sworn in by the President and that afternoon, took over the Chief Justice's chambers while a large number of lawyers stood outside the court holding candles 'to symbolise the onset of darkness'. Dr. Bandaranayake was confined to her residence until her successor was installed in her former chambers and then required to leave in her own car without speaking to the media or (as she had requested) being given an opportunity to thank her staff. She did issue a dignified and moving statement that pointed out that the rule of law to which she had devoted her life had been shattered. She would not resign in order to save her pension, but she could not resist the power of the state to remove her physically from the Court.

In this chapter, I have done my best to recite the facts, which are on record, as objectively as possible. That Dr. Bandaranayake was not even conceivably guilty of misconduct on 12 of the 14 charges is palpable, and the evidence does not support Count 1 (that she made decisions in a case that somehow benefited her sister) and charge 4 (that she had 'assets', in the form of an empty bank account, that were undeclared). The evidence shows that she was impeached as a reprisal for her decision in the *Divineguma* case and perhaps for the outspoken stance that her Judicial Services Commission took in defending against what it saw, not unreasonably, as threats to judicial independence. Some commentators have suggested that the Rajapaske clan had a long-term plan to neuter the independence of the country's judiciary lest it put difficulties in the way of their future hegemony. Others claim that the impeachment removed any danger of unruly judges if the government was forced by international pressure to put a few of its military leaders on trial for war crimes committed during the 2009 conflict: I have no comment to make on these suggestions. I have tried to confine this chapter to the law and practice of judicial independence as applied to Dr. Bandaranayake's case. Although there is an interesting intellectual debate over the precise constitutional borders that separate legislative, executive, and judicial powers, I do not regard it as impinging on the question of whether the Chief Justice was properly impeached. To that question, the only answer is 'no'.

What is to be – or can be – done? It is a calamity for a nation that purports to uphold the rule of law, but it is also an international problem in so far as it may be emulated elsewhere if it passes without consequences and becomes an example for other governments to follow, that is, to sack inconvenient judges and hold the rest in fear of being impeached if they displease their political masters. Politicians, media, and diplomats must be made to understand this, and international bodies that uphold, or purport to uphold, the rule of law must realise just what a corrosive precedent this impeachment sets. There is nothing necessarily wrong with impeachment, which gives a sovereign Parliament representing the people the ultimate power to remove a disgraced judge, but his or her misbehaviour must be proved and by fair means, not foul. Certainly not by a process that has been triggered by dissatisfaction with a judgment that has gone against the ruling party. That this is precisely what has happened in Sri Lanka is a matter of record, and those who have made it happen are on the record. Some of them, regrettably, are lawyers, but all of them must have known that they were embarking on a witch-hunt.

What can be done to deter politicians from exploiting the impeachment process to unfairly remove judges because they have done their duty and ruled against the government? A new tool has become available in 34 democratic countries – such as the US, countries in the EU, Great Britain, and Australia – by which those who abuse human rights can be sanctioned, that is, being denied entry visas, having their property seized, and generally being named, blamed, and shamed. They are called 'Magnitsky Sanctions' after a Russian lawyer was beaten to death in prison after blowing the whistle on official corruption, and they can readily be applied to MPs like those who so maliciously conspired to get rid of Sri Lanka's Chief Justice. Parliamentarians are always fond of travelling to attend overseas conferences, to stash their cash in banks in London or America, and to send their children to schools in other countries: Magnitsky sanctions, by disrupting their ambitions, would serve them right for the wrong that they do to the rule of law. Bad judges, who obey secret government directives, do feature on Magnitsky listings, and so should lickspittle politicians who choose to vilify and humiliate good judges for demonstrating the impartiality and independence required by the rule of law.

12 Impeachment in the Philippines

Politics, Institutions and Leadership

Imelda Deinla and Maria Lulu Reyes

12.1 Introduction

The use of impeachment in removing judges has become a feature of fledgling democracies such as the Philippines. Designed as a mechanism of accountability, impeachment of judges in the highest court, the Supreme Court, has become a tool for consolidating strongman rule. Constitutional guarantees in the 1987 Philippine Constitution were meant to safeguard judicial independence and prevent political assault on the judiciary. The 2018 removal from office of Maria Lourdes Sereno, the first woman Chief Justice of the Philippine Supreme Court, however, provokes us to rethink our assumptions about the power of the judiciary within constitutional democracy. Often regarded as the weakest branch of government, the judiciary does not possess the power of coercion and is dependent on the executive or the legislative branches of government for enforcement or compliance. The democratisation movement that swept many parts of the world in the 1980s brought a new salience for courts in policing constitutional overreach and abuses of power that have been the hallmark of authoritarian regimes. Constitutional developments that granted courts review powers and autonomy have created opportunities for judiciaries to test the efficacy of their authority and reshape their relations with political actors. But the courts' contributions in consolidating democracy and forging the rule of law in democratising countries have been uneven. They sometimes perform as activist courts, but at other times, they acquiesce to executive whims or preferences. More often, the court's authority is under constant challenge or threatened.

The rise of illiberal democracies in contemporary times – and continuing trends towards democratic backsliding – are putting the judiciary under greater stress. How courts relate to political actors and respond to political pressures or demands have become even more critical for countries where liberal democracy is under constant challenge. In the Philippines, the ascendance to power of Rodrigo Duterte ushered in a march towards illiberal democracy. The judiciary and judicial actors have become focal points for political contestation. In a country that had previously overthrown an authoritarian regime (that of Ferdinand Marcos in 1986), the Supreme Court was known to have

DOI: 10.4324/9781003256007-15

resisted attempts at illiberal revival, despite the highs and lows of its democratic consolidation process.[1] The Court and the judiciary have been regarded as the 'beacon of democracy' since the promulgation of the democratic 1987 Philippine Constitution.

When members of the Philippine Supreme Court removed their own Chief Justice in May 2018 through a *quo warranto* procedure that aligned with presidential intentions, does this mean that the Court has become acquiescent to the power of the executive? In practical terms, why would a Court that has gained so much power become so readily compliant with presidential wishes? Is the loss of judicial independence simply a function of executive pressure or dominance?

As with any other institutional setting, courts are weak when there is lack of cohesion, institutionally and among the leadership. Our main argument is that judicial power – and independence – is conditioned by the internal dynamics of the courts as much as by external factors. The manner by which the judiciary has used its power has helped shape the success or failure of constitutional democracy in many democratising countries.[2] However, three factors have been identified as necessary in allowing the court to fulfil its functions in conducting its constitutional mandate and exercising independent judgment: political support,[3] public support,[4] and institutional support.[5] These three conditions are interlinked, but as argued in this chapter, leadership and institutional cohesion are necessary for building the support network necessary for the Court to resist political pressures and assist in forging judicial independence. Moreover, the ability of a Chief Justice to provide capable and strategic judicial leadership has been found to be critical in navigating complex and difficult conditions in building strong judicial institutions and gaining broad support.[6] This leadership is crucial in situations where the Court has been historically weak, as when a Court had been marginalised or undermined by autocratic regimes in the past.[7]

1 I Deinla and B Dressel, 'Introduction' in I Deinla and B Dressel (eds), *From Aquino II to Duterte: Change, Continuity or Rupture* (ISEAS 2019) 1–36.

2 See, for example, T Ginsburg, *Judicial Review in New Democracies: Constitutional Courts in Asian Cases* (CUP 2003); B Dressel, 'Judicialization of Politics or Politicisation of the Judiciary? considerations from Recent Events in Thailand' (2010) 23(5) *The Pacific Review* 671–91; T Moustafa, *The Struggle for Constitutional Power* (CUP 2007).

3 See, for example, J Finkel, *Judicial Reform and Political Insurance* (Notre Dame UP 2008).

4 See, for example, I Deinla, 'Public Support and Judicial Empowerment of the Philippine Supreme Court' (2014) 36(1) *Contemporary Southeast Asia: A Journal of International and Strategic Affairs* 128–58.

5 See, for example, G Helmke and F Rosenbluth, 'Regimes and the Rule of Law: Judicial Independence in Comparative Perspective' (2009) 12 *Annual Review of Political Science* 345–66; T Clark, *The Limits of Judicial Independence* (CUP 2010).

6 See, for example, J Widner, *Building the Rule of Law* (WW Norton 2001).

7 See, for example, S Hendrianto, 'The Rise and Fall of Heroic Chief Justices: Constitutional Politics and Judicial Leadership in Indonesia Asian Courts and the Constitutional Politics of the Twenty-First Century' (2016) 25(3) *Washington International Law Journal* 489–564.

12.2 The Philippine Supreme Court: From 'Kangaroo Court' to the Rise of the 'Gods of *Padre Faura*'

The Philippine Supreme Court underwent institutional evolution after the 1986 People Power EDSA Revolution. It has developed as a 'powerful' court that can leverage its influence with the other branches of government. During the authoritarian regime of former president Ferdinand Marcos, the Court was widely perceived as a 'kangaroo court', a pejorative term for a rubber-stamp court that sustains government actions and those of its agents and allies.[8] The Court was 'empowered' after it was restored as a co-equal branch and essential component of the institution of checks and balances of a democratic government. An independent and empowered court was a key consideration in drafting the 1987 Constitution, a product of broad public consultation to pave the way for reinstalling liberal democracy.

The democratic 1987 Constitution provided for broad powers of the Court, such as the power to determine constitutional boundaries, review and strike down government acts and legislation and exercise exclusive jurisdiction over special legal remedies.[9] Like other judiciaries in democratising countries, these powers have empowered the Court vis-à-vis other branches of government, namely, the executive and the legislative, through its ability to bridge or balance competing political interests or provide judicial solutions to political conflicts.[10] In this way, the judiciary has itself become an object of political disputes.

One way to look at how the Philippine Supreme Court has been 'empowered' can be inferred from how it has regained public trust in the Court after the institution of liberal democracy. In relation to other key institutions of government such as the Senate, the House of Representatives and the Executive as institutions, the Court has made progressive strides towards becoming one of the most trusted institutions over a 20-year period, from 1990–2011. It overtook the Senate as the most trusted between 1993 and 2003, a period that we can call the Court's 'judicial renaissance'. The highest points recorded in this period by the Supreme Court were between 1993 and 1998, which coincided with liberal reformism under President Fidel Ramos (1992–1998), and in 2001, which coincided with the impeachment on grounds of massive corruption and ouster (through the second people power revolution in 2001) of President Joseph Estrada (1998–2001).

A period of 'judicial crisis' can be observed during the impeachment of chief justices: one, during the impeachment of Chief Justice Renato Corona

8 T Moustafa, 'Law and Courts in Authoritarian Regimes' (2014) 10(1) *Annual Review of Law and Social Science* 281–99; W Bello, 'Benigno Aquino: Between Dictatorship and Revolution in the Philippines' (1984) 6(4) *Third World Quarterly* 283–309.

9 Art E5, 1987 Constitution.

10 See T Roux, *The Politics of Principle: The First South African Constitutional Court, 1995–2005* (CUP 2013).

in 2012 under President Benigno Aquino, Jr.'s term in office (2010–2016) and two, during Chief Justice Sereno's impeachment in 2017 under President Rodrigo Duterte's government (2016–2022). Compared with the Sereno impeachment, public satisfaction with the Court recorded the lowest satisfaction during Corona's removal. However, the dip in Court satisfaction during Sereno's impeachment lasted longer compared to Corona's. This could be attributed to the longer proceeding to remove Sereno through impeachment by using the *quo warranto* that ended on 11 May 2018. However, notably, the impeachment proceeding against Chief Justice Hilario Davide in 2003 (in the initial years of Gloria Macapagal-Arroyo's presidency) did not affect the Court's satisfaction standing relative to other state institutions. This could be a subject for a deeper exploration of how the public perceived the legitimacy or illegitimacy of each of these impeachment proceedings and thus affected their trust in the Court.

Individually, the Court members have also become powerful actors in their own right and are highly sought-after for their alliances and loyalties. The Supreme Court, vested with the power to determine with finality what the law is and how it applies to particular situations, has become the 'gods of Padre Faura'.[11] They are so-called 'gods' because the cases become the ultimate law, and the justices are beyond reproach for their decisions. The Court is increasingly seen by politicians as a key ally – or enemy – of government policies or political interests. Hence, Court appointments have become more strategic, calculated and very contentious since the reinstatement of liberal democracy after the people power revolution.[12] In the last 15 years, we have seen that the office of the Chief Justice has become the object of political machinations. Sereno's removal from office is was the third episode since an ouster initiative was unsuccessfully launched in 2003 against Chief Justice Hilario Davide, Jr., during the presidency of Gloria Macapagal-Arroyo (2001–2010). The first successful impeachment in the judiciary was of Chief Justice Renato Corona in 2012 during the administration of Benigno Aquino III.

An examination of Sereno's ouster through the unconventional means of *quo warranto* is important, as this incident points to the weakness of all the three support pillars – political, institutional, and public – during the critical times of the justice's removal. The confluence of these conditions allowed the use of this unprecedented measure without consequent detrimental political and legal backlash. Sereno's removal is exceptional compared to the other two previous impeachment proceedings. The use of a *quo warranto* proceeding

11 Abogado, 'A Look at the New "Olympus" for the "Gods of Padre Faura" '(2018) <https://abogado.com.ph/a-look-at-the-new-olympus-for-the-gods-of-padre-faura/> accessed 6 March 2023.

12 See M Vitug, 'Aftershocks in the Supreme Court' (*Rappler*, 2018) <www.rappler.com/thought-leaders/198489-supreme-court-philippines-appointments-aftershocks> accessed 6 March 2023.

against a high state official has no legal precedent in Philippine jurisprudence. Voting 8–6 (for and against the removal), the 'gods' turned against their own.[13]

Why the justices themselves exercised this power of removal – although most Philippine legal scholars believe that it could only be done through impeachment – can only be explained by the institutional dynamics and personalities within the Court. As we explain in the following, the justices' action in removing a colleague is not a unique phenomenon; this had happened in other jurisdictions where political and institutional support is weak for the courts and judges. The Sereno removal saga also raises questions about the salience of a 'standard' institutional design that had been thought to safeguard or enhance judicial independence, such as the provisions of lifetime (or long) tenure, financial independence and constitutional standards on removing justices from office.

12.2.1 Lack of Political and Institutional Support

Political support, particularly of key political actors and the elites, is critical in resisting the impeachment of a Chief Justice. Support of political actors for an independent bench has been explained in terms of 'insurance' so that the Court will rule fairly toward the incumbent when they are out of office.[14] Sectors of the elites and the general public can also be supportive of the judiciary as a feature of liberal democracy or as part of the political settlement embodied in a democratic constitution after social upheaval, which happened in the Philippines. Support, however, could mean that the public is merely satisfied with the work of the judiciary. In the Philippines, it has been observed that higher public satisfaction with the Court is linked to periods where there is democratic stability that, in turn, allows for the proper functioning of democratic institutions and empowers the Court to perform an 'activist' role.[15]

The Sereno removal saga underscores the emergence of a powerful and highly popular presidency that could command obedience or acquiescence from other political actors, both inside and outside the state system. The Philippines under Rodrigo Duterte had a capricious executive who was bent on going after members of the opposition and critical media by filing criminal cases against them, such as targeting Senator Lilia de Lima, Senator Antonio Trillanes, and Maria Ressa of the online news site Rappler. The saga also demonstrates that institutional division in the Court – as seen from the lack of collegiality, perception of a lack of 'leadership' by the Chief Justice, personal conflicts and administrative issues besetting the office – facilitated the

13 Abogado, 'Pity Sereno! First Time "Gods of Padre Faura" Have Turned Against One of Their Own' (2018) <http://abogado.com.ph/pity-sereno-first-time-gods-padre-faura-turned-one/> accessed 6 March 2023.

14 Ginsburg (n 2).

15 I Deinla, *The development of the rule of law in ASEAN: the state and regional integration* (CUP 2017).

convergence of interests among the executive, the Lower House of Congress, and Justices who opposed Sereno's continued tenure. Hence, the former Presidential spokesperson Harry Roque had to quip, 'She needs no bullying from the President. She has done a magnificent job of alienating her colleagues and her colleagues themselves say she does not deserve her position – not the President.'[16]

Sereno's appointment as Chief Justice by former President Benigno Aquino, Jr. on 24 August 2012 went against the 'norm' of appointing senior Justices to the top post in the judiciary. It was a surprising appointment that was considered a break from tradition. Filipino women judges, however, have been progressively chipping at the male-dominated legal profession and judiciary.[17] Sereno was the first woman Chief Justice and the youngest Chief Justice in the Court's more than 100-year history. When she rose to the highest court in 2010 as Associate Justice, seemingly plucked from obscurity, she was only the 13th woman compared to 169 men who had sat on that Bench before her. While trailblazing for Filipino women, Aquino's selection of Sereno as Chief Justice was unwelcome within a judiciary steeped in the unwritten tradition of seniority, that is, the incumbent justice serving longest on the Court gets the plum prize of the Chief Justice post. She bypassed eleven of the more senior Associate Justices of the Supreme Court. Sereno would have served as Chief Justice for 18 years until she retired at age 70. None of her older colleagues would have had a hope of ever getting a taste of the position. Moreover, her alleged insular leadership style and inexperience in the workings of the judiciary did not help in maintaining collegiality, which is an intrinsic part of the Court's institutional design. In fact, restoring the collegiality of the Court is what the succeeding Chief Justice, Teresita de Castro, has expressed as her legacy to the judiciary.[18]

The Supreme Court was a deeply divided court during Sereno's tenure. The cracks within the Court were an open secret and blamed on the high magistrate's management style, lack of political savvy in bridging divides and failure to create trust. This was evident from allegations of a lack of consultation in decision-making and personal rifts with some judges. Her colleagues asked her to take a leave of absence while the removal proceedings were pending, and five judges went so far as to testify against her during the 2017 impeachment proceedings in the Lower House of Congress. Fissures and cleavages, even among lower court judges and personnel, were apparent in the line-up of those who supported her ouster or resignation and those who advocated for

16 H Roque, *Duterte, not bullying Sereno – Malacañang*, UNTV News & Rescue 2018 <www.untvweb.com/news/duterte-not-bullying-sereno-malacanang/> accessed 6 March 2023.

17 See I Deinla, 'Filipino Women Judges and their Role in Advancing Judicial Independence in the Philippines' in C Crouch (ed), *Women and the Judiciary in the Asia Pacific* (CUP 2021).

18 L Buan, 'CJ De Castro: Collegiality Is Back at the Supreme Court' (*Rappler*, 2018) <www.rappler.com/nation/210560-collegiality-restored-supreme-court-de-castro-chief-justice> accessed 6 March 2023.

maintaining judicial independence.[19] Antonio La Viña, a political analyst and friend of Justice Sereno remarked, 'The chief must honestly look at her way of managing, whether she has to change her tone and practices. They need to go into the process of rebuilding trust.'[20]

The timing for initiating Sereno's ouster could not have been more opportune. When President Duterte picked a very public and rancorous fight with the Philippine Chief Justice over her objections to the war on drugs in 2016, there were many who were only too willing to assist him, including her colleagues in the judiciary. However, weak articles of impeachment, even with the approval of the House of Representatives where Duterte had a supermajority, would not have passed the upper chamber of the legislature, the Senate, which has the power to conduct a trial and vote on Sereno's impeachment. The filing of the *quo warranto* in the Supreme Court itself sidestepped this nearly insurmountable barrier.

12.3 Impeachment: From a Mechanism of Accountability to a Political Weapon

The impeachment process has been in place since the 1935 Constitution, but only in recent memory under the 1987 Constitution did Philippine democracy see it used. Whether the increasing propensity of its use over past and present administrations is a testament to the thriving democracy in the country or an undeniable indicator of the abuse of the process itself is a question that has haunted Philippine constitutional jurisprudence.

The first impeachment proceeding was in pursuit of accountability over a massive corruption scandal involving a sitting president of the republic, Joseph Ejercito Estrada, in 2000. Prior to Estrada's impeachment, only three impeachment complaints were filed in the Philippine Congress, none of which passed beyond the Committee level.[21] As the first impeachment proceeding under the 1987 Constitution, it generated the widest publicity. With the emergence of news about receiving money from *jueteng* sources (a local form of illegal lottery), the president was peppered with allegations of corruption and bribery. In an allusion to the 'Watergate' scandal, President Estrada's name and reputation became saddled with his very own '*Juetengate* Scandal'.[22]

19 L Buan, 'Calida Petitions Supreme Court to Remove Sereno' (*Rappler* 2018) <www.rappler.com/nation/197435-calida-sereno-quo-warranto-supreme-court> accessed 6 March 2023.

20 L Buan, 'Serono Impeachment: Cracks in the Supreme Court' (*Rappler*, 2017) <https://www.rappler.com/newsbreak/in-depth/191150-sereno-impeachment-cracks-supreme-court/#:~:text=But%20La%20Vi%C3%B1a%20believes%20Sereno,themselves%2C%E2%80%9D%20La%20Vi%C3%B1a%20said.> accessed 6 March 2023.

21 J Diaz, 'Estrada Impeached' *Philstar* (2010) <www.philstar.com/headlines/2000/11/14/88756/estrada-impeached> accessed 6 March 2023.

22 F Tatad, 'The Ravages of Impeachment' *Manila Times* (2017) <www.manilatimes.net/the-ravages-of-impeachment/355789/> accessed 6 March 2023.

Not long after this, an impeachment complaint was filed and initiated in the House of Representatives on 12 October 2000. The complaint against Estrada was grounded on bribery, graft and corrupt practices, betrayal of public trust and culpable violation of the Constitution.[23] The House of Representatives, dominated by Estrada allies, was cold to the move. But after the complaint garnered the signature of a minimum one-third of all the members of the House, then-Speaker (and later presidential aspirant) Manuel Villar bypassed the Justice Committee process and immediately sent the Articles of Impeachment to the Senate for the commencement of trial.

For several months, Estrada's impeachment trial was covered live on TV, closely watched and widely followed by a public upset by corruption scandals at the highest echelons of government. It came to an abrupt halt on whether to open key evidence for the prosecution allegedly obtained from questionable sources, the so-called 'envelope' that contained details of Estrada's other secret bank accounts. When a majority of the Senators, sitting as impeachment judges and identified with Estrada, voted to deny opening the said evidence, the prosecutors walked out together with the presiding officer, Supreme Court Chief Justice Hilario Davide, Jr. The walkout sparked thousands of protestors gathered at EDSA demanding Estrada's resignation; the gathering came to be known as EDSA Dos (EDSA 2). Not long after this, Chief Justice Davide swore in Gloria Macapagal-Arroyo as the new President of the Philippines, prompting an embarrassed Estrada to leave the presidential palace.

Although the first-ever impeachment proceeding in the country never came to its full conclusion, it precipitated widespread protest that ended the Estrada presidency. Later, former President Estrada would question Arroyo's presidency by saying that he remained president because he was never convicted and was merely a President on leave. In *Estrada v. Desierto*[24] the Supreme Court ruled that the totality of Estrada's actions taken together, even though an impeachment conviction did not occur, indicated that he had resigned from office.

The next impeachment complaint was directed at the Chief Justice of the Supreme Court, Hilario Divide, Jr. On June 2, 2003, Estrada himself filed an impeachment complaint against Chief Justice Davide on the grounds of corruption and misuse of the Judiciary Development Fund. The impeachment complaint was subsequently referred to the House Committee on Justice, which dismissed the complaint on 22 October 2003.[25] A second complaint was filed the next day by Estrada-loyal members of the House itself, supported by the required endorsement of at least one-third of all its members. Before the House of Representatives could transmit the Articles of Impeachment to

23 Chan Robles, 'Complaint for Impeachment Against President Joseph Ejercito Estrada (2000)' (2018) <www.chanrobles.com/legal11impeachmentcomplaint.htm#.WtiABC5ubIU> accessed 6 March 2023.

24 *Estrada v Desierto*, GR No 146710–15, 2 March 2001.

25 ibid.

the Senate, the second complaint was challenged before the Supreme Court, whose chief was under fire. The main argument in the Supreme Court in *Francisco v. House of Representatives* in 2003 was that the filing of the second complaint violated Section 5 Article XI of the 1987 Constitution providing that no impeachment proceedings shall be initiated against the same official more than twice within a period of one year.

The Supreme Court, in voiding the second impeachment complaint, played a critical role that was perceived as protecting its own. Unlike the later Sereno proceeding, Davide enjoyed wide support from the public and from the judiciary.[26] The Court, however, made a ruling that would also be utilised to defeat the very tenets of accountability that the process of impeachment seeks to approximate and objectify. This legal interpretation would be exploited to the hilt by Arroyo and her supporters over her nine-year corruption-marred and scandal-ridden presidential tenure, creatively skirting multiple attempts to impeach her. Former Presidents Benigno Aquino III and Rodrigo Duterte are also beneficiaries of the decision in *Francisco v. House of Representatives.*

To stop the impeachment of Davide, the Supreme Court ruled that 'initiate' should be construed as the physical act of filing the impeachment complaint coupled with an action by the House of Representatives acknowledging it.[27] Using the constitutionally mandated legislative process, the Supreme Court said that it is the referral of the impeachment complaint to, or resolution by, the proper House Committee (the House Committee on Justice) that 'initiates' an impeachment complaint. Putting the ruling in context, the Court stated that the first complaint by Estrada himself that was eventually dismissed by the House Committee on Justice was considered a properly initiated impeachment complaint. This fact would trigger the one-year constitutional ban against another impeachment complaint, rendering the second complaint filed against Davide, even if endorsed by the one-third of the total members of the House, unconstitutional.[28] The threat of Davide's ouster was thus ended, and he retired as Chief Justice at the mandatory age of 70. He would later occupy the position of Permanent Representative to the United Nations (UN), a job he would have been prevented from assuming had he been impeached.

The Davide impeachment attempt marked the first episode in turning impeachment into a tool for political vendetta. But it was during President Gloria Macapagal-Arroyo's term that impeachment was progressively thwarted or stripped of its accountability model. Starting in 2005, we can see the efficient and effective utilisation of the *Francisco vs. House of Representatives* ruling to tactically avoid legitimate impeachment complaints against President Arroyo. With the public outcry resulting from the 'Hello Garci' scandal that

26 Deinla (n 15).
27 *Francisco Jr v House of Representatives*, GR No 160261 (20 November 2003).
28 ibid.

referred to the alleged cheating in the 2004 presidential elections, impeachment threats against President Arroyo were inevitable. Thus, the public would see the filing of successive complaints against Arroyo in 2005, 2006, 2007 and 2008.[29] Her allies would file impeachment complaints that were deliberately fraught with gaffes, sure to be dismissed by the House Committee on Justice. The one-year prohibition was thereafter triggered, sparing Arroyo. This process was continuously utilised by the Administration until the end of Arroyo's term so that no actual threat of impeachment during her tenure existed. Her term expired as one of the most corruption-ridden and hated administrations. Thus, the Supreme Court ruling that had favoured its own Chief Justice Davide would be abused and exploited to defeat the constitutional mechanism of impeachment in the years that followed, further marring a process that had originally been envisioned to exact accountability for wrongdoing in office.

The subsequent administration of President Benigno Aquino III sought to bring back the accountability function of impeachment. It was intended to carry out his popular anti-corruption crusade *Matuwid na Daan* ('straight path') against officials in the past Arroyo government. But these proceedings were also highly political and capitalised on the weight of executive power. Division within the judiciary also surfaced between the Arroyo appointees and Aquino appointees in the high court. This is seen in the clear division in voting patterns when dealing with the corruption cases that arose under the past Arroyo government.[30]

The first impeachment under Aquino was initiated against Ombudsman Merceditas Gutierrez, an Arroyo appointee whose fixed seven-year term coincided with Aquino's term as president. Gutierrez was considered an obstacle to the prosecution of corruption charges against Arroyo officials. Two impeachment complaints were filed against her in July and August 2010, and both were found to be sufficient in substance and were referred to the House Committee on Justice.[31] Gutierrez challenged the two complaints by filing a petition for certiorari and prohibition in the Supreme Court on the ground that that the one-year ban under Section 5 Article XI of the 1987 Constitution was violated when the House Committee on Justice took on two impeachment complaints at the same time.[32] The Supreme Court issued a status *quo ante* order suspending impeachment proceedings. However, the Court ultimately

29 'Impeachment Complaints Filed Against President Arroyo' *GMA News* (2007) <www.gmanetwork.com/news/news/content/67288/impeachment-complaints-filed-against-president-arroyo-in-2005/story/> accessed 6 March 2023.

30 Supreme Court Voting Patterns Under Duterte Administration (2018) <www.interaksyon.com/breaking-news/2018/05/15/126749/supreme-court-voting-patterns-duterte-administration/> accessed 6 March 2023.

31 L Dalangin-Fernandez, 'Two Impeachment Raps v Ombudsman Sufficient in Form – House Panel' (2010) <https://web.archive.org/web/20100907033857/http://newsinfo.inquirer.net/breakingnews/world/view/20100901-289928/2-impeach-raps-vs-Ombudsman-sufficient-in-formHouse-panel> accessed 6 March 2023.

32 *Gutierrez v House of Representatives*, GR No 193459 (15 February 2011).

ruled that the one-year ban under the Constitution was not violated when the House Committee entertained two complaints. It reasoned that the two complaints were received at the same time. As long as there is only one proceeding regardless of the number of complaints, the impeachment proceeding can go on, and the one-year ban is not violated. The impeachment process against Ombudsman Gutierrez, however, came to a halt in its first step. Before the public display of the political will that the Aquino administration could commence, Ombudsman Gutierrez tendered her resignation personally to President Aquino on 29 April 2011. Aquino accepted it on the same day with a press statement.[33]

The second impeachment under the Aquino Administration was filed against Chief Justice Renato Corona on December 12, 2011, barely a year after the initiation of the Gutierrez impeachment. Corona was a so-called 'midnight appointee' by Arroyo, as he was appointed chief magistrate in the waning days of her presidency, thus depriving then newly-elected President Benigno Aquino his chance of naming his choice for the vacancy. When Benigno Aquino III took his oath as President, Corona was shunned. The swearing-in ceremony is traditionally administered by the Chief Justice, but Aquino asked Associate Justice Conchita Carpio Morales to preside instead. Allegations of corruption and accumulation of ill-gotten wealth propelled the complaint against Corona. In the complaint for impeachment filed in the House of Representatives, he was initially being impeached on eight articles.[34] The eight articles were later reduced to three, and the House focused on only one of the charges. One hundred eighty-eight Congressmen signed the document without purportedly reading the complaint first.[35] The complaint was transmitted to the Senate the next day.

The trial within the Senate chambers revealed the workings of an impeachment process in its political and legal aspects. Evidence dubiously obtained was presented during the trial.[36] This prompted Corona to file a petition for certiorari with the Supreme Court, asking the Court to issue a temporary restraining order claiming that the Senate had acted with grave abuse of discretion in the trial. At the same time, he asked that the Court prohibit the implementation of subpoenas to bank managers in releasing documents for the trial.[37] However, before the Court could act on the subpoenas for bank

33 Official Gazette, President Aquino Accepts Resignation of Ombudsman Gutierrez (2011) <www.officialgazette.gov.ph/2011/04/29/president-aquino-accepts-resignation-of-ombudsman-gutierrez/> accessed 6 March 2023.

34 ibid.

35 Tatad (n 22).

36 K Suarez, 'Corona Trial: Day 12' *Rappler* (2012) <www.rappler.com/nation/special-coverage/1334-coronatrial-day-12> accessed 6 March 2023.

37 A Jerome, 'Corona Asks SC to Stop Impeachment Trial, Bank Subpoenas' (2012) <http://newsinfo.inquirer.net/142077/corona-asks-sc-to-stop-impeachment-trial-bank-subpoenas> accessed 6 March 2023.

records, the Chief Justice surrendered the information to the trial through his execution of a bank waiver.[38]

In May 2012, 20 Senators voted to convict Chief Justice Corona, which was well beyond the two-thirds vote required under the 1987 Constitution. Renato Corona's removal as Chief Justice thus became the first impeachment process to be fully taken to its conclusion in the Philippines. However, the following year, a Senate privilege speech revealed that the executive branch released 50 million pesos or more to each of the Senators who voted to convict the Chief Justice in the form of a 'bribery' through the Disbursement Acceleration Program (DAP).[39] DAP was designed as a mechanism to finance high-impact and priority programs and projects by using savings and unprogrammed funds. It was supposed to be a budget reform intervention to speed-up public spending and to boost economic growth.[40] Aquino's use of DAP was invalidated by the Arroyo-appointees dominating the Supreme Court on 4 February 2015, more than two years after Corona was removed.[41]

After the end of the term of the Aquino administration in 2016, a new and more sinister era of deploying impeachment and other legal rules came with the Duterte government. The first impeachment was filed against Commission on Elections (COMELEC) Chair Andres Bautista. The impeachment complaint was filed on the grounds of betrayal of public trust and culpable violation of the Constitution over allegations of ill-gotten wealth (Cayabyab, 2017). The impeachment complaint was dismissed by the House Committee on Justice. This was overturned by the plenary of the House of Representatives. Seeing the turn of events, Bautista eventually publicly declared his resignation, which would be effective only in December 2017.[42] This pronouncement did not stop the House of Representatives from proceeding with the impeachment. On the same day, he was impeached in the Lower House. The Articles of Impeachment were sent to the Senate for trial. But before the trial could begin, Bautista made his resignation effective immediately, avoiding the trial and the impeachment process entirely.

The second and third impeachment complaints were filed against Chief Justice Sereno on 2 August 2017 and Ombudsman Conchita Carpio-Morales on 13 December 2017, respectively. Both complaints were submitted by the Volunteers against Crime and Corruption (VACC), a private organisation seen as

38 *Philippine Savings Bank v Senate Impeachment Court and others*, GR No 200238 (20 November 2012).

39 F Tatad, 'A Unique Republic of Impeachments?' *Manila Times* (2017) <www.manilatimes.net/unique-republic-impeachments/348909/> accessed 6 March 2023.

40 DBM, 'Disbursement Acceleration Program (Main)' (2018) <www.dbm.gov.ph/index.php/budget-documents/previous-years/35-budget-documents/309-disbursement-acceleration-program-main> accessed 6 March 2023.

41 *Araullo and others v Benigno Aquino III*, GR No 209287 (4 February 2015).

42 B Cupin, 'From Resignation to Impeachment: Chairman Bautista's Longest Day' *Rappler* (2017) <www.rappler.com/newsbreak/inside-track/184990-andres-bautista-resignation-impeachment> accessed 6 March 2023.

unflaggingly supportive of President Duterte, especially of his war on drugs. In the case of Sereno, another complaint was filed on 30 August 2017 by lawyer Larry Gadon, who represented former President Arroyo before the UN Working Group on Arbitrary Detention. In Morales' case, the complaint was not endorsed by any member of the House of Representatives.[43] As a result, the impeachment complaint was not formally acted upon by the House of Representatives and died at its birth. Conchita Carpio-Morales is the sister of the father-in-law of presidential daughter Sara Duterte-Carpio. Impeaching her a few months before her departure from office would have been a futile exercise. Carpio-Morales finished her term as the country's top graft-buster in July 2018.

Prior to these complaints, two impeachment complaints were also lodged against President Rodrigo Duterte due to his alleged roles as Mayor with the Davao Death Squad and President with the mass killings occurring in the country in pursuit of his drug war. However, both impeachment complaints were summarily thrown out by the House Committee on Justice without even conducting a full hearing.[44] An attempt to impeach Vice President Leni Robredo by then-Speaker Pantaleon Alvarez fell through, even as a draft complaint by Marcos lawyer Oliver Lozano, which was circulated in the media, could not find support within the House of Representatives.[45]

12.4 The Supreme Court Removes Its Own Chief Justice

Observers believe that the filing of the *quo warranto* was brought about by the uncertainty of a Senate trial under duly transmitted articles of impeachment. The House of Representatives declared the impeachment complaint sufficient in both form and substance during its final hearing on 8 March 2018. At that point, transmittal of the Articles of Impeachment to the Senate was expected to be a mere formality. However, the intended outcome could not be predicted because 16 senators out of 24 were needed to convict and remove the Chief Justice from office. It was believed that many senators were not sympathetic to having Sereno removed.

The wheels of the meta-constitutional remedy of *quo warranto* began to grind with a petition before the Supreme Court on 1 March 2018 by lawyer Oliver Lozano, the same person who submitted the failed bid for Vice President Robredo's impeachment. Five days later, the Philippine government's chief attorney, Solicitor General Jose Calida, submitted on behalf of the Republic of the Philippines another *quo warranto* petition.[46]

43 L Buan, 'Sereno Impeachment: Cracks in the Supreme Court' *Rappler* (2017) <www.rappler.com/newsbreak/in-depth/191150-sereno-impeachment-cracks-supreme-court> accessed 6 March 2023.

44 Tatad (n 22).

45 M Cepeda, 'Still No Endorsers for Robredo Impeachment Complaint' *Rappler* (2017) <www.rappler.com/nation/168726-impeach-leni-movement-still-no-endorsers-robredo-impeachment-complaint> accessed 6 March 2023.

46 Buan (n 19).

Quo warranto comes from a Latin phrase 'By what right or warrant do you act?'[47] Quo *warranto* proceedings are challenges or claims involving the right to hold a public office. It is a legal remedy for usurpation or intrusion into a public office. It is an action by which the right to an office or franchise is examined and results in the ouster of the holder from enjoying and exercising that office. In Lota v. Court of Appeals (1961), the Court made a distinction between mandamus and quo warranto proceedings. In the Philippines, *quo warranto* may be brought in three instances: (1) against any person who usurps, unlawfully holds or exercises a public office, position or franchise; (2) against any public officer who does or suffers an act, which by provision of law constitutes a ground for forfeiture of office; and (3) any association that acts as a corporation within the Philippines without being legally incorporated or without lawful authority to so act.[48] Thus, a *quo warranto* proceeding is the only manner by which right to an office can be contested. The right to public office cannot be questioned collaterally by any other means, neither through mandamus nor by a motion to set aside or annul an order.[49]

Sereno's *quo warranto* proceeding was anchored in her non-fulfilment of certain ethical requirements. Her fitness and moral integrity to be appointed as chief magistrate was the basis of the action against her, that is, her persistent failure in the past – as required by law, and until she applied for the position of Chief Justice – to file her annual Statement of Assets and Liabilities. The *quo warranto* provides a lower bar for removing a justice than the constitutional provision on impeachment, which needs to be grounded in a culpable violation of the Constitution, treason, bribery, graft and corruption, other high crimes or betrayal of the public trust.[50]

In many ways, the Supreme Court staged a legal-political coup by firing its own Chief Justice in a controversial decision on 11 May 2018.[51] Her ouster by her own colleagues brought to the fore a deeply divided Court, with eight of the 14 justices voting against her, including fellow Aquino appointee Justice Francis Jardeleza, with whom Sereno had a very public squabble that signalled the *quo warranto* outcome. All the associate justices who testified against her in the House Justice Committee in the course of the impeachment proceedings voted to remove her. All Duterte appointees were in favour of her ouster. In the end, with her last-ditch attempt to reverse the vote through a motion for reconsideration being denied, Sereno was declared by her own colleagues in the Supreme Court as ineligible to sit among them.

47 California Attorney General's Office, 'Quo Warranto: Resolution of Disputes – Right to Public Office' (1990) <https://oag.ca.gov/sites/all/files/agweb/pdfs/ag_opinions/quo-warranto-guidelines.pdf> accessed 6 March 2023.

48 Rule 66.

49 *Topacio v Ong*, GR No 179895 (18 December 2008).

50 Sec 2, Art XI 1987 Constitution.

51 *Republic v Sereno*, GR No 237428 (11 May 2018).

Sereno's removal was blowback from President Aquino's disregard of the seniority rule in the Court by appointing a newcomer as Chief Justice. The *quo warranto* decision declared Aquino's appointment of Sereno as Chief Justice to be void. Aquino's failure to appreciate the dynamics and nuances of the relationships and personalities involved, in addition to Sereno's own treacly effort to generate public support for her against the members of the Court, finally doomed her.

Sereno's chief critic in the chamber, Teresita Leonardo-De Castro, would thereafter be selected by President Duterte to replace Sereno for a two-month stint as Chief Justice until De Castro retired at age 70. De Castro vowed to heal the rifts in the judiciary during her short tenure. Subsequent Chief Justice Lucas Bersamin was not an unexpected choice by Duterte for the post, but he bypassed the most senior associate justice, Antonio Carpio, who has taken a very vocal stand against the Philippines' pivot to China in light of the West Philippine Sea issue. Sereno's leaving may have narrowed the cracks within the Supreme Court. Many keen observers, however, are wary. The Court has since decided, with little debate, to extend martial law in Mindanao indefinitely. The Court eventually upheld Duterte's unilateral denunciation of the Rome Statute; dismissed the recount of the 2016 Vice Presidential election; and went on to declare as valid and constitutional various infrastructure loan agreements between the Philippines and China.

12.5 Conclusion

Politics outside – and inside – the Supreme Court spelled doom for Chief Justice Sereno's time in office. A popular executive with power and resources at its disposal and with little respect for the rule of law can tip the scales towards constitutional imbalance. Under the scheme of constitutional democracy, the framework and institutional arrangements are precisely designed to thwart or arrest such a creeping expansion of powers. Judicial power – and judicial independence – are attributes that are built into constitutional design so that this 'least powerful' branch of government, the judiciary, should be able to resist external pressures when determining the law or interpreting constitutional boundaries. It has often been observed that power and independence go hand-in-hand, meaning the capacity for the Court's decision to be obeyed (power) is dependent on its capacity to render decisions in an impartial manner (independence). This chapter argues that judicial power and judicial independence are not mutually dependent and do not work together automatically to sustain judicial integrity. Only when this power is exercised judiciously is the Court's integrity advanced.

The removal through *quo warranto* of Chief Justice Sereno also demonstrates the role that the judiciary plays in undermining its own power – or independence. Although the Philippine Supreme Court gained much judicial power under the 1987 Constitution, its independence was never under more serious doubt than during the Duterte administration. The Court's decision to take on the power of removal, which is not specifically stated in the Constitution, signified its motivation to be part of political initiatives to strip Sereno of her position. Considering that the Lower House voted to approve the Articles of Impeachment, the Court could have chosen to 'defer' to the Senate to proceed with the impeachment trial by ordering the transmittal of the Articles. Instead, the Court willingly drew itself into the political process, with some members even testifying against Sereno, and pre-empted the Senate's opportunity to exercise its prerogatives. Although the *quo warranto* decision tries hard to contextualise the Sereno case to prevent its indiscriminate – or vindictive – use in the future, the Court's decision opens a Pandora's box for using this and other legal devices to unseat other high officials who may have displeased the President or the party in power.

This does not augur well for the stability and functioning of a constitutional government where independent bodies play a crucial role in ensuring accountability and preventing abuses of power. Thus, the use of legal rules as political weapons, with a judiciary that is not prepared to exercise judicial restraint in the use of these tools, can only serve to embolden political leaders intent upon undermining the constitutional balance of power and the rule of law.

A key lesson from this episode is that institutional cohesion and leadership are even more critical than the mere possession of constitutional guarantees to enable the court to be independent. Security of tenure, financial autonomy, and a high bar for the removal of justices are not *ipso facto* guarantees from political intrusions – or the politicisation of the judiciary, as shown in the Philippines. As other jurisdictions have experienced, institutional cohesion and skilful leadership are essential in navigating the ups and downs of democratic transition. Under a climate of strongman rule, the judiciary is highly vulnerable to political machinations and pressure to alter the balance of power in a constitutional democracy. Institutional support from within the Supreme Court for the accused Chief Justice could have provided a barrier against malicious or arbitrary ouster initiatives.

Part IV

Satellite

13 Impeachment in Central and Eastern Europe

Philipp Köker

13.1 Introduction

On 6 April 2004 the Lithuanian Seimas voted to impeach President Rolandas Paksas on three charges of violating the constitution, removing him from office only 15 months after he had been elected as the country's third democratic head of state since the end of Soviet occupation.[1] The impeachment of Paksas was remarkable for several reasons. Central and East European (CEE) presidents and their behaviour in office, especially their attempts to stretch their powers beyond constitutional limits, have long been the subject of both political contention and scholarly debate.[2] Yet, while impeachment attempts had been launched – or at least debated – in several other post-Socialist states,[3] Paksas' removal from office was the first of its kind in the region. Moreover, it was also the first – and hitherto only – successful impeachment of a European head of state.

This chapter surveys the legal and practical aspects of impeachment in CEE, specifically, the 11 formerly Socialist countries that joined the European Union in or after 2004. This set of countries provides a particularly insightful sample for comparison and analysis. They not only share a largely similar historical background and trajectory of socio-economic development but also have faced similar challenges in creating democratic political systems in a short period of time. Nevertheless, the set-up and practices of the new regimes still show remarkable variation.[4] This is particularly true for questions of impeachment. After procedures for the removal of public officials were virtually non-existent under Socialist rule, constitution-makers across CEE included provisions to ensure the accountability of officeholders; despite

1 Terry D Clark and Eglė Verseckaitė, 'Paksasgate: Lithuania Impeaches a President' (2005) 52 *Problems of Post-Communism* 21.

2 Philipp Köker, *Presidential Activism and Veto Power in Central and Eastern Europe* (Palgrave 2017); Vít Hloušek (ed), *Presidents Above Parties? Presidents in Central and Eastern Europe, Their Formal Competencies and Informal Power* (MUNI Press 2013).

3 Young Hun Kim, 'Impeachment and Presidential Politics in New Democracies' (2014) 21 *Democratization* 519.

4 Köker (n 2) 4.

DOI: 10.4324/9781003256007-17

some general similarities, impeachment procedures differ significantly in their accessibility, scope, and frequency of application. Focussing primarily on presidential impeachment, this chapter reviews the constitutional history and rules governing impeachment in CEE and discusses their potential for instrumentalization by political elites.

13.2 Impeachment in Central and Eastern Europe Before 1989

The end of WWI saw the (re-)emergence of a number of independent nations across CEE. Monarchies remained in power across the Balkans, whereas Central European and Baltic nations largely chose republican forms of government.[5] The new constitutions all established parliamentary systems in which executive power was exercised by a cabinet that required the confidence of the legislature. Although monarchs in Bulgaria, Romania, and Yugoslavia retained significant political power,[6] the constitutional and practical role of presidents as heads of state was more ambiguous – they were elected for a fixed term by the legislature or national assembly and possessed only moderate constitutional powers.[7] However, given high levels of political fragmentation and by virtue of the individuals that occupied the office, the presidency often took on a more central role in politics than envisaged by the constitutional text.[8]

Given that cabinets could be removed from office by votes of no confidence, constitutions devoted little space to the legal accountability of officeholders over other concerns. Nevertheless, all republican constitutions foresaw some mechanisms to remove the president – albeit with varying levels of specificity. In Latvia and Lithuania, deputies could remove presidents from office with an absolute two-thirds majority, although it was not clear what would constitute permissible reasons for doing so.[9] In contrast, the Czechoslovak Constitutional Charter of 1920 specified that the President could be impeached following a procedure modelled after the U.S. Constitution, in which the President was indicted by the Chamber of Deputies and convicted by the Senate.[10] In Poland, the President and Members of the Council of Ministers could be

5 RJ Crampton, *Eastern Europe in the Twentieth Century – and After* (2nd edn, Routledge 1997) 31–38.

6 Hungary formally remained a monarchy but was ruled by Admiral Miklós Horthy as Regent.

7 Estonia presents the exception here – the Riigivanem ('State Elder') was head of state and head of government but could be removed from office by the assembly at any time; Lee Kendall Metcalf, 'The Evolution of Presidential Power in Estonia, 1920–1992' (1998) 2 *Journal of Baltic Studies* 333.

8 See, e.g., Tomáš Garrigue Masaryk, founding president of Czechoslovakia (in office 1918–1935).

9 Latvijas Republikas Satversme (1922) art 51; Lietuvos Valstybės Konstituciją (1922) §44; Annija Kārkliņa, 'Valsts prezidenta atlaišanas institūts' (Doctoral thesis, Latvijas Universitāte 2008).

10 Members of the government could be removed using the same procedure; Ústavní listina Československé republiky (1920) §§34, 67, 79.

impeached by parliament, yet judgement was reserved for the State Tribunal (Trybunał Stanu), which consisted of the President of the Supreme Court as chair and twelve additional judges elected by the Sejm and Senate.[11] In monarchies, constitutional accountability naturally excluded the head of state, but cabinet ministers could still be impeached by the legislature and were subsequently tried and convicted by the State Court (Yugoslavia),[12] High Court of Cassation and Justice (Romania),[13] or a special State Tribunal (Bulgaria).[14]

The Communist takeover of CEE after WWII brought not only a change of regimes but also a change of constitutions. Although early drafts and the first, superficially democratic constitutions often still contained some mechanisms of executive accountability, these were subsequently removed.[15] Poland, which had abolished the State Tribunal as part of the 1952 Constitution, notably re-introduced it in 1982 – albeit while still under martial law.[16] Irrespective of the particular type of Socialist regime, the Communist Party and its leadership were – both in theory and practice – the dominant political force that decided the fate of public officials.[17] Nevertheless, as leaders usually served for life and political power was highly personalised, the countries lacked formalised mechanisms to remove incompetent or senile leaders and also failed to develop informal routines.[18] Hence, after the fall of the Iron Curtain, CEE countries had only a fragmentary legacy regarding impeachment. Nevertheless, both early democratic experiences – however short – and executive excesses by authoritarian leaders before and after WWII still served as important reference points in debates about the new constitutional order.[19]

13.3 Instruments of Impeachment in CEE Constitutions

The transition to democracy across CEE necessitated the adoption of new democratic constitutions. Depending on the type of transition and power

11 Konstytucja Rzeczypospolitej Polskiej (1921) arts 51, 59, 64; Jerzy J Wiatr, 'Constitutional Accountability in Poland After 1989' (1996) 5 *East European Constitutional Review* 42.
12 Устав Краљевине Срба, Хрвата и Словенаца (1921) arts 91–93.
13 Constituția României (1923) art 93.
14 Конституцията на Българското княжество (1879) arts 55–58.
15 For instance, while the Czechoslovak Constitution of 1948 still included the same impeachment procedure as its predecessor, it was missing from the first fully communist Constitution of 1960.
16 Wiatr (n 11) 43.
17 Joni Lovenduski and Jean Woodall, *Politics and Society in Eastern Europe* (Palgrave Macmillan 1987) 197ff.
18 Martin McCauley and Stephen Carter, 'Introduction' in Martin McCauley and Stephen Carter (eds), *Leadership and Succession in the Soviet Union, Eastern Europe and China* (Palgrave Macmillan 1986) 13–14; notably, even where regimes sought constitutional solutions, as in the case of severely ill Czechoslovak President Ludvík Svoboda, these were still tailored to individual officeholders, see Philipp Köker, 'The Temporary Transfer of Presidential Powers in the Czech Republic' (2023) 48 *Review of Central and East European Law* 1.
19 Klaus von Beyme, 'Institutional Engineering and Transition to Democracy' in Jan Zielonka (ed), *Democratic Consolidation in Eastern Europe. Volume 1: Institutional Engineering* (OUP 2001).

Table 13.1 Impeachment Instruments in Central and East European Constitutions

Country (constitution)	*President*	*Members of Government*	*Members of Parliament*	*Judges*	*Other Public Officials*
Bulgaria (1991)	✓				
Croatia (1990)	✓				
Czech Republic (1993)	✓				
Estonia (1992)[a)]					
Hungary (2011)	✓		✓		
Latvia (1922/1992)	✓			✓	
Lithuania (1992)	✓		✓	✓[b)]	
Poland (1997)	✓	✓	✓		✓[c)]
Romania (1990)	✓				
Slovakia (1993)	✓				
Slovenia (1990)	✓	✓			

Notes: a) No impeachment procedure; the President, the Chancellor of Justice, the Chief Justice, Judges of the Supreme Court and the Auditor General lose office when a final guilty verdict enters into force; b) only Justices of the Constitutional Court, the Supreme Court, and the Court of Appeal; c) President of the National Bank, President of the National Chamber of Control, Members of the National Broadcasting Council, Commander in Chief of the Armed Forces.

balance between old elites and the democratic opposition, countries not only settled on different distributions of political power but also chose different paths in establishing democratic institutions.[20] Nevertheless, all constitutions contain procedures by which at least some elected or appointed public officials can be removed from office. Table 13.1 summarises the scope of impeachment procedures across CEE. Although all constitutions (except Estonia) include provisions to impeach the president, they differ more widely regarding whether other officials can also be subject to impeachment. Governments in all countries require the confidence of the assembly and can be removed using a (constructive) vote of no confidence; some countries (e.g., Estonia and Poland) even permit no-confidence motions in individual ministers. However, Poland and Slovenia additionally allow for removing the Prime Minister and other members of government from office for violating the constitution in a procedure that is largely analogous to presidential impeachment. Similarly, although members of parliament across CEE enjoy special protection and immunity from prosecution, Lithuania, Poland, and Hungary also allow for their impeachment.[21] Judges may only be impeached in Latvia and

20 ibid.

21 The range of impeachable violations is relatively broad in Lithuania in Poland, whereas Hungarian deputies can only be removed from office if they fail to participate in parliamentary sessions for over a year; Magyarország Alaptörvénye (2011) art 4, para 3 lit f) [4].

Lithuania, but Lithuania limits this to members of the three highest courts (Constitutional Court, Supreme Court, and Court of Appeal). Finally, the Polish constitution also includes the possibility of impeaching a number of other high-ranking public officials, including the President of the National Bank and the Commander in Chief of the Armed Forces.

The wide range of state officials liable to impeachment in Poland results from the historical legacy of the State Tribunal. Since its re-introduction in 1982, it has operated on the basis of the same law, and its organisation and functioning were only fully described in the new Constitution of 1997.[22] Its initial scope was already extensive and covered members of the Council of State (collective presidency), Council of Ministers (government), and high-level civil servants, such as the President of the National Chamber of Control, the President of the Central Bank, and the Prosecutor General. Furthermore, proceedings could be launched up to ten years after an alleged offence had taken place.[23] Given the difficulties on agreeing on a new constitution, the act was merely updated when the 'Small Constitution' of 1992 was adopted and kept its extensive scope.[24] Later amendments then only concerned procedural aspects and did not touch upon the substance of the provisions.[25]

Estonia presents another major exception as the constitution does not include any provisions on impeachment in a narrower sense.[26] Rather, the President, members of government, the Chancellor of Justice, judges of the Supreme Court, and the Auditor General automatically lose office once a final guilty verdict against them enters into force. A majority of the membership of the Riigikogu (parliament) must consent to the preparation of criminal charges, but otherwise, there is no political input, and the process is determined by special provisions of the Criminal Code of Procedure rather than organic law.[27] The reasons for this exception are unclear; nevertheless, the first Estonian interwar constitution similarly did not include any specific impeachment procedures.

13.4 Presidential Impeachment in Central and Eastern Europe

None of the new democracies in CEE established a pure presidential system; however, presidents were nonetheless granted significant powers and became

22 Marek Zubik, 'Trybunały po dziesięciu latach obowiązywania Konstytucji III' (2007) 15 *Przegląd Sejmowy* 151, 169.

23 Ustawa z dnia 26 Marca 1982 r o Trybunale Stanu (1982).

24 Although amendments removed the Prosecutor General from the act, they added the Commander in Chief of the Armed Forces and members of the National Broadcasting Council; Ustawa z dnia 12 grudnia 1992 r o zmianie ustawy o Trybunale Stanu (1993); Ustawa z dnia 29 grudnia 1992 r o radiofonii i telewizji (1992).

25 Zubik (n 22).

26 Ülle Madise and Mall Gramberg, 'Paragrahv 82' in Ülle Madise (ed), *Eesti Varibariigi Põhiseadus. Kommenteeritud Väljaanne* (Iuridicum 2020).

27 Juhan Sarv, 'Paragrahv 85' in Ülle Madise (ed), *Eesti Varibariigi Põhiseadus. Kommenteeritud Väljaanne* (Iuridicum 2020).

crucial – and often controversial – actors, particularly during the first decade of democratisation.[28] Although several scholars have sought to measure and compare presidents' constitutional powers, the constitutional provisions to ensure accountability for their actions generally remain overlooked. Table 13.2 summarises impeachment procedures for CEE presidents; although all countries amended (or replaced) their constitutions at some point, only the Czech Republic and Slovakia altered their impeachment procedures when they switched from indirect to direct presidential elections in 2013 and 1999, respectively.

In the majority of cases, presidential impeachment is initiated and approved in the legislature before being transferred to the Constitutional Court for a final verdict, which reflects wider constitutional trends in the region.[29] Nevertheless, countries still show significant variation in the material and procedural requirements of impeachment proceedings. All countries require a violation of the constitution as grounds for impeachment, yet occasionally include further charges; the Czech Republic is the only country that limits possible charges to high treason. In contrast, Latvia and Slovakia do not fully specify grounds for impeachment. The Latvian constitution lacks any indication of permissible charges, and there is no scholarly or political consensus on what may constitute sufficient grounds for impeachment.[30] In Slovakia, the 1999 amendments to the constitution introduced the possibility to remove the president by plebiscite – but they did not specify on what grounds such a procedure could be launched. As the constitution provides for impeachment in the case of deliberate violation of the Constitution or high treason, scholars have generally argued that charges may only include other actions that violate the president's oath of office.[31]

Legislative thresholds for proposing a motion of impeachment vary greatly, but in most cases, it is less than half the total membership of the legislature. The lowest threshold can be found in Slovakia, where – according to the dominating opinion in the literature – any deputy can propose a motion for presidential impeachment that is to be decided by plebiscite[32] or one-fifth of all deputies in cases tried by the Constitutional Court; one-fifth of deputies is also sufficient in Hungary and Croatia. The highest thresholds can be found in Latvia and Romania (only in the case of high treason), which require that half of the total number of legislators propose a motion to impeach. Although

28 Köker (n 2); Hloušek (n 2).

29 Christoph Hönnige, 'Verfassungsgerichte: Neutrale Verfassungshüter oder Vetospieler?' in Florian Grotz and Ferdinand Müller-Rommel (eds), *Regierungssysteme in Mittel- und Osteuropa: Die neuen EU-Staaten im Vergleich* (VS Verlag 2011).

30 Kārkliņa (n 9) 64ff.

31 Rudolf Manik, 'Zodpovednosť a zánik funkcie prezidenta Slovenskej republiky' (2004) 8–9 *Justičná Revue* 874.

32 Both the constitution and the standing orders of the National Council are silent on the subject.

Table 13.2 Constitutional Provisions on Presidential Impeachment in Central and Eastern Europe

Country (year)	*Permissible charges*	*Who initiates proceedings?*	*Who approves proceedings?*	*Who convicts?*
Bulgaria (1991)	High treason or violation of the Constitution	1/4 of the National Assembly	2/3 of the National Assembly	Constitutional Court
Croatia (1990)	Violation of the Constitution	1/5 of the Sabor	2/3 of the Sabor	Constitutional Court
Czech Republic (1993–2013)	High treason	1/3 of the Senate	1/2 of Senators present	Constitutional Court
Czech Republic (2013)	High treason	3/5 of Senators present	3/5 of the Chamber of Deputies	Constitutional Court
Estonia (1992)[a)]	Any criminal charges	Chancellor of Justice on request of Chief Prosecutor	Majority of members of parliament	Supreme Court
Hungary (1990; 2011)	Violation of the Fundamental Law or committing a crime	1/5 of National Assembly	2/3 of National Assembly	Constitutional Court
Latvia (1992)	Not specified	1/2 of the Seimas	2/3 of the Seimas	Vote in parliament removes president from office
Lithuania (1992)	Gross violation of the Constitution, breach of oath, committing a crime	1/4 of the Seimas	1/2 of the Seimas	3/5 members of parliament following opinion from Constitutional Court
Poland (1989; 1992; 1997)	Violation of the constitution or law, or committing a crime	1/4 of the National Assembly (Sejm & Senate)	2/3 of National Assembly	State Tribunal[b)]

(*Continued*)

Table 13.2 (Continued)

Country (year)	*Permissible charges*	*Who initiates proceedings?*	*Who approves proceedings?*	*Who convicts?*
Romania (1990)	Grave acts infringing upon constitutional provisions	1/3 of all Deputies & Senators	1/2 of Deputies & Senators in Joint Session	Referendum
	High treason	1/2 of all Deputies & Senators	2/3 of Deputies & Senators in Joint Session	High Court of Cassation and Justice
Slovakia (1993–1999)	Activities against the sovereignty and territorial integrity or aimed at eliminating the democratic constitutional order	1/2 of the National Council	3/5 of the National Council	Vote in parliament removes president from office
Slovakia (1999)	Deliberate violation of the Constitution or high treason	1/5 of the National Council	3/5 of the National Council	Constitutional Court
	Not specified	Any member of the National Council	3/5 of the National Council	Referendum
Slovenia (1990)	Serious violation of the law	1/3 of the National Council	1/2 of the National Council	Constitutional Court

Notes: a) The Estonian provisions do not present impeachment proceedings in a strict sense – they are listed here for the sake of completeness; b) President of the Supreme Court, two deputies, and 16 members elected by the Sejm for the duration of the legislative term, half of whom must be qualified to be judges.

a three-fifths majority of Senators is required in the Czech Republic, this only relates to the quorum and not the total membership. Subsequently, the motion is usually passed to the legislature's constitutional or legal affairs committee or a new committee is formed to investigate the claims and make a recommendation to the legislature. Following the committee's report, most countries then require an absolute majority of three-fifths to two-thirds of the membership of the legislature to approve the charges and move to the next stage. An absolute majority of members is sufficient in Lithuania, Slovenia, and Romania (only for constitutional violations other than high treason).

In the vast majority of countries, the final decision to remove a president from office is taken by the Constitutional Court, the High Court of Cassation and Justice (Romania) or a specific tribunal (Poland); Romania and Slovakia also allow the removal of the president through referendum depending on the charges presented. Thereby, Slovakia requires a minimum turnout of 50%+1 of registered voters for any referendum to be valid,[33] whereas Romania has used different thresholds. After applying both no minimum turnout requirement and a 50% minimum in the past,[34] this was lowered to 30% of registered voters in 2013, albeit stipulating that least 25% of registered voters must approve the outcome for it to be valid.[35] Finally, Latvia and Lithuania are alone in placing the final decision solely in the hands of parliament; notably, while the Lithuanian Seimas decides only after consulting the Constitutional Court, no judicial institutions are involved in Latvia.

13.4.1 The Impeachment of President Rolandas Paksas in Lithuania

To date, Lithuanian President Rolandas Paksas remains the only European head of state to be removed from office through impeachment. Arguably, it was also the only attempt to impeach a president that was primarily based on valid legal arguments rather than (purely) political motives. Paksas, former mayor of the capital city Vilnius with two brief stints as prime minister (1999; 2000–2001), was elected as the country's third democratic president in January 2003. Running on a populist anti-establishment platform and with the backing of his newly founded Liberal Democratic Party, he surprisingly defeated first-round frontrunner and incumbent Valdas Adamkus in the run-off. Already during his campaign, Paksas' links with controversial Russian businessman Iurii Borisov who financed much of his presidential campaign aroused suspicion. Subsequently, Paksas' confrontational behaviour in the first months of his presidency further alienated him from erstwhile political allies in parliament and government.[36]

33 Ústava Slovenskej republiky (1992) art 98 [1].

34 Sergiu Gherghina and Sergiu Mişcoiu, 'The Failure of Cohabitation: Explaining the 2007 and 2012 Institutional Crises in Romania' (2013) 4 *East European Politics and Societies* 668, 674f.

35 Lege pentru modificarea şi completarea Legii No 3/2000 privind organizarea şi desfăşurarea referendumului (2013).

36 Clark and Verseckaitė (n 1) 19.

The prelude to Paksas' impeachment were allegations that some of his key advisors maintained ties with criminals; after parliament's subsequent investigation into the matter uncovered evidence that Paksas had made promises to Borisov, and the President refused to heed calls to resign from office, the Seimas approved the formation of an investigatory commission (the first step of impeachment proceedings) on 29 December 2003. Seven weeks later, the commission concluded its work and recommended that Paksas be impeached for (a) illegally granting citizenship to Iurii Borisov, (b) informing Borisov that his phone was wiretapped, and (c) attempting to interfere in the privatization process to benefit his campaign contributors.[37] Parliament approved the recommendation on the same day and turned the report over to the Constitutional Court. The Court ruled that the allegations indeed constituted a violation of the constitution and the President's oath of office.[38] During the subsequent trial in parliament, Paksas' lawyers maintained his innocence (the President himself refused to attend), yet deputies eventually convicted the President on all charges and removed him from office on 6 April 2004.[39] On the whole, the impeachment procedure was arguably completed quickly and effectively. However, it is important to note that this was only due to the shared responsibility of parliament, government, and the judiciary. As *Clark* and *Verseckaitė* point out, none of these institutions was ready to take the blame alone should impeachment fail or wanted to be subject of retaliation by the President.[40]

13.4.2 Unsuccessful Impeachment Attempts

There have been at least nine formal attempts to impeach presidents in other parts of CEE. Nevertheless, these were largely driven by ideological opposition to the president and often proceeded on the basis of constitutionally questionable arguments.

In Romania, three separate attempts to impeach the president ended in failure. In early 1994, opposition parties tried to impeach president Ion Iliescu for his comments on the legality of court decisions on property restitutions. Nevertheless, after the Constitutional Court concluded in a consultative opinion that the president had not violated the constitution, parliament rejected the motion to suspend the president and call for a referendum on his removal by a wide margin.[41] Impeachment proceedings against President Traian Băsescu

37 Terry and Verseckaitė (n 1) 21.

38 Lietuvos Respublikos Konstitucinio Teismo 2004 m kovo 31 d išvada, Valstybės žinios, 2004, No 49–1600.

39 Lietuvos Respublikos Seimo posėdis No 499 (5 April 2004 vakarinis) stenograma; Lietuvos Respublikos Seimo posėdis Nr 500 (6 April 2004 rytinis) stenograma.

40 Terry and Verseckaitė (n 1) 23.

41 Stephen Holmes, 'Constitution Watch: Romania' (1994) 3 *East European Constitutional Review* 2.

advanced further, resulting in two – unsuccessful – impeachment referendums. In 2007, Băsescu was confronted with a whole catalogue of allegations – these included a lack of partisan neutrality, abuse of power and failure to act as a mediator, infringement of powers of parliament and government, and public statements discrediting state institutions.[42] Although the Constitutional Court declared that the charges could in 'content and consequences' not necessarily be regarded as grave violations of the constitution,[43] parliament still voted to call a referendum on the president's impeachment. In a last minute move, the government even amended the procedure so that the vote did not require a minimum turnout to be valid. Nevertheless, voters overwhelmingly rejected impeachment with 75% voting against.[44] In 2012, Băsescu once again faced various allegations of violating the constitution. Although the Constitutional Court dismissed most charges as unfounded, it declared that the president had failed to diligently exercise his role as a mediator between state institutions and state and society.[45] In the subsequent referendum, 89% of voters supported impeachment, yet turnout remained just below the required 50% so that Băsescu remained in office.[46] All three impeachment attempts were largely motivated by partisan opposition against the President rather than actual wrongdoing (as also evidenced by the opinions of the Constitutional Court); the comparatively low threshold to call a referendum thereby clearly facilitated – and perhaps even incentivised – the use of impeachment proceedings as a political tool.

The importance of legislative thresholds, albeit in preventing impeachment proceedings, has also been highlighted in other attempts to use impeachment for political gain. In Slovakia, the illiberal governments of Prime Minister Vladimír Mečiar (1992–94; 1994–98) tried to use impeachment among a range of outright unconstitutional moves to attack President Michal Kováč.[47] Nevertheless, the governing majority managed only to pass a motion of no confidence in the President in early 1995, which failed to fulfil any of the procedural and material conditions for an impeachment vote and was widely condemned as unconstitutional.[48] A formal attempt to impeach Slovakia's third president Ivan Gašparovič in 2013 for failing to appoint the National Council's

42 Gherghina and Mişcoiu (n 34) 674.

43 Aviz consultativ din 5 Aprilie 2007 privind propunerea de suspendare din funcţie a Preşedintelui României, domnul Traian Băsescu, Curtea Constituţională a României, Monitorul Oficial nr 258 din 18 April 2007.

44 Gherghina and Mişcoiu (n 34).

45 Aviz consultativ din 6 iulie 2012 privind propunerea de suspendare din funcţie a Preşedintelui României, domnul Traian Băsescu, Curtea Constituţională a României, Monitorul Oficial nr 456 din 6 July 2012.

46 Gherghina and Mişcoiu (n 34) 675.

47 Köker (n 2) 174.

48 SME, 'Na návrh V. Morica 80 poslancov koalície schválilo uznesenie, ktorým vyslovilo nedôveru prezidentovi, čím podľa opozície porušilo ústavu' *SME* (6 May 1995) <www.sme.sk/c/2121305/na-navrh-v-morica-80-poslancov-koalicie-schvalilo-uznesenie-ktorym-

candidate for general prosecutor likewise failed after only 45 deputies (i.e., less than one-third) voted in favour of impeachment.[49]

In the Czech Republic, a majority of Senators voted to impeach outgoing President Václav Klaus for treason three days before the end of his term in February 2013. Klaus had used his constitutional powers to issue a mass amnesty that expunged or commuted the sentences of up to 30,000 individuals; while this largely affected suspended sentences, it also led to the release of approximately 6,300 prisoners (ca. 27 % of the country's prison population). As the old constitutional provisions were still in force, the Senate's indictment was immediately transferred to the Constitutional Court without requiring the approval of the Chamber of Deputies. However, the Court rejected the case in March 2013 as Klaus had already left office at that point.[50] In 2019, the Senate proposed to impeach Klaus' successor Miloš Zeman for 'continuous violation of the constitution' including failure to appoint or dismiss members of the government and acting contrary to the country's official foreign policy. Although the indictment was supported by 48 out of 75 Senators, it was subsequently supported by only 58 members of the Chamber of Deputies – less than half of the 120 required – and did not proceed further.[51]

In Bulgaria, the government attempted to remove President Georgi Parvanov in 2010 after he first called for the Finance Minister's resignation and later published a transcript of their conversation on his website. Although the initial motion, alleging that Parvanov had violated the Constitution by 'engaging in partisan politics and failing to do his duty as impartial arbitrator', attracted sufficient support, it fell short of the required two-thirds majority in the final vote.[52] Finally, in perhaps the least promising attempt to impeach a president, two Slovenian opposition parties sought to remove president Danilo Türk in 2010. They claimed that by awarding Tomaž Ertl, a Communist-era interior minister and head of the Yugoslav secret police, the Order of Merit, Türk had violated no fewer than 34 articles of the constitution and several provisions of the criminal code.[53] Although the award caused irritation

---

vyslovilo-nedoveru-prezidentovi-cim-podla-opozicie-porusilo-u.html> accessed 25 February 2023.

49 This was only one more than had supported the motion in the first instance; Stenozáznam Národnej rady Slovenskej republiky, 15 Schôdze, 12 Marca 2013.

50 Aktualne.cz, 'Amnestie' *Aktualne.cz* (2 April 2020) <www.aktualne.cz/wiki/domaci/amnestie/r~i:wiki:3575/> accessed 25 February 2023.

51 Anna Kottová, 'Pro 58, proti 62. Poslanci podle očekávání odmítli ústavní žalobu na prezidenta Zemana' *iHROZLAS* (26 September 2019) <www.irozhlas.cz/zpravy-domov/ustavni-zaloba-na-prezidenta-milos-zeman-snemovna_1909261015_zit> accessed 25 February 2023.

52 Rumyana Kolarova and Maria Spirova, 'Bulgaria' (2011) 7–8 *European Journal of Political Research Data Yearbook* 922, 926.

53 Predlog obtožbe predsednika republike pred Ustavnim sodiščem zaradi kršitev Ustave in hujših kršitev zakona, 28 January 2010, Državni zbor EPA 0869-V.

domestically and abroad, the motion was nonetheless easily defeated with the votes of the remaining parties.[54]

13.5 Impeachment of Other Public Officials in CEE

Presidents are not the only public officials that can be subject to impeachment proceedings in CEE. Overall, the application of relevant constitutional provisions tends to be just as infrequent as those for presidential impeachment. However, there are two important exceptions to this rule: (a) attempts to impeach the Prime Minister of Slovenia and (b) the impeachment of members of parliament in Lithuania. Both countries provide particularly interesting insights into the developing constitutional practice of individual countries and the use of impeachment proceedings for political gain.

In Slovenia, the rules for presidential impeachment are applied mutatis mutandis to the Prime Minister, except for a lower threshold for initiating proceedings (only 10 deputies must support the initial motion). Perhaps as a consequence of the different thresholds, deputies sought only once to impeach the president, whereas prime ministers have been subject to a total of six separate impeachment motions so far. The reasons for the motions and the degree of alleged constitutional violations varied greatly, but eventually, all were rejected by the National Council and failed to reach the Constitutional Court.[55] In 1994, opposition parties sought to impeach Prime Minister Janez Drnovšek for his negotiations with Italy on property rights for foreigners, while two further motions against Drnovšek in 1998 claimed that he had violated the constitution over concluding a secret security agreement with Israel.[56] In 2017, several deputies attempted to impeach Prime Minister Miro Cerar for allegedly intervening in the deportation of a Syrian refugee to Croatia,[57] whereas his successor, Marjan Šarec, was accused of hindering the implementation of a ruling by the country's Constitutional Court to provide funding for private primary schools.[58] Finally, in 2021, the opposition alleged that Prime Minister Janez Drnovšek had violated the constitution by using the Covid-19 pandemic as a pretext to extend the government's powers and

54 Državni zbor, 'Postopek obtožbe predsednika republike, predsednika vlade in ministrov' (*Državni zbor Republike Slovenije*, 31 May 2021) <www.dz-rs.si/wps/portal/Home/is/PogostaVprasanja/vprasanje/94f31808-e6f9-46d6-9d2c-5c3f9f5db015/> accessed 25 February 2023.

55 ibid.

56 Alenka Krašovec and Tomaž Krpič, 'Slovenia: Majority Coalitions and the Strategy of Dropping Out of Cabinet' in Torbjörn Bergman, Gabriella Ilonszki and Wolfgang C Müller (eds), *Coalition Governance in Central Eastern Europe* (OUP 2019).

57 Alenka Krašovec, 'Slovenia: Political Development and Data for 2017' (2018) 51 *European Journal of Political Research Data Yearbook* 262, 266.

58 Sandra Hanžič, 'Proti ustavni obtožbi Marjana Šarca glasovalo 53 poslancev' *DELO* (29 January 2019) <www.delo.si/novice/slovenija/proti-ustavni-obtozbi-marjana-sarca-glasovalo-53-poslancev/> accessed 25 February 2023.

by failing to order a sufficient amount of Covid-19 vaccines.[59] The fact that the motions were often based on spurious allegations and always fell considerably short of the required majorities suggests that they were used as a means of generating publicity rather than enforcing the constitutional accountability of officeholders. This is underscored by provisions governing votes of no confidence – these can be initiated and passed by the same number of deputies but lack the additional 'frill' of impeachment charges against the incumbent.

Lithuania not only is the sole country to successfully impeach its president but also has employed impeachment proceedings against members of parliament on several occasions; the procedure followed is exactly the same as for presidential impeachment. The first attempt to impeach a deputy, former Defence Minister Audrius Butkevičius in 1999 for attempted fraud, failed spectacularly – even though Butkevičius, who was elected to the Seimas in 1996, had already been sentenced in 1998 and subsequently served a six and a half year prison term, he remained a deputy for the remainder of the legislative term.[60] In 2010, the Seimas impeached Linas Karalius for violating his oath of office by missing Seimas sessions without justifiable reasons (he was on vacation in Thailand) while the chairman of his party group, Aleksandras Sacharukas, who had voted for Karalius in his absence, narrowly retained his mandate.[61] In 2014, Neringa Venckienė was impeached in her absence after fleeing to the U.S. to avoid prosecution in a highly publicised custody case;[62] two years later, impeachment proceedings against Vytautas Gapšys who had been sentenced for fraudulent bookkeeping were terminated after the Constitutional Court stated that it could not evaluate the actions of MPs before they entered office.[63] Two subsequent impeachment proceedings also had to be terminated before the final vote as the accused – Kęstutis Pūkas (accused of sexual harassment) and Mindaugas Bastis (accused of hiding his connection to former KGB officers) – resigned from office after the Constitutional Court concluded that they had violated their oaths of office.[64]

59 Alenka Krašovec, 'Slovenia: Political Developments and Data in 2021' (2022) 61 *European Journal of Political Research Data Yearbook* 410, 413.

60 Dainoras Lukas, 'Pirmoji apkalta baigėsi šokiruojančiai' *Kauno Diena* (Kaunas, 8 December 2003) <www.delfi.lt/news/daily/lithuania/pirmoji-apkalta-baigesi-sokiruojanciai.d?id=3328996> accessed 25 February 2023.

61 Eglė Samoškaitė and Vytenė Stašaitytė, 'L Karalius neteko Seimo nario mandato, A.Sacharukas išsaugojo' *DELFI* (11 November 2010) <www.delfi.lt/news/daily/lithuania/lkaralius-neteko-seimo-nario-mandato-asacharukas-issaugojo.d?id=38448691> accessed 25 February 2023.

62 Baltic News Service, 'Seimas per apkaltą panaikino N Venckienės mandatą' *Kauno Diena* (Kaunas, 19 June 2014) <https://kauno.diena.lt/naujienos/lietuva/politika/seimas-balsuos-del-n-venckienes-mandato-panaikinimo-635391> accessed 25 February 2023.

63 ELTA, 'Konstitucinis Teismas nenagrinės V Gapšio apkaltos klausimo' *DELFI* (16 May 2016) <www.delfi.lt/news/daily/lithuania/konstitucinis-teismas-nenagrines-v-gapsio-apkaltos-klausimo.d?id=71228838> accessed 25 February 2023; Gapšys nonetheless resigned shortly afterwards when accusations of bribery emerged.

64 Milena Andrukaitytė, 'Taškas: K Pūkas palieka Seimą, apkalta nutraukta' *Diena* (12 January 2018) <www.diena.lt/naujienos/lietuva/politika/k-pukas-atsisako-seimo-nario-mandato-845944>

The last two other attempts to impeach MPs did not even make it to the Constitutional Court, yet highlight that the impeachment procedure is increasingly used as a means to discredit political opponents. In 2018, the investigatory commission of the Seimas concluded that there was no evidence to impeach Artūras Skardžis for using his office for private gain;[65] in 2020, the Seimas declined to investigate Irina Rozova who was accused of concealing contacts with Russian officials.[66] Similar to previous motions, these latter two alleged that the deputies had violated their oaths of office. It could be argued that because the Constitutional Court has established a rather extensive understanding of what such violations may entail through its jurisprudence to date, it has essentially lowered the hurdle for impeachment motions and facilitated their use for political gain.

13.6 Conclusion: The Future of Impeachment in Central and Eastern Europe

Comparative scholarship on the political and legal systems of CEE has hitherto often neglected to give attention to the institution of impeachment. However, the discussion in this chapter has shown that impeachment procedures do possess practical relevance in a number of countries. Nevertheless, in contrast to other third-wave democracies,[67] it has not become a common practice. Regarding presidential impeachment, this can be explained by the fact that no country in CEE has adopted a pure presidential system, meaning that – except for the constitutionally guaranteed leadership roles of the Lithuanian and Romanian presidents in foreign policy – presidents are not the dominant political actors and possess fewer powers than their counterparts in Latin America or elsewhere. Hence, they can be outmanoeuvred more easily when they obstruct legislative majorities and have fewer opportunities to misuse public office. In contrast, prime ministers and cabinet members as the central executive actors can more easily be removed through no-confidence motions even in countries where their impeachment is possible. Based on the constitutional practice in CEE over the last 30 years and the fact that high levels of

accessed 25 February 2023; Rūta Pukenė and Mindaugas Jackevičius, 'Bastys iš Seimo traukiasi pats' *DELFI* (14 March 2018) <www.delfi.lt/news/daily/lithuania/bastys-is-seimo-traukiasi-pats.d?id=77418149> accessed 25 February 2023.

65 The proceedings nonetheless remained controversial due to the removal of a member of the investigatory committee; Dovaidas Pabiržis, 'Skardžiaus apkaltos nebus: parlamentas pritarė komisijos išvadoms' *Verslo Žinios* (30 June 2018) <www.vz.lt/verslo-aplinka/2018/06/30/skardziaus-apkaltos-nebus-parlamentas-pritare-komisijos-isvadoms> accessed 25 February 2023.

66 Paulina Levickytė, 'Rozovos apkaltos klausimas Seime galutinai "uždarytas": Parlamentarė dėkojo kolegoms' *LRT* (2 June 2020) <www.lrt.lt/naujienos/verslas/4/1184390/rozovos-apkaltos-klausimas-seime-galutinai-uzdarytas-parlamentare-dekojo-kolegoms> accessed 25 February 2023.

67 Kim (n 3).

electoral volatility and political fragmentation, which hinder the formation of supermajorities required by most constitutions, continue to characterise the region, impeachment is thus unlikely to become the norm.

The problems of mustering sufficient legislative support for impeachment motions notwithstanding, the case of Lithuania shows that impeachment can indeed function as an effective means to remove officeholders for violations of the constitution. Nevertheless, the frequent use of proceedings against members of parliament also highlights that procedures may easily be abused for short-term political gain and risk becoming a purely political instrument if authoritative interpretations of permissible charges become too broad. As highlighted by the attempted impeachments of Romanian president Ion Iliescu and Lithuanian Seimas deputy Vytautas Gapšys, the involvement of apex courts nonetheless also imposes important limits on politically motivated proceedings.[68] This, however, only works where courts can work independently and judges can do their work without fear of retribution. Thus, although several actions by the right-wing populist governments of Hungary and Poland since 2010 and 2015, respectively, can arguably be classified as being in clear violation of the countries' constitutions,[69] it is questionable whether officials could effectively be removed from office – even in the unlikely case that a legislative majority chose to indict them.

68 Rulings by international courts can further strengthen the rights of the accused and the impeached. For example, the European Court of Human Rights (ECHR) ruled that the lifetime ban on holding public office for Lithuanian President Rolandas Paksas violated the International Covenant on Civil and Political Rights, *Paksas v Lithuania* (ECHR, 2011–I) 35; Lithuanian MP Mindaugas Bastys likewise appealed to the ECHR with a final decision still outstanding.

69 Tímea Drinóczi and Agnieszka Bień-Kacała, 'Illiberal Constitutionalism: The Case of Hungary and Poland' (2019) 8 *German Law Journal* 1140.

14 Impeachment in Nigeria

Process, Practice and Failure

Omololu Fagbadebo

14.1 Introduction

In Nigeria, the process of removal of political leadership under a democratic system manifests the inherent characteristics of the country's politics. At independence on 1 October 1960, the Independence Constitution prescribed a parliamentary system of government fashioned along the British Westminster System.[1] The regime lasted until 15 January 1966, when the military staged a coup that displaced the civilian government. After 13 years of military rule, a transition programme led to the promulgation of the 1979 presidential Constitution for the Second Republic Government. On 31 December 1983, the military struck again to displace the civilian government. Nigeria was plunged into another praetorian system until 29 May 1999, when the 1999 presidential Constitution ushered in the civilian regime of the Fourth Republic. A failed transition programme of the Babangida regime truncated the emerging Third Republic. Leadership was central to this series of political instability in Nigeria.

As argued elsewhere,[2] the attitudinal disposition of Nigeria's political leaders to power rather than the institutional system has remained the bane of political instability in the country. The practice of the parliamentary and presidential systems with similar results since 1960 attests to this assertion. Although the parliamentary system promotes accountability through the doctrine of collective responsibility, the tripartite institutional structures of presidentialism simplify the process of checks and balances, but Nigerian political

1 Larry Diamond, Anthony Kirk-Greene and Oyeleye Oyediran (eds), *Transition Without End: Nigerian Politics and Civil Society Under Babangida* (Lynne Reiner Publishers 1997); Rotimi Ajayi and Joseph Yinka Fashagba (eds), *Nigerian Politics* (Springer 2021) <https://doi.org/10.1007/978-3-030-50509-7_18>.

2 Omololu Fagbadebo, 'Impeachment Procedure and Judicial Intervention in the Legislative Process in Nigeria' in MOA Alabi and WO Egbewole (eds), *Perspectives on the Legislature in the Government of Nigeria* (African Training and Research Centre in Administration for Development (CAFRAD) 2010) 145–68; Omololu Fagbadebo, *Impeachment in the Nigerian Presidential System* (Palgrave Macmillan 2020).

DOI: 10.4324/9781003256007-18

elites are fond of circumventing the rules and procedures to facilitate their pecuniary interests. Thus, with different governing systems, the patterns of the exercise of legislative and executive powers in the First through to the Fourth Republics have been fraught with what has been described as a mercantilist orientation.[3] The two democratic governing systems practised in Nigeria since independence made provisions for the constitutional removal of the heads of the executive arm of the government at the federal and state levels. Nevertheless, the exercise of this power has been in abeyance with the lack of adherence to the statutory procedures by the members of the legislature, especially at the state level.

At the commencement of the Fourth Republic, members of some state legislatures embarked on the removal of their governors and deputies who disregarded the constitutional provisions. Judicial review of the process set a precedent that interpreted the constitutional provisions regarding the impeachment of the head of the executive arm of the government in Nigeria. Until the judicial pronouncement[4] on the impeachment procedure, the exercise of the impeachment power of the legislature has been characterised by an improper interpretation of the constitutional provisions. Previous judicial interventions were characterised by judicial self-restraint. Thus, the dearth of concrete judicial precedents on judicial review of the impeachment process means that the Nigerian politicians of the Second and the early part of the Fourth Republics indulged in the abuse of the constitutional provisions that stipulated the removal of the heads of the executive branch of government by the legislature.[5]

This chapter presents an analysis of the constitutionally prescribed impeachment process in Nigeria, indicating its abuse and misuse. Aside from this introductory section, the chapter has six sections. The second section presents a brief overview of impeachment in presidential systems. The third section discusses the constitutional provisions and practices of impeachment in Nigeria. Section four contains a brief discussion on the removal of the Premier of the Western Region during the First Republic's parliamentary system, while section five discusses the exercise of impeachment power in the Second and

3 ibid. Between 1 October 1960 and 15 January 1966, Nigeria practiced the Westminster version of a parliamentary system. The military intervention of 15 January 1966 terminated the government of the First Republic and was replaced by the military for 13 years. On 1 October 1979, the Second Republic commenced with the practice of a presidential system. This also lasted barely 4 years when another military interregnum truncated the government on 31 December 1983. Attempts by the succeeding military governments to institutionalise another democratic process for the Third Republic were truncated when the military annulled the result of the 1993 presidential election that launched the country into another full military regime until 1998 when the military ruler, Sani Abacha, died. His successor, Abdulsalami Abubakar organised the shortest transition programme that birthed the Fourth Republic, with a presidential system of government, on 29 May 1999.

4 *Inakoju & 17 Ors v Adeleke & 3 Ors* (2007) 1 SC (Pt 1).

5 Fagbadebo, *Impeachment in the Nigerian Presidential System* (n 2).

Fourth Republics.[6] Section six presents an analysis of the politics of the exercise of impeachment power, and section seven concludes.

14.2 Impeachment in Presidential Systems

The seminal work of Juan J. Linz,[7] *The Perils of Presidentialism*, hinges on what he discovered as the peculiar characteristic of the structural operational modalities of the presidential system. His concern, mostly, is the modality for the survival and stability of executive power, which he finds more favourable in parliamentary systems. He therefore concludes that the parliamentary system 'is more conducive to stable democracy' than the presidential system.[8] This, he avers, 'applies especially to nations with deep political cleavages and numerous political parties; for such countries, *parliamentarism* generally offers a better hope of preserving democracy.'[9] Given the fixed term of tenure and being 'independent of parliamentary votes of confidence'[10] because of direct election by the people, the leader of the executive in presidential systems has access to the enormous power of the state. 'He is not only the holder of executive power but also the symbolic head of state and can be removed between elections only by the drastic step of impeachment',[11] a position that makes the struggle to retain and control power more tense.[12] Hence, the need to place a lever to ensure a check on the exercise of power in a manner prescribed by the constitution.

Juan Linz contends that the control measures in presidential systems are complex and rigid, and as such, the struggles among the contending forces could lead to the emergence of a third force, a *poder moderador*,[13] that can reverse democratic gains. Impeachment in presidential systems incorporates measures to insulate the polity from absolute executive power, in either a single individual or a collective.[14] There are other means of ensuring responsible and accountable leadership in presidential systems, depending on the legislative frameworks prescribed by the constitution, as noted in Latin America.[15]

6 The Third Republic did not mature to the extent of full-blown democratic rule. Elected political officials were governed the local and state governments, while the military occupied the national government without any constitution.
7 Juan J Linz, 'The Perils of Presidentialism' (1990) 1(1) *Journal of Democracy* 51.
8 ibid 52.
9 ibid.
10 ibid.
11 ibid.
12 Fagbadebo, *Impeachment in the Nigerian Presidential System* (n 2).
13 Linz (n 7) 54. Linz used this to rationalize the frequency of military coups in Latin America.
14 RZ Ahrens, 'There Shall Be No Kings Upon the Land: Discussions of Monarchy During the Drafting and Ratification of the US Constitution' (2001) Student Research Papers, Paper 233 <http://digitalcommons.law.byu.edu/student_papers/233>; WE Scheuerman, 'American Kingships? Monarchical Origins of Modern Presidentialism' (2005) 37(1) *Polity* 24.
15 Leiv Marsteintredet and Einar Berntzen, 'Reducing the Perils of Presidentialism in Latin America Through Presidential Interruptions' (2008) 41(1) *Comparative Politics* 83.

The essence is to ensure that both the legislature and the executive work together for an accountable government that advances the interests of the public in a system where power is separated but also shared. In Asia,[16] the instability that characterises executive leadership has so far not led to any form of regime-threatening or democratic breakdown. This is because leadership personalisation in the executive arm rather than state policies has been the primary cause of the conflicts.

Impeachment is a procedural instrument that is designed within a presidential system to instil a culture of responsible and accountable leadership in the execution of public policy. Firstly, given its constitutional foundation and procedural process, it connotes a legally binding process. Secondly, the political context of its process and outcomes defines its political character. This is not accidental. Juan and Tiojanco[17] explain the premises of this legal-political status of impeachment. Firstly, the determination of what constitutes impeachment should be within the confines of the political institution, secondly, the impeachable offences and the penalties thereof are political because, thirdly, not all offences are criminal in nature, and fourthly, public opinion and the political capital of the leader will influence the outcomes.

These premises are inherent in the original conception of impeachment as a corrective instrument, but the ambiguity associated with its practice provides the opportunity to expand its scope, as demonstrated in some Latin American countries, and abuse, as in the case of Nigeria.[18] The fact that impeachment is not a criminal trial does not exonerate the leader from criminal prosecution in accordance with extant constitutional provisions regarding the criminal offence committed while in office. That is, the head of the executive whose criminal offence was instrumental to the removal can still be prosecuted for the offence after the impeachment. In the United States, for instance, the

16 Francis Fukuyama, 'Bjorn Dressel ad Boo-Seung Chang: Facing the Perils of Presidentialism?' (2005) 16(2) *Journal of Democracy* 102; Marco Bünte and Mark R Thompson, 'Presidentialism and Democracy in East and Southeast Asia: Between Resilience and Regression' in Marco Bünte and Mark R Thompson (eds), *Presidentialism and Democracy in East and Southeast Asia* (Routledge 2023); Erik Mobrand, 'South Korea: Presidentialism in Historical and Sociological Perspective' in *Presidentialism and Democracy in East and Southeast Asia* (Routledge 2023).

17 Ronald Ray K San Juan and Bryan Dennis G Tiojanco, 'Impeachment' in Rainer Grote, Frauke Lachenmann and Rudiger Wolfrum (eds), *Max Planck Encyclopedia of Comparative Constitutional Law* (OUP 2016) <https://oxcon.ouplaw.com/view/10.1093/law-mpeccol/law-mpeccol-e311?prd=MPECCOL> accessed 10 February 2021.

18 In Latin America, political leaders dread and respect impeachment instruments as an accountability mechanism, whereas in Nigeria, it is an instrument of negotiation between the legislature and the executive susceptible to manipulation for political vendetta. James Madison and his fellow writers of the Federalist Papers and Edmund Randolph devoted their writings and speeches to the need for measures to avert the danger of an absolute head of the executive. One such check and balance measure, which Whittington describes as the 'ultimate and most powerful', is impeachment.

Constitution prescribes that any leader indicted of criminal offences would not escape the law even after removal from office:

> Judgment in cases of impeachment shall not extend further than to removal from office, and disqualification to hold and enjoy any office of honor, trust, or profit under the United States: but the party convicted shall nevertheless be liable and subject to indictment, trial, judgment and punishment, according to law.[19]

Thus, in the United States (US), 'the impeachment trial is not a mechanism for punishment the way the criminal law is; impeachment is primarily a device to enable removal from office of someone who is unfit to continue.'[20] This fitness is defined by the legislature within the context of the constitutionalised oversight responsibilities. Impeachment is one of the instruments of checks and balances to curb the excesses of the executive in the exercise of power.[21]

The US Senate conducts the impeachment trial of a president impeached by Congress. In this form, the Senate, acting on Oath or Affirmation, is akin to a judicial tribunal whose judgment is precluded from judicial review. As Amar and Mazzone note,

> Indeed, it is precisely because the Senate is acting as a sort of judicial tribunal in a trial of impeachment that the federal courts (including the Supreme Court) should respect the judicial decisions made by the Senate and treat the results of impeachment trials as 'political questions' ordinarily not susceptible to federal judicial review.[22]

This is the peculiar nature of the impeachment process in the US, where the Senate is deemed to have considered the activities of Congress leading to the impeachment and has ensured that the process is constitutional. This is the foundation of the political question doctrine that the Nigerian judiciary misinterpreted for several years until 2006 when the Nigerian Supreme Court provided a clear judicial review of infractions that characterised the impeachment of certain governors. In the US, it is established that in the impeachment trial, the Constitution has saddled the Senate with the power to interpret

19 Art I, Section 3, para 7, the Constitution of the United States of America.

20 Vikram D Amar and Jason Mazzone, 'The Power to "Try" "Cases of Impeachment": Some Reflections on the Finality, Transparency and Integrity of Senate Adjudications of Presidential Impeachments (Including That of Donald J. Trump)' (2021) 95(2) *Chicago-Kent Law Review* 455.

21 Keith E Whittington, 'Impeachment in a System of Checks and Balances' (2022) 87 (3) *Missouri Law Review* 835 <https://scholarship.law.missouri.edu/mlr/vol87/iss3/13>; Omololu Fagbadebo and Suzanne Francis, 'Impeachment as an Accountability Measure in a Presidential System? Views from Nigeria's Fourth Republic' (2014) 3(2) *African Journal of Governance and Development* 16 <www.ajol.info/index.php/ajgd/article/view/118359>.

22 Amar and Mazzone (n 20) 456.

the constitutional provisions on impeachment because the 'judicial character of the constitutional language empowering the Senate in impeachment proceedings – helps make political question doctrine less subjective and less capacious.'[23] As Amar and Mazzone observe,

> Indeed, as Justice Byron White pointed out, 'the issue in the political question doctrine is *not* whether the constitutional text commits exclusive responsibility for a particular governmental function to one of the political branches. There are numerous instances of this sort of textual commitment, e.g., Art. I, § 8, and it is not that disputes implicating these provisions are nonjusticiable. Rather, the issue is whether the Constitution has given one of the political branches *final responsibility for interpreting* the scope and nature of such a power.' – in other words, for adjudicating the limits of the power.[24]

Even with this, the Court is still bound to oversee the exercise of the power to ensure that the Senate acts in accordance with the constitutional provisions and not interfere in the impeachment trial. In their analysis of the judicial review of *Nixon v. United States*,[25] Amar and Mazzone submit that

> Under this view, perhaps we should not think of political question doctrine in the impeachment setting as a yes or no determination of whether federal courts can review, but instead think of it more in terms of how much deference the Court will afford the political branches even if the Court does not stay out of the matter entirely.[26]

Ranieri L. Resende[27] has noted some of the challenges associated with these premises:

> a) the attribution to decide on impeachment to a governmental branch other than the Judiciary does not exclude the application of legal criteria; b) sanctions of political nature, such as the suspension and revocation of an electoral mandate and the suspension of political rights, are also enforceable by judicial bodies, especially by electoral courts; c) the acknowledgment of civil and administrative violations seems insufficient to remove illegality as eventual requirement for an impeachment trial; d) political factors

23 ibid 457.
24 ibid 7.
25 *Nixon v United States*, 506 US 224, 240 (1993).
26 Amar and Mazzone (n 20) 458.
27 Ranieri L Resende, 'Impeachment: A Mechanism Between Political Accountability and Legal Responsibility? Common Law Sources and the Brazilian Originalist Model' (2022) 11 *Global Journal of Comparative Law* 222.

may jointly influence constitutional and supreme courts, as cases of judicial review of legislative acts may suggest.[28]

14.3 Impeachment Provisions and Practices in Nigeria

The practice of a presidential system was introduced to the Nigerian political system in the Second Republic from 1979–1983. At independence on 1 October 1960, there was a federal constitution that also contained the constitutions of each of the three regions:[29] North, West and East. Each of these regions had its provisions for the removal of the head of the executive, the Premier, under the inherited Westminster parliamentary system. Similarly, the 1979 and 1999 presidential constitutions incorporate elaborate processes and procedures for the removal of the heads of the executive branches of the government at the state and federal levels. Even though there is no mention of impeachment in these provisions, the use of impeachment to denote the removal of the political heads of the executive has remained the norm in the Nigerian political system.[30]

In the First Republic from 1960–1966, the constitution of each of the three regions contained the process of removal of the premier, the head of the executive and other members of the cabinet.

Section 33 (10) of the Constitution of the Western Region, Eastern Region and Northern Region contained the same provisions regarding the power to remove the Premier and members of the cabinet:

> 33 (10) Subject to the provisions of sub-section (8) and (9) of this section, the Ministers of the Government of the Region shall hold office during the Governor's pleasure: Provided that – (a) the Governor shall not remove the Premier from office unless it appears to him that the Premier no longer commands the support of a majority of the members of the House of Assembly; and (b) the Governor shall not remove a Minister other than the Premier from office except in accordance with the advice of the Premier.[31]

In the 1999 Constitution, the provisions for the procedures to remove the heads of the political leadership of the executive arms of the government at the state and federal levels are replications of the provisions in the 1979 Constitution. Sections 143 and 188 of the 1999 Constitution provide for the

28 ibid 224.

29 According to the arrangement of the 1960 Constitution, each of the three regions had its own constitutions that guided the government. The regions were more autonomous with the practice of a true federal system that devolved power to the component units.

30 Fagbadebo, *Impeachment in the Nigerian Presidential System* (n 2).

31 The Third, Fourth and Fifth Schedules, Nigeria Independence Act, 1960 and Nigeria (Constitution) Order in Council, 1960.

removal of the President and/or his deputy and the state governors and/or their deputies, respectively. Except for the bicameral composition of the National Assembly, the two provisions follow the same procedures. These provisions are found in Sections 132 and 174 of the 1979 Constitution but with slight modification.[32]

Section 188 of the 1999 Constitution states that

> 188. (1) The Governor or Deputy Governor of a state may Removal of Governor be removed from office in accordance with the provisions or the Deputy Governor of this section. from office. (2) Whenever a notice of any allegation in writing is signed by not less than one-third of the members of the House of Assembly. (b) stating that the holder of such office is guilty of gross misconduct in the performance of the functions of his office, detailed particulars of which shall be specified. The speaker of the House of Assembly shall, within seven days of the receipt of the notice, cause a copy of the notice to be served on the holder of the office and on each member of the House of Assembly, and shall also cause any statement made in reply to the allegation by the holder of the office, to be served on each member of the House of Assembly. (3) Within fourteen days of the presentation of the notice to the speaker of the House of Assembly (whether or not any statement was made by the holder of the office in reply to the allegation contained in the notice), the House of Assembly shall resolve by motion, without any debate whether or not the allegation shall be investigated. (4) A motion of the House of Assembly that the allegation be investigated shall not be declared as having been passed unless it is supported by the votes of not less than two-thirds majority of all the members of the House of Assembly. (5) Within seven days of the passing of a motion under the foregoing provisions of this section, the Chief judge of the State shall at the request of the speaker of the House of Assembly, appoint a Panel of seven persons who in his opinion are of unquestionable integrity, not being members of any public service, legislative house or political party, to investigate the allegation as provided in this section. (6) The holder of an office whose conduct is being investigated under this section shall have the right to defend himself in person or be represented before the panel by a legal practitioner of his own choice. (7) A Panel appointed under this section shall – (a) have such powers and exercise its functions in accordance with such procedure as may be prescribed by the House of Assembly; and (b) within three months of its appointment, report its

32 Although the 1979 provisions confine the entire process and procedure to the legislative institution, the 1999 Constitution permits the judiciary, specifically, the Chief Judge of the State and the Chief Justice of the Federation, to be involved in the composition of the panel of investigation.

> findings to the House of Assembly. (8) Where the Panel reports to the House of Assembly that the allegation has not been proved, no further proceedings shall be taken in respect of the matter. (9) Where the report of the Panel is that the allegation against the holder of the office has been proved, then within fourteen days of the receipt of the report, the house of Assembly shall consider the report, and if by a resolution of the House of Assembly supported by not less than two-thirds majority of all its members, the report of the Panel is adopted, then the holder of the office shall stand removed from office as from the date of the adoption of the report. (10) No proceedings or determination of the Panel or of the House of Assembly or any matter relating to such proceedings or determination shall be entertained or questioned in any court. (11) In this section, 'gross misconduct' means a grave violation or breach of the provisions of this Constitution or a misconduct of such nature as amounts in the opinion in the House of Assembly to gross misconduct.[33]

The inclusion of the impeachment provisions in the Nigerian constitutions was intended to statutorily fashion a measure that was 'meant to provide a last resort for the curbing of executive excesses'.[34]

In all cases since 1962, the practice of the constitutional provisions for the removal of the political heads of the executive arms of the government by the legislature has been fraught with abuse and manipulation.

In most cases, deliberate misinterpretation of the statutes was used as a weapon of political vendetta among the elites. Thus, rather than being used as intended by the drafters of the Constitution, the Nigerian lawmakers resorted to outright breaches of the Constitution.

14.4 The Removal of the Western Region Premier in the First Republic

In the First Republic, the Governor of the Western Region, Obas Adesoji Aderemi, in the exercise of his power in Section 33(10) of the Constitution, pronounced the removal of the Premier, Chief Samuel Ladoke Akintola,[35] and

33 Section 188 is quoted in extenso here because it has been the subject of breaches and judicial review. All the impeachment cases in Nigeria since 1979 occurred at the state levels, except for some semblances of veiled threats of removal of the President by members of the National Assembly, especially the House of Representatives.

34 Jinmi Adisa and Adigun Agbaje, 'Impeachment and the Parliamentary Process in Nigeria's Second Republic (1979–1983)' (1985) 27(4) *Journal of the Indian Law Institute* 594.

35 The pronouncement was the sequel to the letter of 21 May 1962, signed by 66 out of the 124-member parliament, indicating that they were no longer in support of the Premier. This letter was predicated on the outcome of the Executive Council meeting of the Action Group (AG), the governing party of the Western region. At the meeting held on 19 May 1962, by a vote of 81 to 29, Chief Akintola was asked to resign his appointment as the deputy leader of the party, as a prelude to his removal as the Premier. This was because of a feud between him

appointed Alhaji Soroye Adegbenro, the regional Minister of Local Government, as the successor.[36] But Chief Akintola refused to accept the decision to remove him from office, and he therefore took the matter to the Regional High Court for adjudication to challenge the Governor in the exercise of his power contained in Section 33(10) of the Constitution. In his submission to the Regional High Court, the Premier raised two fundamental questions about the law:

(1) Can the Governor validly exercise power to remove the Premier from office under section 33 sub-section Io of the Constitution of Western Nigeria without prior decision or resolution on the floor of the House of Assembly, showing that the Premier no longer commands the support of a majority of the House? (2) Can the Governor validly exercise power to remove the Premier from office under section 33 (10) of the Constitution of Western Nigeria on the basis of any materials or information extraneous to the proceedings of the House of Assembly.[37]

Given that this bordered on interpretation of the law, the High Court then referred the matter to the Federal Supreme Court.[38]

The Supreme Court answered the questions in support of Chief Akintola:

> The answer to the first question, therefore, is that the Governor cannot validly exercise power to remove the Premier from office under section 33 sub-section 10 of the Constitution of Western Nigeria except in consequence of proceedings on the floor of the House whether in the shape of a vote of no-confidence or of a defeat on a major measure or of a series of defeats on measures of some importance showing that the

---

and the leader, Chief Obafemi Awolowo. The party leader had accused his deputy of maladministration, anti-party activities and indiscipline. But Akintola refused to resign. Rather, the Premier wrote the Governor to dissolve the parliament and asked that the Speaker convene a parliamentary meeting for a vote of confidence. This contradictory demand threw the government in disarray.

36 *Hon SL Akintola v Sir Adesoji Aderemi & Anor* [1962] LLJR-SC.

37 ibid. Judicial Committee of The Privy Council *Alhaji DS Adegbenro v Chief SL Akintola & Another.* Original Judgment, Privy Council Appeal No 5 of 1963. Judgment delivered on 27 May 1963; *Alhaji DS Adegbenro v Chief SL Akintola & Another* (1 All NLR 1962: 461.

38 Section 108 (2&3) of the 1960 Constitution states: '(2) Where any question as to the interpretation of this Constitution or the constitution of a Region arises in any proceedings in the High Court of a territory and the court is of opinion that the question involves a substantial question of law, the court may, and shall if any party to the proceedings so requests, refer the question to the Federal Supreme Court. (3) Where any question is referred to the Federal Supreme Court in pursuance of this section, the Federal Supreme Court shall give its decision upon the question and the court in which the question arose shall dispose of the case in accordance with that decision'.

> Premier no longer commands the support of a majority of the members of the House of Assembly.[39]

Nevertheless, the Privy Council's interpretation of the phrase, 'unless it appears to him that the Premier no longer commands the support of a majority of the members of the House of Assembly' differed from the position of the Supreme Court. According to the Council, the drafter of the Constitution did not limit the statutory power of the Governor, because 'the limitation is not to be found in the words in which the makers of the Constitution have decided to record their description of his powers.'[40] Akintola and the Supreme Court were of the position that the decisions of the Governor should be based on the record of votes given on the floor of the House, whereas the Privy Council decided otherwise and claimed that

> [U]nless there are compulsive reasons, to be found in the context of the Constitution or to be deduced from obvious general principles, that would impose the more limited meaning for which the respondent contends [but] Their Lordships have not discovered any such reasons.[41]

Consequently, the Council 'will humbly advise Her Majesty that the appeal should be allowed; that the Answer of the Supreme Court given on the 7th July 1962, should be reversed; and that in lieu thereof it should be declared that the Answer to the first Question is Yes.'[42]

> Such frivolous contrasted sharply with the two traditions from which Nigeria had borrowed the impeachment clause – the British, a result of the legacy of colonial rule, and the United States, along the lines of whose experience Nigeria's political elite fashioned the 1979 Constitution – and the most infrequent use of impeachment in these traditions.[43]

Considering the implication of this judgment, the Parliament of the Western Region, under the leadership of Akintola, retroactively passed an amendment

39 Cf. Judicial Committee of The Privy Council *Alhaji DS Adegbenro v Chief SL Akintola & Another*. Original Judgment, Privy Council Appeal No 5 of 1963. Judgment delivered on 27 May 1963. Subsequently, the matter was referred to the Privy Council, the final appellate court in Nigeria at independence.

40 The Privy Council *Alhaji DS. Adegbenro v Chief SL Akintola & Another*. Original Judgment, Privy Council Appeal No 5 of 1963.

41 ibid.

42 ibid.

43 Adisa and Agbaje (n 34) 594.

to Section 33 (10a) of the Constitution on May 27, 1963 to thus read as follows:

> the Governor shall not remove the Premier from office unless it appears to him, *in consequence of the passing of a resolution in the House of Assembly by a majority of the members of the House*, that the Premier no longer commands the support of a majority of the members of the House of Assembly.[44]

Two fundamental issues in this case that have become defining characteristics of Nigerian politics are firstly, the manipulation of legislative frameworks to promote pecuniary interests in settling personal political scores and secondly, the politicisation of judicial review at the expense of the interests of the state. The snowballing effect of the episode in the Western Region was a catalyst for the political crisis that precipitated the first military coup on 15 January 1966.[45] Subsequent decisions to remove the political heads of the executive at the state levels in the Second and Fourth Republics followed similar patterns in Nigeria's presidential systems.[46]

Nigeria's presidential Constitutions of 1979 and 1999 were intended to safeguard the offices of the political heads of the executive arm of the government at the state and federal levels with an immunity clause. Section 308 of the 1999 Constitution precludes the heads of the executive branch of the government at the state and federal levels from any civil or criminal proceedings during their tenure of office:

(1) Notwithstanding anything to the contrary in this Constitution, but subject to subsection (2) of this section (a) no civil or criminal proceedings shall be instituted or continued against a person to whom this section applies during his period of office; (b) a person to whom this section applies shall not be arrested or imprisoned during that period either in pursuance of the process of any court or otherwise; and (c) no process of any court requiring or compelling the appearance of a person to whom this section applies, shall be applied for or issued: Provided that in ascertaining whether any period of limitation has expired for the purposes of any proceedings against a person to whom this section applies, no account shall be taken of his period of office. (2) The provisions of subsection (1) of this section shall not apply to civil proceedings against a person to

44 Cf. Fagbadebo, *Impeachment in the Nigerian Presidential System* (n 2) 392.

45 ibid.

46 ibid. The aborted Third Republic did not have a specific governing system because it was a mixture of the civilian government at the state and local government level and superordinate military leadership at the national level. There were no specific constitutional provisions that guided the governing of the Nigerian state during this period other that the relics of military edicts and decrees.

> whom this section applies in his official capacity or to civil or criminal proceedings in which such a person is only a nominal party. (3) This section applies to a person holding the office of President or Vice-President, Governor or Deputy Governor; and the reference in this section to 'period of office' is a reference to the period during which the person holding such office is required to perform the functions of the office.[47]

This immunity clause, on the one hand, is a necessity to insulate the officeholder from their political opponents who use civil litigation or criminal proceedings to distract the officeholder from state responsibilities.[48] On the other hand, it has remained an abused privilege and has been exploited by the beneficiaries of this immunity clause to perpetuate impunity.[49] In the absence of other remedial measures to curb this phenomenon in Nigeria, the drafters of the presidential Constitutions of 1979 and 1999 incorporated a political process, devoid of judicial intervention and litigation, through the legislature, that would allow the legislature to remove the political heads of the executive arms of the government. Nevertheless, the exercise of this legislative oversight power has been characterised by abuse and manipulation.

14.5 The Exercise of Impeachment Power in the Second and Fourth Republics

The advent of the Second Republic in 1979 ushered in a presidential system unlike the First Republic parliamentary system of collective responsibilities and fusion of the legislative and executive power. Given the nature of the political system with acrimonious intra- and inter-party crises, the political environment was hostile and unfriendly. This was transferred to the government administration, especially in states with divided governments. In the Second Republic, there were three notable episodes of the exercise of the legislative power of removal of the political heads at the state level.[50]

In the aftermath of the 1979 election in Kaduna State, the National Party of Nigeria (NPN) won the majority of seats in the state legislature, while the People Redemption Party (PRP) won the gubernatorial position. The divided government was characterised by Juan Linz's gridlock[51] and immobility as the majority within the legislature sought to frustrate the policies and programmes

47 Constitution of the Federal Republic of Nigeria, 1999 as amended. This is the same wording of Section 267 of the 1979 Constitution.

48 GN Okeke and CE Okeke, 'An Appraisal of the Functional Necessity of the Immunity Clause in the Political Governance of Nigeria' (2015) 59(1) *Journal of African Law* 99.

49 Sesan Fabamise, 'Constitutional Immunity Clause and the Fight Against Corruption in Nigeria' (2017) 8(2) *Journal of Sustainable Development, Law and Policy* 156.

50 Adisa and Agbaje (n 34).

51 Aníbal S Pérez-Liñán, *Presidential Impeachment and the New Political Instability in Latin America* (CUP 2007).

of the government. The intransigent disposition of Governor Balarabe Musa infuriated the NPN-dominated legislature.[52] As a consequence of their majority within the state legislature, the NPN had a comfortable majority to pass any legislation, including the removal of the governor.[53] Ideally, in Kaduna State, the governor needed to be diplomatic in ensuring bipartisan approval of his programmes and policies. Unfortunately, the politics of divided government are usually characterised by acrimonious executive-legislature relations aimed at the removal of the governor. Governor Balarabe Musa fell into this trap, and the NPN-dominated legislature removed him. As argued elsewhere, 'the removal of Governor Balarabe Musa by the legislature was a manifestation of the politics of a divided government rather than an indication of policy failure by his government.'[54]

The second case of impeachment in the Second Republic was the removal of the Deputy Governor, Alhaji Bibi Farouk, on 11 November 1981.[55] The Governor, Alhaji Abubakar Rimi, and his deputy were from the same political party, the PRP. The party was in control of the executive and the legislature. Nevertheless, the internal crisis within the party pitched Farouk against Governor Rimi and hence, the decision to remove him. As Adisa and Agbaje observe,

> Among the offences listed in the notice was the deputy governor's failure to perform functions assigned to him by the governor, and 'flirting' with persons 'hostile' to the state government and thus encouraging its subversion. The notice also charged that he had often travelled out of the state without obtaining clearance from the governor.[56]

In Rivers State, the bitter rivalry between the two main political parties in the legislature triggered the attempt to remove the Governor, Milford Okilo, and his deputy, Frank Eze, who had won the election on the platform of the NPN. The 42-member River State House of Assembly was under the control of the NPN (26 members) and the Nigerian People's Party (NPP). On 2 May 1982, the NPP alleged that the governor and his deputy had committed offences that they considered to amount to gross misconduct.[57] Unfortunately,

52 The Kaduna State House of Assembly had 99 members out of which the PRP had 12 members.

53 Section 170 of the 1979 Constitution stipulated that a two-thirds majority of members of the legislature was required to pass valid legislation regarding the removal of the governor.

54 Fagbadebo, *Impeachment in the Nigerian Presidential System* (n 2).

55 Adisa and Agbaje (n 34); Fagbadebo, *Impeachment in the Nigerian Presidential System* (n 2).

56 Adisa and Agbaje (n 34) 604.

57 Section 170 (2) (b) sets the condition for impeachment that the officeholder must have been alleged to have committed offences that amounted to 'gross misconduct in the performance of the functions of his office, detailed particulars of which shall be specified'. Section 170 (11) defined 'gross misconduct' as meaning a grave violation or breach of the provisions of this Constitution or a misconduct of such nature as amounts in the opinion of the House of Assembly to gross misconduct.

the opposition party could not muster the required two-thirds votes to investigate the allegations. Therefore, on 20 May 1982, the vote failed, and the proceeding ended. Aside from these three cases, legislatures in Niger, Bendel, Cross Rivers, Lagos, Plateau, Gongola and Kwara States, issued threats to commence impeachment proceedings against their respective governors and or deputies.[58]

In the Fourth Republic, the use of impeachment as a weapon for the removal of the political heads of the executive at the state level has been rampant.[59] In December 2005, minority members of the Oyo State House of Assembly initiated an impeachment process against the Governor, Rashidi Ladoja. Both the Governor and the majority members of the legislature were from the same political party, the Peoples Democratic Party (PDP). The process and procedures followed were fraught with breaches of the Constitution.[60] This was the fallout of the intra-party crisis that pitched Governor Ladoja against a frontline member of the party, Chief Lamidi Adedibu. Thus, the manipulation and breaches of the Constitution and the rules were supported by both the national leadership of the party and President Olusegun Obasanjo.[61]

Similarly in Plateau State, Governor Joshua Dariye fell victim to constitutional breaches by the eight members of the 26-member state legislature who initiated and finalised his removal from office. Although his case was complicated and despite the weighty allegations against him, he enjoyed the support of a majority of the members of the legislature.[62] The division within the ruling PDP in Plateau State pitched the Governor against the national leadership of the party, a development that facilitated the mobilisation of the eight legislators to initiate and finalise the removal process. However, given the breaches of the procedures, the Court of Appeal, in *Hon. Michael Dapialong and others v. Chief (Dr.) Joshua Chibi Dariye and another*[63] invalidated his removal, and he was subsequently restored to power.

In Anambra State, Governor Peter Obi was elected on the platform of the All Progressive Grand Alliance (APGA), while a majority of the members of the legislature were from the PDP. This divided government polarised the administration of the state. Most of the members of the legislature (18) initiated an impeachment process on 16 October 2006. Given the circumstances

58 Fagbadebo, *Impeachment in the Nigerian Presidential System* (n 2) 410.

59 For comprehensive details on the cases of impeachment of governors and their deputies between 2005 and 2020, see Fagbadebo, *Impeachment in the Nigerian Presidential System* (n 2).

60 Only 18 out of a 32-member legislature initiated and finalized the process, a development that fell short of the two-thirds requirement of members.

61 PDP was in control of both the executive and National Assembly.

62 The allegations were glaring breaches of the Constitution, including fraud, theft and money laundering. Even though the court nullified his impeachment, he was found guilty of the offences after he left office and was sent to jail.

63 *Hon Michael Dapialong and others v Chief (Dr) Joshua Chibi Dariye and Another* (2007) 8 NWLR.

that led to the emergence of Obi as the governor,[64] the PDP government was not comfortable with the divided government in the state. Hence, the decision to remove him from office because the Governor had refused to accede to the welfare requests of the lawmakers. Eventually, because the removal was in breach of the Constitution, the Court of Appeal, in *Hon. Mike Balonwu & 5 others v Mr. Peter Obi & another*[65] voided the impeachment, and he was restored to complete his terms of office.

14.6 Politics, Constitutional Breaches and Judicial Review of Impeachment Cases

The essence of the tripartite structure of the presidential system incorporating the separation of powers and checks and balances is to avert tyranny and abuse of powers. In the Second Republic, the judiciary did not entertain adjudication of impeachment cases because of the incorrect interpretation of section 170 (10) of the Constitution that stipulates, 'No proceedings or determination of the Panel or the House of Assembly or any matter relating to such proceedings or determination shall be entertained or questioned in any court'. In all cases, the judiciary declined jurisdiction.[66]

Similarly, in the Fourth Republic, the initial judicial intervention on impeachment at the state high courts followed the restraint precedent set in the Second Republic. For instance, in *Abaribe v. Abia State House of Assembly*,[67] Pats-Acholonu, or JCA as he was then known, said that impeachment was a political matter, and as such, judicial intervention would amount 'to brazenly enter into the miasma of the political cauldron and have itself bloodied and thereby losing its respect.'[68] Nevertheless, an appeal to the Supreme Court for a final determination reversed previous judicial restraints on impeachment. The Supreme Court in *Inakoju & 17 Ors vs Adeleke & 3 Ors*[69] declared that although section 188 (10) was an ouster clause, it did not preclude the judiciary from ascertaining that the legislature followed the procedure. Thus, while the ouster clause precludes judicial review of the 'proceedings or determination of the Panel or the House, it does not relate to or affect the procedure spelt out in section 188(1–6).'[70] Subsequent adjudications[71] hinged on this

64 Peter Obi won the election by judicial mandate that voided the election of Chris Ngige of the PDP in the 2003 election after three years of judicial adjudication.

65 *Hon Mike Balonwu & 5 others v M Peter Obi & Another* (2007) 5 NWLR (Pt 1028) 488 CA.

66 *Musa v Speaker, Kaduna State House of Assembly* (1982) 3 NCLR 450; *Musa v Hamza and others* (1982) 3 NCLR 439 (HC); In *Musa v Hamza and others* (1982) 3 NCLR 229 (FCA), Justice Adolphus Karibi-Whyte, said, 'I am satisfied that the moment the legislature commenced removal proceedings and Section 170 (2), the jurisdiction of the court was ousted by Section 170 (10)'.

67 (2002) 14 NWLR (Pt 788) 466 at page 486 paragraphs F-G.

68 ibid.

69 *Inakoju & 17 Ors vs Adeleke & 3 Ors* (2007) 1 SC (Pt 1).

70 ibid.

71 *Hon Michael Dapialong and others v Chief (Dr) Joshua Chibi Dariye and Another* (2007) 8 NWLR; *Hon Mike Balonwu & 5 others v Mr Peter Obi & Another* (2007) 5 NWLR (Pt 1028) 488 CA.

precedent that interpreted the various ambiguities in the impeachment provisions, such as the ouster clause, gross misconduct, and the structural composition of the legislature for impeachment proceedings.

There are common characteristics of elite politics in all the cases of removal of the political heads of the executive since 1960 in Nigeria. The first is the abuse and misuse of statutory instruments of governance. In the case of the removal of Chief Akintola as the premier of the Western Region, the Governor exercised his power as an instrument to settle the political differences between the leader of the party, Chief Awolowo, and his deputy, Chief Akintola, when all his moves for peaceful resolution failed.[72] In the Second Republic, the impeachment of Bibi Farouk was a clear manifestation of abuse and misuse of the provision. Similarly, in the Fourth Republic, the Supreme Court voided the removal of Governors Ladoja, Dariye and Obi because of the abuse and misuse of the provisos. In the cases of Ladoja and Dariye, it was evident that they committed the allegations,[73] but the procedure followed in their removal was an outright breach of the Constitution. The legislators were mobilised not because of the gravity of the allegations but to use the impeachment as an instrument of negotiation in exchange for the pecuniary interests of their sponsors.[74] All the deputy governors that were removed from office through impeachment were victims of this abuse and misuse of the provisions in the Fourth Republic.[75]

Another common characteristic is the politicisation of judicial review. Ideally, the judiciary is expected to be an impartial arbiter in the interpretation of statutes to strengthen governance and public trust. In Nigeria, critical issues of national interests that require definitive judicial pronouncements have been compromised through executive interference in the judicial process and the manipulation of the judicial system.[76] The Supreme Court voided the removal of Akintola because he had the backing of the Federal

72 Emmanuel Ojo, 'The Awolowo – Akintola Leadership Tussle: A Reinterpretation' (2016) 5(1) *Journal of Arts and Humanities* 76.

73 Upon the completion of their terms of office, the Economic and Financial Crime Commission (EFCC) charged Dariye and Ladoja for the offences of mismanagement of state funds while in office. Dariye was found guilty and sentenced to 14 years imprisonment, while Ladoja was acquitted. See A Adesomoju, 'Ex-Plateau Governor, Dariye, Jailed 14 Years for Over N2bn Fraud' *The Punch* (13 June 2018) <http://punchng.com/ex-plateau-gov-dariyejailed-14-years-for-over-n2bn-fraud> accessed 14 June 2018; Ramon Oladimeji, 'Court Discharges, Acquits Ladoja of N4.7bn Fraud 11 Years After' *The Punch* (9 February 2019) <https://punchng.com/court-dischargesacquits-ladoja-of-n4-7bn-fraud-11-years-after/>.

74 The impeachment of Governor Rashidi Ladoja of Oyo State, for instance, was facilitated by the influence of his godfather, Lamidi Adedibu, who mobilisd his supporters in the legislature to initiate the removal of the governor because of their personal differences. For details, see Fagbadebo, *Impeachment in the Nigerian Presidential System* (n 2) 342–50.

75 Fagbadebo, *Impeachment in the Nigerian Presidential System* (n 2).

76 For a detailed discussion on the involvement of the judiciary in the politics of impeachment in Nigeria, see Fagbadebo, *Impeachment in the Nigerian Presidential System* (n 2) especially Ch 6.

Government.[77] In the Second Republic, the lack of definite judicial precedent on the issues of the ouster clause and the interpretation of gross misconduct created an opportunity for political elites to explore impeachment as a weapon of political vendetta, a carry-over from the experience of the First Republic. As noted elsewhere, 'judicial pronouncements, as well as unethical conduct among some judges in the State High Courts, complicated a series of cases of impeachment.'[78] Indeed, the Supreme Court had to reprimand the lower courts for their lack of forthrightness in the interpretation of the statutes and for supporting the frivolities that characterised the exercise of the requisite constitutional provisions regarding impeachment. Indeed, the support of the state judiciary emboldened the legislatures to perpetrate the series of infractions that has characterised the impeachment process in Nigeria.[79]

14.7 Conclusion

Politics rather than policies are the overriding consideration for the exercise of the legislative power of impeachment in Nigeria. While issues of development continue to drag in the polity with the bourgeoning crisis of governance, the legislature has the constitutional mandate to instil the culture of responsible leadership through discipline and adherence to the rule of law. Thus, in Nigeria, the intention of the drafters of the impeachment provisions was to institutionalise a political process regulated by requisite laws 'to empower the people, through their representative to remove them [political heads of the executive arm] mid-term.'[80]

Evidence abounds that the Nigerian political system has the requisite regulatory measures and mechanisms to ensure the promotion of responsible executives and good governance. The proclivity of political leadership to mismanagement of resources with impunity has remained a top priority of the political elites in the absence of an effective legislative institution designed for oversight of the exercise of the power of the state. Hence, the impeachment provisions have remained victims of ineffective institutions to exert their influence to harness their purpose in the public interest.

The challenge is not the system but the operators who circumvent every rule for the promotion of their pecuniary interests. The essence of law is to be

77 The haste at which the case was dismissed and the retractive implementation of the amendment to Section 33(10) of the Constitution of the Western Region attest to this assertion. See also Larry R Jackson, 'Nigeria: The Politics of the First Republic' (1972) 2(3) *Journal of Black Studies* 277.

78 Fagbadebo, *Impeachment in the Nigerian Presidential System* (n 2) 146.

79 In Plateau State, while a judge of the state High Court spotted an infraction in the composition of the impeachment investigation panel, the Acting Chief Judge transferred the case to another court. In Ekiti and Anambra States, the unethical conduct of some judicial officers was met with dismissal and other forms of disciplinary measures. For details, see Fagbadebo, *Impeachment in the Nigerian Presidential System* (n 2).

80 Fagbadebo, *Impeachment in the Nigerian Presidential System* (n 2) 9.

found in the commitment of the stakeholders to its implementation according to prescription. This is when the public will benefit from the intention of the drafters. In Nigeria, the political elites implement the law as prescribed only when it will promote their pecuniary interests. When it does not promote their interests, they resort to its manipulation. Thus, the incessant system failure in the management of the country's public sector is the result. The failure of the political elites to play politics according to the rules has rendered the impeachment provisions weapons of vendetta.

15 The Politics of Impeachment in Pakistan's Hybrid Democracy

Yasser Kureshi

15.1 Introduction

Pakistan belongs to a group of 'hybrid' states in which power remains contested and negotiated between political and bureaucratic power centers.[1] Pakistan's military has been the country's dominant power centre for most of its post-colonial history, shaping the politics and policies of the state. The military has seized political power in military coups four times in Pakistan's history and ruled the state directly for over three decades. During periods of democratic rule, the military has maintained a tutelary role in the political system, constraining the authority of elected governments and ensuring that its interests and preferences are protected in political and policymaking processes.

Pakistan's political history has been marked by repeated disruptions in the development of Pakistan's elected institutions, juxtaposed against the comparative continuity in its unelected institutions; this juxtaposition has effected the strength and legitimacy of elected governments and the perceptions within these unelected branches about their relationship with the elected branches. These unelected institutions sought to establish a political structure that ensured their role overseeing and guiding Pakistan's political system. Kalhan called this the 'viceregal' model, as it was modeled on the colonial state and privileged centralized authority and presidential power.[2] However, several of Pakistan's political parties sought to mobilize popular national and subnational identities and patronage networks in order to win parliamentary elections and gain control over the distribution of political resources.[3] These parties favoured elected parliamentary supremacy and a more decentralized and 'representative' system. Pakistan's constitutional history has been marked by fluctuations between a more presidential system with a constrained parliament and

1 Yasser Kureshi, 'Judicial Politics in Hybrid States: Judiciary and Political Parties in Pakistan' in Mariam Mufti, Niloufer Siddiqui and Sahar Shafqat (eds), *Pakistan's Political Parties: Against All Odds* (Georgetown UP 2020) 235–42.

2 Anil Kalhan, '"Gray Zone" Constitutionalism and the Dilemma of Judicial Independence in Pakistan' (2013) 46(1) *Vanderbilt Journal of Transnational Law* 1.

3 Ian Talbot, *Pakistan: A Modern History* (Hurst and Co 1998).

DOI: 10.4324/9781003256007-19

a parliamentary system with a powerful Prime Minister and a figurehead President. This is the context in which I explore the politics surrounding impeachments in Pakistan, because as I argue in this chapter, impeachments have served strategic goals in contestation over the distribution of power between Pakistan's representative institutions and Pakistan's tutelary institutions.

Therefore, in this chapter, I discuss the history of impeachment proceedings under Pakistan's constitutional framework that has been in place since 1973. I discuss attempts at presidential impeachments, votes of no confidence against Prime Ministers, and the removal of elected leadership through judicial disqualifications. I show that, although there have been no successful presidential impeachments and only one successful parliamentary vote of no confidence, successful and unsuccessful attempts to remove presidents and prime-ministers provide opportunities to understand the politics of hybrid regimes.[4] Impeachment motions, no-confidence motions and even petitions for judicial disqualification may i) provide political parties bargaining leverage against powerful Presidents and Prime Ministers, ii) focus public discourse around the weaknesses, failings, and legitimacy of incumbent leadership, iii) test the popularity of an incumbent leader to signal their political standing, and iv) destabilize incumbent governments to enable a reorganization of political authority between representative and tutelary institutions. The manner in which an impeachment effort is carried out and the goals that it seeks to achieve will depend on the political context in which the measure is initiated, the institutional pathway through which the process is initiated, and the institution and institutional leadership targeted by the effort.

15.2 The Constitutional Framework for Impeachment Procedures in Pakistan

In 1973, Pakistan's civilian government established the constitutional framework that has remained in place to date, albeit with periods of suspension and significant amendments along the way. The 1973 Constitution was originally meant to realize and entrench the 'representative model' of government mentioned earlier. The Constitution establishes a bicameral legislature including a directly elected National Assembly and a Senate elected by the provincial legislatures with equal representation of all Pakistan's provinces.[5] The primary executive offices are a Prime Minister, who is an elected member of the National Assembly who has to secure a majority of votes in the National Assembly, and a President who is the head of state and is indirectly elected by the national and provincial legislatures.[6] The Constitution also grants the superior judiciary the authority of judicial review.[7]

4 Kim (n 1) 519.
5 Constitution of Pakistan (1973) § 59.
6 ibid § 41, 90.
7 ibid § 199.

Under the 1973 Constitution, the President can be removed from office on the ground of physical and mental incapacity or impeached on a charge of gross misconduct or constitutional violations. The process of presidential impeachment involves several steps.[8] First, at least half of the membership of either the National Assembly or the Senate have to provide written notice to the Speaker of the House or the Chairman of the Senate of the intention to move a resolution for the impeachment of the President and detail the charges of incapacity, misconduct, or constitutional violations. The Speaker of the National Assembly must then summon a joint sitting of the National Assembly and Senate within a fixed period of time. The joint sitting would then investigate the president, who could appear before the joint sitting and be represented during the investigation. After the investigation, if over two-thirds of the joint sitting declares that the President is unfit to hold office or is guilty of gross misconduct or of violating the Constitution, then the President shall be deemed impeached.[9] Thus, the process of presidential impeachment in Pakistan is challenging by first requiring a majority of a single house, then an investigative process, and finally, a supermajority of a joint sitting of both houses in order to complete the process.

In contrast, the Prime Minister can be removed from office through a parliamentary vote of no confidence.[10] First, a resolution must be moved by at least 20 per cent of the National Assembly. Then, after the assembly debates the resolution, the resolution must be voted on within a fixed period of time, and if a simple majority passes the resolution, then the Prime Minister ceases to hold office.[11]

Finally, beyond the legislature, through a constitutional amendment passed in 1985, the superior judiciary acquired powers to disqualify political officers including the Prime Minister. The constitutional amendment held that anyone holding elected political office had to meet vaguely defined constitutional standards of morality and sagacity.[12] Pakistan's high courts and Supreme Court were authorized to uphold this constitutional standard, which enabled the courts to disqualify any elected officeholders that the courts found to violate this standard, potentially even enabling the disqualification of the Prime Minister.

Thus, the constitution provides for a particularly difficult procedure for presidential impeachment with multiple veto players positioned to stall the process at different stages, a more doable but still challenging process for removing a prime minister through a vote of no confidence, and a relatively centralized system for judicial disqualification requiring only agreement among the bench of judges issuing the judgment. The variation in the complexity of

8 ibid § 47.
9 ibid.
10 ibid § 91.
11 ibid.
12 ibid § 62–63.

these procedures reflect the constitutional politics surrounding the formulation and evolution of these procedures over time.

15.3 Constitutional Dissonance and Impeachment Procedures in Pakistan's Hybrid Democracy (1985–1999)

In the initial formulation of the 1973 Constitution, the key features of the new constitution were elected parliamentary supremacy, and control over the unelected military and bureaucracy was placed firmly under elected leadership. Executive power in Pakistan was exercised in the name of the President but exercised *by* the federal government consisting of the Prime Minister and the federal ministers of the cabinet, making the Prime Minister the Chief Executive of the country.

The President played a rather ceremonial role in this system and acted as a head of state who represented the 'unity of the republic.' The President theoretically had wide ranging powers including powers to make important judicial and executive appointments and to dissolve the assemblies but could only exercise these powers in line with the advice of the federal government led by the Prime Minister and thus had little independent discretion.

However, this period of civilian rule was short-lived, as the military returned to power in 1977, and Pakistan's military dictator, General Zia, suspended the Constitution, before restoring it in 1985 after making a series of amendments collectively known as the 8th amendment. The purpose of Zia's constitutional framework was to restore the elected parliament but to redistribute power to enable unelected tutelary institutions to constrain the authority and autonomy of the elected institutions. The amended Constitution therefore accommodated features of both the representative model of the original Constitution, and the viceregal model that the military dictatorship preferred. Zia appointed himself as President, and article 90 of the constitution was altered to read: 'The executive authority of the Federation shall vest in the President and shall be exercised by him, either directly or through officers subordinate to him.'[13] The President had to act in accordance with the advice of the Prime Minister but could also reconsider such advice, thus enhancing his discretion. Most importantly, Article 58(2)(b) granted the President the power to dissolve the National Assembly at 'his discretion where in his opinion a situation has arisen in which the Government of the Federation cannot be carried on in accordance with the provisions of the Constitution and an appeal to the electorate is necessary.'[14] Thus, executive power was now shared between the elected Prime Minister and Federal Cabinet, on the one hand, and the unelected or indirectly elected President, on the other hand. Furthermore, Articles 62 and 63 were amended to add new conditions for the disqualification of elected

13 ibid § 8th Amendment (1985).
14 ibid.

representatives, with the Constitution now stating that 'a person shall not be qualified to elected or chosen as a member of (Parliament) if . . . he is sagacious, righteous, and non-profligate, honest and *ameen*.'[15] This vague language about honesty and sagacity placed courts in a position to decide what constitutional standard of morality and sagacity elected representatives had to meet and meant that courts could potentially disqualify elected representatives from standing for election or holding office if there was a legal finding that they violated this standard. Thus, now both the unelected President and the unelected courts were in a powerful position to constrain the authority and autonomy of the elected Prime Minister and legislature, which created an uncomfortable fusion of the representative and viceregal models of government. The elected Parliament represented different peoples of the country, spread across its provinces, and the unelected President, supported by the federal civil-military bureaucracy, represented the unity and ideology of the country.

After Zia's death in 1988, when the Pakistan People's Party won the parliamentary elections in 1988, the elected Prime Minister Benazir Bhutto faced a strong military, a President who was a former bureaucrat and closely aligned with the military, a federal bureaucracy that had mostly been staffed during the era of military rule, a judiciary that had mostly been appointed during military rule, and a strong parliamentary opposition comprised of mostly pro-military parties. The newly elected government had few allies in the unelected sections of the political system and little space to operate given the new constitutional arrangement. Efforts made by the government to expand civilian control over other executive institutions faced strong opposition, and within a year of coming to power, Benazir Bhutto's government faced a parliamentary vote of no confidence.

The opposition alliance of the Islamic Jamhoori Ittehad (IJI) moved a resolution declaring a lack of confidence in the PPP government. The motion required a simple majority in parliament to vote in its favour, and IJI was backed by the powerful President and army leadership working to make sure the motion had enough votes to pass.[16] However, two factors worked against the vote. First, the National Assembly was too fragmented, with the PPP commanding a narrow parliamentary majority, the IJI being an alliance of smaller opposition parties, and a large number of parliamentarians being elected independents without any partisan affiliations. Second, party leaders could not guarantee that their own party members would vote in line with the party leaders or defect and vote based on their own interests. After a decade of repressive dictatorship, political parties had only recently been revived. These parties were weakly institutionalized, with limited organizational depth and coherence, and reliant on attracting local political elites with established

15 ibid § 62–63.
16 Talbot (n 4).

patronage power and limited partisan loyalty.[17] Thus, both the PPP and the IJI, with the help of the military and presidency, competed to offer all sorts of incentives to parliamentarians, especially those who were independent of any partisan affiliations, to support their position. Both parties offered cash payments, government jobs, and land grants to legislators to swing the votes in their favour.[18] Ultimately, the PPP narrowly survived the vote of no confidence, thanks to holding on to its own parliamentarians and a number of independents, while also convincing a number of opposition party members to abstain from the vote.[19] Thus, in a weakly institutionalized and fragmented political environment, building a collective coalition to successfully pass a vote of no confidence proved too challenging.

For the military and presidency, the lesson learned was that maneuvering fragile parliamentary coalitions required aligning the incentives of too many actors; therefore, the simpler solution was to work through more centralized and less fragmented institutions. The ideal institution was, therefore, the presidency. Within a few months of the unsuccessful vote of no confidence, President Ghulam Ishaq Khan used his powers of dissolution to dismiss Bhutto's government and dissolve the parliament on charges of corruption and political horse-trading.[20] The presidential dissolution of elected governments became a recurring occurrence during the 1990s.[21] Once elected governments sought to exercise power independently and bring the unelected institutions under greater political control, they fell out of favour with the military and the presidency and faced presidential dissolution.

Given the presidential prerogative to dissolve the assemblies, when irreconcilable differences emerged between the parliamentary and the military-backed presidential leadership, the tenures of elected governments remained unstable, and the constraints of unelected institutions upon the elected leadership undermined both the institutionalization of elected institutions and the expansion of civilian supremacy in Pakistan. The one weapon that the ruling parties in Parliament could wield when facing a hostile presidency was the threat of impeachment.

After the PPP's government was dissolved, the IJI, the alliance of opposition parties backed by the military, defeated the PPP and came to power, with the largest party in that alliance, the Pakistan Muslim League (PML), forming

17 Shandana Mohmand, 'Losing the Connection: Party-Voter Linkages in Pakistan' (2014) 52(1) *Commonwealth and Comparative Politics* 7.

18 Zahid Hussain, 'Bhutto Expects to Scrape Home in No-Confidence Vote' *The Times* (30 October 1989).

19 John Burns, 'Bhutto Survives as No-Confidence Vote Falls Short' *The New York Times* (2 November 1989).

20 Paula Newberg, *Judging the State: Courts and Constitutional Politics in Pakistan* (CUP 1995).

21 Osama Siddique, 'The Jurisprudence of Dissolutions: Presidential Power to Dissolve Assemblies Under the Pakistani Constitution and Its Discontents' (2006) 23(3) *Arizona Journal of International and Comparative Law* 622.

the new government. However, the new government soon fell out with the presidency, as inevitably, the Prime Minister sought to expand his authority beyond the constraints placed upon him by the powerful presidency. In 1993, when President Khan also fell out with Prime Minister Nawaz Sharif of the PML and dissolved the assemblies, the Supreme Court restored the assemblies holding that the President's grounds for dissolution did not pass constitutional muster.[22] After restoration, Khan continued to seek ways to undermine Sharif's government, which led Sharif's government to publicly mull commencing the process of presidential impeachment.[23] Given the supermajority required for presidential impeachment and Sharif's narrow parliamentary majority, Sharif approached opposition parties for talks. Sharif recognized that bringing together a majority for presidential impeachment would be very challenging, but an alignment with the leading opposition party would make the threat of impeachment credible and thus help convince the President to resign.[24] Ultimately, however, the opposition parties indicated their preference to support the President, and the deadlock persisted, culminating in military intervention. The military leadership stepped in and pressured both the President and Prime Minister to resign and announced new elections.[25] Thus, given the political fragmentation within the assemblies and the level of consensus required across the political system from different veto players, presidential impeachment was always going to prove too challenging, but issuing the threat of presidential impeachment proceedings helped Sharif place pressure on Khan and convince the military of the need to intervene against Khan. Hence, the threat of impeachment was used as a bargaining tool with the presidency and the military, but ultimately, the military's intervention led to the resignation of both the President and the Prime Minister.

The parliamentary majorities required to carry out no-confidence votes and especially presidential impeachments was an almost insurmountable challenge in the fragmented and weakly institutionalized party politics of Pakistan's fragile electoral democracy in the 1990s. An exception to this was Nawaz Sharif's second government from 1997 to 1999. Sharif's PML-N won a decisive parliamentary majority in the 1997 elections after the President dissolved the PPP's second government in 1996. Sharif sought to use his parliamentary majority to shift power away from the unelected institutions and empower the office of the Prime Minister and his parliamentary majority. First, the PML-N-controlled Parliament amended the Constitution and restored the original model of parliamentary supremacy, which removed the President's ability to

22 ibid.

23 Anwar Iqbal, 'Pakistan President Faces Impeachment Call' *United Press International* (31 May 1993).

24 Anwar Iqbal, 'Will Temporary Political Truce Avert Military Takeover in Pakistan?' *United Press International* (2 June 1993).

25 Talbot (n 4).

dissolve the assemblies and shifted executive power from the President to the Prime Minister.[26]

Second, the Parliament amended the constitution to ban Members of Parliament elected on the ticket of a political party from crossing the floor and voting with the opposition.[27] In the weakly institutionalized party system of the 1990s, defections and floor-crossing were a real challenge to political stability and party organization, as illustrated by the experience of the first parliamentary vote of no confidence described previously. Therefore, Sharif's 14th constitutional amendment was designed to remedy this issue and enhance the power of the party leadership by turning defection into grounds for disqualification.

However, the Chief Justice of the Supreme Court attempted to block the passage of the two amendments, leading to a clash between the two institutions.[28] Sharif's government also fell out with the Supreme Court Chief Justice over a dispute pertaining to judicial appointments. This conflict led Sharif to make a speech in Parliament criticizing the Chief Justice for overstepping his limits. The Chief Justice then charged Sharif with contempt of court and compelled him to appear before the Court and defend himself against the charges.[29] If Sharif was found guilty of contempt of court, then he could have faced a possible six-month jail term. In response, Sharif used his parliamentary majority to pass a law that amended the contempt of court rules by giving Sharif the chance to appeal his conviction before a fresh panel of judges if he was convicted by the Supreme Court. However, for a bill to formally become a law, the President needed to sign off on the bill, and while the President could not reject the bill passed by Parliament, he could delay signing the bill.[30] President Leghari, who was known to be close to the Chief Justice, attempted to delay signing the bill, leaving Sharif vulnerable to conviction until he signed the bill. In response, Sharif and his cabinet started preparing a motion for impeaching the President.[31]

This motion for impeachment carried more credibility given that Sharif's party held a decisive majority in Parliament and that Sharif had been moving to make it harder for party members to defect from the party. The threat of impeachment was intended to compel the President to sign the bill and end the delay. However, the Chief of Army Staff intervened to mediate among the

26 Constitution of Pakistan (n 6) § 13th Amendment (1997).

27 ibid § 14th Amendment (1997).

28 'Supreme Court Charges Pakistan Premier with Contempt of Court' *DPA International* (19 May 1997).

29 ibid.

30 'Pakistan's Supreme Court Asks President to Intervene in Power Struggle' *Associated Press* (30 October 1997).

31 Kathy Gannon, 'Agreement Between Pakistan's Leaders Scuttles Cabinet Impeachment' *Associated Press* (20 November 1997).

Prime Minister, President, and Chief Justice.[32] After the Chief's mediation, Sharif agreed to put off impeachment plans, and the Chief Justice postponed hearing the contempt of court charges. However, the institutional clash continued with the President writing a letter to Sharif calling his government an 'abject' failure,' and Sharif responded that the President was lowering the prestige of his office.[33] Ultimately, Sharif, backed by his parliamentary majority, prevailed in the confrontation with the Chief Justice and the President, as both were forced to resign.

Once the President had resigned, the PML-N-controlled Parliament indirectly elected a loyalist of Sharif as President, ensuring that Sharif faced no threat from that office. Thus, Sharif was able to use a strong parliamentary majority and the threat of impeachment to finally bring an end to the dual executive and the constant threat that the presidency posed to parliamentary supremacy. However, Sharif relied heavily on the military leadership to reach this outcome, and this dependence on the military's enhanced tutelary role would cost Sharif when he fell out with the military leadership; he was ousted from power in a military coup in 1999.

What this period shows is that Pakistan's Parliament with its fragmentation and coordination challenges was ill-equipped to use impeachment procedures to deal with hostile officers in the executive branch. However, when a party's parliamentary majority is stronger, the threat of impeachment is more credible. Although impeachment procedures were unlikely to succeed in the context of political fragmentation, they could be used to weaken the Prime Minister or President, apply pressure on the President, or invite military mediation, which made impeachment a potent tool in the inter-institutional bargaining between Pakistan's elected and tutelary institutions during this period of unstable constitutional and political hybridity.

15.4 Impeachment and the End of a Military Regime (1999–2008)

Pakistan was ruled by General Musharraf's military regime from 1999 to 2008. In the first three years of his regime, Musharraf suspended the Constitution and only restored it in 2002 after making himself President and amending the Constitution to restore the powers of the presidency originally established by General Zia. The 17th Amendment restored presidential discretion in key appointments and empowered the President to unilaterally dissolve assemblies once again. However, by 2007, Musharraf's regime faced widespread popular resistance, and in February 2008, his ruling party was trounced in the election, while a coalition of opposition parties, led by the PPP and PML-N, the

32 'Army Chief Steps in to Contempt Case' *The Australian* (22 November 1997).

33 Raymond Bonner, 'Pakistan President Quits in Feud with Prime Minister' *New York Times* (3 December 1997).

parties he had ousted from power in 1999, won the parliamentary elections and returned to power. Musharraf remained President, but he now faced a hostile Parliament, and there were growing calls for presidential impeachment.

Initially, the PPP, which was the largest party in the ruling coalition, was less inclined towards impeachment, with the party leader Asif Zardari saying that a democratic transition required 'unity and not confrontation.'[34] But Sharif and the PML-N were keen on pushing for impeaching the military dictator, and they kept placing pressure on Zardari and the PPP to join their push for impeachment. By August 2008, both parties came to an agreement on preparing a motion for impeachment against Musharraf.[35] The immediate question that came up was whether they could actually impeach him, and although the ruling coalition commanded a majority in the National Assembly, a joint sitting would include the Senate, where Musharraf's former ruling party, which also maintained ties with Pakistan's military, still retained a majority.[36] The fact that a widely unpopular dictator was still in a position to survive an impeachment motion by a ruling coalition that commanded an overwhelming majority in Parliament highlighted just how challenging it was to impeach a president in Pakistan.

The ruling parties set about preparing a charge-sheet against the President and trying to gain the support they needed to make the numbers. The provincial assemblies adopted resolutions calling for the President to resign or take a vote of confidence, and the ruling party submitted a parliamentary motion for impeachment in the Parliament.[37] As the ruling party managed to negotiate the agreement of smaller parties that had formerly backed Musharraf, it became increasingly clear that the military was not informally intervening to pressure these parties to support Musharraf.[38] In this scenario, Musharraf was isolated, and it appeared likely that the ruling parties had the numbers and public support to impeach him. In response, Musharraf decided to avoid facing impeachment and resigned instead, paving the way for a civilian president. Thus, in 2008, Pakistan came closest to witnessing its first presidential impeachment, largely because of the widespread political consensus against the outgoing dictator. Unlike the 1990s, where the political system was fragmented between multiple political, administrative, and military elites spread across elected and unelected institutions, Musharraf's repression of both the PML-N and PPP and the mass mobilization against his increasingly unpopular regime helped bring fragmented political elites across the political system on the same page

34 Masood Haider, 'Asif Says He Will Seek to Work with Musharraf' *Dawn* (26 February 2008).

35 Saeed Shah, 'Pakistan Coalition to Impeach Musharraf' *The Guardian* (7 August 2008).

36 By 2008, Musharraf had retired from the position of Chief of Army Staff, and only held the office of President.

37 'Provincial Assembly in Pakistan Moves to Demand Musharraf Resignation' *New York Times* (11 August 2008).

38 Irfan Bukhari, '"Q" to Face Moral Shock if Musharraf Quits Silently' *The Nation* (17 August 2008).

against him and also likely convinced the military to withdraw support from him. Thus, an unpopular and exclusionary authoritarian presidency unified the political elites required to move an impeachment motion.

15.5 Impeachment in an Era of Parliamentary and Judicial Supremacy

Soon after the fall of Musharraf, the ruling parties came together to pass the largest constitutional amendment package since 1973, known as the 18th Amendment. One key feature of this was to, once again, strip the presidency of the executive powers that Musharraf had assumed and restore the original toothless presidency with limited independent discretion.[39] Given the significant weakening of the president, in this period, the question of presidential impeachments rarely came up.

However, although the importance of the presidency as a tutelary institution constraining parliament diminished, another tutelary institution, the superior judiciary, shaped the hybrid politics of this period. During the later years of Musharraf's regime, Pakistan's superior judiciary embraced an increasingly interventionist approach and populist role conception. Between 2005 and 2009, the judiciary was intervening in all matters of state and justifying this expansion on the grounds of representing the public interest, and this new role placed it at odds with the military regime.[40] Supreme Court judges became increasingly popular public figures, and when Musharraf sought to bring the superior judiciary under control by suspending the Chief Justice, he triggered backlash from Pakistan's courts and bar associations.[41] The demand for the restoration of the Chief Justice and an independent judiciary became the focal point for a growing mass movement against Musharraf's regime. By 2009, Musharraf had been removed, and Chief Justice Chaudhry, the judge who he had ousted, had become a popular household name. The superior judiciary enjoyed a level of visibility and legitimacy it had never enjoyed before.

During the new democratic dispensation, the military carefully managed its withdrawal from power to ensure that it could protect its core interests and continue to more covertly involve itself in the politics of the state. The military maintained its internal and legal autonomy, control of military budgets, autonomy in relations with the executive and legislature, and control over foreign policy, defence policy, and intelligence.[42] However, the judiciary was

39 Constitution of Pakistan (n 6) § 18th Amendment (2010).

40 Maryam Khan, 'Genesis and Evolution of Public Interest Litigation in the Supreme Court of Pakistan: Toward a Dynamic Theory of Judicialization' (2014) 28(2) *Temple Journal of International and Comparative Law* 285.

41 Shoaib Ghias, 'Miscarriage of Chief Justice: Judicial Power and the Legal Complex in Pakistan Under Musharraf' (2010) 25(4) *Law and Social Inquiry* 985.

42 Aqil Shah, 'Constraining Consolidation: Military, Politics and Democracy in Pakistan (2007–2013)' (2014) 26(1) *Democratization* 1007.

rewriting its role in the political system and stepping into the domains of the executive and legislature. Petrol prices, sugar prices, private and public sector corruption, the cutting down of trees, land allotments, and bureaucratic appointments – all of these issues invited interventions by the Supreme Court.[43] Judges summoned public officeholders to the courtrooms and then rebuked them for not carrying out the Court's orders.[44] The restored judiciary had little support for elected governments, and the courts were willing to use all the tools at their disposal to assert their will over the government in all matters of politics and policymaking. Judicial interventions into electoral, bureaucratic, and policymaking processes helped constrain and undermine the elected governments of the time (Waseem 2015). There was an apparent alignment of interests between the military and the superior judiciary in weakening and delegitimizing elected governments.[45]

Under the 18th Amendment, the president's power to dissolve elected assemblies had been removed, but the judiciary's power to oust parliamentarians for not fulfilling vague standards of morality and sagacity, under Articles 62 and 63, remained, and they became vehicles for the unelected judiciary to manipulate the arrangement of elected power, ostensibly to target and eliminate political corruption. Between 2010 and 2018, the Supreme Court removed two elected Prime Ministers from power, during this heyday of judicial populism.

The National Reconciliation Ordinance (NRO) was a US-brokered deal between Musharraf and Bhutto's PPP under which corruption charges against dozens of political leaders and bureaucrats were lifted, which allowed these leaders to return to Pakistan and participate in elections on the condition that they accept that Musharraf remain President. In 2010, after Musharraf was gone, the Court overturned the NRO and reopened corruption cases against political leaders and bureaucrats, including then-President Zardari.[46] The judgment was a foregone conclusion, as the ordinance rested on questionable legal grounds, and the Court had made its opposition towards the NRO evident throughout the proceedings. However, although the NRO involved cases against hundreds of politicians and bureaucrats, the target of the Court's judgment was really the PPP's leader, President Zardari. The Court insisted that the government of the Prime Minister Gilani should write to Swiss authorities asking them to reopen investigations into wealth that Zardari had amassed in Swiss bank accounts.[47] When the PPP government evaded the Court's preference, the Court charged the elected Prime Minister, Yousuf Gilani, with

43 Yasser Kureshi, *Seeking Supremacy: The Pursuit of Judicial Power in Pakistan* (CUP 2022).

44 Mohammad Waseem, 'Judging Democracy in Pakistan: Conflict Between the Executive and Judiciary' (2012) 20(1) *Contemporary South Asia* 19.

45 Kureshi (n 44).

46 Jane Perlez, 'Pakistan Strikes Down Amnesty for Politicians' *New York Times* (2009).

47 'The History of the Swiss Case' *Dawn* (20 June 2012).

contempt of court for failing to implement its order.[48] Under Article 63 of the Constitution, a member of parliament could be disqualified from retaining parliamentary membership

> if he has been convicted by a court of competent jurisdiction for propagating any opinion, or acting in any manner, prejudicial to the ideology of Pakistan, or the sovereignty, integrity or security of Pakistan, or morality, or the maintenance of public order, or the integrity or independence of the judiciary of Pakistan, or which defames or brings into ridicule the judiciary or the Armed Forces of Pakistan, unless a period of five years has elapsed since his release.[49]

An article that was designed to deter elected institutions from taking action that in any way undermined the interests, authority, and legitimacy of Pakistan's tutelary institutions was now used to disqualify an elected Prime Minister. In 2012, the Court held that since the Prime Minister had been convicted of contempt of court, under Article 63, he stood disqualified. The Court's disdain for the state's elected leadership was most evident in the concurring opinion of one of the judges on the bench, where he provided an amended version of a poem by Kahlil Gibran by stating that

> Pity the nation that adopts a Constitution but allows political interests to outweigh constitutional diktat. . . . Pity the nation that demands justice for all but is agitated when justice hurts its political loyalty. . . . Pity the nation that is led by those who laugh at the law.[50]

In 2017, the Supreme Court disqualified another Prime Minister. Nawaz Sharif, who had been ousted by Musharraf in 1999, returned to power with a parliamentary majority in 2013. When the so-called Panama papers (leaked documents containing personal financial information about wealthy individuals and public officials) were made public in 2016, they tied Sharif's children to offshore companies that owned prime real estate in London.[51] Sharif had an acrimonious relationship with the military, and by 2016, the military was increasingly backing a new political party, the Pakistan Tehreek-e-Insaaf (PTI). Led by the charismatic leader Imran Khan and organized around a platform of anti-corruption populism, the PTI had considerable support of the country's urban middle class and a proven capacity to mobilize people.[52] Khan saw the

48 'PM Gilani Indicted for Contempt' *Dawn* (13 February 2012).

49 Constitution of Pakistan (n 6) § 63 (1985).

50 Nasir Iqbal, 'Supreme Court Issues Detailed Judgment in Contempt Case' *Dawn* (8 May 2012).

51 Moeen Cheema, 'Pakistan: The State of Liberal Democracy' (2018) 16(2) *International Journal of Constitutional Law* 635.

52 Rochana Bajpai and Yasser Kureshi, 'Mechanisms of Democratic Authoritarianism: De-Centring the Executive in South Asia and Beyond' (2022) 29(8) *Democratization* 1375.

Panama Papers as an opportunity to push for judicial disqualification as a way to weaken and delegitimize the PML-N government. Khan moved a petition before the Supreme Court calling for Sharif's disqualification from office, under Article 62 of the Pakistan Constitution, based on allegations that these properties were purchased using unexplained and ill-gotten income. Article 62 held that

> A person shall not be qualified to be elected or chosen as a member of Parliament unless . . . he is of good character and is not commonly known as one who violates Islamic Injunctions . . . he is sagacious, righteous and non-profligate, honest and ameen, there being no declaration to the contrary by a court of law.[53]

The Court accepted the petition, and over the course of the widely publicized proceedings, Sharif's assets and financial dealings came under judicial and media scrutiny, and the issue of political corruption became increasingly salient in the build-up to the 2018 elections.[54] The Court's judgment came down in two stages. In the first stage, two judges ruled that there was adequate circumstantial evidence of corruption to disqualify Sharif, while three judges constituted a Joint Investigation Team of civilian and military investigative officers to provide confirmed evidence of Sharif's financial misconduct. By this time, the military leadership had also fallen out with Sharif and was supporting the PTI. The investigation unearthed considerable information about potential corruption and ill-gotten wealth and was information that merited further investigation and scrutiny.[55] But rather than allowing the process of investigation, confirmation, and conviction to go through before disqualifying Sharif, the Court relied on the one minor source of income that Sharif had admitted to not declaring on his election papers as adequate evidence to disqualify him under Article 62 of the Constitution.[56] In subsequent cases, the Supreme Court further expanded the potency of its power and ruled that a disqualification from elected office under Article 62 of the Constitution was a lifetime ban, which also rendered the disqualified individual ineligible to hold a leadership position within a political party. The Court could now purge an elected Prime Minister from political life on the basis of civil charges.

The Court's disqualification of Sharif had a significant political impact. By removing the Prime Minister, the judicial proceedings significantly weakened the PML-N government, and the widely covered court discussion of corruption within the PML-N helped make corruption a salient political issue that weakened the PML-N in the run-up to the 2018 elections. The decision and

53 Constitution of Pakistan (n 6) § 62 (1985).
54 Cheema (n 52) 635.
55 ibid.
56 Kureshi (n 44).

its impact on the PML-N thus significantly strengthened the PTI's electoral fortunes. The combined effect of the Court's judgments, the actions by the military to undermine the PML-N's electoral position, and Khan's anti-corruption populism enabled the PTI to win an electoral plurality in the 2018 election and form a new government.[57] During Khan's rule, the military's political pre-eminence was revived, and the PTI government, backed by the military, used an anti-corruption drive to weaken and dismantle the political opposition of the former ruling parties, namely, the PPP and PML-N, as their leaders were arrested on corruption charges.

Thus, both judicial disqualifications during this period were shaped by the evolving state of hybrid politics in Pakistan. In the context of a weakened presidency, the tutelary authority and legitimacy of the Supreme Court became crucially important in maintaining constraints upon the state's elected government and representative institutions. Moreover, in 2017, Sharif's removal by the judiciary played a critical role in delegitimizing and weakening Pakistan's incumbent political parties, bringing a party aligned with the military to power, and shifting the balance of power in favour of the military once again.

15.6 Impeachment and the End of a Hybrid Regime

In 2022, Pakistan witnessed its first successful vote of no confidence against a sitting Prime Minister. Khan had been the Prime Minister since winning the elections in 2018. For three years, Khan's PTI and the military maintained a close partnership that suited both their interests, but by 2022, this relationship fell apart, as differences over foreign policy and crucial institutional appointments led the military leadership to shift allegiances away from Khan.[58] Taking advantage of the fracturing relationship between Khan and the military leadership, the PPP, PML-N, and other opposition parties came together to prepare grounds for removing Khan from power via a parliamentary motion.

The PTI's parliamentary majority depended not only upon holding on to politicians who had been encouraged by the military to defect to the PTI from the PML-N in the 2018 election but also upon maintaining the support of smaller parties that usually acted in line with the directions and preferences of the military. Once the military withdrew its support for the PTI government, the PPP and PML-N, allegedly backed by the military leadership, worked on securing the support of smaller parties for the vote of no confidence.[59] They also worked to convince several parliamentarians from the PTI to defect and offered them offices within their parties should they leave the PTI.[60] They

57 Bajpai and Kureshi (n 53) 1375.

58 Asfandyar Mir and Yasser Kureshi, 'Imran Khan Dissolved Pakistan's Parliament: How Did That Happen?' *Washington Post* (5 April 2022).

59 'PPP, MQM-P Make Headway in Talks' *Express Tribune* (24 March 2022).

60 Tahir Niaz, 'PTI "Defectors" Assured of Immediate Polls to Avoid by-Election' *Nation* (14 March 2022).

needed to break the PTI's coalition in order to form the parliamentary majority that was necessary to remove Khan. In March 2022, amidst a flurry of parliamentary activity and intense political bargaining both inside and outside parliament, the opposition parties with the support of the military worked to cobble together the parliamentary majority needed to pass their motion to declare no confidence in Khan. The PTI's initial political response was two-fold: i) secure the wavering support of the smaller parties in its coalition and ii) approach the Supreme Court to pre-emptively invalidate the votes of any disgruntled members of the PTI who might vote against the party line and in favour of the no-confidence motion. At the same time, Khan also sought to mobilize and galvanize support by claiming the no-confidence motion was part of a foreign conspiracy seeking to remove him because of his defiance of the west, thus seeking to build and apply public pressure to those supporting the motion.[61] However, by the end of March, it became clear that the opposition parties did not have to worry about an adverse Supreme Court decision on the issue of defections since at least two of the parties who were crucial to Khan's coalition and maintained close ties with the military announced their separation from Khan's coalition and support for the no-confidence motion, leaving him in a minority. Khan could not also not preempt the no-confidence motion by dissolving the assemblies and calling an early election because constitutionally, a Prime Minister facing such a vote could not dissolve the assemblies.

With the writing on the wall and in a last-ditch effort to prevent the vote, the PTI declared that the vote of no confidence was a product of an international conspiracy against Khan, and the Deputy Speaker of the National Assembly, a member of the PTI, chose to dismiss the motion for a vote of no confidence based on these allegations of foreign interference.[62] Upon dismissing the motion, Khan immediately dissolved the assemblies and called an election but stayed in power himself as acting-Prime Minister. This dramatic move was immediately challenged in the Supreme Court, and after five days of hectic litigation, the Court declared the Deputy Speaker's move to reject the motion to be unconstitutional and thus void, restored the assemblies, and compelled the Speaker to hold the vote of no confidence within a fixed number of days.[63] The party's parliamentary leadership remained reluctant to allow the vote to happen, and the consequences of the PTI's defiance of the Court's orders remained unclear. With hours left before the assembly would cross the time limit set by the Court for the vote on the no-confidence motion, the judiciary signaled its willingness to punish the PTI for its defiance. The Supreme Court reopened at 11 pm to signal its willingness to hold the PTI's Speaker and Deputy Speakers in contempt for defying its orders.[64] Around the same

61 Mir and Kureshi (n 59).

62 ibid.

63 Haseeb Bhatti, 'Supreme Court Restores National Assembly' *Dawn* (7 April 2022).

64 Faqir Hussain, 'The Midnight Opening of Courts' *Pakistan Today* (19 June 2022).

time, a petition was filed in the Islamabad High Court restraining Khan from removing the Chief of Army Staff from his position.[65] The two petitions indicated that the two tutelary institutions, the military and the judiciary, had both left Khan isolated and signaled the extent of the deterioration in the relationship between Khan and the Chief of Army Staff. Finally, with no options left, the PTI's Speaker and Deputy Speaker had to end their resistance, and the vote was finally held. Khan became the first Prime Minister to be ousted via a vote of no confidence.

The lessons of this vote of no confidence were three-fold. First, given the broad political consensus required for a no-confidence motion to be successful, the military remained positioned to make or break such a vote. As long as the military supported Khan, any endeavor to bring an end to Khan's government was unlikely to succeed, and once the military withdrew support from Khan, Khan's ability to hold back such a vote disappeared. Thus, the no-confidence motion highlighted the continued role of tutelary institutions in defining the trajectory of Pakistani politics. Second, after Khan's military-backed government aggrandized executive power for three years to weaken and debilitate opposition parties, the parliamentary hearings and bargaining surrounding the vote of no confidence helped revive the relevance and significance of the elected legislature as a site for initiating a political transition. Third, Khan's public campaign to delegitimize the vote of no confidence resonated with large segments of the public, and since being ousted from power, he became a political martyr for his supporters and enjoyed a significant revival of public support. What this indicated was that in the context of Pakistan's hybrid politics, regime change and the removal of governments through legislative and judicial processes enjoyed limited legitimacy and were widely seen as the products of collusion between political and military elites. Indeed, the parties that backed the motion of no confidence have lost support, while Khan's popularity has continued to grow.[66] Hence, this removal provided important insights into how Pakistan's tutelary institutions shift political alliances and the ways in which political parties operate, negotiate, seek to acquire and preserve power, and alter political fortunes in the shadow of powerful tutelary institutions.

15.7 Conclusion

In this book chapter, I reviewed attempts at presidential impeachments, votes of no confidence against Prime Ministers, and the removal of elected leadership through judicial disqualifications since 1973 in Pakistan. Even though impeachment procedures have rarely been successful, different forms of

65 ibid.
66 'Imran Most Popular Leader in Pakistan: Gallup Survey' *Express Tribune* (7 March 2023).

impeachment are strategically deployed as tools to reorganize the distribution of power between elected and tutelary institutions.

The three attempts at presidential impeachment discussed in this chapter each demonstrate not only how the number of veto players required to agree on an impeachment make impeachment highly unlikely but also how the threat of impeachment can be used to bring the offices of the Prime Minister and the President into partisan alignment. The cases discussed here show how impeachment proceedings backed by strong parliamentary majorities were used to compel the military to intervene between the President and Prime Minister or signal the isolation and lack of legitimacy of an incumbent president, thus leading to the resignation of the president and enabling the ruling party to select a new president loyal to the party leadership. Thus, they can play a critical role in expanding the authority of the political leadership in elected institutions over unelected institutions that constrain representative institutions in Pakistan's hybrid system.

Similarly, the two attempts at a no-confidence motion demonstrate how no-confidence motions, whether successful or unsuccessful, have been triggered by the military and elected governments when falling out with each other. Whether it was the PPP government that the military opposed from the outset or the PTI government that the military fell out with after three years, opposition parties can use the fracturing relationship to destabilize the incumbent government, and the military can either directly or covertly intervene to support the no-confidence motion to engineer a shift in political partners. However, the success of a no-confidence motion depends on both military support and the provision of the necessary incentives to engineer a majority coalition and dissuade defections. Thus, once again, understanding both the motivation behind no-confidence motions and the likelihood of their success requires understanding the alignment between and interests of different institutional actors across Pakistan's hybrid arrangement of power.

Finally, the judicial disqualifications reveal how unelected tutelary institutions can destabilize and delegitimize incumbent elected leaders. These judicial disqualifications played a critical role in i) preventing elected governments from consolidating political authority and ii) facilitating a transition towards a more militarized and authoritarian regime structure. The judicial authority to disqualify is a critical tool through which unelected institutions can constrain political institutions in Pakistan, and given the fact that it requires the concurrence among only a plurality of judges on the bench deciding the question of disqualification, it is a far more efficient and, therefore, potent strategy for removing executive leadership and managing the distribution of power across Pakistan's centers of power.

Thus, the recent history of impeachment proceedings in Pakistan, through different institutional pathways and at different political junctures in Pakistan's recent history, highlight the dynamic nature of Pakistan's hybrid politics and reveal the ways in which elected and tutelary institutions contest and negotiate over political authority, autonomy, and legitimacy. Power ebbs and flows between the elected and unelected centers of power, and impeachment proceedings are critical moments that shape this dynamic and dissonant hybrid political order.

16 The United Kingdom and Impeachment

Justification, Renewal, and the House of Commons as a Guardian of the Constitution

*Chris Monaghan**

16.1 Introduction

Impeachment was first used in England in 1376 and ceased to be used after the acquittal of Henry Dundas, Viscount Melville, in 1806. This chapter does not seek to present a historical account of impeachment; rather, it seeks to ask whether impeachment could still serve a role in the 21st century United Kingdom. This chapter makes the case that there is justification for a role for impeachment within the United Kingdom's contemporary constitution. This chapter considers how a revised and modernised form of impeachment could serve a role in buttressing the existing accountability mechanisms, which operate to regulate the conduct of ministers and ensure compliance with the accepted constitutional norms and legal principles of the constitution. Whilst the constitution is regulated by constitutional norms in the form of conventions, the powers of the government (the crown) are regulated by legal principles either developed through the common law (i.e., the limits on the use of prerogative powers) or enacted by Parliament (i.e., the Lord Chancellor's duty under the Constitutional Reform Act 2005).[1] It is argued that amongst the potential justifications, it is possible to see three that support the use of a revised form of impeachment. These three rationales are firstly, enhancing the accountability of the executive in the Westminster system, secondly, enhancing democratic oversight, and thirdly, providing a role for the House of Commons as a guardian of the constitution.

As a consequence of the contested nature of the constitution and the controversy surrounding the approach of the Supreme Court in *R (on the application of Miller) v Prime Minister (No. 2)*,[2] there arguably needs to be a greater

* I am grateful to Professor Robert Blackburn for his feedback on the material upon which this chapter is based. This chapter is based in part on chapter seven of *Accountability, Impeachment and the Constitution: The Case for a Modernised Process in the United Kingdom* (Routledge 2022), and I have taken the opportunity provided to further develop the ideas set out within the original version.

1 Sections 3 and 17 of the Constitutional Reform Act 2005.

2 [2019] UKSC 41.

DOI: 10.4324/9781003256007-20

dialogue about who takes responsibility for the protection and development of the contemporary constitution. This raises the question of how we would define the constitution and the obligations within it that must be followed. The answer is to some extent easier now, in light of the existence of the Cabinet Manual and Ministerial Code (albeit descriptive in nature), but ultimately, the question would need to be answered during the course of the impeachment process, with reference to the opinion of experts, the House of Commons and the proposed Court of Impeachment. The 'partygate' scandal in the United Kingdom arguably demonstrates the willingness of the government to break accepted norms and the determination of the House of Commons to ultimately draw a line under such conduct by referring the issue of whether the Prime Minister misled the House of Commons to the Commons Privileges Committee. However, the fact that such conduct was considered acceptable by the government in the first place demonstrates an increasing deterioration in the operation of the constitutional norms and the need for action to remedy this.

This chapter is not intended to set out in detail how impeachment was used until it fell into disuse after 1806. Rather, this chapter is concerned with accountability within the United Kingdom and how a revised form of impeachment could assist in ensuring that this is improved.

16.2 Defining Impeachment

Before discussing impeachment within a historical context, it is important to understand what exactly is meant by the term impeachment. Within the British system, it means that the House of Commons accuses, that is, impeaches, an individual or individuals on the basis of wrongdoing that is formally known as high crimes or misdemeanours. Thus, the House of Commons will vote on articles of impeachment, and the articles that receive the support of a bare majority of Members of Parliament will then be sent to the House of Lords. The upper chamber acts as a court to determine guilt, and the members of the Lords serve as a jury that votes on each of the articles at the end of the trial. The Lord Chancellor, or Lord High Steward, would traditionally preside over the trial, and the House of Commons would be represented by the Members of Parliament serving as the prosecution managers. The individual who had been impeached would be able to prepare a defence and would be represented by counsel.

Notably, the wrongdoing that an individual can be impeached for includes breaches of the criminal law and conduct that the House of Commons believes to be wrong but that falls outside the scope of the ordinary law. In terms of consequences, the accused, if found guilty by the Lords, could face imprisonment, a fine, and/or removal from office. There was always the possibility that in extreme cases, the accused would be executed, as in the case of Lord Lovat who was impeached in response to his support for Prince Charles Edward Stuart in 1745.[3]

3 For the background, see EM Furgol, 'Fraser, Simon, Eleventh Lord Lovat' in *Oxford Dictionary of National Biography* (OUP 2004).

In terms of the monarch's ability to intervene in an impeachment, a dissolution of Parliament would not bring the impeachment trial to a close,[4] and it would not be possible to pardon the accused until after the finding of guilt by the Lords.[5] Therefore, it is evident that impeachment would offer the House of Commons a forum to proceed against its enemies, which traditionally tended to be members of the ruling administration or other high-ranking officials, without needing the permission of the monarch and under the expectation that the House of Lords would conduct the trial in the event of a successful impeachment in the House of Commons. This is not to say that the House of Lords might not challenge the basis of the impeachment in terms of evidential difficulties in establishing the alleged offences or impeachments that were considered by the Lords to be wholly political.[6]

The problem is that impeachment and its procedures were developed over a long period of time and that this account is based on parliamentary practice, albeit moderated by the influence of the common law in the case of the trial process; therefore, if an impeachment were to occur today, then parliamentarians and the clerks would be forced to refer to earlier editions of *Erskine May* for guidance.[7] This chapter argues that there is a case for the use of impeachment. However, on the basis of the previous definition (and not least the involvement of the House of Lords and Lord Chancellor), it is clear that the traditional approach is far from satisfactory. The point is that it is necessary to separate out what impeachment could offer now, in terms of its normative purpose and providing a role as an accountability mechanism, from how it was used in the past. Impeachment would serve as a way of buttressing the existing accountability mechanisms within the political constitution and act as a way to re-empower Members of Parliament to proceed against breaches of the constitution, whether these be the accepted constitutional norms or legal principles. For example, such an approach would capture a constitutional convention that is either recognised in statute or placed on a statutory footing, such as the Sewel Convention (see Scotland Act 2016 and Wales Act 2017). This is controversial as it is difficult to say with certainty precisely what the constitution demands, or what the boundaries are of a constitutional convention or a legal principle (i.e., the executive's use of prerogative powers and whether this is within the appropriate legal limits). However, I argue that an impeachment procedure should contain mechanisms for determining some

4 This was determined to be the case during the impeachment trial of Warren Hastings, the former governor-general of Bengal. Hastings was impeached in 1787, and his trial took place between 1788–1795. For discussion on the 1791 dissolution of Parliament, see WS Holdsworth, *A History of English Law, Volume XII* (Methuen and Co Ltd 1938) 339.

5 See the Act of Settlement 1701.

6 For a discussion on this point, see C Roberts, 'The Law of Impeachment in Stuart England: A Reply to Raoul Berger' (1975) 84(7) *Yale Law Journal* 1419.

7 See M Jack, *Erskine May Parliamentary Practice* (24th edn, Lexis Nexis Butterworths 2011); T Erskine May, *A Treatise Upon the Law, Privileges, Proceedings and Usage of Parliament* (1st edn, James and Luke J Hansard 1844). It would also be necessary to refer to J Hatsell, *Precedents of Proceedings in the House of Commons*, vol IV (Luke Hansard and Sons 1818).

degree of consensus for what the constitution expects. For example, this could be achieved by the need for independent expert advice prior to the impeachment vote in the House of Commons on whether a breach has occurred and in the way that expert opinion is relied upon during the trial. How impeachment might be reconceptualised as a modernised accountability procedure is explored in the following.

The approach set out by the British practice of impeachment influenced the drafters of the United States Constitution. The United States Constitution empowers a bare majority of the House of Representatives to impeach the President and other executive officers (and federal judges), and if the House of Representatives votes to impeach, then the individual accused of high crimes and misdemeanours is tried by the Senate. If convicted by the required two-thirds majority of senators, then the sanction is either to remove the individual from office and possibly to disqualify them from holding future office. In terms of high-profile presidential impeachments, there have only been four, and two of these were of President Donald Trump. In terms of the Senate impeachment trials, these occurred once while Trump was serving as President and the other after he had left office.[8] Interestingly, the debate as to whether a former President could be impeached for acts committed whilst in office relied on the British precedent of Warren Hastings, the former governor-general of Bengal, who was impeached after resigning his position and returning to Britain.[9] Needless to say, no President has been convicted by the Senate, and arguably in most situations, party loyalty would serve as a way to render the requirement of a two-thirds majority impossible to achieve. However, it should be noted that the impeachment mechanism permits a formal spotlight to be cast on presidential conduct that is deemed contrary to the law and Constitution, which in the case of the President's immunity from criminal prosecution in the ordinary courts during their term in office, is extremely important in calling out conduct that the House of Representatives views as objectionable.

16.3 Impeachment in a Historical Context

This next section briefly considers the use of impeachment within a historical context. Impeachment originated in 1376 during the meeting of the

8 The other two examples of presidential impeachment are Andrew Johnson in 1868 and William Clinton in 1998. As was the case with Donald Trump, both Johnson and Clinton were acquitted by the Senate. However, note the broad cross-party support in the House of Representatives for the impeachment of Richard Nixon and how this threat of impeachment led to Nixon's resignation.

9 J Marcus, 'Why a Corrupt 18th Century English Governor of Bengal Is at the Heart of Trump's Impeachment' *The Independent* (9 February 2021) <www.independent.co.uk/news/world/americas/us-politics/trump-impeachment-warren-hastings-b1800015.html> accessed 30 May 2023.

so-called Good Parliament.[10] Parliament met at a time when England's fortunes were approaching a nadir, and Members of Parliament were keen to allocate blame to those deemed to be responsible.[11] Somehow during the course of parliamentary deliberations, the Commons, led by its first speaker, Thomas de la Mare, impeached Lord William Latimer, a leading official at the court of King Edward III.[12] Whilst they never intended to proceed directly against the king, the Members of Parliament accused (as one body rather than as individual Members of Parliament) the individuals viewed as responsible for the present military and economic failures besetting England. This was significant and was a major innovation in terms of creating an accountability mechanism that could be deployed by the Commons. Having accused Latimer, the Commons was then able to persuade the Lords (in the absence of John of Gaunt, the Duke of Lancaster and Edward III's son, who would have blocked such an initiative) to try Latimer with the Commons acting as the prosecutor and the Lords serving as the court.[13] Whilst the Lords had agreed to put Latimer on trial, they were clear that there were certain procedural safeguards that would need to be satisfied in order to prevent a pronouncement of guilt solely on the basis of the Commons' decision to impeach. Thus, impeachment was devised (or perhaps this is a later interpretation) as creating a mechanism to hold senior government officials, not the monarch, to account.

Impeachment continued to be developed during the reign of Edward III's successor, Richard II, and was for a time adopted by the crown to proceed against the king's enemies. Despite much debate as to whether certain prosecutions were or were not actual impeachments, the pivotal development was in the use of impeachment by the Commons against Michael de la Pole, Richard II's

10 A balanced account of why the Good Parliament met and the situation facing England is provided by M McKisack, *The Fourteenth Century 1307–1399: The Oxford History of England* (OUP 1959, reprinted 1988). There is an interesting academic debate as to how and when impeachment originated. For differing accounts, see B Wilkinson, *Studies in the Constitutional History of the Thirteenth and Fourteenth Centuries* (Manchester UP 1937); TFT Plucknett, 'The Origin of Impeachment' (1942) 2 *Transactions of the Royal Historical Society* 47; MV Clarke, *Fourteenth Century Studies* (LS Sutherland and M McKisack eds, Clarendon Press 1968).

11 For an interesting account of the circumstances leading to the Good Parliament, see G Dodd, 'Corruption in the Fourteenth-Century English State' (2011) 34 *International Journal of Public Administration* 720. For an overview of the military situation and the consequences that this would have during the Good Parliament, see CC Bayley, 'The Campaign of 1375 and the Good Parliament' (1940) 55 (219) *The English Historical Review* 370.

12 See GL Harris, 'The Formation of Parliament, 1272–1377' in RG Davies and JH Denton (eds), *The English Parliament in the Middle Ages* (Manchester UP 1981). See also G Holmes, 'Latimer, William, Fourth Baron Latimer' in *Oxford Dictionary of National Biography* (OUP 2004).

13 For an argument as to why the Lords played a pivotal role in the impeachments of 1376, see Wilkinson (n 10).

Lord Chancellor.[14] As a consequence of Henry IV's usurpation of the throne in 1399, impeachment ceased to be a feature of the political and constitutional life of England, with impeachment only remerging towards the end of Henry VI's reign when the Commons impeached William de la Pole, the Duke of Suffolk.[15] The York and Tudor monarchies led to the abeyance of impeachment until the later years of James I's reign. The reasons for why impeachment ceased to be used during this period are complex and can be partly explained by a strong monarchy and careful control of Parliament.[16] That is not to say that impeachment was not discussed, as historians have made reference to the attempt to impeach several leading Tudor officials, but these do not appear to resemble impeachment as understood in the later medieval period.[17] The so-called revival of impeachment in 1621 saw a series of impeachments against leading Jacobean officials, such as Francis Bacon, Viscount St. Alban, and

14 JS Roskell, *The impeachment of Michael de la Pole Earl of Suffolk in 1386 in the context of the reign of Richard II* (Manchester UP 1984).

15 See J Watts, 'Pole, William de la, First Duke of Suffolk' in *Oxford Dictionary of National Biography* (OUP 2004); A Tuck, *Crown and Nobility 1272–1461: Political Conflict in Late Medieval England* (Fontana 1985) 297.

16 See, for example, Raoul Berger, who observed that '[w]hat emerges is that Parliament bent before the wind of Tudor power and prudently refrained from confrontations with royal favorites' (R Berger, *Impeachment: The Constitutional Problems* (Harvard UP 1973) 28.

17 For example, in the reign of Edward VI, the political rivalries that arose during the minority of a young king resulted in the fall from power and execution of two of the king's maternal uncles, Thomas Seymour, Lord Sudeley, and Edward Seymour, Duke of Somerset. Thomas Seymour was accused of trying to seize power and of attempting to gain the affections of Princess Elizabeth, the youngest daughter of Henry VIII. Thomas was regarded as a rival to his brother, Edward, whose authority he endeavoured to undermine. The efforts to proceed against Thomas Seymour are said by the author of an anonymous eighteenth-century pamphlet on impeachment to have begun as an impeachment, 'but upon second Thoughts the other Method was chosen, and a Bill passed for his Attainder' (see *An Enquiry into the Origin of Parliamentary Impeachments: With A History of the Moft Remarkable Proceedings of that Kind from the Beginning to Out Time* (J Peele at Locke's Head, in Pater-Nofter-Row 1745). The entry for Thomas Seymour in the *Oxford Dictionary of National Biography* does not expressly refer to impeachment (GW Bernard, 'Seymour, Thomas, Baron Seymour of Sudeley (*b.* in or before 1509, *d.* 1549)' in *Oxford Dictionary of National Biography* (OUP 2004)). However, it does state that 'Seymour was arrested on 17 January 1549. Examined on 25 January, he wrote an abject submission to Somerset on 27 January. Many were interrogated. Some members of the privy council were *clearly turning this information into articles* against Seymour' (Bernard, 'Seymour, Thomas'). Eventually, Parliament voted for a bill of attainder, and this led to his execution. The attainder and execution of Thomas Seymour was approved by his brother, Edward Seymour. References to the attempt to impeach Thomas Seymour are contained in other sources (Bernard, 'Seymour, Thomas'). Although in other sources, it is Thomas' brother Edward, Duke of Somerset and the Protector of England, who had Articles of impeachment drafted for use against him. John Guy interestingly notes that Thomas Seymour was attained for 'attempting to seize [King] Edward . . . and also with attempting to marry the king's half-sister Elizabeth' (61), but he does not refer to impeachment within the context of Thomas Seymour. Rather, it is his brother, Edward Seymour, the Duke of Somerset and the Protector of England, who had articles of impeachment drawn up against him (61) (see *The Tudors: A Very Short Introduction* (2nd edn, OUP 2013).

George Villiers, the Duke of Buckingham. As a consequence of the tensions between Charles I and parliamentarians and the eventual meeting of what became known as the Long Parliament in 1640, there were further impeachments against royal officials, most notably Thomas Wentworth, Earl of Strafford, and William Laud, the Archbishop of Canterbury. However, the House of Commons abandoned the impeachment trial of Strafford and Laud and opted instead to proceed against both men by way of a bill of attainder.[18] This resulted in the execution of both Strafford and Laud. The switch to a bill of attainder had overcome the shortcomings of impeachment (at least from the House of Commons' perspective), which was the need for a trial, whereas attainder simply required a parliamentary vote on a bill.

Perhaps the most notable impeachment after Strafford and Laud was that of Warren Hastings, who had been the first governor-general of Bengal. Hastings had been appointed as a result of the Regulating Act 1773, which had been a statutory attempt by Lord North's administration to reform the management of the East India Company's Indian territories and the financial problems besetting the company.[19] Hastings was criticised by his opponents for ignoring the East India Company's orders to tackle corruption by the company's employees,[20] and he himself was accused of corruption, abuse of position and acting in a despotic manner.[21] The impeachment owed much to Hastings' rivalry with Sir Philip Francis, who had served with Hastings on the Supreme Council of Bengal.[22] Upon his return to Britain, Francis had managed to gain the support of parliamentarians including Edmund Burke and Charles James Fox to support the impeachment.[23] Finding broad support

18 For commentary, see P Christianson, 'The Peers, the People and Parliamentary Management in the First Six Months of the Long Parliament' (1977) 49(4) *Journal of Modern History* 575; S Lambert, 'The Opening of the Long Parliament' (1984) 27(2) *The Historical Journal* 265; JP Greene, *Evaluating Empire and Confronting Colonialism in Eighteenth-Century Britain* (CUP 2013); JH Timmis, 'The Basis of the Lord's Decision in the Trial of Strafford: Contravention of the Two-Witnesses Rule' (1976) 8(4) *Albion: A Quarterly Journal Concerned with British Studies* 311.

19 Further reform was attempted by the Fox-North coalition government in 1783, albeit unsuccessful due to the influence of George III in calling on the House of Lords to defeat the bill that would have introduced the planned reform.

20 For the public's concern over the conduct of the company's employees, see P Lawson and J Phillips, '"Our Execrable Banditti": Perceptions of Nabobs in Mid-Eighteenth Century England' (1984) 16(3) *Albion* 225; TW Nechtman, *Nabobs and Identity in Eighteenth-Century Britain* (CUP 2013).

21 For an account of Hastings' alleged misconduct, see NB Dirks, *The Scandal of Empire: India and the Creation of Imperial Britain* (Permanent Black 2008); Conor Cruise O'Brien, *Edmund Burke* (Vintage 2002).

22 See S Weitzman, *Warren Hastings and Philip Francis* (Manchester UP 1929); TH Bowyer, 'Philip Francis and the Government of Bengal: Parliament and Personality in the Frustration of an Ambition' (1999) 18(2) *Parliamentary History* 1.

23 ibid. On Francis' hostility and campaigning, see CH Phillips, 'The East India Company "Interest" and the English Government, 1783–4' (1937) 20 *Transactions of the Royal Historical Company* 83.

in the Commons, with even William Pitt the Younger,[24] the Prime Minister, voting for certain articles of impeachment, the impeachment was successful, and Hastings was tried before the Lords. What is truly significant about Hastings' trial was not that it lasted seven years, the longest impeachment trial in history, but that it confirmed the usage of the common law and the rules of evidence over parliamentary practice and offered a more legalistic approach to the procedure used at the trial.[25] This had the consequence of significantly hampering the prosecution managers' case, and in 1795, Hastings was acquitted by the Lords.

The final use of impeachment was in 1806, when the House of Commons impeached Henry Dundas, Viscount Melville, who was the First Lord of the Admiralty. The charges against Melville were that he had misappropriated funds belonging to the navy whilst he had been Treasurer of the Navy.[26] The fact that Melville was a long-time ally of William Pitt the Younger, did not prevent him from being impeached. Melville was acquitted by the House of Lords in 1806. Following Melville's acquittal, other forms of accountability mechanisms superseded impeachment, with impeachment being considered obsolete.[27] These included the need for the government to retain the confidence of the House of Commons and ministerial responsibility to Parliament.

The last attempt at impeachment was in 2004, when a number of Members of Parliament were able to place a motion on the House of Common's Order Paper to impeach the then-Prime Minister, Tony Blair, in response to the invasion of Iraq in 2003. The motion was drafted by parliamentarians including Douglas Hogg (now Viscount Hailsham) and Edward Garnier. The attempt proceeded no further, although it was debated in the House of Commons. Impeachment was clearly understood by a minority of Members of Parliament, including amongst them trained lawyers, to not be obsolete, and this was also the view of Conor Gearty and Rabinder Singh QC in their legal opinion on the matter.[28] However, in parliamentary reports, impeachment was held to be obsolete, even if it was still a live sanction but one that was no longer considered appropriate to use.[29]

24 See CC Davies, 'Warren Hastings and the Younger Pitt (1955) 70 *The English Historical Review* 609, 609–10, 614–15.

25 See GM Ditchfield, 'The House of Lords and the Impeachment of Warren Hastings' (1994) 13(3) *Parliamentary History* 277; PJ Marshall, *The Impeachment of Warren Hastings* (OUP 1965).

26 For an account of the impeachment, see M Fry, *The Dundas Despotism* (John Donald 2004); JA Lovat-Fraser, 'The Impeachment of Lord Melville' (1912–13) 24 *Juridical Review* 235.

27 For differing views on whether impeachment is obsolete, see W McKay and CW Johnson, *Parliament and Congress: Representation and Scrutiny in the Twenty-First Century* (OUP 2010); R Singh QC and C Gearty, 'In the Matter of an Impeachment of the Prime Minister: Arising from the War Against Iraq' (*Legal Opinion*, 22 September 2004).

28 Singh QC and Gearty (n 28).

29 For example, see Joint Committee on Parliamentary Privilege Report, vol 1 – Report and Proceedings of the Committee (HL 43-I, HC 214-I) [16].

16.4 What Would a Modern Impeachment Look Like?

The purpose of this chapter is to argue that impeachment could be reimagined to focus on protecting the constitution and to permit the House of Commons to undertake the role as a guardian of the constitution. Impeachment, at least in the modernised version that is being proposed, should not be seen as a way to threaten political rivals with criminal sanctions, to undermine the rule of law, to impede the operation of the ordinary courts or to replicate the existing criminal sanctions that are available. The proposed mechanism would empower the House of Commons and serve as a way to firstly, ensure the executive's compliance with accepted constitutional norms and legal principles, secondly, secure a way to tackle non-compliance in a manner that places the House of Commons at the centre, and thirdly, through the prospect of a trial before a Court of Impeachment, serve as a deterrent. This determinantal element is crucial, as the point would be not just to measure success with the numbers of actual impeachments but rather to see impeachment as a deterrent and something that could take place as a last resort in the event of ministerial non-compliance with accepted constitutional norms and legal principles. This would reimagine what is meant by impeachment and confront the issue of executive dominance within the Westminster system by looking for a novel solution to rebalance the executive-House of Commons relationship. The rationale for using impeachment within the United Kingdom's constitutional system is explored later; however, at this stage, it is important to sketch out what is proposed in terms of a modernised process. This is important as the arguments that follow are very much dependent on this reconceptualization of the traditional understanding of impeachment.

It is proposed that the House of Commons would retain the power to impeach, and its powers to do so would be placed on a statutory footing. The proposed Impeachment Act would abolish high crimes and misdemeanours and therefore explicitly shift the focus of impeachment towards non-compliance with the accepted constitutional norms and legal principles of the constitution by the executive, which is arguably where there is a more pressing case for enhanced parliamentary control, and leave criminal conduct to the ordinary courts. This raises many issues such as how do we define the constitution and determine the scope of a legal principle. For example, when precisely will the use of a prerogative power give rise to a breach of the constitution (in the sense that the lawfulness of the use of the prerogative can be challenged) and fall within the ambit of impeachment? However, these problems are not unsurmountable, and within the United Kingdom, a broad spectrum of expert opinion exists to be drawn upon to answer such a question. When deciding whether to impeach a minister, the House of Commons will be guided by informed expert opinion.

In terms of empowering Members of Parliament to enforce the constitution, the proposed process would offer a mechanism for a small number of Members of Parliament to start the impeachment process, and even if the majority of the House of Commons does not support the impeachment, then there would still be the possibility to commission an expedited review by experts to determine whether a minister's conduct was contrary to an accepted constitutional norm. The 'partygate' scandal and the decision of the House of Commons in April 2022 to refer the Prime Minister for investigation by the Commons Committee of Privileges does demonstrate a willingness to act, but it is also an exceptional event, and crucially, the referral was due to the government allowing its Members of Parliament a free vote. This alternative way of addressing alleged misconduct should not be seen as excluding the prospect of the use of impeachment, as what I propose would allow an investigation without the need for the support of a majority of Members of Parliament. There is quite rightly the concern that Members of Parliament could use the process to pursue political grievances and that there would be a risk once again that impeachment could be misused for partisan reasons. The solution would be to create sufficient filters, such as needing the permission of the Speaker of the House of Commons to initiate the impeachment proceedings and other safeguards, to prevent overt partisanship. This chapter does not argue that political gameplaying would not be a factor in Members of Parliament trying to bring an impeachment; rather, it acknowledges that this is to be expected of politics, and, therefore, checks and balances should be put in place to prevent abuse. There is quite rightly a concern with the way that politics is going, with personal attacks and a willingness to disrespect the rules. However, impeachment should not be seen as just another way to attack an opponent, as misguided and unsound attempts would fail to proceed. That is, bluster and threats of impeachment would only be political hot air unless there was a genuine case that could be made out.

The proposed Impeachment Act would remove both the Lord Chancellor and the House of Lords from the impeachment process. The House of Lords would no longer be involved and would have no role in determining guilt. In place of the House of Lords, it is proposed that the function of trying an impeachment would be undertaken by a specially constituted Court of Impeachment. Such a court would be constituted of both judicial and lay members and would be partly based on the use of a hybrid impeachment court in Denmark. The advantages of having such a Court of Impeachment would be that this would instil political knowledge through the lay members, whilst bringing in judicial expertise and offering a blended tribunal to determine if an impeachable offence has been committed. Furthermore, the use of a Court of Impeachment reduces the risks that the result is seen as unfair and a violation of the accused's rights under the European Convention on Human Rights. For example, the impeachment of Erik Ninn-Hansen, the Danish Minister of Justice, in 1995 was challenged before the European Court of Human Rights, with the court finding that the Erik Ninn-Hansen's Convention rights had not be violated.[30] Thus, it is possible to safeguard Convention rights, such as the Article 6 right to a fair trial, within an impeachment process.

30 *Ninn-Hansen v Denmark* (1999) (admissibility decision No 28972/95). See also the application of the former Prime Minister of Iceland in relation to his impeachment and conviction (*Haarde v Iceland* (Application No 66847/12)).

Having focused on whether the conduct of the minister amounted to a breach of the constitution, this would then limit the sanction to the official performance of that individual's role. Therefore, a minister could face the prospect of the Court of Impeachment ordering that they are removed from office and possibly disqualified from holding office in the future. This reconceptualization of impeachment would mean that only a minister or the Prime Minister could be impeached (which would also include former minsters and Prime Ministers) and have an exclusive focus on the central United Kingdom executive.

16.5 The Rationale: Enhancing Accountability, Democratic Oversight, and Providing a Role for the House of Commons as the Guardian of the Constitution

In this section, it is necessary to consider the rationale for modernising impeachment and for arguing that it should be part of the contemporary constitutional landscape of the United Kingdom. The rationale for the retention and modernisation of impeachment could be viewed as threefold. The first rationale for this is the role impeachment could play in enhancing accountability, specifically of the executive, and ensuring the effective regulation of executive power. The importance of ensuring the accountability and democratic regulation of executive power cannot be underestimated, and it should not be taken for granted that the status quo can be improved upon through the use of impeachment.

The second rationale is the inherent legitimacy of the House of Commons in having such an oversight of the use of executive power and the ability of the House of Commons to impose tangible sanctions if there has been serious misconduct through the abuse of this power. The House of Commons has considerable legitimacy due to its democratic nature and the importance of representative democracy in the Westminster system. This makes the House of Commons the most legitimate institution, both in a constitutional and a democratic sense, of checking and regulating executive power and ministerial compliance with the accepted constitutional norms. As to compliance with the legal principles of the constitution, whilst this can be regulated by the courts (i.e., *Miller (No. 2)*), there is a strong case for the House of Commons to have a role in ensuring that the laws that Parliament enacts are observed and that the legal principles developed through the common law are respected by the government, given the importance of these in the operation of the constitution.

The third rationale is that impeachment would provide a role for the House of Commons as the guardian of the constitution and reinstate the House of Commons as the institution that should be able to determine the scope of, and compliance with, the constitution. This is essentially about re-empowering the House of Commons through the modernisation of impeachment and the explicit recognition that impeachment can be used where there has been a breach of accepted constitutional norms and non-compliance with legal principles. Thus, it envisages a partnership between the House of Commons and the courts. It is now necessary to explore these three rationales in more detail.

16.5.1 Enhancing Accountability

The first rationale is enhancing executive accountability. A useful approach when addressing accountability is that of the editors of the *Oxford Handbook of Public Accountability*, where they pose five questions for thinking about accountability: (i) who, (ii) to whom, (iii) for what, (iv) which standards, and (v) why.[31] The rationale for impeachment is that it serves a purpose in reinforcing the constitutional accountability of the executive. With the five questions regarding accountability, it is possible to consider whether impeachment, as reimagined within this chapter, could provide for greater accountability.

The first question to consider is who would be accountable when impeachment is used. Impeachment in England, and then Britain, has traditionally seen a broad range of individuals fall within the scope of those who could be impeached. These individuals included judges, royal advisers, ministers, Lord Chancellors, merchants, bishops, a Governor-General of Bengal, ambassadors, Members of Parliament, a Queen Consort and a minister of religion. It needs to be emphasised that any revised formulation of impeachment would only be concerned with the Head of Government and ministers of the Crown at Westminster. It is appropriate that ministers, as senior actors within the political constitution who exercise considerable statutory and prerogative powers, implement policies, and direct the business of state, should be the focus of impeachment as a constitutional accountability mechanism. The exclusion of the monarch can be justified by the operation of the constitutional monarchy and the limited discretion that the monarch has in the use of his personal prerogative powers.[32] In the case of a monarch who may be perceived to be acting unconstitutionally, the appropriate sanction would be for the government to advise the monarch to abdicate. Even in the case of Edward VIII where there are serious questions about his conduct, there were mechanisms to encourage his abdication, and even if the king had chosen to act in an unconstitutional manner, the government, by relying on its support in Parliament, could have acted without needing to impeach the monarch. Today, it is almost impossible to imagine such a scenario occurring, even if there were some concerns over the activist nature of the then Prince of Wales (now King Charles III) when he became king. The reason for the exclusion of the judiciary from the scope of a revised form of impeachment is that statutory accountability mechanisms already exist in the form of disciplinary measures, for example, in the case of junior judges, by the Lord Chancellor and the Lord Chief Justice in England and Wales; moreover, both Houses of Parliament possess the ability to request the removal of senior judges by way of a resolution.[33]

31 M Bovens, R Goodin and T Schillemans, 'Public Accountability' in M Bovens, R Goodin and T Schillemans (eds), *The Oxford Handbook of Public Accountability* (OUP 2016) 10–13.

32 Impeachment has never been used against a monarch, although it has been used against a Queen Consort.

33 Senior Courts Act 1981 and the Act of Settlement 1701.

Furthermore, if impeachment were to focus on constitutional accountability and the judiciary were to be included within its scope, then there would be the possibility that, in the event of a controversial judicial decision, Members of Parliament could threaten judges with impeachment.[34] If this were to happen, then it would undermine judicial independence, although it is conceded that in the same circumstances, Members of Parliament may seek a resolution to remove the judges concerned.[35] Finally, senior civil servants would not be subject to impeachment, as they can already be dismissed from their position, and within the constitution, it is the minister who is responsible to Parliament.

The second question is to consider to who these individuals are accountable too. As noted earlier, impeachment originated in 1376 and was concerned with the accountability of royal advisors and minor officials to the Commons, in their capacity as the representatives of the country. It was the novel idea that grievances could be presented before the Commons and then brought before the Lords by the Commons, where the Commons would demand a trial and the determination of wrongdoing. There was some uncertainty during the 1370s and 1380s over who controlled the procedure; however, it is clear that the Commons controls the procedure. Central to the justification of the accountability of officials and advisers remains the notion of representative democracy and the role of Members of Parliament in representing their constituents and collectively, the country.[36] This would explain the exclusion of the Lords from the process. It is important to reiterate that whilst the initial impeachment would be brought by the Commons, the Commons would not determine guilt. Therefore, in any revised form of impeachment, guilt would be determined by a Court of Impeachment. Impeachment can be viewed as a hybrid form of accountability that is essentially political in its initial stages but increasingly legal in terms of the determination of wrongdoing.

The third question is for what are they accountable? Traditionally, individuals were impeached for treason and high crimes and misdemeanours, and the definition of an impeachable offence was very wide and could include non-criminal conduct.[37] However, political charges were often rooted out by the Lords,[38] and in the penultimate impeachment, the Lord Chancellor, Lord Thurlow, played a significant role in holding that ordinary law and rules of evidence applied during the trial of Warren Hastings. It is important to note

34 This happened, for example, after Richard II sought advice from his judges as to the use of impeachment, and a number of Charles I's judges were impeached for having supported the king in their judicial decisions.

35 For example, see the motion by nearly 200 Labour Members of Parliament to remove Sir John Donaldson in the 1970s.

36 For further discussion, see AH Birch, *Representative and Responsible Government: An Essay on the British Constitution* (U of Toronto P 1964) 13–17.

37 See the debate between Raoul Berger and Clayton Roberts (Berger (n 16) 67–69; Roberts (n 6) 1419, 1439.

38 See Roberts (n 6) 1419, 1433–34.

that this debate continues in the United States.[39] It is argued here that ministers should be accountable for their official conduct and ensuring that they and their departments, when following official policy, comply with accepted constitutional norms. The revised form of impeachment would not be concerned with the criminal conduct of ministers, as this is best left to the ordinary courts, and it would thus not expedient to retain the formulation of high crimes and misdemeanours. The key aspect of accountability would protect the integrity of the constitution and safeguard important constitutional principles such as the rule of law.

The fourth question is which standards would be applied when the accused is judged. The standards against which an individual would be judged are subject to contrary interpretation. This is because the United Kingdom possesses an uncodified constitution and there is considerable debate about its extent and scope. Therefore, it would be reliant on expert determination, and this would be built into the impeachment process, firstly, through an initial investigation before the House of Commons votes to impeach and secondly, in the form of the Court of Impeachment. This could be problematic, but there would be safeguards built in to protect ministers from a draconian application of constitutional principles that make no allowance for reasonableness.

The final question is why ministers of the Crown should be accountable and why do they believe that they are held to account? Ministers exercise considerable power and through the exercise of their duties, can act contrary to accepted constitutional norms and legal principles. Given the importance of executive accountability in the Westminster system, it could be argued that there is merit in looking at additional ways to complement the existing accountability mechanisms, such as through the use of impeachment as a mechanism to enhance executive accountability.

Impeachment would promote constitutional integrity, as protecting the integrity of the uncodified constitution is central to the rationale of impeachment. Through the ability to sanction breaches of the constitution, impeachment would serve as a deterrent and importantly, would promote a dialogue between the House of Commons and the executive as to the nature and scope of the constitution and the obligations that Members of Parliament would impose upon ministers. Impeachment would be concerned with where a minister is personally blameworthy within the area of ministerial responsibility. It would not be appropriate to impeach a minister for all matters for which they are accountable, such as failings within their department, although a refusal to take responsibility for a policy failure might give rise to an impeachment. It is submitted that impeachment would reinforce the obligations and duties

39 See Berger (n 16) 67–69. Regarding the debate as to whether the offence in the United States needed to be an offence within the ordinary criminal law, see CS Potts, 'Impeachment as a Remedy' (1926) 12 *Saint Louis University Public Law Review* 15; W Lawrence, 'The Law of Impeachment' (1867) 15(11) *The American Law Register* 641.

within the Ministerial Code and empower Parliament in the most extreme cases of constitutional misconduct to hold a minister to account and to be responsible for their conduct.

16.5.2 Impeachment Is Democratic

The second rationale would be that impeachment is democratic, as the impeachment proceedings are brought by the democratically elected lower house. It could be argued that impeachment could be an intrinsically democratic accountability mechanism; this is because the charges would be brought on behalf of the elected House of Commons, and the decision to impeach would be theirs, while it is argued that the House of Lords should no longer be involved with the actual determination of wrongdoing. Impeachment would offer an in-house mechanism to enforce constitutional accountability, which could be instigated by a small number of Members of Parliament and see the House of Commons as the driver behind the process.

A further understanding of this rationale for impeachment is that it counters areas of democratic concern that relate to fears that Parliament is weak and fears about the presidentialism of the executive. There is a genuine concern over the presidentialism of the office of the Prime Minister, which emerged during Tony Blair's premiership and has resurfaced due to Boris Johnson's initial unwillingness to engage with the House of Commons and the short-lived creation of a White House-style press briefing at Downing Street. There are also concerns about the threat of popularism, with the executive willing to erode the rule of law, breach international law or breach constitutional norms to achieve policy.

16.5.3 Guardians of the Constitution

The final rationale, discussed previously, is that Members of Parliament would act as the guardians of the constitution. The role of enforcing accepted constitutional norms and the legal principles of the constitution would be undertaken by the elected representatives rather than left solely to the courts, as it is currently, and this could be useful in negating concerns about judicial power and the increased legalisation of the constitution. To enable Members of Parliament to undertake this role, impeachment would strengthen the powers of the House of Commons, which would have a strong punitive and deterrent factor. This would buttress the existing powers of the House of Commons, which is further explored in the following.

Impeachment would reassert the House of Commons' role as the guardian of the constitution. Just which institution within the United Kingdom has this role and should actively seek to define the accepted the nature and scope of the constitution is a moot point. Historically, impeachment had provided a way for the House of Commons to check the actions of the executive, and it served an important role. Philip Norton has observed that 'impeachment provided the basis for the development of Parliament's scrutiny of administrative actions.'[40] Parliament has been viewed as the grand inquest of the nation to review grievances and misconduct, which was discharged by its ability to impeach, and the development and meanings of this term were considered by Geoffrey Marshall and Graeme Moodie in *Some Problems of the Constitution*.[41]

The Supreme Court's decision in *R (on the application of Miller) v Prime Minister (No. 2)*[42] serves as an illustrative example of the problems of constitutional accountability, the question of which institution should determine the scope of the constitution, and the limitations to the political constitution. The decision to advise the monarch to prorogue Parliament in 2019 was challenged through the courts by ordinary citizens and by a large number of parliamentarians who, because Parliament was prorogued, could not challenge this use of the prerogative through the political constitution. It was the political constitution that the Supreme Court turned to by way of justification when it found that the decision to prorogue Parliament was unlawful as, in addition to restricting parliamentary sovereignty, it also prevented political accountability through the House of Commons being able to hold the government to account. This central role played by the House of Commons in scrutinising executive decision-making was recognised as a principle of the constitution and given legal protection.

A particular criticism of the Supreme Court's decision in *Miller (No. 2)* was that the court was seeking to exercise an improper role in defining the nature of the constitution and acting as a quasi-constitutional court.[43] Given the controversy, it is necessary to briefly consider some of this criticism, which I do not agree with, but it illustrates a certain view that exists among a section of scholars and lawyers. There is, however, considerable support for the Supreme Court in this role, with Mark Elliot arguing that the decision, 'is capable of being simultaneously rooted in orthodoxy ***and*** path-breaking' and was also in part 'mundane'.[44] Furthermore, in a view that I fully support, Elliot notes that

> [i]ndeed, for the Court to have declined to play its part, and to have refused to determine and enforce the legal limits upon the government's authority to suspend Parliament, would have been nothing other than a dereliction of its constitutional duty.[45]

40 P Norton, *Parliament in British Politics* (2nd edn, Palgrave Macmillan 2013) 19.

41 G Marshall and GC Moodie, *Some Problems of the Constitution* (4th edn, Hutchinson University Library 1967) 139.

42 [2019] UKSC 41.

43 For example, see D Wyatt and R Ekins, 'Reforming the Supreme Court' *Policy Exchange* (July 2020) <https://policyexchange.org.uk/wp-content/uploads/Reforming-the-Supreme-Court.pdf> accessed 30 May 2023.

44 M Elliot, 'Constitutional Adjudication and Constitutional Politics in the UK' (2020) 16 *European Constitutional Law Review* 625, 643. See also Paul Craig's critique of the criticism levelled against the decision in 'The Supreme Court, Propagation and Constitutional Principle' (2020) 2 *Public Law* 248.

45 ibid.

Returning to the criticism, John Finnis views the decision as an unnecessary constitutional development: 'This exercise of judicial constitutional creativity is not an authentic constitutional development because there was *no need for it*. There was *no need* – no constitutional need.'[46] Furthermore, according to Finnis, the decision damaged democracy and undermined the rule of law. This is a view that I reject and upon my own reading of the decision, and it cannot be substantiated by the actual judgment. Stephen Laws QC, writing for the Judicial Power Project, regarded the decision in *Miller (No. 2)* as being without reason and 'damaging to the UK's constitutional arrangements.' This in my opinion is clearly not the case and had the opposite effect.[47] Richard Ekins has advocated for wholesale reform of the Supreme Court and has raised concerns regarding the court's role as guardian of the constitution:

> There are reasons to fear that the Supreme Court has begun to understand itself to be a constitutional court, with a responsibility to serve as *the* guardian of the constitution. The Court has been invited to play this role and to some extent has accepted the invitation, with damaging consequences for the rule of law and the integrity of the political constitution.[48]

However, is there anything wrong with the Supreme Court acting as a guardian of the constitution, given the historic role of the courts in defining the constitutional landscape? My answer would be no, and it would not be appropriate to use this and the wider criticism as a justification for reforming the Supreme Court.

This criticism is founded on long-standing concerns over judicial power and the constitutional legitimacy of the judiciary's role in shaping the constitution, especially where this involves the judicial oversight of inherently political decisions. Whilst this can be presented as a threat to the separation of powers, the rule of law and respective institutional competence, notably, this criticism can be countered on the premise of the legitimacy of the Supreme Court in upholding the accepted norms of the constitution and giving effect to key constitutional principles through the protection of the law. I do not agree with this criticism, but I acknowledge that some do agree with the concerns raised. Therefore, what is the point of highlighting concerns over the Supreme

46 J Finnis, 'The Law of the Constitution Before the Court' *Policy Exchange* (2019) 24 <https://policyexchange.org.uk/wp-content/uploads/The-Law-of-the-Constitution-before-the-Court.pdf> accessed 30 May 2023.

47 S Laws, 'The Supreme Court's Unjustified Lawmaking' *Judicial Power Project* (4 October 2019) <https://judicialpowerproject.org.uk/stephen-laws-the-supreme-courts-unjustified-lawmaking/> accessed 30 May 2023.

48 R Ekins, 'Protecting the Constitution: How and Why Parliament Should Limit Judicial Power' *Policy Exchange* (2019) 19 <https://policyexchange.org.uk/wp-content/uploads/2020/01/Protecting-the-Constitution.pdf> accessed 30 May 2023.

Court as a guardian of the constitution and how does impeachment relate to these concerns? The point is that there is scope for empowering politicians by giving them a role in protecting the constitution. Therefore, a form of impeachment that gives the House of Commons the power to determine whether the constitution has been breached would explicitly give the House of Commons an overt role in protecting, defining the scope of, and evolving the constitution (this would operate alongside the ability of Parliament to introduce legislative reforms). One possible advantage of this is that it would counter concerns about the role of the Supreme Court by making it clear that the task of protecting the constitution belongs not only to the courts, through the legal constitution, but also to the House of Commons through the political constitution. This should not be taken as a criticism of the Supreme Court. In my opinion, the Supreme Court has a perfectly valid approach to constitutionalism, and this new approach would be a way of recruiting reinforcements (rather than restricting the court's role) and encouraging a partnership between the House of Commons and the courts.

By reasserting the role of the House of Commons as a guardian of the constitution, this would provide an additional mechanism to protect the constitution. This chapter now explores how impeachment could buttress the existing accountability mechanisms, and the importance of the political constitution (which is dependent on non-legally enforceable constitutional conventions and the inherent discretion of ministers) being protected through the use of impeachment cannot be underestimated. This is the case where the revised form of impeachment, firstly, empowers a small number of Members of Parliament to instigate impeachment proceedings; secondly, such instigation could lead to a time-sensitive review by experts of the perceived wrongdoing even if there are not enough votes in the House of Commons to support impeachment; and thirdly, it carries a range of serious sanctions that may act as a deterrent to ensure initial compliance with accepted constitutional norms.

16.6 Application: How Impeachment Could Buttress Existing Executive Political Accountability Mechanisms

This final section of the chapter considers how impeachment could buttress the existing executive political accountability mechanisms by applying impeachment to recent events that have been argued as amounting to actual or possible breaches of the accepted constitutional norms or legal principles of the constitution. I now outline how impeachment in these examples might be used to enhance accountability in relation to the other accountability mechanisms.

16.6.1 Failure to Comply with a Constitutional Convention

The first example where impeachment could serve a role is the failure of the executive to comply with a constitutional convention. Notably, ministerial performance of duties and impeachment were once connected before the emergence of the convention of individual ministerial responsibility. Birch observed:

> [i]n the early part of the eighteenth century . . . ministers were liable to be impeached by Parliament for the mismanagement of public affairs . . . Impeachment fell into disuse because politicians had come to regard 'the loss of office and public disapprobation as punishments sufficient for errors in the administration not imputable to public corruption'. This clear assumption that a minister would have to resign if an administrative error in his department were exposed and criticized in Parliament was shared by most constitutional lawyers and commentators in the second half of the nineteenth century. It forms the basis of the doctrine of the individual ministerial responsibility of ministers for the work of their departments.[49]

Dicey was clear that impeachment would not be used to enforce conventions as they are not laws,[50] and Marshall and Moodie gave an interesting account of the political and legal aspects of ministerial responsibility, which concerned the use of impeachment.[51]

In terms of a specific example of where impeachment could possibly be used, the following example arguably provides this given the seriousness of the subject matter and evidence for a breach of the convention. In 2018, Theresa May deployed the United Kingdom military to take part in airstrikes against Syria. This military action had not been approved by the House of Commons before it took place, as is required by the constitutional convention that regulates military action. Theresa May was accused of breaching the convention, and Jeremy Corbyn, the Leader of the Opposition, stated that

> [i]t seems the convention established in 2003 and that is in the Cabinet manual is being tossed aside as simply inconvenient. It is necessary and urgent that the House has the opportunity to discuss its rights and responsibilities in respect of decisions on UK military intervention.[52]

A vote was subsequently held. However, it was clear that the Prime Minister did not consider herself in the present circumstances to be bound by the convention and did not believe that it covered the situation. Whilst demonstrating the uncertainty and plurality of views as to what is required by a convention,

49 Birch (n 36) 139.
50 AV Dicey, *Introduction to the Study of the Law of the Constitution* (8th edn, Palgrave Macmillan 1915) 276.
51 Marshall and Moodie (n 41) 59.
52 HC Deb 17 April 2018, vol 639, col 195.

there clearly did appear to be breach of the convention, and impeachment might have been used as a way to register disapproval of the Prime Minister's decision.

16.6.2 Failure to Enforce the Ministerial Code

This next example focuses not on a breach of the Ministerial Code by a minister or the minister's failure to comply with the requirements of the convention of individual ministerial responsibility but with the Prime Minister's failure to enforce the Ministerial Code. The Ministerial Code outlines the duties and requirements that ministers must comply with. It is an important constitutional document, despite not being legal in nature, and supports the political constitution. The only person who can enforce the Code, short of a minister resigning without being told to do so, is the Prime Minister. Priti Patel, the Home Secretary, was accused of bullying civil servants in her role as a minister, and the most senior civil servant in her department resigned and commenced legal proceedings. In 2020, Sir Alex Allan, the Prime Minister's ethics advisor carried out an inquiry that concluded that the Home Secretary's conduct amounted to bullying and that she had breached the Ministerial Code. The Prime Minister decided that the conduct did not in fact breach the Code. In response, Sir Alex Allan resigned.[53] The Prime Minister's decision not to enforce the Ministerial Code has been criticised as undermining accountability, the operation of the Code and a system that is based on principle.[54]

The issue here in terms of where impeachment could possibly play a role could apply not only to Priti Patel's conduct, which if true, is a breach of her duties under the Ministerial Code, but also crucially, to the Prime Minister's refusal to enforce the Code and accept that it had been breached. This is because of the Prime Minister's pivotal role as the enforcer of the Code. It could be argued that the Prime Minister's conduct was contrary to the accepted constitutional norms and that this might be an appropriate matter for impeachment to have been initiated, especially given the importance of the Code in ensuring ministerial accountability and the discretion accorded to the Prime Minister under the current system. Patel's conduct, if found to have breached the Ministerial Code, could be suitable for impeachment, but I would argue the larger issue is the Prime Minister's decision not to find that there has been a breach of the Code.[55]

53 S Murphy, 'Alex Allan: The Veteran Windsurfing Mandarin Who Quit Over Patel Row' *The Guardian* (20 November 2020) <www.theguardian.com/politics/2020/nov/20/alex-allan-the-veteran-windsurfing-mandarin-who-quit-over-bullying> accessed 30 May 2023.

54 C Haddon, 'The Handling of the Priti Patel Bullying Inquiry Has Fatally Undermined the Ministerial Code' *Institute for Government* (20 November 2020) <www.instituteforgovernment.org.uk/blog/priti-patel-bullying-inquiry-undermined-ministerial-code> accessed 30 May 2023.

55 See the recent High Court decision concerning this matter, *R (on the Application of the FDA) v The Prime Minister and Minister for the Civil Service* [2021] EWHC 3279 (Admin).

16.6.3 The Prime Minister's Decision to Advise the Monarch to Prorogue Parliament

Another example where impeachment could have been used is the prorogation controversy, where the Prime Minister advised the monarch to prorogue Parliament for five weeks. This is the use of the prerogative powers in a manner that is inconsistent with the constitution. Traditionally, this has been determined by the courts, but it would be possible for the House of Commons to check the executive's lawful compliance with the accepted limits of prorogation. The Prime Minister's advice was found to be unconstitutional by the Supreme Court in *Miller (No. 2)* and the prorogation void. However, to challenge the decision to prorogue, ordinary citizens and parliamentarians had to rely on the courts, here, the legal mechanism of judicial review, and this led to criticisms of the Supreme Court adjudicating on a political issue and acting as the guardian of the constitution, and it reinforced long-standing concerns about judicial power. I do not think that criticism of the Supreme Court's role as discussed earlier justifies excluding the ability to bring judicial review in these circumstances, and the courts performed a valuable function. I would argue that the availability of a modernised form of impeachment would give parliamentarians another option, which depending on the circumstances, might perhaps be preferable to relying solely on judicial review. At the time of prorogation, the wider political context saw the House of Commons divided along partisan grounds and the then-Speaker of the House of Commons was viewed as having taken a partisan position. However, on a matter of this nature, there will more likely than not be such a division, even if the position of the Speaker is less likely to be as controversial. Even if the then-Speaker had given permission for an impeachment motion to proceed, this would only have been one step in the process, with a specially constituted committee of the House of Commons and independent experts being asked to consider the motion and the strength of the allegations. This would have been the case even if in the exceptional circumstances surrounding Brexit and the position of John Bercow, the granting of permission by the Speaker would have been seen as driven by partisan considerations.

Impeachment in a situation like *Miller (No. 2)* could have been used in three ways: firstly, following the Supreme Court's decision in *Miller (No. 2)*, Members of Parliament could have responded by initiating an impeachment proceeding, which would have kept the issue of unconstitutional action alive and, even if it had not been successful (which it most likely would not have been), it would have demonstrated the seriousness of the Prime Minister's conduct. This is crucial as it would have reinforced the view that the prorogation was unlawful and had a serious impact upon the way in which the constitution operated. Secondly, the existence of impeachment might have been used by parliamentarians as an alternative to litigation. This would have removed the need for the Supreme Court to adjudicate on political matters and would have allowed Parliament, once it was no longer prorogued, to enquire into the probity of the Prime Minister's advice. However, I would reiterate that criticism of the court should not be grounds for removing its role in these circumstances. Thirdly, had impeachment been modernised prior to 2019, then it might have been possible for impeachment to act as a deterrent and moderate the Prime Minister's decision-making. In reality, there were calls to impeach Johnson over prorogation.[56] However, had any impeachment taken place without first engaging in a wholesale reform of the process, this would have reduced the effectiveness of the procedure and highlighted the historical shortcomings.

16.6.4 Failure to Uphold the Rule of Law and Judicial Independence

The next example of where impeachment could have been used is in relation to the perceived failure of Liz Truss, the then-Secretary of State for Justice and Lord Chancellor, to take sufficient steps to support the judiciary following the 'Enemies of the People' headline published by the *Daily Mail* in November 2016.[57] The headline was in response to the High Court's decision to find against the government in *Miller (No. 1)*.[58] It is first necessary to consider the Lord Chancellor's constitutional obligations as outlined in statute. Section 17(2) of the Constitutional Reform Act 2005 requires that the Lord Chancellor take the following oath:

> I [name] do swear that in the office of Lord High Chancellor of Great Britain I will respect the rule of law, defend the independence of the judiciary and discharge my duty to ensure the provision of resources for the efficient and effective support of the courts for which I am responsible. So help me God.

This oath is intended to protect two important constitutional principles, specifically, the rule of law and judicial independence. The Lord Chancellor, due to the nature of the office, is in a unique position as a minister, and the role requires officeholders to take their constitutional obligations seriously.

Returning to the aftermath of the 'Enemies of the People' headline, Liz Truss delayed responding to the headline and eventually gave what was perceived to be an unsatisfactory response. Senior judges were critical of the

56 L Saville Roberts, 'Boris Johnson Led the Charge to Impeach Tony Blair for Betraying Our Trust: What's so Different Now?' *The Times* (29 September 2019) <www.thetimes.co.uk/article/boris-johnson-led-the-charge-to-impeach-tony-blair-over-iraq-qrl9zhz2k> accessed 30 May 2023.

57 J Slack, 'Enemies of the People: Fury Over "Out of Touch" Judges Who Have "Declared War on Democracy" by Defying 17.4m Brexit Voters and Who Could Trigger Constitutional Crisis' *Daily Mail* (4 November 2016) <www.dailymail.co.uk/news/article-3903436/Enemies-people-Fury-touch-judges-defied-17-4m-Brexit-voters-trigger-constitutional-crisis.html> accessed 30 May 2023.

58 *R (on the Application of Miller) v Secretary of State for Exiting the European Union* [2016] EWHC 2768 (Admin).

Lord Chancellor's conduct. A former judge, Sir Stephen Sedley, criticised Truss by observing that '[t]he failure of . . . Liz Truss . . . to do anything to defend the three senior judges . . . is evidence enough of the fragility of judicial independence.'[59] In March 2017, Lord Thomas, the Lord Chief Justice of England and Wales, criticised Liz Truss's failure to defend judicial independence as required by her statutory oath:

> 'I regret to have to criticise her as severely as I have, but to my mind she was completely and absolutely wrong. And I am very disappointed,' he said. 'I can understand how the pressures were on in November, but she has taken a position that is constitutionally, absolutely wrong.' It was Truss's duty, as lord chancellor, to defend the judges, he said.[60]

Despite the criticism of Truss and conduct that was arguably against accepted constitutional norms, Truss remained in office as she had the support of the Prime Minister. Impeachment could have been used here as an initial deterrent or used by Members of Parliament to commence an investigation into Truss's perceived failure, which, even if it had not proceeded and only reached the report stage, would have been a public condemnation of the Lord Chancellor's response. This would be an example of where impeachment could protect the legal principles of the constitution, which Parliament had enacted, and where there might not be a prospect of bringing the matter to the courts.

16.6.5 An Inquiry into the Legality of the Iraq War

The next example is controversy surrounding the legality of the Iraq War and the decision to hold a public inquiry. The Chilcot Inquiry was criticised as being too costly and too slow, and the findings were obscured by delay and the depth of coverage.[61] Whilst there was an attempt to impeach Tony Blair in 2004 in relation to the invasion of Iraq in 2003, had a revised form of impeachment been available, then this could have served as an alternative to a public inquiry and could have considered the constitutional conduct of the Prime Minister.[62]

59 S Sedley, 'Judicial Independence Is a Fragile Thing' *The Financial Times* (27 January 2017) <www.ft.com/content/abd56378-e3e0-11e6-9645-c9357a75844a> accessed 30 May 2023.

60 O Bowcott, 'Lord Chief Justice Attacks Liz Truss for Failing to Back Article 50 Judges' *The Guardian* (22 March 2017) <www.theguardian.com/politics/2017/mar/22/lord-chief-justice-castigates-liz-truss-for-failing-to-defend-judges> accessed 30 May 2023.

61 See 'Iraq War: Everything You Need to Know About the Chilcot Inquiry' *ITV News* (5 July 2016) <www.itv.com/news/2016-07-05/iraq-war-what-is-the-chilcot-inquiry> accessed 30 May 2023; A Beckett, 'Revelation or Whitewash – What Can We Expect from the Chilcot Inquiry?' *The Guardian* (4 July 2016) <www.theguardian.com/uk-news/2016/jul/04/chilcot-inquiry-iraq-war-whitewash> accessed 30 May 2023.

62 For commentary on this attempt, see G Rangwala and D Plesch, 'A Case to Answer: A First Report on the Potential Impeachment of the Prime Minister for High Crimes and Misdemeanours in Relation to the Invasion of Iraq' (August 2004); O Gay and N Davies, 'Impeachment'

The advantage of impeachment would be to take the impetus for reviewing misconduct and controversies away from the executive. Public inquiries are at the discretion of the government and are criticised as too long-winded and costly, which buys time for the government and does not address problems at the relevant time. A modernised form of impeachment would give the power to initiate proceedings to the House of Commons. It would contain a process to permit an independent review of the alleged misconduct within a specific period of time, even if the Members of Parliament initiating the impeachment ultimately lack the votes in the House of Commons to impeach the Prime Minister.

16.6.6 Misleading the House of Commons

Finally, the allegations that the Prime Minister misled the House of Commons in December 2021 over his knowledge of parties happening in Downing Street, during a period in which people in England were subject to legal restrictions because of the Covid-19 pandemic, is clear evidence of a breach of the Ministerial Code. This view in my opinion is reinforced by the fact the Prime Minster (amongst others) was issued with (and paid) a Fixed Penalty Notice by the Metropolitan Police. It is arguable that a modernised form of impeachment could be used in conjunction with, or separately to, the investigation that is carried out by the Commons Privileges Committee. Here, the government permitted its Members of Parliament a free vote on whether to refer the Prime Minister's conduct for investigation, but there may be situations where this would not be the case, and any attempt at a referral could fail. In these circumstances, an impeachment attempt could be initiated by a small number of Members of Parliament, and under the procedure that I propose, this would include an investigation and a report by experts, even where the actual vote on whether to impeach would not succeed due to the government's majority.

16.7 Conclusion

It is acknowledged that the subject matter of this chapter may appear to be controversial and raise questions as to whether there is any need for the use of impeachment (albeit in a modernised form) and whether any reforms could overcome the longstanding concerns over political partisanship, the rule of law, human rights and due process. Furthermore, it invites the question as to whether, in reality, there is a real problem with the exercise of executive power by the government and as a consequence, whether there are shortcomings in the ability of the House of Commons to hold the government to account.

House of Commons Library, Standard Note (16 November 2011). Note that an updated version is available.

It was argued in this chapter that there are justifications for the use of a modernised form of impeachment that would draw heavily on the use of impeachment in Denmark (which has a hybrid Court of Impeachment, but unlike Denmark, I am not proposing that the court should be able to impose a custodial sentence). This chapter is intended to encourage debate as to whether the accountability of the executive is insufficient within the Westminster system, whether the accepted norms of the constitution require safeguarding, whether there is legitimacy in empowering the House of Commons to take on a greater role as a guardian of the constitution, and whether impeachment might in part help to remedy any deficiencies and achieve the desired goals in terms of accountability and respect for the constitution.

Part V

Futures

17 Impeachment in Comparative Perspective

An Empirical View

*Tom Ginsburg, Aziz Z. Huq and David Landau**

17.1 Introduction

Removal of a chief executive is a necessary power in any political system, whether presidential, parliamentary, or otherwise. Even traditional monarchies had procedures for removing kings who were incapacitated or incompetent. During the Middle Ages, the question of monarchical removal became a central problem for English constitutional theory: between 1327 and 1485, five English monarchs were deposed.[1] Today, however, the removal of a president from office by a mechanism other than through the regular operation of elections, term limits, and the normal apparatus of political selection goes to the core of democratic governance. It is, by any measure, an extreme action. But this is a moment of increasing popular discontent with established regimes, coupled with a growing polarization within the voting public of many democracies.[2] The legitimacy of chief executives is being strained, and claims against them include anti-democratic entrenchment, corruption, and sometimes even stolen elections. Under such conditions, it is perhaps unsurprising that elected tenures would prove to be fragile and talk of preemptive removal and impeachment endemic.

This chapter examines impeachment from a global perspective by accounting for the ways in which it is set up and used in diverse national contexts. Primarily, this is a matter of constitutional law: the design of removal procedures for chief executives is almost uniformly a matter of constitutional text, not statutory policy. This reflects an assumption that the question is an important one to be insulated, to some extent, from transient politics. The examination

* This chapter draws, with permission, from T Ginsburg, AZ Huq and D Landau, 'The Comparative Constitutional Law of Presidential Impeachment' (2021) 88 *University of Chicago Law Review* 81.

1 WH Dunham and CT Wood, 'The Right to Rule in England: Depositions and the Kingdom's Authority, 1327–1485' [1976] *The American Historical Review* <https://doi.org/10.1086/ahr/81.4.738>.

2 J McCoy, T Rahman and M Somer, 'Polarization and the Global Crisis of Democracy: Common Patterns, Dynamics, and Pernicious Consequences for Democratic Polities' (2018) 62(1) *American Behavioral Scientist* 16.

DOI: 10.4324/9781003256007-22

of impeachment provisions and practices globally is relevant to a number of questions fundamental to a democracy. A global view of impeachment can illuminate its potential function in a constitutional democracy and hence suggest how its scope and mechanisms might be reconciled with electoral democracy. This sets up the following questions. When should a democratic mandate be superseded because of the perceived costs of allowing the people's choice to remain in power after some form of wrongdoing? If supersession is to be allowed, should it be through a political process (defined and judged according to partisan standards) or a more formalized, law-governed process (for example, as defined by the criminal law)?

The focus of this chapter is primarily on fixed-term executives who tend to be called presidents. Such officials are found in an array of political systems, including presidential systems, semi-presidential systems,[3] and even some parliamentary systems. It includes heads of state in parliamentary systems who tend to have a more ceremonial role but excludes prime ministers (who are typically disciplined instead through a parliamentary 'vote of confidence' mechanism).[4]

A global survey reveals that impeachment does not always focus on the criminal behavior or bad acts of an individual president. Rather, it also serves as a response to a particular kind of political crisis in a presidential system, usually occurring when public support for the leader has collapsed. Some recent impeachments, such as that of Park Geun-hye in South Korea, include crisis combined with evidence of criminality to oust a president from office. But in other cases, such as in Brazil and Paraguay, presidents were removed with scant evidence of apex criminality. Removal was instead used to push out weak presidents who had lost the ability to govern. Consistent with this practice, many constitutions around the world include a textual standard for removal that explicitly goes beyond criminality to include governance failures or poor performance in office, while other provisions enable such an approach through ambiguity. Impeachment globally is, in practice, a device to mitigate the risk of paralyzing political gridlock rather than simply a way to deal with individual malfeasance. A second important empirical conclusion follows. When examining measures of democratic quality in the wake of impeachment, we find no evidence (at least in the small sample of extant cases) that impeachment of a president reduces the quality of democracy in countries where it is carried out. The same holds true when removal through impeachment is attempted but not completed. The fear that a more political impeachment process would necessarily be destabilizing has no empirical support in the recent comparative experience. Rather than undermining or circumventing democracy, impeachment may play an important role in its stabilization.

3 R Elgie, 'Variations on a Theme' (2005) 16(3) *Journal of Democracy* 98 <https://doi.org/10.1353/jod.2005.0045>.

4 JD Huber, 'The Vote of Confidence in Parliamentary Democracies' (1996) 90 *American Political Science Review* 269.

17.2 Impeachment in Constitutional Design

It is very common for democratic constitutions to provide for removal of the head of state under some conditions. As of 2017, 90 percent of presidential and semi-presidential regimes had constitutional rules that laid out a process for removal, either for incompetence, criminal action, or some other basis. The procedures differ widely on issues such as the basis for dismissal, the process of proposal for dismissal, the process of approval, the period of the term of office within which the President's mandate can be revoked, and the timing of different steps. The fact of constitutional entrenchment does not necessarily preclude the enactment of statutes with important effects on the process. We mainly focus here on constitutional text but note that due caution should be exercised in drawing inferences about how this text interacts with statutory supplements or institutional cultures. We ask three questions. First, what warrants impeachment? Second, what process is utilized? And third, what is the effect of impeachment?

On the first question, Table 17.1 summarizes the bases for removal of heads of state as of 2017, as set forth in national constitutional texts. Note that many constitutions provide for multiple alternative grounds for removal, and so there is no reason we would expect the percentages to sum to one.

Table 17.1 Basis for Removing Heads of State[5]

Basis	*Number of all constitutions providing for removal (n=149)*	*%*	*Presidential & semi-presidential democracies only (n=68)*	*%*
Crimes	88	59	43	63
Violations of the Constitution	69	46	19	28
Incapacity	55	37	19	28
Treason	51	34	19	28
General dissatisfaction	20	13	7	10
Other	29	19	10	15

5 Presidential and semi-presidential democracies are coded by the Democracy and Dictatorship Dataset, as supplemented by Christian Bjørnskov and Martin Rode. JA Cheibub, J Gandhi and JR Vreeland, 'Democracy and Dictatorship Revisited' (2010) 143 *Public Choice* 67 <https://doi.org/10.1007/s11127-009-9491-2>; Christian Bjørnskov and Martin Rode, 'Regime Types and Regime Changes: A New Dataset' manuscript, August 2018 <www.christianbjoernskov.com/wp-content/uploads/2018/08/Regimes-and-Regime-Change-August-2018.pdf> accessed 23 February 2023.

Table 17.1 illustrates that the most common basis for head of state removal is criminal misconduct. But apart from the United States, constitutions generally do not stipulate a requirement that crimes be 'high.' Indeed, the phrase 'high crimes' seems to be limited to constitutions directly influenced by the American one, including those of Palau, the Marshall Islands, and the Philippines. Of these, only the Philippines is a true presidential system. Its formulation is that the president and other high officials can be removed 'on impeachment for, and conviction of, culpable violation of the Constitution, treason, bribery, graft and corruption, other **high crimes,** or betrayal of public trust.'[6] At first glance, this seems quite similar to the language of the U.S. Constitution. But the Philippines model of impeachment sweeps beyond the domain of criminal offenses to cover *constitutional* wrongs and 'corruption,' which might include but not be exhausted by formal criminal offenses. In this regard, even the Philippines model may extend beyond the focus on individual criminality.

Beyond criminal offenses, violations of the constitution or the president's oath of office are also a common predicate for removal. A violation of the constitution may or may not be a crime in a particular political system, but nonetheless, such a violation obviously goes to the core of the constitutional order. Several countries in Africa stipulate that the violation must be 'willful.'[7] This possibility has gradually fallen out of constitutional practice in the United States.

The most interesting category is what we label 'general dissatisfaction' in Table 17.1, which covers a variety of situations. In many countries, more general grounds for removal blur the canonical distinction between presidential and parliamentary systems. For example, the Constitution of Ghana allows the President to be removed by a two-thirds vote in the legislative assembly for conducting himself in a manner 'i. which brings or is likely to bring the high office of President into disrepute, ridicule or contempt; or ii. prejudicial or inimical to the economy or the security of the State,' and for reasons of incapacity or 'violations of the oath of office'.[8] This formulation blends two different grounds for removal: policy dissatisfaction and misconduct. Similarly, in Tanzania, the President can be removed if he 'has conducted himself in a manner which lowers the esteem of the office of President of the United Republic.'[9] Uganda's Constitution allows the president to be removed for 'conduct that brings hatred or contempt to office of president.'[10] Honduras allows impeachment to proceed against 'actions contrary to the Constitution of the Republic or the national interest and for manifest negligence, inability,

6 Constitution of Philippines, art IX, sec 2 (1987).
7 See Constitution of Gambia, art 67(1) (1996); Constitution of Uganda, art 107(1) (1995); Constitution of Zimbabwe, art 97(1) (2013); Constitution of Ghana, art 69(1)(a) (1996).
8 Constitution of Ghana, art 69(1)(b) (1996).
9 Constitution of Tanzania, art 46A (1977).
10 Constitution of Uganda, art 107(1)(b)(i) (1995).

Table 17.2 Most Common Removal Procedures as of 2017 for All Constitutions (n = 194)

Who can propose? (n)	*Legislative threshold to propose (n)*	*Who approves? (n)*	*Legislative threshold to approve (n)*
Lower house (100)	2/3 (53)	*Court/constitutional council (61)*	2/3 (54)
Both houses required (19)	Majority (20)	*Lower house (50)*	3/4 (10)
Court/constitutional council (9)	3/4 (7)	*Upper house (17)*	Majority (7)
Upper house (6)	3/5 (3)	*Both houses required (17)*	Other (3)
Cabinet (5)	Other (30)	*Public through referendum (12)*	–
Prime minister (4)	–	*Cabinet (2)*	–
Public through recall (4)	–	–	–

or incompetence in the exercise of office.'[11] These standards seem to spill over into the distinctly political bases of removal that characterize the parliamentary system, in which the head of government is dependent on the parliament for continued tenure. Like parliamentary systems, in many cases, a legislature in a presidential system can remove the executive under relatively broad criteria.

The second question concerns the process by which impeachment occurs. Processes of removal typically involve multiple phases and different institutions. They are also characterized by different voting thresholds (sometimes within the same document) and time limits. These procedural details also sometimes vary along with the basis of the charge for removal. This means that there is a good deal of complexity and variety. Table 17.2 provides the most common thresholds and actors for all independent countries as of 2017.

Impeachment is, as Table 17.2 suggests, a predominantly legislative procedure. This means that it requires the aggregation of votes in one or more houses of a legislative body. Even if not called impeachment, head of state removal typically begins with action in the legislature, either in the lower house, the upper house, or both houses acting jointly. The most common vote threshold is a two-thirds vote. Whether or not the legislature proposes removal, it often has a role in approving the process. Again, the modal threshold is a two-thirds vote. There are some interesting variations. When the legislature is bicameral, it is quite common for an upper house or the two chambers acting jointly to be the body to approve the motion to remove a leader. In Ireland, which has a non-executive president, two-thirds of either house can propose impeachment, in which case the other house tries the case and can

11 Constitution of Hond, art 234 (1982).

remove with a two-thirds vote. In a small number of cases, the legislative role is also nondiscretionary. For example, in Fiji, the Prime Minister can propose the removal of the President. Whether removal occurs in the case of allegations of misbehavior is then determined by a tribunal of three judges.[12] Parliament is required to accept the judgment of the panel.[13]

Legislative procedures sometimes involve constitutionally mandated actions by legislative committees or other subparts of the chamber. In Tanzania, a written notice must be signed and backed by at least 20 percent of the Members of Parliament to be submitted to the Speaker of Parliament at least 30 days prior to the sitting at which the motion of dismissal is to be moved.[14] The next stage entails a Special Committee of Inquiry, whose membership is to be voted upon by members of Parliament.[15] This is formed to investigate the charges levied against the President. During this period of inquiry, the office of President is deemed vacant. After receiving a report from the Special Committee, the National Assembly discusses the report and can approve the charges by a two-thirds supermajority vote of all MPs, in which case the President is removed.[16]

The role of the judiciary in impeachment processes is complex and varied. At one end of the spectrum is the United States, where the Constitution gives no role to the courts.[17] On the other end of the scale is Honduras. There, until a 2013 amendment, the *only* body with the power to remove high officials such as the president was the country's Supreme Court. Most constitutions steer a middle course between these poles. Rather than adopting a corner solution and more in keeping with a quasi-legal conception of impeachment, courts in many countries have a role in approving the removal of the president. But the judicial role in impeachment varies quite widely. In some cases, courts may be limited to ensuring that impeachment procedures are being carried out using the proper procedures by political actors. In others, such as the South Korean constitution, courts may become involved at the final, trial-like stage of impeachment, after the legislature has made an initial decision as to whether impeachment is justified. A few constitutions also have multiple tracks for impeachment, with some dominated by the courts and some dominated by legislators. For example, the Colombian constitution provides that if the President is impeached for a 'crime in the exercise of functions' or 'unworthiness for bad conduct,' the House impeaches, and the final trial for removal is before the Senate.[18] But where a president is impeached for a com-

12 See Constitution of Fiji, art 89.

13 ibid ('In deciding whether to remove the President from office, Parliament must act in accordance with the advice given by the tribunal').

14 See Constitution of Tanzania, art 46A(3)(a).

15 ibid art 46A(3)(b), (4).

16 ibid art 46A(9).

17 This has been affirmed by the US Supreme Court, *Nixon v United States*, 506 US 224 (1993).

18 Constitution of Colombia, art 175 (1991).

mon crime, the final trial instead occurs before the Criminal Chamber of the Supreme Court. The Brazilian constitution contains a similar provision, with roughly the same bifurcation of trial procedures between the Supreme Court and the Senate.[19]

The identity of the judicial body tasked with impeachment-related functions can also vary. In some cases, a special chamber is established, while in others, a constitutional court takes on the role as one of its ancillary powers. Lebanon utilizes a mixed committee, called a Supreme Council, whose sole task is to impeach the President and Ministers.[20] This Council comprises seven Deputies specially elected by the Chamber of Deputies and the eight highest-ranking judges in the country. These 15 members can then make final impeachment decisions with a two-thirds vote.

Finally, the public has a role in impeachment in several countries. In some cases, the public must approve the removal of the President by referendum. For example, in the Gambia, the Constitution allows a vote of no confidence by the legislature, proposed by one-third of members and approved by a two-thirds majority, in which case a referendum is called for the public to endorse or reject the decision.[21] In the Austrian semi-presidential system, the legislature can call a referendum on the president's impeachment, which requires a two-thirds vote of the upper house; if the referendum fails, the upper house is disbanded.[22] In Colombia, members the public may file complaints against the President or other officials in the House of Representatives, which must then assess them as the basis for any impeachment resolution before the Senate.[23] A two-thirds vote in the Senate is also required.

In keeping with their populist rhetorical emphasis on the 'people,' several of the so-called Bolivarian constitutions of Latin America also give the public a role in a recall procedure that shares some features with impeachment. In Bolivia and Ecuador, the public can initiate the revocation of the mandate of the President with 15 percent of registered voters proposing it.[24] There are temporal restrictions: in Bolivia it can only be invoked after at least half the term has elapsed, while in Ecuador, it can be initiated only after the first year (and in both countries so long as at least one year remains in the presidential term).[25] Similarly, in Venezuela, 20 percent of registered voters can petition for a referendum to dismiss the President after at least half the term has elapsed.[26] Only one petition to remove the President can be filed during the term of office. The absolute number of voters in favor of dismissal must be

19 See Constitution of Brazil, art 86 (1988).
20 See Constitution of Lebanon, art 80 (1926).
21 See Constitution of Gambia, art 63 (1997).
22 See Constitution of Austria, art 60(6) (1920).
23 See Constitution of Colombia, art 178(4) (1991).
24 See Constitution of Bolivia, art 250 (2009); Constitution of Ecuador, art 105 (2008).
25 ibid.
26 See Constitution of Venezuela, art 72 (1999).

equal to or greater than the number of voters who elected the President, and voters in favor of the dismissal must be equal to or greater than 25 percent of the total number of registered voters.

The third and final question relates to the consequences of impeachment. Often, this is simple: a successful impeachment process typically leads to the immediate removal of the chief executive. Sometimes, the president is suspended from serving after the initial vote until the final resolution of the process. Failed procedures can also have formal and informal consequences, however. For example, Tanzania also has a feature of removal procedures that looks parliamentary in character.[27] If at the end of the process the vote for removal fails, no new motion can be brought for 20 months. This means that the president can be somewhat insulated from repeated use of impeachment procedures via an institutional design that resembles parliamentary systems, which often insulate prime ministers from votes of no confidence for a period of time after a failed attempt.

In contrast, where an impeachment does go through, ouster may not be its sole effect. In addition to removal from office, constitutional impeachment provisions also envisage lifetime (or more limited) bans on holding public office, criminal punishment, and new elections. Hence, a first important constitutional choice concerns whether an impeached executive may run again. Some constitutions ban a convicted president from ever running again for the presidency. In 2004, shortly after being impeached, Rolandas Paksas of Lithuania made clear his desire to run again in the next presidential election. In anticipation, the legislature passed a constitutional amendment prohibiting an impeached leader from competing again for office. The European Court of Human Rights struck down this ban in 2011, holding that it was disproportionate.[28] Other constitutions impose shorter prohibitions. In Brazil, for instance, the constitutional text states an eight-year ban from office upon removal.[29] This ban was imposed after Fernando Collor was removed in 2002. During the impeachment of Dilma Rousseff in 2016, the Congress was allowed to hold two separate votes: the first removed her from office, but the second imposed no ban on future runs.

A second important design choice involves the interaction between removal from office and criminal prosecution. Generally, removed presidents are not protected from criminal responsibility for their actions, but as in the United States, the process of prosecution is often separated from that of removal from office. For example, in Ukraine,[30] a president can

27 See Constitution of Tanzania, art 46A(2) ('[N]o such motion shall be moved within twenty months from the time when a similar motion was previously moved and rejected by the National Assembly').

28 Case of *Paksas v Lithuania*, Judgment 34932/04, 6 January 2011 (Grand Chamber, ECHR).

29 Constitution of Brazil, art 52 sole paragraph.

30 Constitution of Ukraine, art 175 (1996).

be removed from office by the Senate after a hearing. Although the Senate cannot impose criminal charges, it can refer the matter to a court for prosecution after removal. Many constitutions allow for prosecution after leaving office.

A third, particularly important design decision about removal is whether or not it triggers a new election. In the United States, for example, removal leads to the Vice President assuming the office of the presidency for the remainder of the term. Brazil, which has removed two presidents since its return to democracy, follows the same design. But this practice is neither necessary nor particularly common. It is actually far more common for presidential and semi-presidential systems to respond to the removal of a president with new elections rather than to allow a substitute (such as a vice president) to serve out the remainder of the term automatically. For example, in South Korea, the removal of Park Geun-hye in 2017 was followed by a new presidential election. In presidential or semi-presidential constitutions that speak to the issue, 74 percent (51 out of 69) provide for new elections within a short period; the remainder provide for a vice president or other official to complete the remaining term automatically.

17.3 Impeachment in Practice

The ubiquity of constitutional text on impeachment is matched by a similar pervasiveness of attempts to remove presidents. Although attempts are not rare, they are rarely successful. Writing in 2010, Samuels and Shugart reported that out of 223 individuals elected in presidential democracies from 1946 to 2007, only six were ultimately impeached.[31] More recently, Young Hun Kim noted that some 45 percent of new presidential democracies faced an impeachment attempt in the period of 1974–2003 and that nearly a quarter of presidents who served in this period were subjected to an attempt.[32] These attempts vary widely in seriousness, ranging from mere calls by some set of legislators for impeachment to full formal votes in the parliament. When defined as a mere proposal in the legislature, attempts are exceedingly common. Supplementing Kim's data, we gathered data on all such attempts since 1990 and found at least 154 proposals in 63 countries against 132 different heads of state. Using Kim's fourfold framework for level of attempt, we identified the highest level of seriousness in each attempt and report these in Table 17.3. Although there is some difficulty distinguishing different attempts, the overall data indicate well over 200 proposals of various levels of seriousness.

31 DJ Samuels and MS Shugart, *Presidents, Parties, and Prime Ministers: How the Separation of Powers Affects Party Organization and Behavior* (CUP 2011).

32 HK Young, 'Impeachment and Presidential Politics in New Democracies' (2014) 21(3) *Democratization 519* <https://doi.org/10.1080/13510347.2012.751973>.

Table 17.3 Frequency of Impeachment Attempts 1990–2018

Level	*1990–99*	*2000–2009*	*2010–18*	*Total*
1=proposal by some deputies to impeach	38	81	35	154
2=attempt to place the question on the parliamentary agenda	26	36	10	72
3=parliament votes on whether to impeach	3	11	6	20
4=parliament passes an impeachment vote	7	8	8	23
Head of state actually leaves office[33]	5	7	8	17
Removal through impeachment	3	4	3	10

These attempts are not uniformly distributed. Impeachment is quite common in some countries: Ukraine, for example, has featured 25 different proposals in the 28 year-period we examine. Other countries with frequent calls include Nigeria (17), South Korea (14), Ecuador (13), the Philippines (12), and Brazil (11). Russia had 14 attempts in the tumultuous 1990s but none since Vladimir Putin came to power.

As the last row in Table 17.3 demonstrates, successful removal by impeachment is a rarity. We identify 10 total cases since 1990. Close inspection of these cases suggests that successful removal typically involves a situation in which the opposition has control of the parliament and is also able to convince some members of the president's party to defect. But this is not likely to occur because of certain structural features. Both attempts and removals are more frequent when the president is unpopular and does not have a majority of support in the legislature. They often occur in the context of structural shifts in the larger party system.

Presidential systems are characterized by single individuals who enjoy popular appeal but may not necessarily have strong roles within their own parties. Party leaders may have a good deal of trouble controlling their presidential candidate once in office. Although one might assume that this would lead to parties turning against their presidents on occasion, the linked electoral fates of parties in the legislative and executive branches mean that they have relatively weak incentives to do so (even if they control the levers of impeachment or removal). At the very least, to impeach one's own party leader implies that the party was incompetent in choosing the person as a candidate. Worse, it might catalyze a fragmentation of the party, as the spurned leader breaks off with his or her own political coalition.

33 This row includes some cases in which an impeachment vote was held, but the president was either removed beforehand or resigned and so does not count as being formally removed by impeachment. For example, President Victor Yanukovych was deposed in Ukraine's Orange Revolution of 2014 and fled Ukraine. Parliament voted to remove him from office for being unable to fulfill his duties but did not pass formal articles of impeachment.

To illustrate why removing presidents is so difficult even when their own party turns against them, consider the attempt to dismiss President Ranasinghe Premadasa of Sri Lanka. In 1991, a motion to impeach Premadasa was raised in the parliament and was supported by some members of his own party who came from a higher caste. Premadasa was able to expel dissident members, who then, in accordance with the text of the Sri Lankan Constitution, lost their seats in parliament. Another instance of a failed attempt in a presidential system to use impeachment for intraparty conflict includes South Korea's Roh Moo-hyun. After a party split left him with minority support in the National Assembly, Roh was impeached, but the country's Constitutional Court found that the violations were insufficiently severe to justify removal from office. An election held between the National Assembly decision and the proceedings before the Court indicated that the public still supported Roh. Under these circumstances, removal was unlikely to occur.

In the context of pure presidential systems, we were able to locate one case of a party's legislative majority voting to remove its own president. This case was Raul Cubas Grau in Paraguay, in 1999, who resigned after his impeachment by the Chamber of Deputies and just before a Senate vote that would have completed his removal from office. Cubas had won the party's nomination only because the party leader had been jailed for a coup attempt. After a political assassination, another faction in his party attempted to impeach him in favor of its preferred candidate. This was successful after a period of political turmoil. This is a rare instance in which the party in question truly dominates the political scene and all levers of power. Intraparty fights thus take the place without the specter of party-against-party competition that typically characterizes general elections.

At the same time, it is sometimes the case that a handful of members of a president's party will join with others in an impeachment motion or threat. Such was the case when Richard Nixon resigned under threat of impeachment in 1974. Other examples involving impeachment or related mechanisms include Ecuador's Abdala Bucaram in 1997 and Jamil Mahuad in 2000, Paraguay's Cubas Grau (discussed earlier) in 1999, Venezuela's Carlos Andres Perez in 1993, and Guatemala's Otto Perez Molina in 2015.[34] In 2005, Ecuador's Congress deposed Lucio Gutierrez from office for abandoning his duties, though it did not have to complete the impeachment process because of his resignation. In these cases, individual legislators' interests plainly diverged from those of the party, perhaps because of differences in the consistencies represented by different legislators within the same party or perhaps because of ideological divisions within the party.

What happens in the rare circumstances in which an impeachment is successful? Table 17.4 presents all the cases of successful removal of directly elected presidents through impeachment since 1990 (and goes beyond the

34 In 2015 in Guatemala, the country's Attorney General presented a motion for impeachment that was unanimously approved by the Supreme Court. The President was facing allegations of corruption. After the vote by the Supreme Court, the President submitted a resignation that was unanimously accepted by Congress. Congress also unanimously voted to strip him of his immunity from prosecution. This vote by Congress can thus be seen as akin to impeachment.

Table 17.4 Successful Presidential Removals Involving Impeachment Since 1990

Country	*Year*	*President*	*Change in Polity score from t–2 to t+2*
Brazil	1992	Fernando Collor	0
Venezuela	1993	Carlos Andres Perez[35]	0
Madagascar	1996	Albert Zafy	–2
Peru	2000	Alberto Fujimori[36]	+8
Philippines	2001	Joseph Estrada	0
Indonesia	2001	Abdurrahman Wahid	0
Lithuania	2004	Rolandes Paksas[37]	0
Paraguay	2012	Fernando Lugo	+1
Brazil	2016	Dilma Rouseff	0
South Korea	2017	Park Geun-hye	0
Peru	2020	Martin Vizcaira	Not available

Source: Archigos dataset supplemented by authors

data in Table 17.3 which end in 2018). It shows that the phenomenon is not unknown. But it is also not particularly common. It represents well less than half of 1% of all country-years in which impeachment might have occurred.

The final column also offers a threshold piece of evidence of the impact of impeachment on the political system. It does this by tracking whether the country's level of democracy improves or declines as a result of impeachment. To measure democracy, we use the widely utilized Polity2 index, which rates democratic quality on a 21-point scale ranging from -10 (total autocracy) to +10 (total democracy). By convention, scores of 6 or higher are considered full democracies. Notably, *every* country that successfully impeached a president remained a full democracy thereafter, in most cases, without any change in the level of democracy. Even Madagascar, where President Albert Zafy was impeached in 1996, remained a full democracy a few years later. The impeachment of Abdurrahman Wahid in Indonesia, which occurred just two years after the country became a democracy, was part of the country's democratic growing pains. As a result, it soon thereafter moved from the marginal score of 6 to an 8. Peru's impeachment of Alberto Fujimori occurred as part of the restoration of democracy after his period of autocratic rule, and we therefore see a similar movement in that case.

35 The Perez removal may have been irregular. Congress declared the post 'permanently vacant' after Perez fled the country without waiting for the Court's impeachment trial to finish, and the Supreme Court issued a preliminary ruling declaring the complaint to be well-founded.

36 Paksas was impeached for violating the Lithuanian constitution and his oath of office. His impeachment followed news that he had granted citizenship to a Russian businessman who was the main contributor to his campaign. After being found guilty by the Seimas (National Parliament), he was removed from office on the same day. See TD Clark and E Verseckaitė, 'PaksasGate: Lithuania Impeaches a President' (2005) 52(3) *Problems of Post-Communism* 16 <https://doi.org/10.1080/10758216.2005.11052200>.

37 Fujimori had already fled the country in response to allegations of corruption and attempted to resign, but Congress insisted on completing the impeachment proceeding.

To this list could be added several instances in which impeachment occurred, but the President was not removed, either because he or she was not convicted or because of extraconstitutional action. Of course, U.S. Presidents Bill Clinton and Donald Trump are examples of impeached but not convicted presidents. Russian president Boris Yeltsin was impeached in the early 1990s but dissolved parliament to stay in office. Similarly, Alberto Fujimori's 'self-coup' in 1992 was followed by a vote to remove him, but Fujimori had already dissolved Congress. There are also cases in which some kind of vote was held, and the president departed but not through impeachment. In addition, there have been at least eight formal impeachment attempts since 1990 that did not pass the legislature. Only the Russian case led to a significant decline in the Polity score, which occurred when Russia could be characterized as a semi-democracy during a tenuous (and ultimately failed) transition from authoritarianism.

17.4 Implications

A first lesson of the previous empirical evidence reviewed is that impeachment is not, or at least not only, about removing a bad actor from office. Rather, impeachment occurs when there are systemic problems in the political environment, either in addition to or instead of evidence of serious individual wrongdoing by the chief executive. This is because politics typically forms a difficult constraint on executive removal. Even a bad actor will not be removed if she has sufficient support.[38] Indeed, without a very high level of opposition, presidents tend to survive in office regardless of the individually culpable act they have committed. Typically, a successful removal involves not only an attack by the opposition party or coalition but also the president's former party, coalition, or allies turning against him or her. This suggests that a chief executive is most likely to be successfully ousted when he or she is perceived to be linked to a governance situation perceived as fundamentally unacceptable across the partisan spectrum rather than as a function of individual foibles. There are a number of different ways in which 'fundamentally unacceptable' can be understood. No doubt the way in which systemic problems are perceived, described, and evaluated will vary. The important point here is that absent a sufficiently shared sense of such a crisis, impeachment is unlikely to occur in practice – even if the impeachable actions involve severe misconduct.

Is this broader model of impeachment, which is focused on systemic problems rather than individual wrongdoing, a good or a bad thing from a normative perspective? This is a difficult question to answer. But we tend to answer the question, at least tentatively, that it is a good thing. It is useful to develop the case for a 'systemic problem' conception of impeachment by situating that conception within the contrast between presidential and parliamentary systems of government. Recognition of the 'systemic problem' paradigm, in effect,

38 Aníbal S Pérez-Liñán, *Presidential Impeachment and the New Political Instability in Latin America* (CUP 2007) (referring to this as the 'legislative shield' enjoyed by chief executives).

is a way of seeing how the two forms of governance can converge toward each other in practice, even as they remain formally distinct. Parliamentarism, according to one representative definition, is 'a system of government in which the executive is chosen by, and responsible to, an elective body (the legislature), thus creating a single locus of sovereignty at the national level.'[39] The essence of parliamentarism is a logic of mutual dependence between the legislative and executive branches: either institution has the ability to bring down the other. The government can dissolve the legislature. Likewise, a legislature can bring down the government by a vote of no confidence in it. In contrast, presidentialism has a logic of mutual independence, where the president and the legislature are separately elected for fixed terms. Under ordinary conditions, neither branch has the ability to curtail the term of the other.

Impeachment is an exception to this rule of independent and durable electoral mandates. The opposite is supposed to be true in a parliamentary system. Indeed, the very fact that in parliamentary systems, the legislature may generally vote no confidence in the government for any reason at all is indicative of the very different conception of legislative/executive relations as mediated through removal protocols. Presidential systems, of course, are quite distinct from appointment-related arrangements. This shows that the arrangements for executive removal are a core element of the distinction between presidential and parliamentary systems.

The contest between presidentialism and parliamentarism has spurred an enormous literature with few clear conclusions. At the very minimum, the performance of each regime type clearly depends on many other variables, including the nature of the political party system in which the regime is embedded.[40] However, one of the core arguments against presidentialism rests on the personalization and centralization of power in a single individual. Concentration of power may pose a heightened risk of moves towards authoritarianism. Especially when the president and legislature are dominated by different parties or movements, presidential systems may calcify into policy gridlock. Gridlock may feed perceptions that government is ineffective or stimulate expansions in executive power that spark moves towards authoritarianism.

Some of the criticisms of presidential systems can be blunted by tweaking the design and practice of impeachment to avoid or mitigate the kind of deep crisis to which presidentialism sometimes seems to succumb. Impeachment can instead play the same sort of 'resetting' function that is achieved through votes of no confidence or dissolutions in well-functioning parliamentary systems. It does not follow that impeachment should be 'easy' or become routinized. In comparative terms, impeachment is a relatively rare and potentially

39 J Gerring, SC Thacker and C Moreno, 'Centripetal Democratic Governance: A Theory and Global Inquiry' (2005) 99 American *Political Science Review* 567.

40 For an elegant demonstration of the difficult of drawing simple comparisons, see Cheibub José Antônio, *Presidentialism, Parliamentarism, and Democracy* (CUP 2009).

traumatic event in essentially all presidential democracies. But so too are no-confidence motions in parliamentary democracies, as they tend to be deployed rarely. Rather than thinking of impeachment as distinct and more infrequent than a no-confidence motion, impeachment can be conceptualized as a similar tool for navigating between the rigid and undesirable extremes of, on the one hand, a strict rule of fixed-term electoral independence for the executive, and on the other hand, the complete reliance on legislative confidence. At least in certain deep, systemic crises, permitting the legislature to remove the executive may ameliorate some of the most problematic features of a presidential system of government. Exactly which such crises should trigger the use of impeachment is primarily a question for constitutional designers and practitioners in individual countries. But the main point here is that the 'systemic problems' conception of impeachment should be recognized as a useful adaption that may ameliorate one of the weaknesses of presidentialism.

Of course, moving towards a 'systemic' conception of impeachment is not without costs. One is that impeachment may exacerbate rather than defuse political crises. Consider Brazil, where the removal of Rousseff drew Brazil deeper into a crisis of political distrust and corruption. This is an important concern, but it can be partially addressed through other procedural designs, such as requiring that impeachment trigger new elections immediately rather than allowing automatic accession by a pre-set successor such as a vice president. A related problem is that a broader use of impeachment could increase political polarization, thus begetting cycles of ever more-frequent removals. Some systems, such as that of Peru or pre-invasion Ukraine seem to use impeachment quite frequently, indicating grave partisan escalation. However, although countries do seem to differ in the frequency with which they resort to impeachment, successful removals are fairly rare everywhere. Even where a more flexible standard is employed, there do not appear to be countries where impeachment has been successfully used with great frequency. As shown previously, impeachment can be initiated as a purely partisan exercise supported by one party or movement, but it rarely succeeds unless it has substantial cross-partisan support, often from within the president's own party. In contrast, there are countries where irregular removals of presidents are commonplace and highly destabilizing. Encouraging the use of impeachment as a removal tool may in fact lessen reliance on these alternatives, whether they are dubious legal substitutes or extralegal maneuvers. But there is no reason to think that successful impeachments beget a destabilizing dynamic over the long term (and some contrary reason to think that the current global rate of impeachment is too low).

What, however, should happen in the wake of impeachment? We think that the evidence suggests that impeachment can play a useful, hard reset function in cases of political crisis. Holding a new election shortly after an impeachment reduces the possibility of strategic initiation of a removal process. The relevant players will be more uncertain about who will benefit from the impeachment. In particular, supporters of impeachment will need to worry that backers of the deposed president may win the subsequent election, especially if there is a perception that impeachment was undertaken abusively or for a narrow agenda. A new election is also more likely to create an exit from a political crisis, since a new president will be able to claim a renewed popular mandate.

In this way, impeachment followed by new elections helps to ease the much-criticized rigidity of presidentialism by giving it a bit of the flavor of parliamentarism. In parliamentary systems, governmental crises and drastic losses of governmental support by the legislature are often, albeit not inevitably, resolved not only through a change in the executive cabinet but also through new popular elections. Even if new elections do not occur after a change in government, the new government is reliant on at least implicit legislative support. In contrast, the fixed electoral calendar of presidentialism generally prevents the holding of new elections as an escape valve, even during a deep crisis. Indeed, this fixed calendar is often seen as one of the greatest vulnerabilities of presidentialism, sometimes feeding deadlock and even leading to breakdown. The removal of a chief executive through an extraordinary process such as impeachment seems to us to be a useful exception to the general rule of a fixed calendar: it allows a new election to help provide an exit from a crisis, but at the same time, impeachment is too rare an event to lead to very frequent elections that might themselves destabilize the system.

17.5 Conclusion

Presidential impeachment in practice is about far more than removing criminals or other bad actors; it often serves as an exit from the deep structural crises that presidential (and semi-presidential) systems of government sometimes undergo. Such a conceptualization of impeachment is not only descriptively accurate in comparative terms but also normatively desirable. There is no evidence that impeachment generates immediate destabilizing consequences or is correlated with reductions in democratic quality. Increasing the availability of impeachments for regimes facing systemic problems thus holds the prospect of mitigating some of the worst aspects of presidential democracy without generating new costs. That is, it is a constitutional possibility that seems well worth exploring.

Index

Note: Page numbers in *italics* indicate a figure and page numbers in **bold** indicate a table on the corresponding page.

For Product Safety Concerns and Information please contact our EU
representative GPSR@taylorandfrancis.com
Taylor & Francis Verlag GmbH, Kaufingerstraße 24, 80331 München, Germany

www.ingramcontent.com/pod-product-compliance
Ingram Content Group UK Ltd.
Pitfield, Milton Keynes, MK11 3LW, UK
UKHW020155200926
475702UK00016B/2713
9781032187457